Business Data Communications

C0-DAP-473

Business Data Communications

Allen Dooley
Woodbury University
Pasadena City College

PEARSON

Prentice
Hall

Upper Saddle River, New Jersey 07458

Library of Congress Cataloging-in-Publication Data

Dooley, Allen
    Business data communications/Allen Dooley.
      p. cm.
    Includes index.
    ISBN 0-13-142429-7
      Business—Data processing.
      1. Business. 2. Communication systems—Data processing. 3. Local area networks (Computer networks).
      4. Data tranmission systems. I. Title.

  HF5548.2.D593 2004
  004.6—dc22

2004049275

Executive Editor: Robert Horan
VP/Editorial Director: Jeff Shelstad
Project Manager: Lori Cerreto
Editorial Assistant: Robyn Goldenberg
Senior Media Project Manager: Nancy Welcher
Managing Editor: John Roberts
Production Editor: Suzanne Grappi
Production Manager, Manufacturing: Arnold Vila
Design Manager: Maria Lange
Art Director: Pat Smythe
Cover Designer: Brian Salisbury
Interior Design: Debbie Iverson
Director, Image Resource Center: Melinda Reo
Manager, IRC Rights and Permissions: Zina Arabia
Manager, Visual Research: Beth Brenzel
Image Permission Coordinator: Nancy Seise
Manager, Print Production: Christy Mahon
Composition: Integra Software Services
Full-Service Project Management: Jennifer Welsch,
  BookMasters, Inc
Printer/Binder: Courier/Kendalville

Credits and acknowledgments borrowed from other sources and reproduced, with permission, in this textbook appear on page 428.

Microsoft® and Windows® are registered trademarks of the Microsoft Corporation in the U.S.A. and other countries. Screen shots and icons reprinted with permission from the Microsoft Corporation. This book is not sponsored or endorsed by or affiliated with the Microsoft Corporation.

Copyright © 2005 by Pearson Education, Inc., Upper Saddle River, New Jersey 07458.
Pearson Prentice Hall. All rights reserved. Printed in the United States of America. This publication is protected by Copyright and permission should be obtained from the publisher prior to any prohibited reproduction, storage in a retrieval system, or transmission in any form or by any means, electronic, mechanical, photocopying, recording, or likewise. For information regarding permission(s), write to: Rights and Permissions Department.

Pearson Prentice Hall™ is a trademark of Pearson Education, Inc.
Pearson® is a registered trademark of Pearson plc
Prentice Hall® is a registered trademark of Pearson Education, Inc.

Pearson Education LTD.
Pearson Education Singapore, Pte. Ltd
Pearson Education, Canada, Ltd
Pearson Education–Japan

Pearson Education Australia PTY, Limited
Pearson Education North Asia Ltd
Pearson Educación de Mexico, S.A. de C.V.
Pearson Education Malaysia, Pte. Ltd

10 9 8 7 6 5 4 3 2 1
ISBN 0-13-142429-7

For reasons close to my heart, this text is dedicated
in memory of my father, Bennie Dooley.

WITHDRAWN

SHATFORD LIBRARY

JUN   2005

1570 E. Colorado Blvd.
Pasadena, CA 91106

Brief Contents

Contents

Preface

Data communications covers a wide range of topics that can at first glance seem overwhelming. Many of these topics appear to be especially challenging because they are highly theoretical in nature and do not lend themselves to easy comprehension or explanation. To facilitate understanding of this subject, this text presents the topics in a student-focused manner. Concepts and content are not sacrificed, but the language used is student-friendly, with an emphasis on clarity, simplicity, and example. In addition, reviewers of this text were of the opinion that faculty also will find that essential material is presented thoroughly, yet in a manner that engages and interests students.

Audience

This text is primarily addressed to the university-level undergraduate student pursuing a program in business information technology related to data communications and networking. Providing the data communications foundation theory critical for university credit, the text also offers a practical how-to approach for applying theory to the real world. The straightforward, but detailed, presentation of the material will also appeal to students returning to the university or community college to enhance their career skills in the field of networking technology.

How the Text Is Organized

The text is divided into five parts, each a set of logically related chapters. The approach enables students to see how a data communications infrastructure builds from standards, to protocols, to networks of various sizes and purposes.

Part One, Data Communication Fundamentals, includes Chapters 1 through 3. These chapters cover layered modeling (OSI and TCP/IP) and standards-setting bodies, as well as essential physical and data link layer details.

Part Two, Local Area Networks, is composed of Chapters 4 and 5. Topics range from LAN components, design considerations, topologies, logical IP addressing and subnetting to network and application layer services.

Part Three, Backbone, Metropolitan, and Wide Area Networks, is composed of Chapters 6 and 7. The principle topics presented are how these networking models vary and are yet related. The implementation of each type of network is also covered. These chapters also examine Gigabit Ethernet, backbone architectures and fault tolerance, wiring closets, circuit versus packet switching, and versions of DSL, trunk services, ISDN, Frame Relay, and ATM.

Part Four, Integrating the Enterprise, includes Chapters 8, 9, and 10. The intent of these chapters is to show students how the various topics they have been studying—networking models, standards, protocols, and devices—are integrated into a total enterprise solution. Chapter 8 focuses on server technology. Chapter 9 emphasizes such enterprise solutions as Storage Area Networks, VPNs, and VoIP. Chapter 10 covers how an enterprise can be secured through RAID, encryption, firewalls, and proxy servers. These chapters demonstrate how varied data communications technologies relate to each other, providing students an important contextual connection.

Part Five, Looking Ahead, peers into future trends and technologies. Addressed are convergence technologies such as unified messaging, wireless implementations, and IPv6. And very importantly, it examines careers for data communications technologists.

Special Features

This text provides several special features that differentiate it from other, similar materials:

- Every chapter includes a feature entitled "The Ethical Perspective." This feature asks students to reflect on chapter content in an ethical context. Without proposing a right or wrong answer, this unique special feature can be used to generate class discussion on the implications of information technology in a modern society

- At the end of every chapter is another feature, the "Topic in Focus." Related specifically to the chapter being presented, this feature provides a more detailed discussion on a particular concept or technology. Each "Topic in Focus" stands alone; chapter exercises and questions do not include material covered by the "Topic in Focus." In this way, faculty can choose to present all, some, or none of the "Topics in Focus" without being concerned that the core content of the chapter is affected. This feature is also useful to students who want to know more about the particular topic being presented.

- Starting with Chapter 1, a continuous business case study is presented. This business case study, if assigned, asks students to develop a data communications solution for a mid-sized, entertainment-based business—Sheehan Marketing and Public Relations (SMPR). The case study activities, although chapter specific, connect concepts presented from one chapter to the next. This connectivity offers students a big-picture context. Although not required, the case study lends itself to a group analysis approach, so that students have an opportunity of working in small teams in developing a total business data communications solution. By its nature, the case study allows for many varying solutions so that students can be creative and flexible in their solutions.

- Each chapter presents a set of "Research in Brief" questions and activities that are unrelated to other chapters in the text. The intent of these questions and activities is to enable a student to research a chapter-specific topic. Student responses to each question and/or activity will typically be between two and five pages, depending on faculty requirements.

- This text provides several chapters that are unique in their content approach. For example, Chapter 6, although presenting material related to metropolitan area networks, focuses on backbone networks. Chapter 8 provides extensive coverage of the various types of servers. Chapter 9 introduces integrated enterprise-level solutions. Chapter 10, which examines enterprise security, covers encryption, physical security, network policies, disaster recovery planning, and how they relate, all in one chapter.

- While presenting the OSI layer model early in the text, and referring to it consistently throughout other chapters, this text emphasizes the TCP/IP layer model as a data communications model solution. The advantage of this approach is that virtually all students are familiar in some way with the Internet and the World Wide Web. Using TCP/IP as the layered model of choice, while still presenting OSI concepts, gives students an immediately familiar subject to which to relate other data communications and networking topics.

- The text covers several current areas of development such as storage area networks, Network-Attached Storage, unified messaging, and IPv6, among others.

Standard Features

The text incorporates a number of standard features that are also important. The following bulleted list identifies these features:

- Every chapter begins with a bulleted list of learning objectives.

- Every chapter ends with a detailed summary.

- Throughout each chapter, key words are denoted in bold.

- At the end of every chapter, key words used in the chapter are identified.

- Each chapter includes context-relevant graphics and images that further explain chapter concepts.

- Every chapter includes 4 end-of-chapter short answer discussion questions, for a total of 44 such questions. These questions typically require a one-paragraph response.

- The text proper incorporates a total of 745 multiple-choice/true-false questions. For each chapter, with the exception of Chapter 11, 50 multiple-choice and 20 true/false questions are provided at the end of each chapter.

- An easy-to-find acronym list is provided on the inside front and back covers of the text.

- At the end of every chapter, a Web site reference page is provided that summarizes at a glance the Web sites referenced in a chapter.

The Supplement Resource Package:

www.prenhall.com/dooley

A comprehensive and flexible technology support package is available to enhance the teaching and learning experience. All instructor and student supplements are available on the text's Web site: **www. prenhall.com/ dooley**

- ***Instructor's Manual.*** The Instructor's Manual includes learning objectives, answers to the questions and exercises at the end of the chapters, and teaching suggestions. It is available on the secure faculty section of the Dooley catalog page.

- ***Test Item File and TestGen Software***. The Test Item File is a comprehensive collection of over 600 true-false, multiple-choice, and short-answer questions. The questions are rated by difficulty level and the answers are referenced by page number. The Test Item File is available in Microsoft Word and as the computerized Prentice Hall TestGen. TestGen is a comprehensive suite of tools for testing and assessment. It allows instructors to easily create and distribute tests for their courses, either by printing and distributing through traditional methods or by online delivery via a Local Area Network (LAN) server. TestGen features Screen Wizards to assist you as you move through the program, and the software is backed with full technical support. Both the Test Item File and TestGen software are available on the secure faculty section of the Dooley catalog page.

- ***PowerPoint Slides.*** PowerPoint slides are available that illuminate and build on key concepts in the text. Both student and faculty can download the PowerPoint slides from the Dooley Web site.

- ***Materials for Your Online Course.*** Prentice Hall supports our adopters using online courses by providing files ready for upload into both WebCT and Blackboard course management systems for our testing, quizzing, and other supplements. Please contact your local PH representative or **mis_service@prenhall.com** for further information on your particular course.

Acknowledgments

The reviewers of this text provided much in-depth and beneficial criticism and guidance. Without their good work, professional expertise, and challenging, though helpful, comments, this text would not have been possible.

Barbara Carpenter, Temple College

David Easton, Waubonsee Community College

Xisheng Fang, Ohlone College

Jeremy Graves, Jones County Junior College

Jeff Gullion, Des Moines Area Community College

Rassule Hadidi, University of Illinois–Springfield

Norman Hahn, Thomas Nelson Community College

Barbara Holt, Northern Virginia Community College

Anita Krsak, Lakeland Community College

Tim Mason, Tacoma Community College

Bill Morey, University of Central Oklahoma

Vincent J. Motto, Asnuntuck Community College

David Weirscham, Texas A&M University

Steven H. White, Anne Arundel Community College

I also thank, with real gratitude, my Executive Editor, Robert Horan, who allowed me to present to him my ideas for this text and who graciously gave me guidance in its implementation.

Allen Dooley
Woodbury University, Burbank, California
Pasadena City College, Pasadena, California

chapterone

Introduction to Data Communications

Learning Objectives	After studying this chapter, you should be able to:
	• Identify five phases in the evolution of data communications.
	• Explain the difference between data communications and telecommunications.
	• Understand what a protocol is and why protocols are used.
	• Recognize the importance of standards and standards-setting bodies.
	• Understand the OSI and TCP/IP networking models.
	• Describe the benefits of layered architectures.
	• Know the four general categories of networks.

This chapter is only a beginning, as a first chapter should be. It will present terms and concepts with which you are probably not familiar, but that is to be expected. Don't panic if at first much seems unclear. Each chapter will introduce new vocabulary, concepts, and technologies that you will master. This first chapter provides background and perspective on some of the key components that make up the data communications world, including protocols, standards, and networking models.

As you read these materials, we hope to stimulate your curiosity. The theory and implementation of data communications is a challenging subject, but one of great importance, and very interesting, too. We can't promise that the topics will get easier as you work through the chapters of this book, but we certainly hope they will be clearly presented and inspire you to learn more. You are on a great voyage of discovery. In your hands is a map. Data communications technology is your ocean. You are the captain charting unknown territory. Good sailing!

The Changing World of Communications

It is 5:00 A.M. and you are sound asleep. On your front lawn, however, something curious is occurring. Silently, an electronically controlled sprinkler head with a sensor containing a small microchip rises 2 inches above ground level. The sprinkler sensor's microchip controller has been programmed to activate the twice-a-day watering of your lawn. Using wireless communications, the sprinkler's sensor controller sends an inquiry to an orbiting weather satellite. In response, the weather satellite informs the sprinkler's sensor controller that your area has an 85 percent probability of rain. Previously, you had programmed your sprinkler's sensor controller to activate watering only if the likelihood of rain is less than 75 percent. Based on your programmed commands, the sensor controller directs your sprinklers to postpone watering. The sensor controller then, like you, goes back to sleep until its next programmed activation. A light rain begins to fall.

This is but one example of how data communications are changing our world. In fact, this technology, illustrated in Figure 1.1, is available now from such vendors as HydroPoint Data Systems (**www.hydropoint.com**). Just how much have things changed? In 700 B.C., the Greeks used homing pigeons to carry messages. Today, programmed devices, such as smart sprinkler systems, work invisibly based on wireless communications. One popular option for automobiles is a global positioning system (GPS), Figure 1.2, that can provide instant directions and assistance, regardless of where the driver is, at the push of a dashboard button. Automobiles have become mobile communication devices. Of course, these technologies took time to evolve, even though they evolved very rapidly. The evolution of data communications can be divided into five phases:

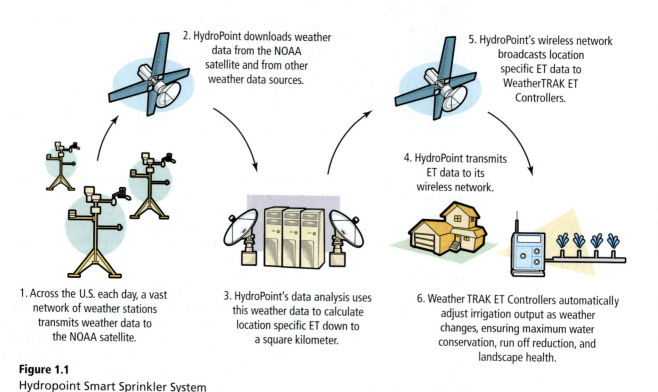

2. HydroPoint downloads weather data from the NOAA satellite and from other weather data sources.

5. HydroPoint's wireless network broadcasts location specific ET data to WeatherTRAK ET Controllers.

4. HydroPoint transmits ET data to its wireless network.

1. Across the U.S. each day, a vast network of weather stations transmits weather data to the NOAA satellite.

3. HydroPoint's data analysis uses this weather data to calculate location specific ET down to a square kilometer.

6. Weather TRAK ET Controllers automatically adjust irrigation output as weather changes, ensuring maximum water conservation, run off reduction, and landscape health.

Figure 1.1
Hydropoint Smart Sprinkler System

Figure 1.2
Automotive manufacturers are increasingly including GPS technology as a standard feature in many vehicles, such as this Lexus.

1 Digitization in the 1960s

2 Growth of data communications in the 1970s

3 An era of deregulation in the 1980s

4 The Internet as a common tool in the 1990s

5 Pervasive computing in the 2000s

Phase 1: Digitization

In the 1960s, computer technology began to transform our social, economic, and governmental infrastructures. Data, formerly transcribed or maintained primarily in paper form, were instead being captured electronically as binary digits understandable to computers (Figure 1.3). The process of transcribing data into binary form is called **digitization**. This period witnessed the beginnings of extensive digitization, with processing and communications being highly centralized.

The computers in use at that time, called mainframes, Figure 1.4, were very large and expensive and used proprietary architectures that did not support cross-platform communications. **Proprietary** generally refers to a technology or product that is copyrighted and not available for use without some type of fee or payment to its owner. As a result, an organization's mainframe from one vendor could not directly interact with the software and hardware of a different vendor's mainframe, creating a closed architecture

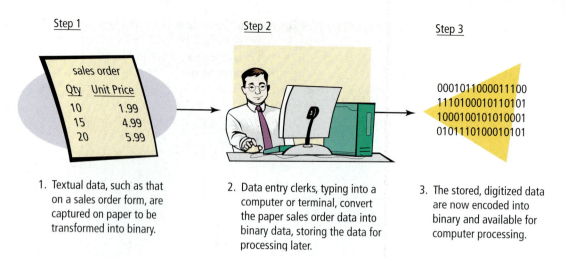

sales order

Qty	Unit Price
10	1.99
15	4.99
20	5.99

0001011000011100
1110100010110101
1000100101010001
0101110100010101

1. Textual data, such as that on a sales order form, are captured on paper to be transformed into binary.

2. Data entry clerks, typing into a computer or terminal, convert the paper sales order data into binary data, storing the data for processing later.

3. The stored, digitized data are now encoded into binary and available for computer processing.

Figure 1.3
Digitization: From Paper to Binary

Figure 1.4
A typical facility for housing mainframe computers. Mainframes require specialized environmental controls, including air conditioning and air filtration.

technology. A **closed architecture technology** does not permit competing technologies to directly interface or interact with it.

Because they were large, expensive, and complex, mainframes were used mostly by governments, major research institutes, and large corporations. Users connected to the mainframe by way of dumb terminals. All work and communications were controlled through the mainframe. The dumb terminals were simply the way that users accessed the mainframe's computing power.

In this environment, when a business bought into a computer vendor's technology, it bought into one vendor's implementation of that technology. Today, for both software and hardware, as well as data communications models and protocols, the trend has been toward open architecture systems. **Open architecture systems** enable the use of technologies that are conversant across platforms. For consumers, open architecture systems offer many advantages, including greater competition for their dollars as more vendors enter the market.

Phase 2: Growth of Data Communications

Electronic data must be transported from one location to another over some type of transmission infrastructure in order to be widely available. An **infrastructure** is like a roadway, Figure 1.5, in that it conveys data from one location to another. The first data communications infrastructures used the existing circuit-based telephone system. This system was owned and run as a monopoly by Bell Telephone/AT&T, meaning that Bell was the only provider of this critical infrastructure.

As technology improved in the 1970s, and as the importance of computer technology became apparent, especially to the business world, solutions were pursued that would enable computers to more efficiently communicate and share information with each other. Smaller-scale

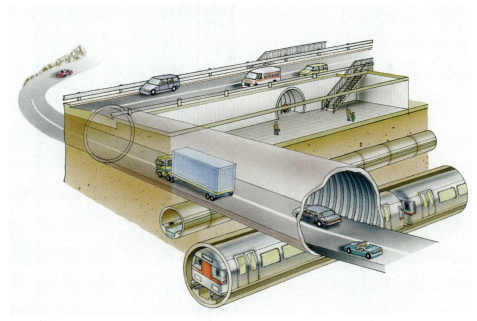

Figure 1.5
Human infrastructures, such as the ones conceptualized in this illustration, allow goods to be transported from one point to another. Data communications requires similar infrastructures to move data from one point to another.

computers, minicomputers, were introduced. Processing and communications became more decentralized. The microprocessor became commercially available. Also, packet-switching networks, first created in the 1960s, began to be extensively deployed and implemented.

Briefly stated, packet-switched circuits are more efficient for transporting data, whereas circuit-switched circuits are more efficient for voice transmission. (We find out why in Chapter 7.) With increased digitization of data through computer technology, communication networks were needed that could support more than voice. The development of packet-switching technologies was the solution to this problem (Figure 1.6). Packet-switching networks, in turn, because of their ability to more efficiently transport digitized data, ignited the growth of extensive data communications networks. Users of technology now expected their communications systems to provide real-time, online capabilities over great distances.

Phase 3: Deregulation

As the economic impact and power of capable and reliable data communications infrastructures became apparent, more players sought to enter the field of providing data communication technologies for profit. Until 1968, Bell Telephone/AT&T, operating as a monopoly, controlled the entire U.S. telephone system. A series of legal battles, beginning in the late 1960s and continuing into the 1970s, introduced an era of deregulation that in 1984 resulted in the federally mandated breakup of Bell Telephone/AT&T into two components. One component resulted in seven *regional Bell operating companies* (RBOCs) that were to provide only local telephone services to

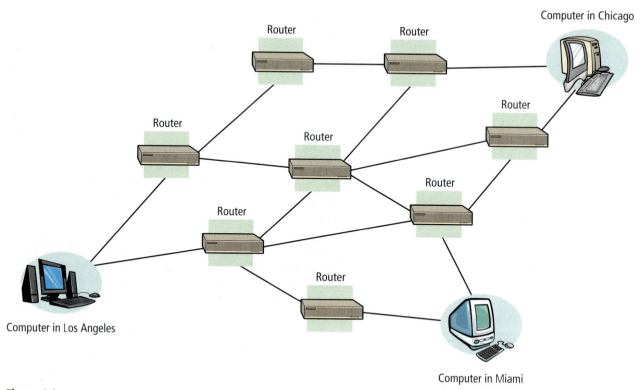

Figure 1.6
Simple Packet-Switching Network
In this illustration, multiple potential "packet switching" routes are available for a communication between a device in Los Angeles and one in Chicago.

businesses and homes. The second component created a new AT&T that was permitted to provide only long-distance telephone services, but in competition with other providers. A key goal of **deregulation** is to allow competition to enter a market so that consumers in that market can have a wider selection of service providers from which to choose.

The 1980s saw the beginnings of much greater competition among service providers in the areas of telecommunications and data communications. In 1996, the U.S. Congress passed the Telecommunications Competition and Deregulation Act. This act resulted in changing the highly regulated and monopolistic industry of providing local telephone service into one of open competition. The issue of deregulation is politically charged and has become a global topic of concern. International competition to provide telecommunication services has intensified as for-profit organizations seek to increase their market share. The trend, especially in the United States, has been toward greater deregulation.

Phase 4: The Internet as a Common Tool

In 1958, in response to the Soviet Union's launch of Sputnik, Figure 1.7, the U.S. Department of Defense established the Advanced Research Projects Agency (ARPA). One of ARPA's primary missions was to find a way for computers to communicate with each other, regardless of the computers' manufacturers. Recall that in the 1960s mainframe computers were not cross-platform conversant and were a closed architecture technology. Researchers knew that by designing a communication model that enabled different types of computers to communicate with each other over great distances, researchers could more easily exchange ideas and knowledge, thus reducing duplication of effort.

By 1969, ARPA, Figure 1.8, would evolve into **ARPANET**. That same year, the first two nodes of ARPANET, which would eventually become the Internet, were connected to each other. One node was located at the Stanford Research Institute and the second was at UCLA. Things have changed. As of June 2002, the Internet had more than 200,000,000 million nodes. Another way of stating this is that the **Internet** is a great network of networks based upon a common architecture. From its origin as a research tool, the Internet has been transformed into an infrastructure that is increasingly viewed as the single most important universal information transport and service tool ever created. However, the Internet's very success

Figure 1.7
Spurred by the launch of Sputnik, United States Department of Defense creates ARPA.

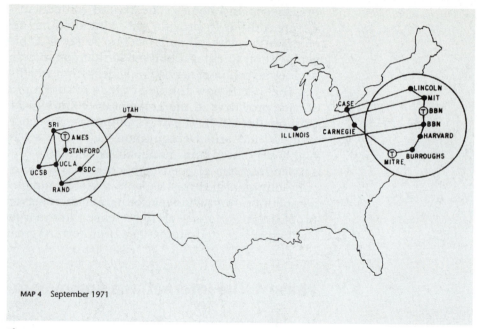

MAP 4   September 1971

Figure 1.8
A figure illustrating the simple beginnings of what would ultimately become the Internet.

has led many to believe that the Internet as we now know it is nearing a meltdown.

The Internet in use today is known as version **IPv4** (Internetworking Protocol version 4). When this version of the Internet was created, researchers had no way of knowing how wildly successful the Internet would become. Also, the types of data that IPv4 was designed to carry did not include such relatively resource-intensive kinds of files such as those carrying video and sound. Users have come to expect a rich multimedia experience, and they expect computer and communication infrastructures to support such use. In addition, in the future, users will increasingly want to connect many other types of devices to the Internet, including computers, cell phones, pagers, cameras, cars, and other devices, so that they are always "plugged-in."

Business has also been an aggressive adopter of Internet technologies. Through the Internet, businesses seek solutions that allow hardware, software, and services to be integrated into one secure, reliable, and scalable infrastructure. The Internet is evolving into an intelligent network that will be capable of providing Web services, policy management, network management, security, and mobility. In the long run, for all of this to happen, IPv4 will ultimately be replaced with the new improved Internet, **IPv6** (Internetworking Protocol version 6). This transition will take time, but IPv6 is a solution to many of the significant problems that IPv4 cannot address. For those who cannot wait to discover how IPv6 differs from IPv4, and why IPv6 was needed, Chapter 11 provides an overview of how IPv4 and IPv6 differ.

Phase 5: Pervasive Computing

The nature of what we mean by communications and how we communicate is rapidly changing. A major discussion under way in today's business world revolves around the convergence of communications. The Internet,

Figure 1.9
An illustration of the current complexity of the Internet or the Information Super Highway.

Figure 1.9, and wireless technologies are playing a major role in how this convergence is being implemented. We are fast approaching a society in which pervasive, and some say invasive, computing is the norm. From your watch to your phone to perhaps the buttons on your shirt—all of which could serve as digital receivers—we are an increasingly connected society and carry our connections with us wherever we go. A technology so commonly used that it is taken for granted within a society is referred to as a **pervasive technology**. A famous example of a commonly used pervasive technology in industrial countries is the traditional telephone system. Residents of the United States expect to hear a dial tone when they pick up the telephone, whether they are in a metropolis such as Los Angeles or a tiny rural community in the mountains of Montana. The following discussion of telemetry provides a few examples of this relatively new pervasive technology.

Telemetry is the wireless transmission and reception of data for the purpose of remotely monitoring environmental conditions or equipment parameters. Telemetry is used with mobile robots, satellites, and space probes. Both the Space Shuttle and the International Space Station use telemetry to monitor the physical condition of astronauts and ensure the maintenance of their working environment.

Telemetry can be used to monitor security and fire alarm systems, read utility meters, track and locate vehicles or inventory, or poll remote candy vending machines to determine if they require replenishment. Industrial manufacturers use telemetry to streamline maintenance tasks, prolonging machine life and reducing product support, and to improve asset utilization. The health-care industry uses telemetry to minimize human error in recording patient data at its point of capture, to improve doctor–hospital workflow processes, and to better manage individual patient health-care services and data. For businesses, telemetry is an efficient way to control and access critical data, saving time and money. Each of these examples is a form of pervasive computing.

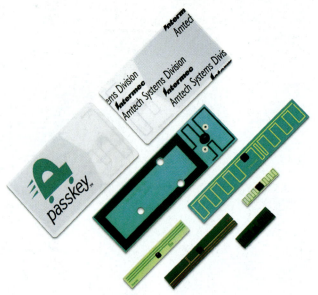

Figure 1.10

RFID tags such as these are increasingly being used by businesses to track and monitor the movement of goods and inventory.

Let's consider a practical business use for telemetry in data communications. ACME, Inc. produces three styles of living room furniture: Santa Fe, English Provincial, and French Modern. Wireless Radio Frequency Identification (RFID) tags, Figure 1.10, are placed on each piece of furniture manufactured by ACME. The furniture is stored in warehouses on inventory shelves. The telemetry tags, tracked by satellite, enable the production manager to quickly analyze which products are moving out of the warehouse and which are not. She adjusts her production schedule accordingly, knowing she needs to produce more of those items that are selling and fewer of those that are not. The production manager's schedule will affect her orders for parts from outside vendors as well as other ACME departments.

For example, the ACME marketing department manager has access to the production schedule. With this information, the marketing staff makes decisions on how to better market slow-moving inventory and how to increase the market share of those items selling successfully. Management, on the other hand, uses both production and marketing data to set strategic goals for ACME. At the heart of all this, however, is the wireless telemetry technology used on ACME's inventory. Perhaps management, based on the data, decides that the Santa Fe line is on its way out due to poor sales, so they stop production of Santa Fe and pursue another furniture line. Figure 1.11 demonstrates ACME's use of telemetry.

The Internet will be a key vehicle for such communications convergence. Originally used for remote access, file sharing, and e-mail, the Internet, by way of the World Wide Web (WWW), has become an information repository. The Internet has made e-commerce a multi-billion-dollar reality. Common communications today include instant messaging as well as online gaming, music, movies, and voice/video conferencing.

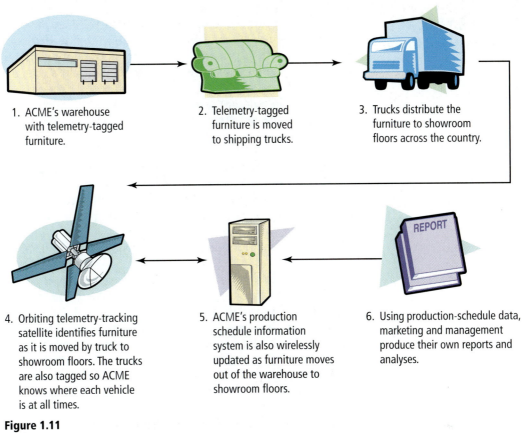

1. ACME's warehouse with telemetry-tagged furniture.

2. Telemetry-tagged furniture is moved to shipping trucks.

3. Trucks distribute the furniture to showroom floors across the country.

4. Orbiting telemetry-tracking satellite identifies furniture as it is moved by truck to showroom floors. The trucks are also tagged so ACME knows where each vehicle is at all times.

5. ACME's production schedule information system is also wirelessly updated as furniture moves out of the warehouse to showroom floors.

6. Using production-schedule data, marketing and management produce their own reports and analyses.

Figure 1.11
ACME's Use of Telemetry

Increasingly, users will expect to use these communications anywhere and everywhere they go, sometimes to the displeasure of those around them.

Of course, supporting these types of communications presents a number of challenges, especially those relating to privacy, security, cost, and access.

Defining Data Communications

Data communications is properly considered a subset of telecommunications, meaning that data communications is included within telecommunications, not the other way around. Even so, data communications covers a very large territory. Let's look first at what is meant by *telecommunications*, so that we can then see why data communications has a more narrow focus.

The word *tele* comes from the Greek word for *distance*, and in telecommunications, we are usually talking about great distances. **Telecommunications** includes many different types of communication besides data, such as voice and video, and includes telephony, telegraphy, and television. Therefore, telecommunications historically has supported other purposes beyond communications between computers and networks. A number of standards-setting bodies, both national and international, specify how, where, when, what, and who can provide telecommunications services. We will identify a few of these standards organizations in a moment.

Data communications, as the name implies, is focused on the communication of data and information between computers and computer

The Ethical Perspective

Technology continues to provide us with increasing convenience. Yet, this very convenience in many ways may require that we surrender, knowingly or not, data and information that many of us might consider to be private. How much management over a technology should a user, or consumer, of that technology be able to regulate and control? The issue of control and access over data and information involves a code of conduct, or code of ethics, for those who manage this data and information.

Ethics is the study of the standards of conduct that a society uses as guidelines on what that society believes is right or wrong. Evolving data communications technologies, which are pervasive or invasive depending on how one views them, are having dramatic effects on the ethical standards of conduct within our society. These technologies are changing our society's standards of what is ethically considered right and wrong in terms of the use of data and information. Consider the following scenario.

Should a clothing manufacturer be able to stitch tags into the labels of its garments that track, through wireless technology, where the garments go once they are taken off store shelves? This technology is already available through the use of RFID, a type of telemetry. From a business perspective, such tracking makes a lot of sense. A business wants to be able to keep accurate records of its inventory. If a business knows what is in its warehouse or selling from its shelves, it will have a better understanding of what items it should be increasing, or decreasing, production of. RFID can help a business do that. Yet, as a consumer of that clothing product, when you buy a shirt, jacket, or pair of socks, are you concerned about the *possibility* of your movements being tracked and identified?

What do you think about this? What implications, beyond clothing, do you foresee? Might this affect our legal system? What about our medical system? Is this type of market tracking what you had in mind when you bought your last pair of shoes? From a business perspective, though, how is this type of tracking beneficial? Can this data be ethically used? How might it be ethically abused?

The Electronic Privacy Information Center, a nonprofit organization located in Washington, D.C., has posted a warning regarding RFID technology on its Web site (**www.epic.org/privacy/rfid**). The warning makes for interesting reading.

networks. Today, the term *data* encompasses a much broader range of elements, no longer consisting of just numbers and text. Data might include graphic images, sound files, or video elements. Because of the broader context that data now includes, and with newer technologies such as Voice over IP (VoIP), the distinction between the worlds of telecommunications and data communications are blurring. The difference between telecommunications and data communications may soon be one that is no difference at all. Regardless of the kind of data, that data will ultimately be expressed in binary code (a coding notation we cover later in our text) so that computers can process it. **Binary** coding schemes, using elements called bits, represent the data in the form of zeroes and ones, Figure 1.12. Binary coding schemes are examined more closely in Chapter 2. One binary coding scheme in particular that will affect data communications technologies is Unicode, a relatively new technology that is receiving a lot of attention.

Figure 1.12
Ultimately, data processed by a computer must be expressed in binary format.

After being expressed in binary format, the data may need to be transmitted from one computer to another, or from one network to another, in order to be processed. Data communications networks have been built to handle this transition. Data communications networks may use many different types of computers and other devices that enable data to be processed and routed. A data communications network may also have many different types of transmission media that permit the data to be carried from one location to another. The medium may be wired or wireless. Besides the devices that process the data, and the transmission media that carry the data, the data communications network will also have rules or protocols that determine how the devices and transmission media work with each other. These rules and protocols are defined by standards that are set by formal and informal controlling organizations; many of these organizations are the same ones that define telecommunication standards.

All of these elements affect and determine the quality of the data communications infrastructure. The three questions that must be considered with regards to data communications are (1) how the data are delivered, (2) how accurate the data are once delivered, and (3) how accessible the data are to those who need to use it. This text will discuss the many types of devices, transmission media, rules or protocols, and standards that allow the data communications infrastructure to exist. As you can see, data communications is itself a vast topic.

Protocols

Simply stated, a **protocol** is a set of rules that determine how something is performed or accomplished. Many kinds of protocols rule our daily lives, some formal, some casual. For example, when a customer goes into a bank to make a transaction, protocol states that the customer politely wait in line until it is his or her turn to speak with a teller. We have language protocols, called rules of grammar, that make it possible for people who speak and read the same language to understand each other. Without human protocols, our lives would be even more complicated than they already are, and social institutions as we know them would not be possible. Like people, computers, and the networks they use, need protocols in order to understand and work with each other. Also, as with human protocols, different types of protocols exist for different needs.

In data communications, protocols must possess four key characteristics in order for communications to successfully and effectively occur. First, an agreement, or protocol, must specify how the data are to be packaged, or formatted, so that they can be sent between sending and receiving devices. If a person were to write an English-language letter and send it to a business associate in Moscow, that person would follow the formatting, or syntax, protocol rules for English grammar. Having a formatting protocol, however, does not necessarily imply that the sender and receiver will understand each other. For example, the Russian business associate may not read English. The same is true with communicating devices. Such devices, of course, will not be using a language such as English or Russian to communicate, but rather some type of binary encoding scheme, as discussed earlier. An **encoding scheme** is a way of transforming one type of data or information into another. Translating English into Russian, for example, requires an encoding scheme that follows a formatting protocol. A binary encoding scheme will also follow a formatting protocol.

However, if a receiving device does not understand the binary data format of the sending device, communication will not occur. Just as someone who reads only Russian would not be able to understand a letter written in English, so, too, a protocol should address a second characteristic, the ability of the communicating devices to understand the formatting protocols being used. Within the binary encoding schemes, or protocols, that are in use, sending and receiving devices will have to agree, for the sake of understanding, as to what particular patterns of bits mean within the bit stream being sent. Formatting of the data according to a protocol is one thing; the two communicating devices must also understand the meaning of the format. For the Russian associate discussed earlier, when the sender sends the letter, the sender better also send an English-to-Russian dictionary and grammar book so that the Russian business associate can understand and interpret what has been written.

A third characteristic that data communication protocols should address is the speed of the communication. When a sending device sends its data to a receiving device, the two devices must agree on the rate of speed that will be used in the transmission. For example, one device may be faster than the other, and without controlling for this, transmission overload could occur. Imagine what would likely happen if all the cars driving on a busy highway were suddenly detoured to a two-lane country road! The two-lane country road would suffer serious transmission overload. Protocols determine the speed at which sending and receiving devices can communicate based on the capabilities of each device.

Finally, when two devices need to communicate, one of the devices may not be available for a variety of reasons: hardware failure, a downed communication link, system repair, or software upgrading. Communication protocols determine when, and if, communications can occur. Devices are not like people; they require specific control over not only the speed at which they can communicate, but when they can communicate as well. A sending device needs to know if a receiving device is available for communications. If available, both sender and receiver have to agree on the speed of the communication.

Standards and Standards-Setting Bodies

Protocols, as stated earlier, are the rules that determine how devices communicate. The question then is, who determines the rules? The answer is that **standards** are defined that establish the essential rules, functionalities, and operations a protocol must fulfill. Standards-setting organizational bodies usually create and define the standards. We say "usually" because there are two kinds of standards: formal and informal. First, let's describe why standards are desirable.

Standards provide well-known and published guidelines upon which a technology can be based. By following standards, providers of data and telecommunications technologies ensure the interoperability of their software and hardware. Owing to this interoperability, consumers of the technology have a more competitive and open market from which to select their services and products. Developers of a technology know that by following standards they will create a product of much greater appeal to their market of interest. Managers of a technology appreciate standards because it makes for easier maintenance, upgrade, and troubleshooting of their technology infrastructures. Standards are well documented, and, in general, rigorously tested and evaluated before they can become standards.

Formal standards are those standards that have been authorized by either an officially recognized body or by law and regulation. It is not unusual for formal standards to evolve from informal **de facto standards**. De facto standards are either proprietary or nonproprietary. The trend in most industries over the past couple of decades has been toward **nonproprietary**, meaning "open," standards. A technology may, because of its pervasiveness, or because it is the only model of that technology, become a de facto standard simply by its existence and use. These types of de facto standards will occasionally evolve into formal standards. A famous example of a de facto standard that later became a formal standard is the Ethernet protocol. Ethernet was created by Xerox Corporation and later formalized by the Institute of Electrical and Electronics Engineers (IEEE; **www.ieee.org**) as the 802.3 standard.

The IEEE is one example of a standards-setting body; there are, of course, many more. In addition, many standards-setting bodies are managed by professional organizations, not by formal governmental agencies. We will identify only those that are of primary importance in North America, but be aware that there are standards-setting bodies for Europe, Asia, and other parts of the world. The following lists the key North American standards-setting groups:

- The International Standards Organization (ISO; **www.iso.org**)

- The International Telecommunications Union-Telecommunication Standards Sector (ITU-T; **www.itu.int**)

- The American National Standards Institute (ANSI; **www.ansi.org**)

- The Institute of Electrical and Electronics Engineers (IEEE; **www.ieee.org**)

- The Electronics Industries Association (EIA; **www.eia.org**)

- The Internet Society (ISOC; **www.isoc.org**)

- The Internet Engineering Task Force (IETF; **www.ietf.org**)

- The Internet Engineering Steering Group (IESG; **www.iesg.org**)

- The Internet Architecture Board (IAB; **www.iab.org**)

- The Internet Assigned Numbers Authority (IANA; **www.iana.org**)

The ISO is an international body of voluntary organizations with great influence in the field of information technology. The ISO attempts to create international technological compatibility by supporting and establishing worldwide standards.

The ITU-T concerns itself with international telecommunications issues. The ITU-T's particular areas of interest are phone and data systems. The ITU-T has established standards that define data transmission over phone lines, e-mail and directory services, and transmission over public digital networks.

ANSI represents the United States on the ISO. However, ANSI does not have a formal affiliation with the federal government; it is a nonprofit, private corporation. ANSI's membership list includes industry associations, consumer groups, governmental bodies, professional associations, and other interested parties. ANSI is the principal standards-setting body in the United States.

The IEEE defines many standards for both local area networks (LANs) and backbone networks (BNs). With an emphasis on electronics and electrical engineering, the IEEE is the largest professional engineering society in the world. The IEEE is playing a critical part in establishing new wireless communication standards.

The EIA, like ANSI, is a nonprofit organization that defines physical connection interfaces, electronic signaling specifications, and serial communications between two digital devices, among other technologies. The EIA plays a fundamental role in the defining of standards for electrical and functional characteristics of interface equipment.

There are numerous Internet-related organizations, each with its particular responsibility and area of interest; here we identify just a few. The ISOC, an open-member professional society, meaning you could join it if you wanted to, is the closest the Internet has to an owning organization. It represents more than 100 countries. The IETF is also an international community, consisting of researchers, vendors, and network designers. Its concern is with the evolution of the Internet's architecture and its efficient functioning. The IETF spearheaded the development of the Simple Network Management Protocol (SNMP) and reviews performance standards for bridges, routers, and router protocols. The Internet Engineering Steering Group (IESG) is the technical, management arm of the IETF. The IESG is responsible for actions associated with, and the final specifications of, Internet standards. The IESG manages the Internet standards process. The Internet Architecture Board (IAB) provides strategic direction and guidance to the IESG and IETF. Finally, the IANA governs the assignment of IP (Internet Protocol) numbers.

Although not a standards-setting body, the U.S. Federal Communications Commission (FCC; **www.fcc.gov**) is a very important regulatory agency. The FCC oversees and authorizes interstate and international electrical communication systems originating in the United States. FCC approval is required before a piece of communication technology equipment can be marketed in the United States. The FCC plays a major role in ensuring that the national telephone system operates effectively.

Networking Models

Computers and other devices process data and then may route that data from one location to another. In order to get the data from point A to point B, an infrastructure must be used. Recall that an infrastructure is like a highway that provides a means of transporting goods from one city to another. In data communications, various types of networks are used as a transporting infrastructure.

Networks have both physical and logical components: the hardware devices that make them up and the software that drives them. The physical aspects of a network will also include the media used to transport data from one location to another. The media might be wired or wireless. Many of the physical components that make up a network can be seen and touched, but not all. For example, microwave transmissions are not visible to the human eye, and yet microwaves are a physical reality. Consider that dogs can hear sound frequencies that humans cannot. The fact that we cannot hear these sound frequencies does not mean that they do not physically exist. Physical and logical components within the network work with each other based on standards and protocols. Above and beyond their standards and protocols, networks have another dimension that describes how they function. This extra dimension is the model upon which the network is based.

When a builder wants to build a house, he or she usually starts with an architectural blueprint. The blueprint is not the house itself, of course, but rather a conceptual, logical model of what the house will be. As a model, the blueprint can be modified, perhaps as the builder adds or removes rooms during the design process. Eventually, the house is built based on the final model described by the blueprint. The end result may vary from the model as originally drawn, because the concept, in this case the blueprint, which is logical, and the physical construction, the house, are not the same thing.

The model is a guideline. Depending on what is being built, the builder may follow the model precisely, to its last detail, or more generally, deviating from the model's specifications. If the model is good, it provides good guidelines, and the builder will end up with, in this example, a sound building. If the model is bad, then the house will also be bad or flawed. In this case, the house may not survive the next big storm.

Open architecture models share similar advantages to open standards in that they are available for public comment, review, and varying implementations. Open models provide a common basis of understanding because their functionalities are documented and available. Open models lend themselves to duplication; this means that the designers of technologies that use these models do not have to take on the cost and labor of creating new ones. Models, because they are conceptual, can be modified to fit varying conditions. Technologies based on established models provide known advantages and disadvantages. Software and hardware vendors who create products based on accepted models can produce products that have a wider consumer appeal.

Data communications networks, like houses, are also built from models. Several data communications network models have been developed, but two in particular have won wide acceptance. The first is the Open Systems Interconnection, or OSI, model. The second is the Transmission Control Protocol/Internet Protocol, or TCP/IP, model. Perhaps these models are new to you. However, if you have ever used a bank's automated teller machine (ATM) machine, paid for gasoline at an automated gas pump using a charge card, made an airline reservation over the phone, paid a restaurant check using a credit card, or surfed the World Wide Web, then you have used a data communications network that is based on one of these two models.

Both models have several characteristics in common. First, they are both open architecture models. This means that anyone, anywhere, at any time, can freely design or create technologies based on these models, which is a real advantage. Second, both models are based on a **layered architecture**. This means that each model can be broken into several distinct components, called *layers.* Each layer within the model has its own particular and specific responsibilities and functionalities. A major topic discussed throughout this text is what these layers do, how they do it, and why. And finally, each model is well established and accepted by the data and telecommunications industries as models that provide clear guidelines as to how to build a data communications network that works. But remember, models are conceptual guidelines; how they are physically implemented can vary.

This chapter introduces you to both the OSI and the TCP/IP models, but the emphasis in this text will be on the TCP/IP model. The TCP/IP model has become the model of choice throughout the world not only for wide area networks (WANs), but also for local area networks (LANs) and backbone networks (BNs). Throughout the text we attempt to point out the similarities between the two models. And, in fact, they have much in common. Perhaps the most important feature they share is that both the OSI and the TCP/IP models have layered architectures. Let's discuss briefly why this layered architecture is so advantageous.

Layered Architectures

In a layered architecture, each layer is assigned a specific set of functionalities and responsibilities. This means that one layer does not have to do the work of all the other layers or understand what the other layers are doing. Instead, each layer is responsible only for its assigned duties, no more, no less. Let's look at this in a real-world scenario.

You have been hired as a "generalist" at ACME, a business with 1,000 employees. As ACME's "generalist" you have many duties. You are responsible for running accounts receivable, managing payroll, developing marketing brochures, presenting staff development training, and improving employee relations. All of these are important functions that ACME requires to be an effective business. After the first week, you go to your president and say, "This is crazy. You can't have one person being responsible for all these different functions. It is simply not efficient. I quit."

As you head out the door, the president calls out, "Wait, ACME's in real trouble. We're about to go under! What do you recommend?" You reply, "Well, separating or layering out these responsibilities would be much more efficient. Each organizational layer would have its own specific responsibilities. For example, the accounts receivable manager wouldn't have to know what the payroll manager's job duties are or how they are done. Each functional area would be responsible for its own duties, although each functional area would still need to communicate with other functional areas in the organization."

While this is an extreme example, it gets the point across. Different functional areas can be responsible for their specific duties. This works for networking models as well as for human organizations. In the layered network model approach, each layer has a set of functions that it is responsible for. Each layer only needs to be able to communicate with the layer immediately above or below itself. The layer does not have to understand what happens above or below it, but it must know the proper format to pass information up or down. Again, let's look at a real-world scenario.

A secretary gathers financial sales data from individual department employees. He uses the data to type, in a company-required format, a financial analysis statement that he then passes up to his manager. The secretary is not required or expected to explain or understand the analysis he typed. The secretary is responsible only for accurately typing the financial analysis in the required format and passing the analysis up to his manager.

The manager accepts the printed analysis. The manager is not concerned with how it was typed or on what computer, only that it is accurate and produced in a timely manner. The manager takes the analysis and other data and summarizes the information for the Vice President of Finance. The Vice President of Finance, who wants her data in a specific summarized format, does not care or ask who typed the data or how. What she wants is for the data to be in an accurate format appropriate to her level in the organization. She will then process the data and pass it up to the next level of organizational hierarchy. Here we see that one layer of the organization does not need to know the detail of how a different layer produced its results. And yet, layers that touch do require that data that are passed back and forth be in a specific presentation format for the information to be usable.

The network layer model works in much the same way. Let's take a closer look at the layers that make up the OSI and TCP/IP models.

The OSI Model

Developed by the ISO, one of the major standards groups we presented earlier, the **Open Systems Interconnection (OSI) model** has seven distinct layers. Each layer has a specific set of functionalities and responsibilities. Starting from the bottom of the model, the physical and data link layers are low-level layers that are responsible for placing the data on a physical medium and then framing, or formatting, the data bits into a form that can be passed from one computer to another. The mid-level layers, the network and transport layers, are responsible for the complete delivery of a message, and the data packets that make it up, between the sender and receiver. The top, high-level layers, the application, presentation, and session layers, represent functions that involve the user or user applications. The order of these layers, from top to bottom, is shown in Table 1.1.

Notice in Table 1.1 that both the sender and receiver have the same set of layers in the exact same order. We call this type of architecture a **layer stack**, which is like a stack of pancakes. (In a later chapter, you will learn that there are also stacks called protocol stacks.) The layers on the sender's side do the same work as the layers on the receiver's side. A popular phrase for remembering these layers in their correct order is: **A**ll **P**eople **S**eem **T**o **N**eed **D**ata **P**rocessing. Of course, the term data processing is now fairly dated, so maybe we can update it to the following: **A**ll **P**eople **S**eem **T**o **N**eed **D**igital **P**ower. Each layer represents a type of function that a protocol should support if that protocol is designed to work at that particular layer.

Table 1.1 The Seven Layers of the OSI Model

Sender	Receiver
7. Application	7. Application
6. Presentation	6. Presentation
5. Session	5. Session
4. Transport	4. Transport
3. Network	3. Network
2. Data link	2. Data link
1. Physical	1. Physical

(As each layer is examined more closely, you will probably find that there are terms or concepts that are unfamiliar or that you do not yet understand. Don't be too concerned at this point; remember, this is only Chapter 1. As you move through the remainder of the text, these terms, concepts, and functionalities will be described in much greater detail.)

Application Layer

Here, the term *application* does not refer to an end-user application, such as a word processor, but refers to how a user or a user application would gain network access. Users and end-user applications gain network access by cooperating with a process running at the application layer of the OSI. Some of the services supported at this layer include e-mail, remote file access and transfer, and shared database management. No header or trailer data are added at this layer.

Presentation Layer

This layer ensures that data passed up to the application layer is in a format understandable to that layer. The presentation layer is responsible for the interoperability between a sender and receiver who might be using different encoding schemes. Recall that data have to be encoded into some binary form so that the data can be used by computer systems. The presentation layer might perform translation, but it can also, if required, perform encryption and compression. **Encryption** scrambles data so that only those with a decryption key can use the data. Encrypted data must be unscrambled in order for the data to be available for use. **Compression**, which occurs at the sender's end, reduces the number of bits to be transmitted based on some type of compression scheme. The receiver would have to have the proper decompression software to then use the transmitted data in its original, uncompressed form.

Session Layer

The sender and receiver may need to establish a connection, or session, before they can begin to communicate. The session layer is responsible for establishing, maintaining, and terminating communications running between processes or applications across the network. In essence, the session layer manages the dialog that occurs between two communicating devices.

Transport Layer

The transport layer ensures that the entire message sent from a sender to a receiver has been delivered. By providing connection control, the transport layer can be either connectionless or connection-oriented. (Explaining connectionless or connection-oriented at this point would be too involved, but you will see in later chapters exactly what is meant by these terms.) In addition, the transport layer reassembles or segments data based on whether it is passing the data up (reassembly) or down (segmentation) the layer stack.

Network Layer

Whereas the transport layer is responsible for determining if the entire message has been delivered, the network layer is concerned about the delivery of individual packets across network links. This layer is responsible for ensuring that each packet that makes up a message gets from its point of origin, the sender, to its final destination, the receiver. The network layer also handles the **logical addressing** of a packet, attaching to the packet the logical addresses of both the sender and receiver. Something that is "logical," as in a logical address, can be changed or modified. Something that is "physical," as in a physical address, is fixed, or set, and cannot be changed. Based on where the sender and receiver are in relation to each other, on the same or different logical networks, the network layer may also perform routing services.

Data Link Layer

The data link layer has several key responsibilities. This layer takes unpackaged bit stream data arriving from the physical layer and packages the bits into units called *frames.* The data link layer attaches a physical address to each frame. This layer is responsible for getting each frame from one node to another on its way from sender to receiver. This layer also provides flow control, error control, and access control. So, whereas the network layer provides for logical addressing, the data link layer provides for physical addressing. In data communications, as you will discover, there are many types of addressing schemes, each serving a particular purpose.

Physical Layer

The physical layer concerns itself with transmitting an unpackaged bit stream over some type of physical medium. The medium might be wired or wireless. This layer deals with the mechanical and electrical specifications that define the connection between devices and the transmission medium they use. This layer is responsible for the synchronization of bits, line configuration, physical topology, and the transmission mode. (Again, it is not expected at this point that any of these terms are meaningful to you, but by the end of this text they will be.)

The TCP/IP Model

The **Transmission Control Protocol/Internet Protocol (TCP/IP) model** was developed prior to the OSI model. The layers of the two models are similar, but they are not exactly the same. Note that data communications

How the Layers Work

All chapters will have "Topic in Focus" features. Each "Topic in Focus" explains a particular subject in greater detail. For those who want to know a little more, this extended topic coverage will be interesting and informative. (Check with your instructor as to whether some or all of these special topic discussions will be part of your formal course.) Each "Topic in Focus" appears at the end of a chapter. In this chapter, the "Topic in Focus" describes how layers in the OSI models cooperate using a typical business application scenario.

networks that use TCP/IP as their model refer to network devices as *hosts*. Therefore, any device, whether a computer, printer, or smart terminal, that is connected to a TCP/IP network is called a **host**.

One feature shared by TCP/IP and OSI is that they are both layered models. One difference, however, is that while everyone, everywhere agrees that the OSI model has seven layers, TCP/IP, depending on who you speak to or what reference you are reading, may be presented as either a four- or a five-layer model. Either approach will include all of the functionalities of the TCP/IP model; the difference is in how some of those functionalities are divided between the layers. For purposes of clarity, this text will present TCP/IP as a five-layer model.

Another significant difference between TCP/IP and OSI is that with TCP/IP, several of the protocols are relatively independent of the layer that they are generally associated with. This means that some protocols, depending on the needs of the network, can appear in one or another of the TCP/IP layers. With the OSI model, protocol functions are dependent, or tied, to the layer they are associated with.

In our approach, the TCP/IP model is presented as having five distinct layers, as shown in Table 1.2. Each layer has a set of functionalities and responsibilities. As with the OSI model, the lower-level layers, the physical and data link layers, are responsible for placing the data on a physical medium and then framing, or formatting, the data bits into a form that can be passed from one computer to another. The mid-level layers, the network and transport layers, are responsible for complete delivery of a message, and the data packets that make it up, between sender and receiver. The top-most layer, the application layer, represents functions that involve the user or user applications. The application layer of TCP/IP includes the functionalities of the OSI application, presentation, and session layers. Table 1.2 shows the layers, from top to bottom, of the TCP/IP model.

Table 1.2 The Five Layers of the TCP/IP Model

Sender	Receiver
5. Application	5. Application
4. Transport	4. Transport
3. Network	3. Network
2. Data link	2. Data link
1. Physical	1. Physical

Let's look at each of these TCP/IP layers. You probably will not be surprised to discover that they have many of the same functionalities as those identified in the OSI model.

Application Layer

The TCP/IP application layer is equivalent to the application, presentation, and session layers of the OSI model. In TCP/IP, this layer is also sometimes referred to as the *process layer*, because this is where a protocol stack interfaces with processes on a host machine, enabling that host to communicate across the network. Simply stated, this layer is the user's access to the network.

Transport Layer

The transport layer of the TCP/IP model has two key protocols that are identified with it: TCP (Transmission Control Protocol) and UDP (User Datagram Protocol). Both TCP and UDP are responsible for the delivery of a message from one process to another, or in other words, from the sender to the receiver. (A later chapter explores how TCP and UDP differ in this delivery.) This layer's primary responsibility is establishing and maintaining end-to-end communication between the sender and receiver.

Network Layer

The network layer of TCP/IP supports IP, the Internetworking Protocol. Four protocols are associated with the IP protocol: the Address Resolution Protocol (ARP), the Reverse Address Resolution Protocol (RARP), the Internet Control Message Protocol (ICMP), and the Internet Group Message Protocol (IGMP). The key here is that IP, working within the network layer, is the transmission mechanism used by the other TCP/IP protocols. IP is formally called an "unreliable" and "connectionless" protocol, but that does not mean that it is bad or weak. IP is used at the network layer to send units of data called datagrams from one network to the next. You will learn more about datagrams in a later chapter.

Data Link Layer

As in the OSI model, the data link layer is responsible for moving data from one host to the next in the network path from the sender to the receiver. Bear in mind that between the sending host and the receiving host there may be, and probably are, many intermediary hosts. The data link layer will frame the data bits and perform flow and error control.

Physical Layer

This TCP/IP layer serves the same purpose as its OSI twin. At the physical layer, the physical connections between the sender and receiver are specified. The physical layer will detail all of the hardware devices and physical mediums used to transport data from one host to another.

Networking Categories

Up to this point, you have discovered that there are data communication protocols, standards, and models, each of which is logical, defined, and documented. That is all very well and good, but as of yet nothing physically exists. You have the theory but not the product. What we must do next is implement the theory into a real, live, physical data communications network. But it is not, of course, quite that easy. The problem is that no one-size-fits-all network solutions are available. In the physical implementation of the logical theory, many factors must be considered in order to determine the type of network that will be built. Very likely, as a curious professional networking technologist, you are already asking several questions: What is the purpose of the network? What services will this network be expected to provide? What types of connectivity, 10 people or 100,000, are required? What are the physical dimensions the network is bounded by, a room or a country? What type of business and user applications will this network have to support? Are the applications online real-time, 24/7 as they say, or are they batched? Based on business requirements, what bandwidth and transmission issues need to be addressed? Will there be a need for remote accessibility? What size budget is available? Will there be a qualified staff to support the network? Does management understand the types of resources the network might require, and is management willing to support those needs? Do any regulatory issues—city, state, county, national, and/or international—need to be addressed? Have we run out of questions yet? The answer is, no.

There will always be more questions with more problems, or as an optimist would say, more challenges. But these are just a sampling of the questions networking professionals ask themselves when designing a network. Likely, the answers will require more than one type, or category, of network. Answering the questions just presented will go a long way toward defining what category of network is needed, and in some cases, several different types of networks may be required.

A network will fall into one of four categories:

1 Local area network

2 Backbone network

3 Metropolitan area network

4 Wide area network

Each type of network will be discussed in much greater detail in later chapters. This introductory chapter provides a very simple set of characteristics associated with each type of network. Keep in mind that each category of network is in itself a very large topic. Entire courses are designed around subtopics relating to each of these four categories. In today's world, a networking technologist will usually end up concentrating his or her technical skills in one of these four networking categories, and probably within a subtopic area of the category. It is to the advantage of the technologist, however, that he or she understand, at least in general, something about each of the four categories of networks that make up a complete data communications system.

This text provides a detailed overview of the critical factors that touch on each of these networking categories. Keep in mind that sometimes the distinction between where one category of network begins and another ends can be blurry. This is especially true when technologies designed to support one category of network are applied to a different category.

Local Area Networks

A **local area network (LAN)** is a network that is usually bounded by a relatively small geographical space, for example, a room, a building, or a complex of buildings. LANs are generally inexpensive to set up, especially compared to the other types of networks. Of great importance is that, because LANs typically do not cross public thoroughfares or property, they are not regulated by the FCC or state public utility commissions. Depending on the type of LAN, a LAN might include devices such as printers, microcomputers, workstations, servers, hubs, bridges, and routers. We describe these different devices in greater detail in later chapters. For now, be aware that a LAN can have differing configurations based on the specific needs of a business. An organization may have one LAN, or hundreds, based on its business needs. Figure 1.13 illustrates a simple LAN.

Backbone Networks

Organizations that have more than one network, and especially more than one LAN, may want to connect these networks so that they can share resources. All of the networks that belong to one organization are collectively called the **enterprise**. An organization's enterprise network may consist of dozens, or hundreds, of networks. The networks of the enterprise are typically connected through a **backbone network (BN)**. A BN is usually a high-speed circuit that connects all of the networks within the enterprise, allowing them to communicate with each other. Figure 1.14 demonstrates how a BN might be used.

Metropolitan Area Networks

A **metropolitan area network (MAN)** is a network that spans a city. An organization can use a MAN to cover greater distances at higher data rates than those offered by a LAN. A MAN can be used to connect BNs and LANs. An organization may find, if justified by transmission-volume needs, that having a private MAN may be less expensive than leasing

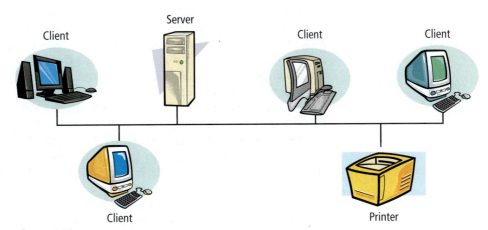

Figure 1.13
Simple Local Area Network (LAN)
A local area network (LAN) is typically limited in size, for example, to a room or building. Also, a LAN will usually have no more than 50 connected devices.

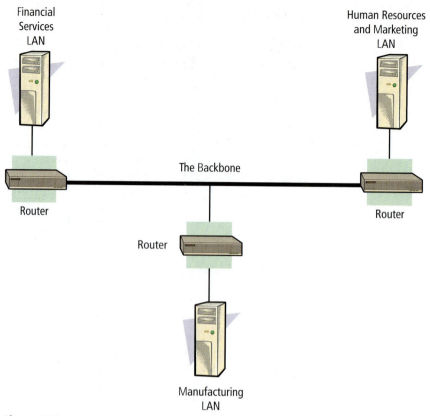

Financial
Services
LAN

Human Resources
and Marketing
LAN

The Backbone

Router

Router

Router

Manufacturing
LAN

Figure 1.14
Simple Backbone Network (BN) in a Single Building
A backbone is a network used to connect other networks of the enterprise.
The backbone is typically a high-speed circuit. In this example, routers
connect the networks of the enterprise to the backbone.

these services from a local telephone company. A MAN is between a LAN and a WAN in terms of its geographic scope. However, MANs, unlike LANs, may be subject to federal and state regulations.

At this point, the term *cloud* must be introduced. A cloud to most people is a fluffy, beautiful object floating in a blue sky. To a data communications technologist though, a **cloud** is a term used to logically represent connecting to a network infrastructure without being concerned as to how that infrastructure is configured, maintained, or controlled. For many users of MAN and WAN infrastructures, how the infrastructure works is not their concern. These users are simply leasing or renting the right to use the infrastructure, and they generally leave the details of how it works to others. The inner workings of the infrastructure, the details that are hidden from the user, are called the cloud. Figure 1.15 shows a three-LAN organization connecting through a MAN cloud.

Wide Area Networks

Business data communication needs may require that data be transported over great geographic distances, such as across a state, several states, a country, or even around the world. A network on this scale is called a **wide area network (WAN)**. A WAN will very commonly use

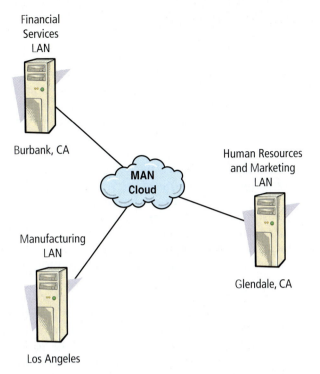

Figure 1.15
Simple Metropolitan Area Network (MAN)
*Los Angeles County is a very large metropolitan area
that includes the cities of Burbank, Glendale, and
Los Angeles.*

circuits provided by **common carriers**. Common carriers include such
organizations as Sprint, MCI, AT&T, and SBC, among others. A WAN
can connect BNs and MANs. The infrastructures that create and support a WAN are heavily regulated. Figure 1.16 illustrates a WAN that
spans a continent.

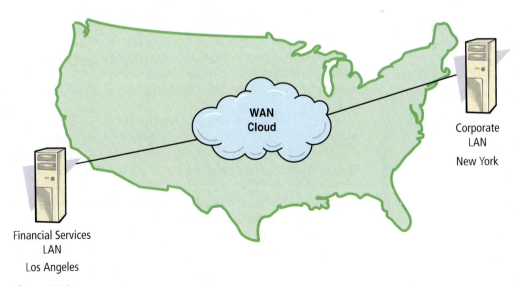

Figure 1.16
Simple Wide Area Network (WAN)
*A WAN spans great geographic distances, including states, provinces, countries,
continents, or the globe.*

Five phases characterize the evolution of data communications over the past five decades: (1) digitization, (2) expansion, (3) deregulation, (4) Internet as a common tool, and (5) pervasive computing. Technology continues to change, altering our definition of what is meant by "communications."

Data communications is a subset of telecommunications. Whereas telecommunications involves such technologies as telephony and television, data communications is more specifically concerned with the transmission of data between computers and computer networks. In the transmission of data from one location to another, data are first transformed using binary coding schemes. Binary coding schemes use the binary digits 0 and 1, which are called bits, to represent data.

Data communications uses protocols, or rules, that establish how the communications occur. There are many different types of protocols that fulfill different purposes and functionalities. Protocols state how the data are to be formatted, how the format is to be interpreted, the rate at which the data are to be transmitted, and whether communications between two devices can be established.

Protocols become established or defined through a standards process. Both formal and informal standards exist. The trend is for standards to be open and publicly available for all to use. There are numerous standards-setting bodies; many of them are nongovernmental, private nonprofit organizations.

Networks have both physical and logical components, the hardware devices that make them up and the software that drives them. Networks are also based on models. Open architecture models have some of the same advantages as open standards. Two major models used in data communications are the Open Systems Interconnection, or OSI, model and the Transmission Control Protocol/Internet Protocol, or TCP/IP, model. The two models share several characteristics, and each model is well established and accepted by the data and telecommunications industries. One of the most important features they share is that both models are based on the concept of layered architectures.

A model is based on theory. The theoretical model must then be implemented into a physical data communications network. In general, a network falls into one of four categories, based on the network's characteristics. A local area network (LAN) is usually contained within a limited geographic area. A backbone network (BN) is usually a high-speed circuit that connects all the networks within an enterprise. A metropolitan area network (MAN) can connect BNs and LANs. Wide area networks (WANs) are used to transport data over great geographic distances, such as across a state, a country, or even the globe.

chapter one | Keywords

ARPANET **(7)**

Backbone network (BN) **(25)**

Binary **(12)**

Closed architecture technology **(5)**

Cloud **(26)**

Common carrier **(27)**

Compression **(20)**

Data communications **(11)**

De facto standard **(15)**

Deregulation **(7)**

Digitization **(3)**

Encoding scheme **(14)**

Encryption **(20)**

Enterprise **(25)**

Host **(22)**

Infrastructure **(5)**

Internet **(7)**

IPv4 **(8)**

IPv6 **(8)**

Layered architecture **(18)**

Layer stack **(19)**

Local area network (LAN) **(25)**

Logical addressing **(21)**

Metropolitan area network (MAN) **(25)**

Nonproprietary **(15)**

Open architecture technology **(5)**

Open System Interconnection (OSI) model **(19)**

Pervasive technology **(9)**

Proprietary **(3)**

Protocol **(13)**

Standards **(15)**

Telecommunications **(11)**

Telemetry **(9)**

Transmission Control Protocol/Internet Protocol (TCP/IP) model **(21)**

Wide area network (WAN) **(26)**

Short Answer

1. What are open standards, and what, if any, are the advantages of such standards?

2. In general, why would a layered architecture be viewed as beneficial?

3. What is a protocol and why would one be used? Provide an example of a technological protocol or a society-based protocol.

4. What are the four different types of networks and what are the key characteristics of each?

5. How are the OSI and TCP/IP models similar? How do they differ?

Multiple Choice

For each of the following select the one best answer.

1. During which decade did the process of extensive digitization begin?
   a. 1940s **b.** 1950s **c.** 1960s **d.** 1970s

2. During which decade did the widespread growth of data communications begin?
   a. 1940s **b.** 1950s **c.** 1960s **d.** 1970s

3. Early mainframe computers were based on what type of architecture technology?
   a. Closed **b.** Open **c.** Proprietary **d.** a or c

4. The trend today is toward architecture technologies that are
   a. closed. **b.** open. **c.** proprietary. **d.** a or c

5. Which of the following is a key goal of deregulation?
   a. To allow more competition to enter a market
   b. To decrease competition in a market
   c. To stabilize the market
   d. Deregulation is not applicable to telecommunication services.

6. Which of the following describes the level of international competition among telecommunication providers?
   a. Competition is low. **b.** Competition is moderate.
   c. Competition is high. **d.** Competition is not an issue.

7. Which of the following sparked the creation of the Advanced Research Projects Agency?
   a. Lawsuits brought against Bell Telephone
   b. The launch of Sputnik by the Soviet Union
   c. Demands for technology from big business
   d. None of the above

8. Currently, which of the following is the most widely implemented version of the Internet?
   a. IPv2 **b.** IPv3 **c.** IPv4 **d.** IPv6

9. Which of the following is the most recent version of the Internet?

    a. IPv2   **b.** IPv3   **c.** IPv4   **d.** IPv6

10. Which of the following is a wireless communication technology that can be used to remotely monitor environmental conditions or equipment parameters?

    a. Fiber optics   **b.** IPv4   **c.** Telemetry   **d.** TCP/IP

11. Which of the following was one of the original purposes of the Internet?

    a. To provide advanced database functions
    b. To provide security for common business applications
    c. To enable remote file sharing among researchers
    d. None of the above

12. Data communications is a subset of

    a. telecommunications.   **b.** communications.
    c. Either a or b   **d.** Neither a nor b

13. Traditional data communications includes such technologies as

    a. television.   **b.** telegraphy.   **c.** telephony.   **d.** None of the above

14. Which of the following can be represented as data?

    a. Text   **b.** Graphic images
    c. Sound and video files   **d.** All the above

15. How many distinct values are used by a binary coding scheme?

    a. 1   **b.** 2   **c.** 4   **d.** 8

16. Which of the following describes a protocol?

    a. A set of rules that determine how something is performed
    b. A computer that performs a task in a certain way
    c. Information that is not used in data communications
    d. Information that is not part of the OSI or TCP/IP models

17. Which of the following is true of formal standards?

    a. They are never proprietary.
    b. They are always proprietary.
    c. Either a or b, depending on the standard.
    d. They are just like de facto standards.

18. Which of the following is true of a formal standard?

    a. It might evolve from a de facto standard.
    b. It never evolves from a de facto standard.
    c. It always begins as a de facto standard.
    d. None of the above

19. Networks have

    a. only a physical component.
    b. only a logical component.
    c. both physical and logical components.
    d. a or b, but not both at the same time.

20. Which of the following is true of the Federal Communications Commission (FCC)?

    a. It is a major standards-setting body.
    b. It is a United Nations regulatory body.
    c. It is a United States regulatory body.
    d. Both b and c

21. International standards-setting bodies can affect standards

    a. only outside the United States.
    b. sometimes inside the United States.
    c. always inside the United States.
    d. There are no international standards-setting bodies.

22. Which of the following is true of the OSI or TCP/IP models?

    a. Only OSI is based on layers. **b.** Only TCP/IP is based on layers.
    c. Neither is based on layers. **d.** Both are based on layers.

23. Which of the following is true of the physical layers of the TCP/IP and OSI models?

    a. The physical layers of the TCP/IP and OSI models are very different.
    b. The physical layers of the TCP/IP and OSI models are very similar.
    c. The OSI model does not have a physical layer.
    d. The TCP/IP model does not have a physical layer.

24. A layer in a model needs to communicate with

    a. the layers directly above it. **b.** the layers directly below it.
    c. all layers in the model. **d.** a and b

25. Which of the following is true of the OSI model?

    a. It is older than the TCP/IP model.
    b. It is newer than the TCP/IP model.
    c. It is the same age as the TCP/IP model.
    d. The OSI and TCP/IP are essentially the same model.

26. Which of the following is a network that is restricted in size to a room or a building?

    a. LAN **b.** BN **c.** MAN **d.** WAN

27. Which of the following is used to connect the networks of an enterprise?

    a. LAN **b.** BN **c.** MAN **d.** WAN

28. Global networks commonly fall into which category?

    a. LAN **b.** BN **c.** MAN **d.** WAN

29. A LAN may connect to which of the following?

    a. BN **b.** MAN **c.** WAN **d.** All the above

30. Standards-setting bodies

    a. are always run by a governmental agency.
    b. are never run by a governmental agency.
    c. may or may not be run by a governmental agency.
    d. are not relevant to data communications.

31. How many phases characterize the evolution of data communications?

    a. 2 **b.** 3 **c.** 4 **d.** 5

32. The use of the Internet as a common tool is associated with which decade?

    a. 1960s **b.** 1970s **c.** 1980s **d.** 1990s

33. Early large-scale computers were called

    a. data frames. **b.** mainframes.
    c. data stores. **d.** data warehouses.

34. During which decade were packet-switching networks created?

    a. 1960s **b.** 1970s **c.** 1980s **d.** 1990s

35. Which year saw the federally mandated breakup of Bell Telephone?
a. 1974 **b.** 1984 **c.** 1994 **d.** 2001

36. How many companies were created from the breakup of Bell Telephone?
a. 1 **b.** 8 **c.** 5 **d.** 7

37. Binary coding schemes use elements called
a. frames. **b.** packets. **c.** addresses. **d.** bits.

38. Which term refers to set of rules that determine how something is performed or accomplished?
a. Code **b.** Protocol **c.** Etiquette **d.** Procedure

39. Which of the following is NOT a key data communication protocol characteristic?
a. Specifying how data is formatted or packaged
b. An agreement as to the meaning of a given data format
c. Determining when communications can begin
d. The name of the protocol

40. Which of the following is another term for an informal standard?
a. De facto standard **b.** In facto standard
c. Ad hoc standard **d.** None of the above

41. Which of the following is an international body with great influence in the field of information technology?
a. ANSI **b.** EIA **c.** FCC **d.** ISO

42. Which of the following is an important regulatory agency that controls communication technologies in the United States?
a. CCC **b.** SCC **c.** FCC **d.** DCC

43. How many layers does the OSI have?
a. 4 **b.** 5 **c.** 6 **d.** 7

44. Which layer in the OSI model is responsible for encryption and compression?
a. Application **b.** Session **c.** Presentation **d.** Compression

45. Which layer in the TCP/IP model maintains end-to-end communication between the sender and receiver?
a. Application **b.** Transport **c.** Network **d.** Data link

46. Networks can be categorized into how many categories?
a. 2 **b.** 3 **c.** 4 **d.** 5

47. Which type of network is used as a high-speed connection to connect other networks?
a. LAN **b.** BN **c.** MAN **d.** WAN

48. Which type of network would span a city but not a state?
a. LAN **b.** BN **c.** MAN **d.** WAN

49. The study of the standards of conduct between right and wrong is called
a. anthropology. **b.** semantics. **c.** ethics. **d.** biography.

50. A term used to logically represent connecting to a network infrastructure without being concerned as to how that infrastructure is configured, maintained, or controlled is
a. network. **b.** cloud. **c.** protocol. **d.** standard.

True or False

For each of the following select either True or False.

1. Extensive digitization is a process that began in the 1940s.
2. Early mainframe computers were based on an open architecture technology.
3. The trend today is toward the use of open architecture technologies.
4. There is little international competition among telecommunication providers.
5. The Advanced Research Projects Agency was created in response to lawsuits brought against Bell Telephone.
6. Telemetry is as a wireless communication technology that can be used to remotely monitor environmental conditions or equipment parameters.
7. One of the original purposes of the Internet was to enable remote file sharing among researchers.
8. Data communications includes such technologies as television and telegraphy.
9. Data might include text, graphic images, and sound or video files.
10. Binary coding schemes use at least four distinct values.
11. A protocol is a set of rules that determine how something is performed or accomplished.
12. Formal standards are never proprietary.
13. It is not unusual for a formal standard to evolve from a de facto standard.
14. Networks have both physical and logical components.
15. The Federal Communications Commission is a major standards-setting body.
16. The OSI and TCP/IP are both layered models.
17. The physical layers of the OSI and TCP/IP models are very different.
18. Layers in a model only need to communicate with layers that they directly border or touch.
19. A LAN is usually limited in size, restricted to a building or campus.
20. BNs are primarily used to connect the networks of an enterprise.

Exercises

Research in Brief

As a data communications professional your researching skills will be very important, whether in troubleshooting a jabbering network host, finding the latest software driver, or providing a cost-benefit analysis for a technical solution to your

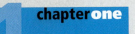

management. At the end or every chapter four questions will be presented that require additional research and analysis on your part. For one or more of the questions below, provide a one- to two-page report based on your findings.

1. Select one of the standards-setting bodies introduced in this chapter and answer the following questions:

   - What is the history of this body?

   - What technologies does this body concentrate on?

   - What recent developments has this body been involved with either to recommend or establish new standards?

   - Why is this body important to the area of data communications?

2. Describe what a protocol is and detail the process of how a protocol might become a standard. Discuss the advantages of open protocols.

3. Unicode provides for extensive new character-set definitions. Visit and explore the Unicode Web site at **www.unicode.org**. Answer the following based on your findings:

   - Who belongs to the Unicode consortium?

   - What is the current version of Unicode and what does it include or not include?

   - What future changes to Unicode are planned?

   - What are the benefits of a coding scheme such as Unicode?

4. Pervasive computing will transform how we think of communications technology. The following three Web sites address pervasive computing: **www.computer.org**, **www.ibm.com/pvc**, and **www.nist.gov**. Visit these sites, or others that you find, and answer the following questions:

   - What organizations are involved in pervasive computing?

   - How do you think pervasive computing might change a society?

   - What types of issues are being discussed with regard to pervasive computing?

Case Study

Each chapter ends with a case study. The case study presents a scenario that will be a continuing work in progress, building from one chapter to the next using the same business problem. As you work through the case study at the end of each chapter, you will create a total business solution that will require you to understand how the information you are learning fits into the "big picture." You may work on this case study alone or in small groups.

Sheehan Marketing and Public Relations

Sheehan Marketing and Public Relations (SMPR) is a mid-sized public relations firm that focuses on the entertainment industry, primarily film and music. Based in Los Angeles, SMPR also has branch offices in New York and Chicago, with plans for expansion in Miami and Nashville. Each office has an internal network; the offices' internal networks are not currently connected to one another. SMPR's office networks were implemented 6 years ago. Each office network is based on UTP Ethernet 10 Mbps traffic using hubs. Currently, the branch offices depend on telephone and United Parcel Post (UPS) for cross-country communications.

Tom Sheehan, SMPR president, recognizes that to remain competitive, the corporate and branch offices need much greater integration of their technology and improved communications between branch offices. Each office has data and information resources that the others do not. The offices must be able to collaborate and share music, video, and text files. Each office currently maintains it own database of clients and projects. However, SMPR account executives working from different offices increasingly need to work, as a team, on a given client's marketing and public relations program.

Each SMPR branch has a manager who reports directly to the company's president. Each branch manages its own payroll, accounting, and other services. Only the LA office has a dedicated LAN administrator. However, the LAN administrator, Karla, was never trained in her job, but "grew" into it because "she understands computers." The New York and Chicago offices are frequently frustrated by the lack of on-site technical support, which is needed to keep their LANs up and running. At the last quarterly branch managers retreat meeting, held of-site in Phoenix, a major topic was how data communications technology could help SMPR not only improve, but also survive. President Sheehan informed his managers that he would aggressively pursue solutions to their problems. He stated that one of his first goals would be hiring a network technologist who would oversee and manage SMPR's data communication technology operations.

Although pleased with this decision, the branch managers also expressed concern that their individual offices would be neglected or not have their needs immediately addressed. In fact, Sheehan was surprised at how strongly each branch manager insisted that his or her branch office must be the first linked to the Los Angeles office. There was also much discussion about what skills a corporate networking technology manager should have. Before ending the retreat, it was agreed that a major strategic goal of SMPR would be the integration and coordination of data communication technology needs across all offices. As he concluded the session, President Sheehan reflected that he would need to know much more about the data communications industry in order to guide his business wisely.

Case Questions

Using the information just provided, answer the following questions.

1. What are SMPR's data communication needs?

2. Based on the information provided, do you foresee any significant problems in integrating and coordinating the needed networks? If so, what are they?

3. What skills do you think should be included in a job description for SMPR's new corporate networking technology manager?

4. How much do you think the owner of a business like SMPR needs to know about data communications? Detailed information? General information? Justify your answer.

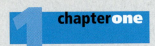

5. Mr. Sheehan is also contemplating the creation of a mission statement for his organization that would describe how SMPR uses client data. List three things you believe should be addressed by such a statement.

Web References

The links presented here, and in other chapters, were active and operational at the time this text was published. However, because of the dynamic nature of the World Wide Web, sites come and go. We apologize should one or more of the links referenced no longer be operational.

www.hydropoint.com

www.epic.org/privacy/rfid

www.ieee.org

www.iso.org

www.itu.int

www.ansi.org

www.eia.org

www.isoc.org

www.ietf.org

www.iesg.org

www.iab.org

www.iana.org

www.fcc.gov

www.unicode.org

www.computer.org

www.ibm.com/pvc

www.nist.gov

How the Layers Work

The following discussion is simplified in order to make the topic more approachable. Most significantly, the term *envelope* is used to describe how data might be processed in a layered model. Many students relate to the intent of a private letter being enclosed in an envelope, stamped, and only, ideally, being read by those meant to read it! The layered models are in some ways similar to the concept of addressing private handwritten mailed communications. Greater detail as to how the data communications layers work is provided in later chapters.

This chapter introduced two of the world's most popular data communication models, OSI and TCP/IP. Both models use a layered architecture. In a layered architecture, each layer is responsible for a particular set of functions and operations. A given layer is only required to communicate with the layers immediately above or below it. This means, in the 7-layer OSI model, layer 3 needs to communicate only with layers 2 and 4. Layer 3 has nothing directly to do with layers 1, 5, 6, or 7. In fact, layer 3 doesn't know, or care, that the other layers, other than 2 and 4, exist.

With this highly conceptual topic, understanding how these layers work can be challenging. By placing the layers into the context of a common business need—for example, sending a payments-due-and-paid report electronically from one network in an organization to another—we expect to make clearer just what these mysterious layers are doing and why. The following discussion focuses on the OSI model and its seven layers, explicitly detailing how and what each layer is doing and why. Also, because the focus of this text is on TCP/IP, this OSI example will provide needed exposure to this model. TCP/IP layers, though, operate in a manner similar to how the OSI layers operate.

In the OSI model, the seven layers, from top to bottom, are application, presentation, session, transport, network, data link, and physical. The sender and receiver each have identical layer stacks on their networked workstations. With the OSI model, the seven layers can be divided into two categories: end-to-end layers and chained layers. The top four layers are the end-to-end layers: application, presentation, session, and transport. These four layers are "end-to-end" because the layers on the sender's "end" and receiver's "end" directly communicate with each other. The four top layers on each "end" establish a communication. This communication provides an "end-to-end" connectivity.

The remaining three lower layers—network, data link, and physical—are the chained layers. These three layers are "chained" in that they are used to link, or chain, one physical device to another in a communication path. The number of devices that need to be linked, or chained, depends on the number of intermediary devices or networks between the sender and receiver of a communication. In a network or enterprise, there may be many intermediary devices or networks between a sender and receiver. The lower three layers provide the chain of links that permits the sender and receiver to have a communication. Figure 1.17 shows the OSI layers in an end-to-end and chained illustration. Notice in this figure how the end-to-end layers appear only in the layer stacks of the sender and receiver, whereas the chained layers are on all devices, especially those that "link" the sender and receiver to each other. Let's consider how this might work with a common business application.

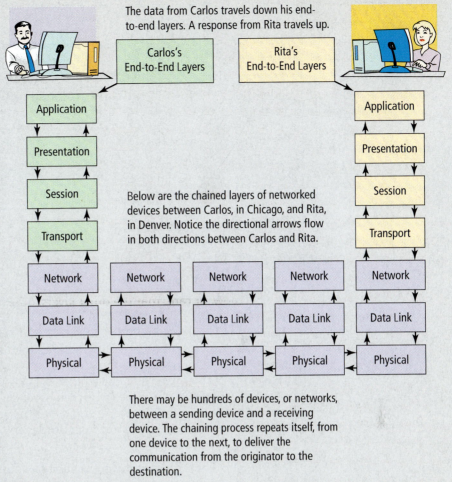

The data from Carlos travels down his end-to-end layers. A response from Rita travels up.

Carlos's End-to-End Layers

Rita's End-to-End Layers

Application

Presentation

Session

Transport

Below are the chained layers of networked devices between Carlos, in Chicago, and Rita, in Denver. Notice the directional arrows flow in both directions between Carlos and Rita.

Network	Network	Network	Network	Network
Data Link	Data Link	Data Link	Data Link	Data Link
Physical	Physical	Physical	Physical	Physical

Application

Presentation

Session

Transport

There may be hundreds of devices, or networks, between a sending device and a receiving device. The chaining process repeats itself, from one device to the next, to deliver the communication from the originator to the destination.

Figure 1.17
OSI End-to-End and Chaining Layers

Carlos and Rita are both employed by ACME, Inc. Carlos works in Accounts Payable (AP) at the Chicago branch office. Rita works in Financial Services (FS) at the company's Denver office. From his workstation in Chicago on the AP LAN, Carlos sends a large report file to Rita regarding outstanding payments owed and amounts paid to various vendors for the last fiscal quarter. Rita, in Denver, receives the report file at her workstation, which is part of the FS LAN. As you can imagine, there are likely numerous intermediary devices and networks between Carlos's workstation in Chicago and Rita's in Denver. How does Carlos's report file get to Rita? And how do the OSI layers assist in this process?

In Chicago, at his "end," Carlos's workstation has a report-generating program associated with a database, such as Microsoft's SQL Server or Oracle's Oracle9i. At her "end," Rita has the same, or similar, reporting program and database. To send his large report file, Carlos uses a file transfer protocol program. The user interface in this file transfer program serves as the "application layer" mechanism that permits Carlos and Rita to exchange the data file over the network. (Other common types of application layer protocols include e-mail and Web browsers, which are covered in detail elsewhere in the text.) From his workstation, Carlos uses the file transfer program to submit his data for transmittal. When Carlos clicks the Send button or presses the Enter key on his keyboard, the file transfer application layer protocol takes over.

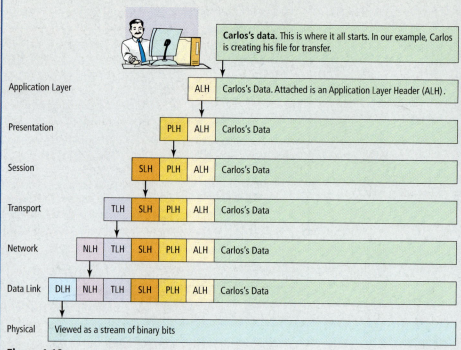

								Carlos's data. This is where it all starts. In our example, Carlos is creating his file for transfer.
Application Layer							ALH	Carlos's Data. Attached is an Application Layer Header (ALH).
Presentation						PLH	ALH	Carlos's Data
Session					SLH	PLH	ALH	Carlos's Data
Transport				TLH	SLH	PLH	ALH	Carlos's Data
Network			NLH	TLH	SLH	PLH	ALH	Carlos's Data
Data Link		DLH	NLH	TLH	SLH	PLH	ALH	Carlos's Data
Physical	Viewed as a stream of binary bits							

Figure 1.18

OSI Layers with Enveloping and Headers

As Carlos's data travels down the layers, each layer envelopes and adds its own header. As the data travels up the layers on Rita's device, each layer recognizes the header created by its equivalent from Carlos's end.

The file transfer program at the application layer of Carlos's workstation puts his data into what we can think of as an "envelope." The program also writes a note, or header, on the outside of this electronic envelope. The matching file transfer application layer protocol on Rita's receiving "end" workstation reads the header and data created by Carlos's application to interpret the application protocol being used. (Because the sender might be using one of many application layer protocols, an e-mail client or Web browser for example, a header provides specific information on the protocol being used.) Other layers ignore this application layer header, recognizing that it is not addressed to their level. An envelope created by one layer is read and processed only by its matching layer on the other side of the communication. This is the magic of how the layers work with each other. Look at Figure 1.18 to see how each layer provides for its own envelope and header.

From the sender's perspective, each layer accepts an "envelope" of data from the layer above it. Upon acceptance, without reading the contents of the envelope, each accepting layer puts the unread envelope into a new envelope that it creates. The accepting layer then attaches its own header and other relevant information to the envelope it creates. An envelope created at one layer is not processed or read by the other layers. The different layers recognize which layer created an envelope by reviewing the attached header information. Let's continue with Carlos's file transfer.

Carlos's application layer file transfer protocol puts his data into an envelope, stamps the envelope with a header, and then hands that stamped envelope down to the presentation layer. You may recall that the presentation layer takes application layer data and transforms it into a form agreeable to both the sender and receiver. The presentation layer can also encrypt the data if it is flagged as being sensitive. In our example, Carlos creates his report file using an English-character-based alphabet, meaning simply the report is in text, not binary. After all, the report is not for a machine to read, but for Rita! Even so, as discussed earlier in this chapter, data must be encoded into a binary form before it can be transmitted over a communication infrastructure. This is where the presentation layer comes in. Carlos's presentation layer transforms the received application layer's English text data into binary data, encrypts it, packages the transformed data into a presentation layer envelope, stamps the envelop with its own presentation layer header, and passes this newly created envelope down to the session layer.

The job of the session layer on Carlos's end is to ensure that the session layer at Rita's end is available for a communication. If, for some reason, Rita's workstation is not available for communication (a bad data link, her workstation is turned off, some type of hardware or software failure, etc.), a session will not be established and the process will stop. But, let's assume that Rita's workstation is up and running properly and ready for communications. Carlos's session layer makes the initial contact with Rita's session layer, establishes a connection, monitors its progress throughout the communication, and eventually terminates the communication. If the connection is not terminated when data transfer is finished, valuable bandwidth or circuit capacity could be wasted. However, for the session layer to be successful in establishing a communication, the session layer hands down a "connection request" to the transport layer. Once the connection request has been fulfilled, meaning a successful connection has been established, the session layer on Carlos's end creates an envelope. Carlos's session layer places his presentation data into a session layer envelope, stamps the envelope with a session layer header, and hands the envelope down to the transport layer.

The transport layer, as we just saw, assists the session layer by first making the initial connection request. In our example, we need to connect Carlos's workstation in Chicago to Rita's in Denver. Once the link is established, the session layer hands down its stamped envelope to the transport layer. If the session layer data envelope is too large, the transport layer may need to segment the data into smaller units. In fact, this is one of the transport layer's essential duties. On Carlos's end, the transport layer takes Carlos's session layer data and disassembles this data into segments and sequences these segments with a number. The disassembled segments must be given a sequence number so that they can be put back into correct order by the transport layer on Rita's receiving end. In this way, the transport layer on the sender's end creates segmented envelopes; each envelope is stamped with a sequence number and other transport layer header information. These transport layer enveloped segments are then passed down to the network layer.

In our example, the end-to-end layers have done their work, and now the chained layers take over. The chained layers are concerned with getting the data from one device to another in the chain of devices between a sender and receiver. In Carlos and Rita's case, there are likely many intermediary devices, and networks, between them. The network layer on Carlos's workstation receives its transport layer data, envelopes the data, and stamps the envelope with network layer header routing information. (Later chapters discuss how this routing information is determined. For now, let's simply say that the network layer maintains routing information that allows it to know where to send a data envelope on its way from the original sender to the ultimate receiver.) With this routing information, the network layer is ready to pass down its stamped header envelopes to the data link layer.

The network layer may need to route data from one network to another. The data link layer, however, is only concerned with passing data from one single device to another. The data link layer envelopes the data, stamps it with a header, and then passes the data down to the physical layer. The physical layer is the one layer that does not create an envelope and stamp it with a header. Instead, the physical layer, which we look at in greater detail in Chapter 2, is simply a means of getting the physical data bits from one point to another, whether the two computers are 5 feet or 500 hundred miles apart. The physical layer does not evaluate or analyze the data bits; it is only concerned with transmitting these bits along a physical media.

Let's assume that there are 100 networks between Carlos and Rita, and that each network has 20 devices. A communication between Carols and Rita must go through multiple devices and networks to get to where it needs to go. The number of devices and networks between Carlos and Rita depends on how the enterprise is set up. The important idea here is that there is a chain of devices and networks between Carlos and Rita that have to be navigated in order for a communication to be delivered. Imagine that you are telling a friend in Florida how to drive to your house in Los Angeles. Such a trip would require several days, with different "linking" or "chaining" highways or roadways to get from point A to point B. That is a chaining process. You are planning out to your friends, by links, how to get to your house. Our data communication example is not so different, except that instead of friends in a "car" envelope we have data bits in an "electronic" envelope. This chaining process continues over and over again (network, data link, physical) until eventually the data arrives at its ultimate destination, in our example, to Rita's computer in Denver from Carlos's computer in Chicago.

This discussion has described the flow of data from the application layer to the physical layer. From the sender's end, each layer envelopes and attaches headers (except at the physical layer). Once the receiver receives the data, the opposite occurs. Instead of headers being attached as they pass down through the layer stack, as they do at the sender's end, the reverse occurs as data flows up the layer stack at the receiver's end. For the receiver, headers are evaluated and stripped off as the data passes up the layer stack on the receiver's end. Each layer in the stack processes the envelope appropriate to its layer, identified by the envelope header, and then strips off, or removes, its own layer header and envelope before passing the data up the stack to the next-higher layer.

The physical layer at the receiver's end, in this case Rita's workstation, takes the binary bits coming in from her physical layer and passes them up to her workstation's data link layer. Rita's data link layer evaluates the data received in their appropriate data link layer format. Assuming no problems are encountered, the data link layer removes its layer-specific information and passes the data up to the network layer. The network layer does the same, evaluating and removing its layer-specific information and passing the data up to its next-higher layer, the transport layer. The other layers continue the process. Eventually, Rita is looking at a report on her workstation's display screen in an application-friendly format, very likely without realizing the amount of layer-stack teamwork required to get it there. But that is, after all, how it should be in a well-run enterprise.

2 chapter two

Physical Layer Fundamentals

Learning Objectives

After studying this chapter, you should be able to:

- Understand the general purpose of the physical layer.
- Identify four components of the physical layer.
- Describe the differences between analog and digital signaling.
- Understand amplitude, frequency, and phase modulation in analog signaling.
- Describe the differences between simple and complex analog signaling.
- Understand general digital signal encoding schemes.
- Describe two digital transmission modes.
- Explain two circuit configurations.
- Explain three methods of data flow.
- Identify common types of conducted media.
- Identify common types of radiated media.
- List the factors that affect medium selection.
- Identify common physical layer devices.
- Describe four types of multiplexing.

Chapter 1 described how physical data communications networks are based on logical models. These models propose that physical networks be built using a layered approach. Both the OSI and TCP/IP models identify lower-level layers. These lower-level layers are responsible for the physical media and the devices that make up a network and the initial framing of data bits so that these bits can be passed from one computer or network to another. The two lower-level layers are the physical and the data link layers. This chapter looks in greater detail at the physical layer.

Physical Layer Concepts

The **physical layers** of the OSI and TCP/IP models serve the same function in a very similar manner. Both identify the physical characteristics of the network. Such physical characteristics may include the types of cables and **connectors** that are used to join devices. For example, when using a cable, how long should the cable segment be? In this chapter, you will learn that the segment length depends on the type of cable used. A cable might be coaxial, twisted-wire pair, or fiber-optic. Based on the type of cable, particular types of connectors will be required. Connectors create physical links between communicating devices. Data transmission may also be wireless.

The physical layer converses or talks directly with the data link layer. The data link layer passes *frames* of data bits down to the physical layer. The physical layer then transmits these frames as an unformatted stream of electrical, optical, or electromagnetic signals represented by the binary bits 0 and 1. (A **frame** is a specially formatted sequence of bits. Framing occurs at the data link layer and is discussed in the next chapter.) In effect, the physical layer does not "see" a frame, only a stream of data bits. The physical layer is responsible for transmitting this unformatted bit stream across a **transmission medium**, from one device to another, until ultimately the data bits travel from sender to receiver.

Data bits are frequently passed through pins in the connectors. It is the physical layer's function to make pin-signal assignments for the cable and connectors. ISO (**www.iso.org**) standard 2110 defines connector-pin assignments for 25-pin serial connectors. This means that each of these 25 pins has a particular purpose and function. The DB-25 connector, for example, is frequently used in modems, and each of its pins is associated with a particular signal. Figure 2.1 shows a standard DB-25 connector and its pin designations. There are, of course, many other kinds of connectors (see **www.cablesdirect.com**).

Transmission properties are also defined at the physical layer that indicate how a binary 0 or 1 signal is to be represented in either an analog or digital encoding scheme. A 0 or 1 can be represented either electronically or optically. Most networks make use of some type of digital encoding scheme. We take a closer look at a couple of digital encoding schemes later in this chapter.

Note that the physical layer assigns no meaning to the data bits it is transferring. This means that the physical layer does not interpret the bit stream. That is not its job. The physical layer serves as a means of getting the data bits from point A to point B. It is the function of the higher-level layers of the OSI and the TCP/IP models to provide meaning to the bits being transmitted.

Physical Layer Components

The four physical layer components are (1) the signaling methods used for conveying or representing data and translating between them, (2) the circuit configuration that carries the data, (3) the transmission medium used, which is wired or wireless, upon which the circuits are based, and (4) the devices typically associated with this layer.

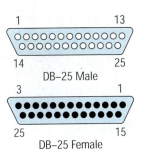

DB–25 Pin	Centronics Pin	Signal Description	Signal Direction (at the PC)	Signal Function
1	1	STROBE	Output	Clocks data
2	2	DATA BIT 0	Output	Data line
3	3	DATA BIT 1	Output	Data line
4	4	DATA BIT 2	Output	Data line
5	5	DATA BIT 3	Output	Data line
6	6	DATA BIT 4	Output	Data line
7	7	DATA BIT 5	Output	Data line
8	8	DATA BIT 6	Output	Data line
9	9	DATA BIT 7	Output	Data line
10	10	ACKNLG	Input	Acknowledge receipt of data
11	11	BUSY	Input	Printer is busy
12	12	POUT	Input	Printer is out of paper
13	13	SEL	Input	Printer is online
14	14	Auto Feed XT	Input	Autofeed
15	32	FAULT	Input	Indicates printer fault (or when printer is offline)
16	31	Input Prime or INIT	Output	Resets printer, clears printer buffer and initializes it
17	36	SLCT IN	Output	TTL high level
18–25	16, 17, 19–30, 33	Ground	N/A	Ground reference for signal pins 1–12, in most cables as twisted pairs.

Figure 2.1
Standard DB-25 Connector with Pin Designations

Each component is equally important in fulfilling the functions of the physical layer. Understanding what these components do, and why, will be essential in designing a networking infrastructure that is both effective and efficient.

In terms of management, when something is **effective**, it is performed correctly. When something is **efficient**, it is cost-effective. The two terms are not the same, and a networking technologist will pay close attention to both. Furthermore, from a business perspective, we want our data communication systems to be a balance of efficiency and effectiveness. Achieving an ideal balance can be challenging, especially when there are so many varying technologies from which to choose.

Signaling

A **signaling method** defines a set of rules for representing how a 0 or 1 is to be represented electromagnetically. The question is: Why would one need to do that? Recall that networks transmit data from one location to another. A physical transmission medium connects the devices with the networks. However, the data are not always in a form that can be transmitted across the medium. For example, the data may initially take the form of a paper document, such as a sales invoice. Obviously, a paper document cannot be directly transmitted across a network in its original form. For that reason, the original data must be encoded into a form that the medium can support.

The binary bits 0 and 1 are used to encode the data. However, our transmission medium is a physical path that conducts energy in the form of electromagnetic signals, not literally 0s and 1s. Therefore, these binary bits will have to be further transformed into electromagnetic form. This transformation turns the physical layer's data bit stream into energy in the form of electromagnetic signals. These signals may be either analog or digital. Let's look more closely at each type of signal representation, beginning with analog.

Analog Signaling

The term **analog** refers to a measure, form, or expression that is continuous and has a range of magnitude between one value and another. Temperature, for example, is analog. If we have a finely calibrated Fahrenheit thermometer, we could measure a continuous range of temperatures from 98.000 to 98.999. In fact, humans live in an analog world. Things such as smell, sound, and touch, as we experience them, are all analog. When using analog transmission, the signal sent over the transmission medium will continuously vary from one state to another in a smooth, wavelike pattern. An analog wave is capable of having an infinite number of values as it travels along its path.

Analog communications are used extensively. Phones (both landline and cellular), modems, fax machines, cable television, and many other devices and network services are based on analog communications. Our first telephone networks were designed for analog communications— human speech, not data. When we speak, our voices generate sound waves. The plain old telephone system, or POTS, was originally built to transmit voice sound waves in an electrical form. A telephone on the sender's end will translate the sound wave produced by a human voice into electrical signals. These signals are then passed to and travel along a voice communication circuit. A telephone on the receiving end will then reverse the process, taking incoming electrical signals and converting them back into sound for the listener to hear.

In analog communications, signals flow across a copper wire in the form of electromagnetic waves. Analog signals can also use fiber-optic or wireless (e.g., radio, microwave, infrared) transmission media. Taking the

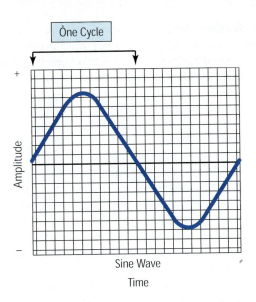

Figure 2.2
Simple Sine Wave Modulated by Amplitude, Frequency, and Phase

One Cycle

Amplitude

Sine Wave

Time

form of a sine wave, analog signals may be simple or complex. A sine wave is usually represented as a smooth oscillating curve with a continuous rolling flow, as shown in Figure 2.2. Whether simple or complex, sine wave analog signals have three basic characteristics that can be manipulated, or modulated, to represent the binary bits 0 and 1. These modulated characteristics are amplitude, frequency, and phase. Let's look at each of these characteristics, first in their simple form, and then as a complex signal.

Amplitude Modulation

The amplitude of a sound wave defines the height, or strength, of the wave. In terms of your own voice, if you speak loudly, amplitude increases; when you speak softly, amplitude decreases. **Amplitude modulation (AM)** takes place when the height of a sound wave is manipulated to encode a binary 0 or 1. Amplitude modulation is also called *amplitude shift keying (ASK)*. Simple amplitude modulation defines one amplitude or height of a wave as representing a binary 0 and the second amplitude as defining a 1. Amplitude modulation is measured in watts, volts, or amperes, depending on the type of signal. See Figure 2.3 to see how amplitude is used to encode 0s and 1s.

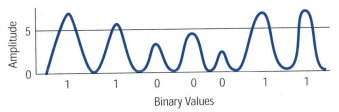

Amplitude

5

0

1   1   0   0   0   1   1

Binary Values

Figure 2.3
Amplitude Modulation
In this figure, note that different ranges of amplitude, measured in voltage, can be used to identify equivalent binary 0s and 1s. Voltage values between 0 and up to and including 5 are identified as a binary 0, any voltage value greater than 5 is a binary 1.

Frequency Modulation

When you speak in a higher or lower pitched voice, you are demonstrating a form of frequency modulation. **Frequency modulation (FM)** uses **frequency**, the number of waves per second, to differentiate between 0 and 1. Frequency modulation is also called *frequency shift keying (FSK)*. With simple frequency modulation, the amplitude of the wave remains constant and only two different frequencies are defined. One frequency encodes a 0, the second encodes a 1. Frequency modulation also has an element called the **period**, which is the amount of time, in seconds, that a signal needs to complete one cycle. A cycle is the completion of one full pattern of a wave. Thus, frequency modulation is based on two concepts: frequency and period. Figure 2.4 shows how FM is used to encode 0s and 1s to depict both period and frequency.

The communications industry has defined five units of measurement for both frequency and period. Frequency is measured in hertz, kilohertz, megahertz, gigahertz, or terahertz. A **hertz** is a unit of frequency. The following prefixes are also used: kilo for thousand, mega for million, giga for billion, and tera for trillion. A kilohertz, then, has a unit frequency of 1,000. A period is measured in seconds, milliseconds, microseconds, nanoseconds, or picoseconds. See Table 2.1 to see how these values are expressed exponentially.

It just so happens that frequency and period are the multiplicative inverse of each other, so if you know one, you can determine the other. Following are a few examples. When you see them, don't panic. Realize that in a typical business setting, it is unlikely you will be called upon to do this type of computation. Still, it is to your benefit to know something about the physics of FM. And besides, you can dazzle the boss with your grasp of a tough subject.

Let's assume we have a wave with a frequency of 8 hertz. Its period, expressed as a multiplicative inverse, is 1/8, or .125, second. A wave with a frequency of 8 kilohertz has a period of 1/8000, or .000125, second. A wave with a period of 8 seconds has a frequency of 1/8, or .125, hertz. If a wave has a period of 80 microseconds, its frequency

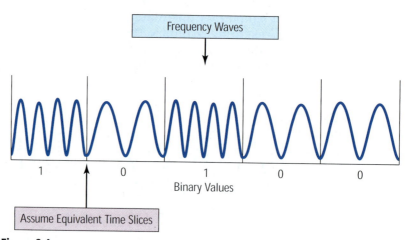

Figure 2.4

Frequency Modulation

Frequency modulation also has a time component. In this example, assume that within the same time period if four or more frequency waves are generated then a binary 1 is represented. If three or fewer frequency waves are generated, a binary 0 results.

Table 2.1 Frequency and Period Unit Measurements

Frequency Unit	Frequency Unit Exponential	Period Unit	Period Unit Exponential
Hertz (Hz)	1 Hz	Seconds (s)	1s
Kilohertz (KHz)	10^3Hz	Milliseconds (ms)	10^{-3}s
Megahertz (MHz)	10^6Hz	Microseconds (µs)	10^{-6}s
Gigahertz (GHz)	10^9Hz	Nanoseconds (ns)	10^{-9}s
Terahertz (THz)	10^2 Hz	Picoseconds (ps)	10^{-12}s

is 1/.000080, or 12,500 hertz, which is equal to 12.5 kilohertz (12,500/1000).

Phase Modulation

Phase modulation, which is also called *phase shift keying (PSK)*, is a bit more complicated. With **phase modulation (PM)**, a wave begins in a given direction, called its phase, and then creates a baseline, or reference wave. Look at Figure 2.5 as you read so that you can see what is being described. As shown in Figure 2.5, the baseline begins at zero. As the wave starts at the baseline and moves up and to the right, it reaches phase degree zero (0°). As the wave starts at the baseline and moves down and to the right, it reaches phase degree 180 (180°). We can define phase 0° as being a binary 0 and phase 180° as being a binary 1. As the phase shifts, or modulates, it changes from 0 to 1, and then back again.

In Figure 2.5, the first time period wave is the baseline wave and is defined as binary 0. When the phase shifts, in time period two, a binary 1 is expressed. Unlike amplitude or frequency modulation, phase modulation

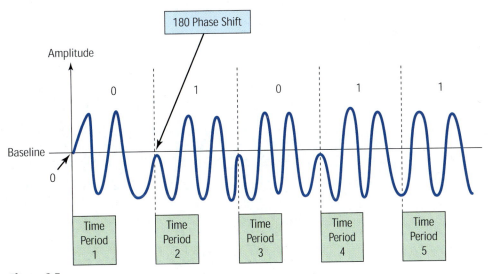

Figure 2.5
Phase Modulation
Note that the wave's amplitude, frequency, and time periods are the same. The phase shift causes the change in value from 0 to 1.

is not readily intelligible to the human ear. Fortunately, electronic devices can easily recognize phase changes.

Of the three modulation techniques, amplitude modulation is the most susceptible to noise and distortion during transmission. Amplitude, frequency, and phase modulation can all be used in radio and television broadcasting. For satellite communications, though, only frequency and phase modulation are used. With **simple signal modulation**, which is what has been discussed thus far, each signal sent represents only one binary bit. In this case, the bit rate and the symbol rate are the same. The term *bit rate* refers to the number of bits transmitted per second, per signal. The **symbol rate** refers to the number of bits that can be encoded in a single signal.

With simple signal modulation, the ratio is one-to-one, meaning that one signal symbol represents one bit. Some techniques, however, allow a single signal symbol to represent more than one bit. Such techniques are referred to as complex signal modulation.

Complex Signal Modulation

In **complex signal modulation**, the symbol rate and the bit rate are not the same. Instead, the bit rate becomes a multiple of the symbol rate. Before continuing, let's look again at what we mean by the symbol rate.

The symbol rate is also called the *baud rate*, but symbol rate is the term recommended for use by the ITU-T. In simple signal modulation, one bit is encoded per symbol, so the bit rate and the symbol rate are the same, one-to-one. Complex signal modulation, however, allows a single signal symbol to encode more than one bit. In that case, one symbol may have two, four, or more bits encoded within it. This can be accomplished in several ways.

With amplitude modulation, it is possible, for example, to define not two, but four different amplitudes. Each of the four amplitudes would represent one pair of two bits: 00, 01, 10, or 11. Figure 2.6 shows the definition of four distinct amplitudes. Each single amplitude, or symbol, represents

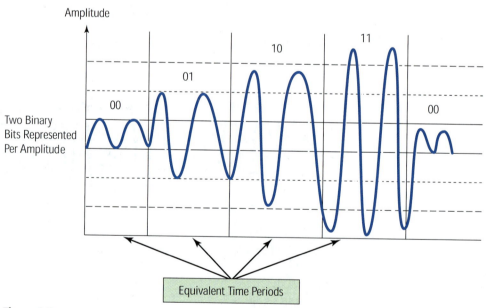

Figure 2.6

Expression of Two Bits per Symbol by Complex Signal Amplitude Modulation two bits. If eight amplitudes were defined, four bits per symbol could be encoded. At some point though, if too many amplitudes are defined, it may become difficult to differentiate between them. If a communication system cannot differentiate one amplitude from another, the significance of the different amplitudes becomes lost and the communication fails.

This concept also works with frequency and phase modulation. Defining four frequencies or four phases allows each single frequency or phase to represent two bits. Modulation techniques can also be combined. Quadrature amplitude modulation (QAM) is one popular combination method. QAM uses two different amplitudes and eight different phases. Each amplitude is capable of representing one bit and each phase three bits, for a total of four bits. The bit rate would be four times the symbol or baud rate. A major advantage of combination techniques such as QAM is that more bits can be sent at the same time, resulting in faster transmissions.

A tremendous volume of data is carried on analog communication circuits. From this discussion, you can see that it is possible for analog signals to be translated into digital signals. This translation is necessary so that analog signals can be processed by computers, which are digital. However, computers frequently need to send their digital signals across analog lines, again requiring a translation, but in this case the translation is digital to analog. Both analog and digital signaling are important. Now that we know something about analog signaling, let's take a closer look at digital signaling.

Digital Signaling

Digital signaling is, in several ways, more straightforward than analog signaling. With **digital signaling**, only two values are used, 0 and 1. These values are represented electronically. Because digital signals are one value or the other, with no variance in between, they are a discrete representation. This discrete representation means that digital signals have only a given, specific value. Digital signaling is usually less expensive than analog signaling because it requires less complex circuitry. Noise interference is less of a problem in digital signaling, making error detection and correction easier. A disadvantage is that digital signals are more susceptible to attenuation. **Attenuation** can be defined as the weakening of a signal's strength as it travels through a circuit. This weakening of the signal is caused by friction. The longer the distance that a signal needs to travel though a circuit the more probable attenuation becomes. Different media, however, will suffer from attenuation at varying distances. Digital signals can be carried over copper or fiber-optic cables.

Two other characteristics of digital signaling are bit interval and bit rate. **Bit interval** is the time required to send a single bit. **Bit rate** is the number of bit intervals per second. It is usually measured in bps (bits per second).

One of the most common ways of electronically encoding digital signals is to use two different voltage levels, one for each of the two binary digits. A positive voltage is usually used for 0, and a negative voltage for 1. A number of digital encoding schemes are available; each has advantages and disadvantages. To better understand these advantages and disadvantages, we first discuss signal timing and the ability of an encoding scheme to be self-clocking.

Signal Timing and Clocking

Each bit signal sent in a digital transmission has a specific duration. This duration is called the bit interval, or the time required to send one single bit. The sender and receiver in a communication can use the bit interval to clock their transmission with each other. **Clocking** allows the sender and receiver to synchronize their transmission. In a communication, a sender and receiver need to clock, or synchronize, each bit's duration because the bit stream transmitted may, and likely will, contain a string of bits in a series with the same value. This presents a problem.

Bits of the same binary value are identified using the same voltage. So if 20 binary 1s are in a series in the bit stream, one after the other, and each binary 1 is represented by −5 volts, how does the receiver know when one binary 1 ends and another binary 1 begins, since they all look the same? If the bits are clocked, meaning each bit's duration is known, the receiver will be able to determine when one bit begins and ends. This is where the bit interval comes into play.

The sender and receiver may rely on their own external clocks to keep data bits synchronized, based on the bit interval, but would require resynchronizing millions of times per second, which eats up valuable transmission time. Or, extra clocking bits could be inserted into the data stream. But this means that the amount of data will have to be increased, eating up valuable transmission capacity. Both are inefficient solutions. It would be better if the encoding scheme itself had a self-clocking mechanism built into it. An encoding scheme that has clocking "built into" it is referred to as being **self-clocking**. And in fact, many encoding schemes are self-clocking, making external clocks or additional clocking bits unnecessary.

Some encoding schemes use a more sophisticated method called transition coding. With **transition coding**, a value is encoded by means of a voltage transition during the bit interval, not before or after it. The advantage of transition-coding schemes is that they are less susceptible to noise. Noise can distort or corrupt the data bits on a transmission line. Vendors that provide physical layer hardware that use encoding schemes should be able to provide sample timing diagrams for their products; however, you may have to ask for one. (See **www.nuhorizons.com/products/Clock.html** to see some interesting clock and timing devices.) Following are brief descriptions of several digital encoding schemes.

Unipolar encoding has a direct current (DC) component. It uses either a positive or negative voltage, but never both, to represent one value, usually a binary 1, and zero voltage to represent a second value, usually binary 0. Unipolar does not provide transition coding and requires communicators to use their own external clocks for synchronization. As an encoding scheme, Unipolar is mostly obsolete because it is fairly primitive, has problems with synchronization, and cannot be used on media that do not support DC components.

Bipolar encoding uses positive, negative, and zero voltages. Generally, zero voltage is used to represent one value and a nonzero voltage the other. The bipolar encoding schemes non-return-to-zero level (NRZ-L) and non-return-to-zero invert (NRZ-I) do not use transition coding and require external clocks. Both of these forms of NRZ have a disadvantage in that it is difficult to determine within a bit stream where one bit ends and another begins. However, NRZ is inexpensive to implement and does not suffer the DC-component problem presented by Unipolar encoding. Figure 2.7 provides examples of NRZ-L and NRZ-I.

Biphase encoding includes at least one transition per bit interval and provides for a self-clocking mechanism, giving these encoding schemes an advantage over NRZ ones. Also, transition coding makes it easier for these schemes to detect errors. Two common biphase schemes in use are Manchester and Differential Manchester.

Manchester is used in Ethernet and other LANs, whereas Differential Manchester is used in token ring LANs. With **Manchester**, the direction

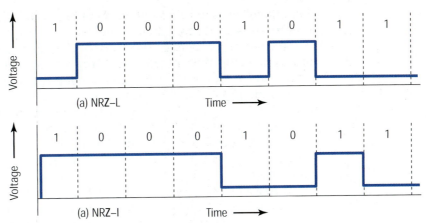

Figure 2.7
Non-Return-to-Zero Level and Non-Return-to-Zero Invert

of the transition in mid-interval, negative to positive or positive to negative, indicates the binary bit value. For a 1 bit, the transition is always from negative to positive; for a 0 bit, it is from positive to negative. This mid-bit transition serves not only to represent data, but also provides clocking. With **Differential Manchester**, the presence or absence of a transition at the beginning of a bit interval indicates the bit value. The transition in mid-interval is used only for self-clocking, not to provide data, which is an advantage. Figure 2.8 illustrates Manchester and Differential Manchester.

Digital Transmission Modes

Digital signaling has another characteristic, the transmission mode. Transmission mode is either serial or parallel. **Transmission mode** determines how many bits will transmit at one time as a block. For transmission mode, the block is usually one or eight bits. Recall that binary bits are used to represent digital data. These binary bits are organized into units called bytes. Each byte is able to represent one, and only

Manchester encoding: With Manchester, the direction of the transition in mid-interval, negative to positive or positive to negative, indicate the binary bit value.

Differential Manchester encoding: With Differential Manchester, the presence or absence of a transition at the beginning of a bit interval indicates the bit value.

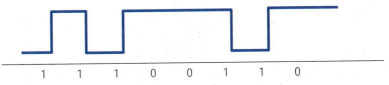

Figure 2.8
Manchester and Differential Manchester Encoding

one, character, such as the characters a, A, 1, 9, #, and $, among others. Binary bits are put together into bytes based on an encoding scheme.

The two most widely used encoding schemes are **ASCII** (American Standard Code for Information Interchange) and **EBCDIC** (Extended Binary Coded Decimal Interchange Code). EBCDIC was created by IBM for use with its large-scale mainframe computers and is based on an eight-bit byte. ASCII is the more common encoding scheme and is used much more extensively, especially by terminals and microcomputers. ASCII has two versions, **Standard ASCII**, based on a seven-bit byte, and **Extended ASCII**, based on an eight-bit byte. Of the two, Extended ASCII is used more often.

In EBCDIC or Extended ASCII, a byte has eight bits. Both EBCDIC and Extended ASCII are capable of encoding, or defining, up to 256 different characters using these eight bits. The limit is 256 because there is a maximum of 256 different ways that eight 0s and 1s can be put together. Two possible ways are 00000000 and 11111111. See Figure 2.9 for other possible ASCII combinations.

In digital transmissions, a byte with its eight bits is transmitted in one of two modes, serial or parallel. In **serial transmission mode**, which is more common because it only requires one wire, each bit of the byte is

Decimal	Octal	Hex	Binary	Value	
000	000	000	00000000	NULL	
048	060	030	00110000	0	
049	061	031	00110001	1	
050	062	032	00110010	2	
051	063	033	00110011	3	
052	064	034	00110100	4	
053	065	035	00110101	5	
054	066	036	00110110	6	
055	067	037	00110111	7	
056	070	038	00111000	8	
057	071	039	00111001	9	
058	072	03A	00111010	:	(colon)
059	073	03B	00111011	;	(semicolon)
060	074	03C	00111100	<	(less than)
061	075	03D	00111101	=	(equal sign)
062	076	03E	00111110	>	(greater than)
063	077	03F	00111111	?	(question mark)
064	100	040	01000000	@	(AT symbol)
065	101	041	01000001	A	
066	102	042	01000010	B	
067	103	043	01000011	C	
068	104	044	01000100	D	
069	105	045	01000101	E	
070	106	046	01000110	F	
071	107	047	01000111	G	

Figure 2.9
Some Extended ASCII Binary Characters

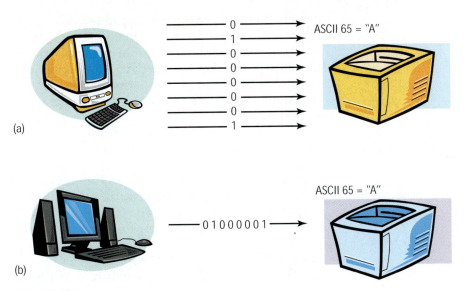

Figure 2.10
Serial and Parallel Modes
In ASCII, the capital letter "A" is represented by the value 01000001. Part (a) of the figure shows the parallel transmission of the letter "A" from a computer to a printer. Note that the bits all travel together at one time. Part (b) shows the serial transmission of the same letter. Note the bits are sent one at a time in single file.

sent single file, one after the other. In **parallel transmission mode**, all eight bits of the byte are sent at one time in parallel, thus this mode is eight times as fast as serial mode. The catch is that parallel mode requires eight separate wires for each of the eight bits of the byte to travel upon. Because of the need and expense for additional wiring, parallel mode is used almost exclusively within the confines of the computer's internal architecture or to connect a computer to a high-speed device, such as a laser printer. Parallel mode is also sometimes used to connect two high-speed devices that are in close proximity to each other. Serial mode, because it only requires one wire, is the more common form used by communication circuits. See Figure 2.10 to see how these two modes differ in how they transmit a byte.

Interestingly, a third encoding scheme has been established, Unicode. **Unicode (www.unicode.org)** uses a 16-bit character code that can support up to 64,000 different characters. This is a big enough character set to represent most, if not all, human languages, something not possible with EBCDIC or ASCII. In addition, Unicode contains the EBCDIC and ASCII coding schemes. Technologies that use Unicode can be **backward compatible** with the proper software engineering. A backward-compatible technology is one that will function with earlier versions of that technology. A backward-compatible technology will cost a business less in that older hardware and/or software may not need to be immediately replaced.

From your reading, you now understand that data signals can be either analog or digital and that both are important in data communications. Digital signals have several advantages over analog signals. Because digital signals are binary, with only two values, they produce fewer errors. Higher maximum transmission rates are possible with digital signaling. More data can be sent through a digital circuit than an analog one; therefore, digital transmission is more efficient. It is also possible with digital circuits to combine data, voice, and video onto the same circuit, allowing for greater integration.

Whether the signals are digital or analog, they have to be transmitted along some type of physical medium. A signal is transmitted through a medium over a circuit. A circuit is simply the path over which data and information travels. Circuits have to be configured in a manner that is effective and appropriate for the network. The next section looks at circuit configuration, the second physical layer component covered in this chapter.

Circuit Configuration

A circuit is the link that provides the physical means by which data are transferred. **Circuit configuration** affects the way in which two or more communicating devices share their connection or link with each other. The two basic circuit configurations are point-to-point and multipoint.

Point-to-Point Configuration

In a **point-to-point configuration**, a dedicated circuit is established between two devices. Circuit dedication means that the circuit's entire capacity is reserved for the two communicating devices; no other devices can use that dedicated circuit. This type of link is most efficient when the two communicating devices are using most, if not all, the capacity of the circuit. If this were not the case, then the circuit's capacity would be seriously underutilized. A point-to-point circuit might also be appropriate between two devices that must be able to communicate with each other whenever they need to. Most point-to-point circuits use a length of wire or cable to connect two devices, but other media are possible, such as microwave, satellite, or infrared. For example, if you use an automatic garage door opener, the device you click, the door opener, is using a wireless point-to-point circuit to communicate with its controller. Figure 2.11 offers an example of point-to-point wired connections.

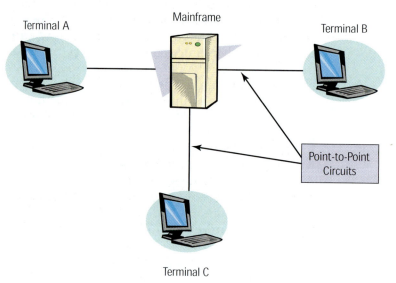

Figure 2.11

Point-to-Point Circuit

In this example, each terminal has a direct point-to-point link, or circuit, to the mainframe computer. For terminal A to communicate with B, A must go through the mainframe. Likewise for B and C. Also, A, B, and C do not share their circuit with each other. This type of circuit is common with mainframe and terminal configurations.

In a typical network, most devices are not in constant communication with other devices. Someone sitting at a typical networked computer is not constantly pressing the Send button or Receive button every 30 seconds to do their work. Instead, most users of these devices only need to send or receive a communication once in a while, not constantly. Therefore, having point-to-point circuit configurations for all devices is not only expensive, because of wiring and other hardware costs, but inefficient as well. Point-to-point circuits should be reserved for devices that require a dedicated link because their communication needs demand it. A pair of multiplexers will, for example, need to be connected by a single link. Multiplexers are devices that let other, slower devices share a higher-speed circuit. Sharing a high-speed circuit is more efficient in terms of utilizing that circuit's capacity. Multiplexing is examined in greater detail later in the chapter.

Multipoint Configuration

Most devices in a network do not require the dedicated capacity of a point-to-point circuit. For the organization, then, it is more efficient and cost-effective for devices to share a circuit. Multiple devices sharing a single circuit are using a **multipoint configuration**. Multipoint is also sometimes referred to as a *multidrop*. With a multipoint circuit, many devices can be connected to the same physical circuit.

Multipoint circuits require that a method be established that determines how devices will share a single circuit resource. One common way for sharing this single resource is for devices to wait turns to use the circuit. The next chapter will describe how Media Access Controls specify how devices share a single physical circuit. Figure 2.12 shows an example of a multipoint configuration.

Bandwidth

Whether point-to-point or multipoint, every circuit has a key characteristic associated with it called bandwidth. For many, this mysterious concept of bandwidth is irritatingly vague and confusing. It can be difficult to

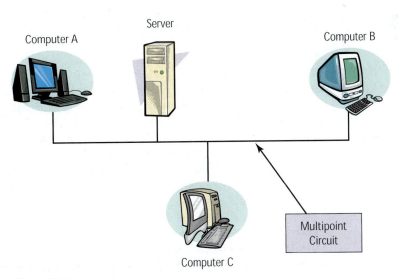

Figure 2.12
Multipoint Configuration
With multipoint circuits, all devices share the same circuit. Multipoint circuits are common in LANs.

grasp something that cannot be seen or touched. Simply stated, **bandwidth** is the capacity of a circuit to carry data. The more data that a circuit can carry, the greater that circuit's bandwidth capacity. And, different types of data require different types of bandwidth capacity.

Consider a river that carries water, with the water being the river's data. A small river will have less capacity, or bandwidth, to carry water than a large river. A small river will also be limited in the types of boat traffic that it can handle. For example, a small river might accommodate a canoe very easily but not be able to support a massive ocean-going cruise ship. A geographer comparing the water capacity of the Sacramento River in the United Sates with the Amazon River in Brazil would say that the capacity, or bandwidth, of the gigantic Amazon to carry water is far greater than that of the tiny, in comparison, Sacramento River. Data communication circuits are conceptually similar, but of course they carry data, not water or canoes. And the data of a small, simple text file will require far less capacity, or bandwidth, than the data of even a small video file.

With an analog circuit, bandwidth is the difference between the circuit's highest and lowest frequencies. The wider this value, the greater the bandwidth. With a digital circuit, bandwidth is usually measured in bps (bits per second). A formula to determine bps using bit interval and bit rate is: bps = 1 / (bit interval * period unit exponential value). (A table of period unit exponential values was provided earlier.) As an example, a digital signal with a bit interval of 60 microseconds has a bps bandwidth of: $1 / (60 * 10^{-6})$ = 16.6 Kbps. The higher the result, the greater the bandwidth. For some, this may be all they want or need to know about bandwidth. However, those who want to know more about this intriguing topic should read the "Topic in Focus" at the end of the chapter.

Data Flow

Whether using a point-to-point or multipoint circuit, data flows over the circuit. The data may flow in one or two directions, based on how the circuit is configured. Data can flow over a circuit in three ways: simplex, half-duplex, or full-duplex. The method chosen depends on how the circuit is to be used. Each method is appropriate under particular circumstances, and a medium- to large-scale network will likely utilize all three.

Simplex

With **simplex** communication, data travel in one direction only; data can be sent or received, but not both. The direction depends on the purpose of the communication. It may be that a central computer receives data from remote sources on a simplex circuit but never sends data back out. When you drive a car and listen to the car stereo, you are experiencing a simplex transmission—you receive but do not send sound. Keyboards and monitors are two common examples of simplex devices; one is used for input, the other for output. The entire bandwidth is used either for input or output.

Half-Duplex

A **half-duplex** circuit can transmit data in either direction, but in only one direction at a time. The circuit is either used to send or receive, but never simultaneously. An example of a half-duplex communication is the use of walkie-talkies that permit two users to speak or listen, but not both at the same time. A network may have a central computer that remotely receives data but that cannot send data while it is receiving. After analyzing the received data, the central computer sends the data back to its source for correction or modification; but while it is transmitting, it cannot receive new data.

Full-Duplex

In a **full-duplex** communication, data can be sent and received simultaneously. An everyday example of full-duplex is a telephone conversation. It may not be polite, but you and your friend can both be talking, or listening, at the same time. To permit this simultaneous two-way communication, one of two things must occur. Either two physically separate transmission paths can be established, in effect creating two circuits, one for sending and one for receiving, or the capacity of the circuit is divided so that the sending and receiving signals can travel together but in opposite directions.

Depending on the needs of the network, simplex, half-duplex, or full-duplex might each be appropriate. Circuits, though, regardless of the type of data flow selected, have to be based on some type of wired or wireless physical medium. **Wired** media are often referred to as *conducted*; **wireless** media are often called *radiated*. The next section examines the third component of the physical layer, the medium used to transmit data.

Transmission Media

Transmission media make up the physical path that data travels over to get from point A to point B. This medium might be wired, or **conducted**, and be one of several different types of cable. The medium might be wireless, or **radiated**, in which case the physical path is said to be "in the air." Data can be radiated in several different ways. Each of these two categories of media, conducted and radiated, have advantages and disadvantages. Based on the needs of the network, both types of media might be required. Some of the characteristics that must be considered when selecting a medium are security, cost, bandwidth, distance, and susceptibility to error.

Certain types of transmission media are used for baseband communications and others are used for broadband. In networking, a **baseband** connection is one that uses digital signals. With baseband connections, one digital stream is transmitted over the single baseband channel. Baseband, by definition, has only a single channel, although within that channel there may be multiple, interleaved signals (this is examined more closely later in the chapter during the discussion on multiplexing). In a traditional sense, **broadband** communication sends analog signals over multiple frequency channels at the same time. However, today broadband is widely marketed and viewed as a digital technology. Broadband offers multiple channels, and each channel is allocated a specific frequency range or bandwidth. Therefore, one physical cable might have separate channels for sound, video, and data. Figure 2.13 shows how baseband and broadband differ. The next section considers different types of conducted and radiated media.

Conducted Media

Conducted media are composed of some type of cable. We will look at three types of cable: twisted-wire pair, coaxial, and fiber-optic. Of these three, twisted-wire pair and fiber-optic are used extensively in data

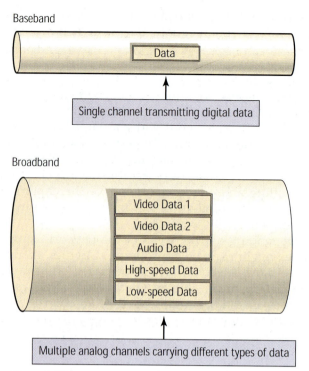

Figure 2.13
Baseband Versus Broadband

communication networks. Coaxial is more likely to be found in older, legacy networks. Networking technologists need to be familiar with all three types of conducted media. Regardless of the cable type, every cable has a conductor, insulation, and sheathing.

Common Cable Components

First, a cable must have a **conductor** over which a signal can be conducted. The conductor will either be copper wire for twisted-wire pair and coaxial cables or glass or plastic strands for fiber-optic cables. For copper, the conductor, called the **carrier wire**, might be solid or stranded, and the conductor's diameter might be measured in inches, centimeters, or millimeters. The **American Wire Gauge (AWG)** is another common means for specifying the diameter of a wire conductor. For fiber-optic cables, the conductor is called the **core**. The core can be either a glass or plastic tube that runs through the cable. The core's diameter is measured in microns, which are millionths of a meter.

Secondly, a cable's conductor has some type of **insulation** that is used to keep the signal in and external interferences out. For electrical wire, the insulation is usually made from some type of nonconductor, such as polyethylene. Fiber-optic insulation is called **cladding**. The cladding is made of a material with a lower refraction index than the core's material. The **refraction index** measures the ability of a material to reflect light rays. For fiber-optic cables, a cladding with a lower refraction index than the core ensures that light bounces back off the cladding and remains in the core.

Finally, a cable also has some type of outer **sheath**, or jacket, that encases the cable's elements and keeps them together. The sheath can also serve to provide some measure of protection from environmental forces such as water, pressure, or heat.

Twisted-Wire Pair

The signal wires for **twisted-wire pair** come in pairs that are wrapped around each other. By twisting wires around each other at regular intervals, usually between 2 and 12 twists per foot, noise on an individual wire is significantly reduced. A twisted-wire pair cable might contain 2, 4, 6, 8, 25, 50, or 100 twisted pair bundles. The more pairs there are per bundle, the more care that must be given to prevent crosstalk by providing adequate shielding and proper wire termination to the connector. Figure 2.14 shows a typical unshielded twisted-wire pair cable.

Unshielded twisted-wire pair cables are connected to network devices using a snap-like plug-in called an RJ-45 connector. These connectors are slightly larger than standard telephone jacks, because they contain more wires. RJ-45s have eight conductors, one for each wire of four twisted pairs. Connectors of any type have what are currently called plugs and jacks. A plug fits, or is inserted, into a jack. In the past, plugs were referred to as male and the jacks as female.

For networking, two- and four-pair cables are the most common. Twisted-pair wire comes in two flavors: **shielded twisted pair (STP)** and **unshielded twisted pair (UTP)**. Of the two, UTP is by far the most commonly used. UTP's cost is significantly less than STP's. Also, because STP uses more shielding to protect its internal copper wiring, it is bulky and can be difficult to work with in tight spaces. UTP, however, is very inexpensive, easy to install, and highly flexible. One potential problem with both types is a moderate risk of security violation. An unauthorized individual could, with the right equipment and opportunity, tap into the copper cabling that UTP and STP are based on. The signals that flow over the copper wire make no distinction between authorized and unauthorized taps. Security is thus a factor to be considered.

UTP is far more susceptible to noise and electromagnetic interference than either coaxial or fiber-optic cabling. Also, UTP signals cannot travel as far as signals on the other cable types before they need to be boosted. Even so, due to its low cost and ease of installation, UTP is the most common medium used in data communications networks. A UTP cable has two conductors, each with its own colored plastic insulation. The colors provide information about the specific conductors in the cable and show which wires belong in pairs. For a standard UTP segment, the length of the cable should not be greater than 100 meters (about 330 feet).

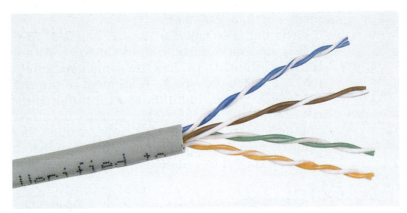

Figure 2.14
Unshielded Twisted-Wire Pair
This is an example of a category 5 unshielded twisted-wire pair. Notice that there are four pairs of two twisted wires.

The EIA (**www.eia.org**), one of the standards-setting bodies identified in Chapter 1, has specified UTP standards by category. The categories range from one to seven, from lowest to highest quality. Because UTP is inexpensive, many networks use Category 5, or Cat 5, which supports data transmission speeds of up to 100 Mbps (million bits per second). Standard Cat 5 has four pairs of 24 American Wire Gage copper wire. Category 1 is basic twisted-wire pair cable used in telephone systems. More than adequate for voice, Category 1 UTP is not sufficient for data communications.

Coaxial Cable

For home use, a type of coaxial cable, RG-11, is a popular choice for connecting to cable television broadcasting and for linking to the Internet. But for data communications networks, coaxial cable is more likely to be encountered in older, legacy systems. Two of the most common forms of coaxial cable are **thinnet** (RG-58) and **thicknet** (RG-8). In enterprise networks, thinnet has mostly been replaced by UTP, whereas fiber-optic cables have replaced thicknet. Recall that the term enterprise refers to the collection of all networks of a single organization.

A standard **coaxial** cable has five layers. The innermost layer is the conductor wire, typically made of copper or copper treated with tin or silver. The conductor wire is wrapped in a dielectric, which is made of a nonconductive material, such as polyethylene or Teflon. The dielectric is wrapped in a foil shield. The foil shield is then wrapped in a braid shield, a flexible conductive wire braid made of aluminum or bare or treated copper. Finally, the braid shield is wrapped in the outermost layer, the jacket or sheath. As you can see, coaxial provides much more shielding than UTP. Figure 2.15 shows a diagram of a typical coaxial cable.

Thicknet, which has a 3/8-inch diameter, is relatively expensive, heavy, hard to work with and install, very inflexible, and has pretty much gone the way of the dinosaur. A segment can be as long as 500 meters. Each computer attached to a thicknet cable uses a connector called a transceiver. The transceiver then uses what is called a "vampire tap" to connect to the thicknet's copper core. Also referred to as 10Base5, thicknet has a maximum data rate of 10 Mbps and is a baseband circuit. The 10 in 10Base5 refers to the speed in Mbps (millions of bits per second), The Base stands for baseband, and 5 refers to hundreds of meters per segment length, or 500 meters.

Thinnet, also called 10Base2, has a 3/16-inch diameter. It is much lighter and more flexible than thicknet. Although less expensive than thicknet, thinnet also has the same maximum data rate of 10 Mbps. It, too, is a baseband circuit. A segment of thinnet runs not 200 meters as you might expect, but 185, several hundred meters shorter than thicknet. Rather than transceivers, thinnet uses BNC or barrel connectors to link devices to its cable. UTP cable, though, is even less expensive then thinnet. Also, most modern buildings are wired with UTP. The low cost and widespread installation of UTP have caused thinnet to lose out to its

Figure 2.15

Baseband Coaxial Channel

With baseband coaxial cables, the copper core provides a single channel.

UTP competitor. The following Web links offer interesting insight into cable selection:

- **www.linktionary.com/c/cabling.html**
- **www.serverworldmagazine.com/monthly/2003/03/kvm.shtml**
- **www.firewall.cx/cabling_10baseT.php**
- **www.windowsitlibrary.com/Content/405/02/1.html**

Fiber-Optics

Fiber-optic cable, unlike twisted-wire pair or coaxial, transmits signals using light rather than electricity. This type of cabling operates in the range of about 10^{14} to 10^{15} hertz. Because light signals are used, fiber-optic cables do not suffer from electromagnetic interferences—a major advantage. Also, fiber-optic cables experience much less resistance to the signals they carry; therefore, signals travel much farther before they need to be boosted. Consequently, fiber-optic signals encounter much less attenuation than those transmitted over a copper medium—a second major advantage. In addition, fiber-optic cable provides excellent bandwidth. Speeds of up to 50 Gbps (billion bits per second) are possible—a third advantage. And finally, fiber-optic cables are extremely hard to tap into—a fourth advantage. With a fiber-optic strand, if the strand is broken, which will likely occur if someone tries to tap into it, the link itself is broken, and communication stops. Fiber-optic circuits provide excellent security. Given all these advantages, why then isn't everything fiber-optic? One word answers that question: cost.

Fiber-optic technology, with all its benefits, is also quite expensive. Network Interface Cards (NICs) (discussed in the next chapter) for fiber connections can cost hundreds of dollars per card. An NIC is essential for connecting to the network. An NIC for a UTP connection might cost as little as $20. If 1,000 devices must be connected to the network, and each device must have an NIC, you can see how cost might be an important decision factor. In evaluating their needs, businesses often select to go with the technology that is the most cost-effective rather than the most technology efficient. Recall that effectiveness and efficiency are two different considerations. Each must be balanced.

Fiber-optic cables have one or more glass or plastic fibers through which light moves. Plastic is less expensive to manufacture, but works over shorter distances. Glass is more expensive, but works over greater distances. Distance, then, may be a deciding factor over what type of fiber-optic cable is selected. Do you need to connect a campus of a few buildings or branches across a state? In either case, the fiber core will range from 2 to several hundred microns. One micron is about 1/25,000 of an inch. Most core sizes for networking are 60, 62.5, and 100 microns. Also, most fiber-optic cable has at least two strands in its core, one for receiving and one for sending. You may recall that fiber-optic cable has a cladding for its insulation. The core and the cladding are frequently manufactured as a single unit. The fiber-optic cable can be either single mode or multimode. A mode is a possible path through which light can travel through a cable.

When single-mode fiber-optic cable is used, the core is very narrow, usually less then 10 microns. Single-mode cable has the least signal attenuation, but it is the most costly to install. Using single-mode cable, speeds of greater than 50 Gbps are possible. To put this in context, one 10 Gbps line can carry up to 130,000 voice channels. Because there is only one transmission path, distortion of the signal, which can occur with multimode, will not happen. Single-mode fiber-optic cable with a glass core and cladding will be of the highest quality and the highest expense.

Multimode cabling has a wider core. Because the core is wider, multiple beams of light have more paths to follow, resulting in the transmission of greater amounts of data. However, in a multilight path, signal distortion at the receiving end of the transmission is also more likely. Multimode is particularly useful in wavelength division multiplexing (WDM). In 1997, Bell Laboratories developed a WDM system that used 100 light beams to generate a total data rate of 1 trillion bits per second.

The light source for fiber-optic is either a laser or a light-emitting diode (LED). Although laser light sources provide better quality, LEDs are cheaper. LEDs are also less likely to fail, and thus are more reliable. Because of cost and reliability, LEDs are more commonly used. Whether single- or multimode, fiber-optics has become the medium of choice for backbone networks. Figure 2.16 contrasts single and multimode fiber-optic strands.

Fiber-optic technology is expensive and has its own special requirements. See the following Web sites for more information about fiber-optics.

- **www.corning.com/opticalfiber/discovery_center/tutorials/fiber_101/**
- **www.fiber-optics.info/glossary-a.htm**
- **www.fiber-optics.info/default.htm**
- **www.arcelect.com/Telebyte_Fiber_frame_page.htm**

So far we have discussed conducted, or wired, media. The other category type of media is radiated, or wireless. Whereas conducted media can be physically seen and touched, radiated media is, under normal circumstances, invisible to the human eye and said to be "in the air." For certain data communication needs, radiated media may provide the best, and

Figure 2.16
Single and Multimode Fiber-Optic Cables

sometimes the only, solution. We look now at the common forms of radiated media.

Radiated Medium

Radiated or wireless media has four general forms: earth-based **terrestrial microwave**, space-based **satellite microwave**, **radio**, and **infrared**. All of these forms are based on frequency waves, electromagnetic or light. Radio and microwave transmission and reception are achieved by use of antenna. During transmission, the antenna radiates electromagnetic energy into the air. For reception, the antenna picks up the electromagnetic energy. With infrared media, transmitters and receivers are used that modulate infrared light. As with the different conducted media, each type of radiated medium has advantages and disadvantages.

One disadvantage that all radiated media share is low security. Because transmissions are carried in the air, anyone with the proper equipment can intercept these transmissions. Therefore, for data that are sensitive or critical, some type of encryption is typically used. Data that are **encrypted** are scrambled or altered in order to prevent unauthorized users from understanding the message. Encrypted data, however, require that both the sender and the receiver have the necessary **software keys** to unlock the meaning of the scrambled messages. Encryption has a time element. It takes time to encrypt and then unencrypt data so that the data can be used. There is a saying that "time is money." Encryption is used with selected data, not all data. The same is true with compression, when data are squeezed into a smaller form so that the data can be transmitted more quickly. Again, compressed data must be uncompressed before it can be used. Again, this takes time.

Terrestrial Microwave

In a terrestrial microwave application, a microwave signal is beamed over a line-of-sight path to a parabolic antenna. Microwave frequencies follow a straight line and do not bend with the curvature of the Earth. Because microwave frequencies do not bend, **line-of-sight antennas** are required. The sending antennas must be precisely placed in order for the transmitting frequency to be passed and caught by the receiving antenna. If the antennas are not in line of sight of each other, a transmitting frequency will continue on a straight line into space, and ultimately into the next galaxy and beyond—which is not good when we are trying to communicate here on Earth.

Transmission frequencies used in terrestrial microwave generally range from 2 to 40 GHz (Gigahertz, billions of hertz). Higher frequencies provide higher potential bandwidth and data rates. But, higher data rates are also more likely to experience errors. As is true with any transmission medium, attenuation can be a problem. Microwave boosters are usually placed between 10 to 100 kilometers apart. These boosters, also called repeaters, can be installed with each antenna. Environmental influences such as heavy rain, snow, or fog can negatively impair a microwave's performance, whether terrestrial or satellite. Terrestrial microwave is an essential and critical component in global telephone systems.

Microwave relay stations are typically placed at high positions, such as on skyscrapers or hills or mountains, in order to extend the range between the sending and receiving antennas. For long distances, a series of microwave relay towers are required. This type of transmission, as with satellite transmission, crosses public thoroughfares and

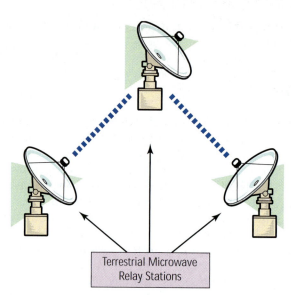

Figure 2.17
Terrestrial Microwave Relay Stations
Terrestrial microwave relay stations must be in line of sight of each other. The microwave frequencies they transmit do not bend with the curvature of the Earth, but instead travel in a straight line. One relay station captures and passes a transmission to the next relay station. The dotted lines represent data being transmitted.

Terrestrial Microwave Relay Stations

is highly regulated. Cost in establishing a microwave network is high. Figure 2.17 diagrams how a series of microwave relay stations might work. See the following Web sites for more information on terrestrial microwave:

- **www.andrew.com/products**
- **www.microstar-antennas.com**
- **www.photoconnect.net/imgIndustryTelecoms/index.php**
- **www.antenna-tower.com**

Satellite Microwave

Satellite microwave is also a line-of-sight technology, but in this case one of the stations is on Earth and the other is in orbit. The satellite, in effect, is the antenna and the receiver. The satellite also serves as an amplifier, so intermediate amplifiers are not needed as they are with terrestrial microwave. When transmission signals need to span a continent or an ocean, satellite is a good choice. However, satellite microwave can also be negatively affected by the same environmental conditions as terrestrial microwave: heavy rain, fog, snow, or solar flares from the Sun.

Transmitting over two bands, satellites have an uplink and a downlink. The **uplink** is from the Earth station to the satellite. The **downlink** is from the satellite to the Earth station. The optimum frequency range for satellite communications is from 1 to 10 GHz. A satellite in geosynchronous orbit is fixed about 23,000 miles above the Earth's surface. Note that there are only a limited number of spaces available to place satellites in geosynchronous orbit. It takes at least three geosynchronous satellites, equally spaced from one another, to provide complete global coverage.

The long distances traveled by signals transmitted by satellite results in propagation delay. **Propagation delay** is the time it takes a transmission to get from Earth to the satellite, or vice versa. This delay is significant enough that it can be noticed in a satellite-based telephone conversations. Propagation delay can also result in problems related to data flow and error control. As with terrestrial microwave, satellite communications are heavily regulated and very expensive to implement. Most users of microwave technologies, whether terrestrial or satellite, lease the

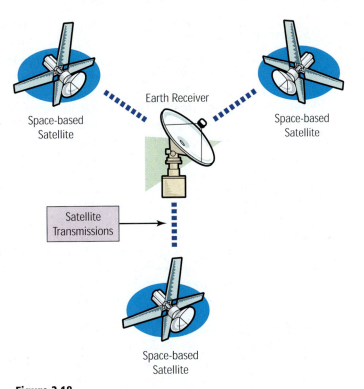

Figure 2.18
Satellite Communications
*Three geosynchronous satellites are required for
global communication coverage. An Earth-based
station communicates with its space-based satellite
partner and can then relay that communication to another
space-based satellite. The satellites are in line of sight
with their Earth-based receiver.*

use of the infrastructure from a common carrier rather than build their
own. Leasing the infrastructure is only moderately expensive. Figure 2.18
shows what a possible satellite communication might look like.

Because of cost and the limited number of locations to position geosynchronous satellites, low-earth-orbiting satellites, or LEOs, are
another option. LEOs are much closer to the Earth, typically between
435 and 1,500 miles. This closer distance means that propagation delay
is not a problem. However, this type of satellite also covers a much
smaller area of the Earth in terms of communications capability. This, in
turn, means that many more LEOs are required to cover the same
amount of territory that a geosynchronous satellite could cover. In addition, LEOs travel faster than the rotation of the Earth. This means that a
ground station that uses a LEO must track the satellite before beginning
a communication. See the following Web sites for more information on
satellite technology:

- **www.satdx.com**
- **www.windows.ucar.edu/cgi-bin/tour_def/space_missions/
  sputnik.html**
- **www.amsat.org**
- **www.metoffice.com/satpics/latest_VIS.html**
- **noaasis.noaa.gov/NOAASIS**

The Ethical Perspective

Satellites and You

Satellite technology has proven to be an invaluable tool for modern man, assisting in weather tracking, global communications, environmental research on global climate change, and exploration of the universe, as well as other uses. Satellite technology, however, also allows the users of that technology, primarily governments, major research institutions, and large businesses, to use the technology in ways that not all may be in agreement with.

For example, one country may use its satellite technology to observe and track the events taking place in another country, in a highly detailed manner. Buildings, vehicles, and people can be tracked with almost pinpoint accuracy from anywhere in the world. Some are concerned that a government might use this technology to track its own population in ways that its citizens are unaware of. Many consider the use of satellite technology for such purposes to be a violation of a government's international sovereign rights and an invasion of privacy of the populace at large.

What do you think? Should international law stipulate how satellite technology is used? Are there ethical issues of conduct related to privacy and security that should be considered by those who either control or have access to satellite technology? What is your ethical perspective?

Radio

Radio transmissions, in terms of data communications, generally fall in the VHF (very high frequency) and UHF (ultrahigh frequency) ranges. Together, they range from 30 MHz to 1GHz. VHF frequencies are associated with VHF television, FM radio, aircraft AM radio, and aircraft navigational aids. UHF is associated with UHF television, mobile telephones, cellular radio (which can be used in wireless networks), and paging. Because of their low frequencies, VHF and UHF are less susceptible to environmental attenuation caused by rain, fog, and snow.

The tremendous popularity of mobile telephones and other mobile devices is driving the convergence of the telephone and the Internet. Emerging radio-based technologies include Bluetooth and IEEE 802.11g, two topics we return to in a later chapter. Radio solutions can accommodate the relatively short distances associated with a LAN. In addition, such technologies are low in cost. However, the speed of data transmission is also slow—from 1 to 10 Mbps.

Infrared

Infrared communications use transmitters and receivers, which have to be in line of sight of each other. The frequency used is just below the visible light spectrum. Unlike microwave transmissions, infrared light does not penetrate or pass through solid substances such as walls. Because transmission does not go beyond a room, security problems are lessened compared with other wireless solutions. However, this also limits the mobility of the user linked to an infrared network. Like radio, infrared has a relatively low cost and is used for short distances appropriate to a LAN. Although infrared can potentially provide significant bandwidth, as a technology it can be difficult to implement, especially with its line-of-sight requirements.

Transmission Impairment

Many factors can negatively affect a medium's transmission performance. Cable performance can be impaired by attenuation, crosstalk, and distortion. Radiated media are affected by fog, rain, snow, and solar disturbances. Transmission impairment can result in the transmission signal sent not being the transmission signal received.

Attenuation

Attenuation is the decrease of a signal's strength as it travels over a wire. This happens because the signal loses some of its energy as it tries to overcome the resistance of the cable. The greater the distance the signal must travel over a segment of cable, the more likely it is that a loss of signal strength, or attenuation, will result. Attenuation occurs more often in transmissions of higher frequencies or when the cable's resistance is higher. Devices such as repeaters can prevent attenuation. Repeaters intercept and boost a signal before passing it on to the next cable segment. However, repeaters may also boost any noise traveling on the cable.

Crosstalk

Crosstalk occurs when one cable or circuit's transmission interferes with the transmission of a different cable or circuit. For example, different pairs of twisted wire in an UPT cable may interfere with each other. If this occurs, the signals from each pair of wires, in effect, step on each other, making one or both of their transmissions unintelligible. One means of correcting for crosstalk is to use cables that have additional shielding so that the wires and circuits are better protected from each other. For radiated media, guardbands, or buffer frequencies, can be used to separate signals from each other.

Distortion

Sometimes a signal changes its form or shape as it travels from its source to its destination. The signal arrives, but not as it was originally sent. This is called **distortion**. Distortion is a particular problem with complex signals. Recall that a complex signal may include multiple types of modulation, such as QAM, which uses amplitude and phase modulation. Individual signal components that make up a complex signal each have their own propagation speed. Propagation speed is the distance a signal can travel through a medium in 1 second. Distortion could occur if all of the signals that make up a complex signal do not arrive at their destination at the same time.

Now that we know something about the common components and problems that might affect transmission, let's look more closely at how to select a medium.

Choosing a Medium

After examining both conducted and radiated media, the question becomes: How do you choose a medium for a particular data communication need? To answer that, five factors need to be considered:

1. **Cost**. Cost includes not only the materials, but also the labor for installation, which is often one of the most expensive elements in implementation.

Table 2.2 Advantages and Disadvantages of Different Media

Medium	Security	Transmission Distance	Cost	Error Potential	Difficulty of Installation
Twisted-wire pair	Moderate	Short	Low	Moderate	Low
Coaxial cable	Moderate	Short	Moderate	Low	Low
Fiber-optic	High	Moderate to long	High	Very low	High
Radio	Low	Short	Low	Moderate	Moderate
Terrestrial microwave	Low	Long	Moderate	Low to moderate	Low to moderate
Satellite	Low	Long	Moderate	Low to moderate	Low to moderate

2 **Bandwidth**. What are the data speed requirements? Bandwidth should be based on business needs. Which medium provides sufficient bandwidth to support organizational requirements?

3 **Security**. Is security critical, or just desirable?

4 **Transmission impairment**. What level of transmission impairment can be tolerated? What physical environment will the medium be placed into?

5 **Distance**. Does the medium need to provide transmission between rooms in a building or between states or provinces in a country? Is the medium for a LAN, BN, MAN, or WAN?

In a large enterprise, you will likely need several types of media, and they should be placed where they are used best. Again, efficiency and effectiveness are important, and your recommendation may need to balance the two. Table 2.2 summarizes the advantages and disadvantages of the various media that have been considered. Keep in mind that the medium selected must address economic business requirements. Most likely, a business will use a variety of media throughout its enterprise. One of your jobs might be advising the enterprise as to where and why a particular medium would or would not be appropriate.

Physical Layer Devices

The selected transmission medium is one element in the overall design of a data communications network. You also need to be aware of the many types of devices that allow a data communications network to function. Each layer of the OSI and TCP/IP models has devices that are either specifically or generally associated with that layer. Some devices are more flexible in their functionality and thus can be positioned or used in more than one layer of the model. Several devices are associated with the physical layer. This section addresses the devices used at the physical layer. The intent is not to list every possible type of device, but only those most commonly associated with the physical layer.

Hubs or Repeaters

Hubs, also referred to as **repeaters**, are devices that pass signals that transmit through them to an adjoining section of the same logical network (see **www.3com.com/corpinfo/en_US/pressbox/resources/hubs.html**). Hubs connect devices that share a common architecture, such as Ethernet or token ring. These architectures are explored later in the text. A hub is either *active* or *passive*.

If active, the hub not only transmits signals, but boosts and cleans the signals before it passes them on. In order to do this, an active hub must have its own power supply. A passive hub does not clean or boost the signals, so it does not have its own power supply. A passive hub simply passes the signals on to the next segment of transmission medium it is connected to. Another term for boosting a signal is *amplifying*. Passive hubs, because they have no power supply, are limited to connecting shorter segments of the network.

Modems

Modems are devices that modulate a digital signal into an analog signal on the sending end, and then, at the receiving end, demodulate the signal from analog back to digital. A digital device is at each end of the communication. The term *modem* stands for modulator/demodulator. As you read earlier, analog signals can be modulated using amplitude, frequency, or phase modulation. Modems also use simplex, half-duplex, or full-duplex connections, depending on the type of modem.

Both the sending and the receiving modems will have to agree on the speed of their communication. The slower of the two modems will control the speed at which they both communicate. Capable of performing error correction, modems can save on retransmission. Modems are data circuit-terminating equipment (DCE) devices, meaning that they are connected at one end to a data terminal equipment (DTE) device. The DTE device, usually a personal computer, sends instructions and data to the DCE equipment. The days of the dial-up modem being the device of choice for users to connect to the Internet are probably numbered. Newer high-speed technologies such as DSL (digital subscriber line), cable, and satellite are becoming cost-effective for the average consumer. Figure 2.19

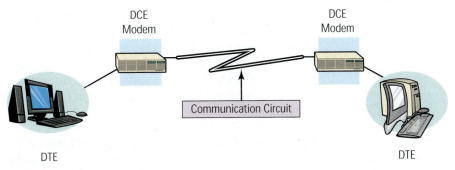

Figure 2.19
DTE and DCE Equipment
DTE and DCE are based on the RS232 standard. The figure shows the placement of DTE and DCE equipment with which you are probably familiar—a desktop computer and an external modem.

illustrates where a DCE and a DTE would be placed in a typical data communication configuration.

Codecs

The term **codec** stands for coder/decoder. Codecs do the reverse of what a modem does. They take analog signals on the sending end, convert them to digital signals for transmission, and then translate the signals back from digital to analog on the receiving end. Codecs are used in such technologies as ISDN (Integrated Services Digital Network). A codec typically converts the transmission through pulse amplitude modulation (PAM). Using PAM, samples of an analog signal's amplitude are converted into discrete, corresponding digital signals. A codec, using PAM, samples the analog signal at a rate at least twice the frequency's signal. In this way, a PAM device samples a voice signal with a 4 KHz bandwidth at least 8,000 times.

Multiplexers

A **multiplexer** is a device that can take communications from several slow-speed devices on the sending end and combine them so that these several communications can pass over a single high-speed circuit. Another multiplexer is at the receiving end. Its job is to take the single high-speed circuit's combined communications and break it back down into the original individual communications. Multiplexers are frequently used with multiples of four slower circuits that have devices connected to them. Sending and receiving multiplexers might be assembling and disassembling communications from 4, 8, 16, or more slower-speed circuit devices.

Assume that there are four slow-speed devices in Los Angeles. It would not be cost-effective to give each of them a high-speed connection to a central computer in Boston, especially if the Los Angeles devices are not communicating that frequently. In this case, it makes sense to multiplex the four devices. The four individual communications are combined and then the combined communication is passed over a single high-speed circuit. At the receiving end, the communications are split back apart so that they are understandable. Note that there are two multiplexers, one at the sending end and another at the receiving end. Multiplexing requires either hardware or software at both the sending and receiving ends that works as a team to combine and take apart the multiplexed signals.

To recap, a multiplexer at the sending end is connected to several slower-speed devices. The sending multiplexer takes the transmissions from the slower devices, combines them, and places these transmissions onto a single high-speed circuit. At the receiving end, another multiplexer separates out the individual transmissions. This can be done in one of four ways: frequency-division multiplexing, time-division multiplexing, statistical time-division multiplexing, and wavelength division multiplexing.

Frequency-Division Multiplexing

Frequency-division multiplexing (FDM) divides a single high-speed circuit horizontally, creating a series of separate channels, each on a different frequency. Frequency-division multiplexers can use either amplitude or frequency modulation. Each sending device connected to the frequency-division multiplexer has its own channel, sharing the single high-speed circuit. The combined bandwidth of the individual channels cannot be greater than the total bandwidth of the single high-speed

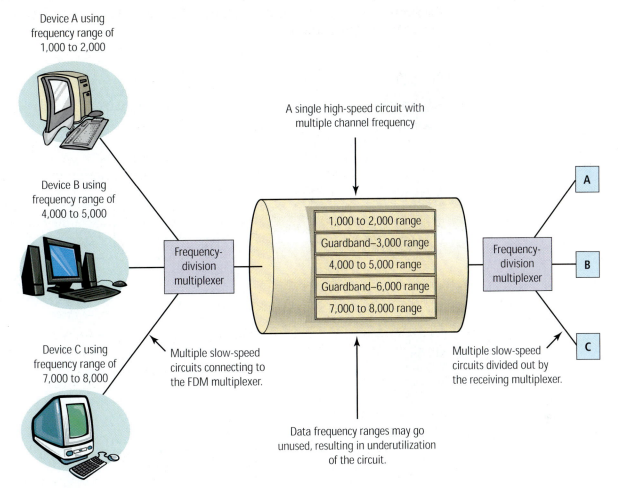

Device A using
frequency range of
1,000 to 2,000

A single high-speed circuit with
multiple channel frequency

A

Device B using
frequency range of
4,000 to 5,000

Frequency-
division
multiplexer

1,000 to 2,000 range

Guardband–3,000 range

4,000 to 5,000 range

Guardband–6,000 range

7,000 to 8,000 range

Frequency-
division
multiplexer

B

C

Device C using
frequency range of
7,000 to 8,000

Multiple slow-speed
circuits connecting to
the FDM multiplexer.

Multiple slow-speed
circuits divided out by
the receiving multiplexer.

Data frequency ranges may go
unused, resulting in underutilization
of the circuit.

Figure 2.20

Frequency-Division Multiplexing

With frequency-division multiplexing, each device has an allocated frequency range. A range may go unused if a device has nothing to send or receive. Guardbands carry no data and are used only for separating data ranges from one another. The data are represented as analog not digital and carried on frequency channels not frames. Bandwidth is measured in hertz not bps.

circuit. And, in fact, the combined bandwidths need to be less due to the need for guardbands.

The tradeoff here is that between each of the frequency channels, a guardband of frequency has to be inserted. The guardband is an unused portion of the circuit. No data are carried in the guardbands. The purpose of the guardband is to prevent the separate channels from interfering with each other, which would result in crosstalk. The guardband is necessary so that individual channels remain distinct within the single circuit. This means that the total capacity of the circuit cannot be used because guardbands are required to ensure that individual channels maintain their integrity. Guardbands are a form of overhead. **Overhead** is an additional element that must be added to a technology in order for that technology to work. As a rule, lower overhead is more desirable because it is more efficient. Figure 2.20 shows a diagram of frequency-division multiplexing.

Time-Division Multiplexing

Time-division multiplexing (TDM) divides the circuit vertically into time slots. Each of the slower devices connected by time-division multiplexing is given an allocated, specific time slot over which it can communicate.

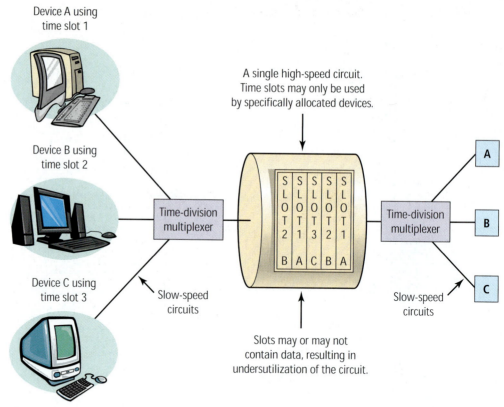

Figure 2.21

Time-Division Multiplexing

With time-division multiplexing, each device has an allocated time slot that only it can use. Slots may go unused if a device has nothing to send or receive.

Devices cannot use or share another device's time slot. If a device has nothing to transmit, its time slot goes unused. Time-division multiplexing is useful when the data rate capacity of the high-speed circuit is greater than the data rate required by the individual sending and receiving devices.

Keep in mind that the time slots are preallocated: Each time slot can be used only by the device defined for it. TDM does not need guardbands, because each device owns a predetermined portion of the high-speed circuit. The tradeoff here is that when devices are not communicating or transmitting, their time slot of the circuit goes unused. So, even if a device has nothing to send, it will be granted a time slot on the circuit. Idle devices cause overhead. Even so, TDM is generally more efficient than FDM. See Figure 2.21 for an illustration of time-division multiplexing.

Statistical Time-Division Multiplexing

The problem with time-division multiplexing is that circuit capacity is underutilized if a device has nothing to send over its allotted time slot. **Statistical time-division multiplexing (STDM)** can evaluate each device's transmission needs and, based on those needs, allocate or not allocate a portion of the high-speed circuit. In this way, devices that need to transmit can do so, and those that are idle are not wasting circuit capacity. In order to do this, statistical time-division multiplexing encodes each individual transmission it sends with an identifier so that the senders and receivers are kept in sync. With STDM, the overhead is in the identifier information that must be encoded on each signal. Recall that with any type of multiplexing, identification of the individual

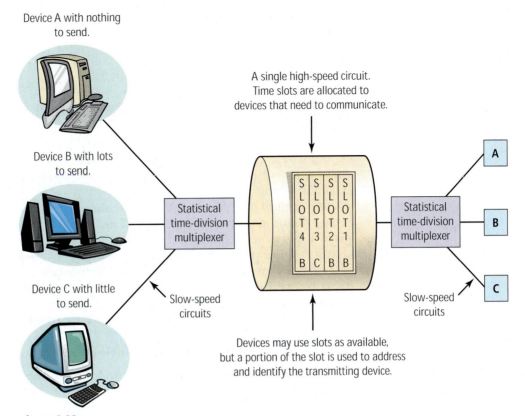

Figure 2.22
Statistical Time-Division Multiplexing
With statistical time-division multiplexing, time slots are used by those devices that need to communicate. Time slots are not preallocated, but are distributed based on the need of a device to communicate. The data are represented as analog not digital and carried on frequency channels not frames. Bandwidth is measured in hertz not bps.

devices must be provided for both the sending and receiving ends. Even so, statistical time-division multiplexing is more efficient then time-division multiplexing.

With statistical time-division multiplexing, the combined bandwidth capacity of the individual devices communicating can be greater than the single high-speed circuit they are sharing. Usually this works. However, when demand exceeds capacity, meaning that all devices want to send immediately, statistical time-division multiplexing must have internal memory that it can use to store data that it cannot immediately transmit. In general, though, statistical time-division multiplexing is more efficient and cost-effective then either frequency- or time-division multiplexing. See Figure 2.22 for an illustration of statistical time-division multiplexing.

Wavelength Division Multiplexing

Wavelength division multiplexing (WDM) is used with fiber-optics in a manner similar to how frequency-division multiplexing is used with copper. Wavelength division multiplexing uses lasers to transmit different frequencies of light through the same fiber-optic cable. At the sending end, narrow bands of light are combined into a wider band. The wider band is the high-speed circuit. At the receiving end, the signals are separated. A more complex form of wavelength division multiplexing is dense wavelength division multiplexing. **Dense wavelength division multiplexing (DWDM)** combines wavelength division multiplexing with time-division multiplexing. Using DWDM, one fiber-optic cable can send up to 400 Gbps (billions of bits per second).

Cabling Tools

Cabling tools are not physical layer devices, but they are used in working with and testing the physical layer medium. A standard tool kit might include wire strippers, dies (which are used in crimping wire), and crimping tools that are used to attach connectors to the ends of cable segments. Fiber-optic cabling requires its own set of specialized, and generally more expensive, tools and testing devices.

For copper media, scanners and monitors are available for testing cable conditions. The simplest and least expensive ones can determine if there is any electrical activity between one location in a network and another. More expensive and sophisticated devices can test not only for cable faults, but also check whether performance specifications for the network are being met. For fiber-optics, an optical power meter can be used to read levels of optical signals on the fiber line. See the following Web sites for more information on networking tool kits:

- **www.lashen.com/vendors/ideal/default.asp**
- **www.cables-and-networks.com/kits/cabling-tool-vogo.html**
- **www.tecratools.com**
- **www.flmicro.com/Products/toolkits.htm**
- **www.belkin.com/**

Chapter Summary

The physical layers of the OSI and TCP/IP models are virtually the same. The physical layer identifies the physical characteristics of the network. These characteristics include the types of cables and connectors used to join devices together. Transmission properties are also defined at the physical layer that indicate the ways in which a binary 0 or 1 signal is to be represented in either an analog or digital encoding scheme. A 0 or 1 can be represented either electronically or optically.

Four important physical layer components are (1) the signaling methods used for conveying or representing data and translating between them, (2) the circuit configuration used to carry the data, (3) the transmission medium used, wired or wireless, on which the circuits are based, and (4) the devices typically associated with this layer.

Data can be represented as analog or digital signals. In analog communications, signals flow across a copper wire in the form of electromagnetic waves. Analog signals can also use transmission media such as fiber-optics or wireless (radio, microwave, infrared). Digital signaling is more straightforward than analog signaling. With digital signaling, only two values are used, 0 and 1. With analog signaling, modulation techniques include amplitude, frequency, and phase. These modulation techniques can be simple or complex. For digital signaling, encoding schemes such as bipolar, biphase, Manchester, and Differential Manchester are used.

Whether analog or digital, signals are carried over a transmission medium. The transmission medium has a circuit configuration, point-to-point or multipoint, and a data flow, simplex, half-duplex, or full-duplex. Based on the needs and size of the network, one or all of these might be used. Transmission media fall into one of two categories: conducted or radiated. Conducted media use cables: twisted-wire pair, coaxial, or fiber-optic. Radiated, or wireless, media include microwave, radio, or infrared. Each type of transmission medium has advantages and disadvantages. Factors to consider when selecting a medium include cost, bandwidth, security, transmission impairment, and distance.

A number of different devices are associated with the physical layer. These include hubs, modems, codecs, and multiplexers. Multiplexers at the sending end of a communication combine several slower-speed circuits onto one high-speed link. At the receiving end, multiplexers disassemble the high-speed transmission back into its slower-circuit component parts. Multiplexers are frequently configured with multiples of four slower-speed circuit devices. Types of multiplexing include frequency-division, time-division, statistical time-division, and wavelength division multiplexing.

Although not physical layer devices, tools and special equipment are used that help a networking technologist monitor and maintain the network.

American Wire Gauge (AWG)   **(60)**

Amplitude modulation (AM)   **(47)**

Analog   **(46)**

ASCII   **(54)**

Attenuation   **(51)**

Backward compatible   **(55)**

Bandwidth   **(58)**

Baseband   **(59)**

Biphase encoding   **(52)**

Bipolar encoding   **(52)**

Bit interval   **(51)**

Bit rate   **(51)**

Broadband   **(59)**

Carrier wire   **(60)**

Circuit configuration   **(56)**

Cladding   **(60)**

Clocking   **(52)**

Coaxial   **(62)**

Codec   **(72)**

Complex signal modulation   **(50)**

Conducted   **(59)**

Conductor   **(60)**

Connectors   **(44)**

Core   **(60)**

Crosstalk   **(69)**

Dense wavelength division multiplexing (DWDM)   **(75)**

Differential Manchester   **(53)**

Digital signaling   **(51)**

Distortion   **(69)**

Downlink   **(66)**

EBCDIC   **(54)**

Effective   **(45)**

Efficient   **(45)**

Encrypted   **(65)**

Extended ASCII   **(54)**

Fiber-optic   **(63)**

Frame   **(44)**

Frequency   **(48)**

Frequency-division multiplexing (FDM)   **(72)**

Frequency modulation (FM)   **(48)**

Full-duplex   **(59)**

Half-duplex   **(58)**

Hertz (Hz)   **(48)**

Hub   **(71)**

Infrared   **(65)**

Insulation   **(60)**

Line-of-sight antennas   **(65)**

Manchester   **(52)**

Modem   **(71)**

Multiplexer   **(72)**

Multipoint configuration   **(57)**

Overhead   **(73)**

Parallel transmission mode   **(55)**

Period   **(48)**

Phase modulation (PM)   **(49)**

Physical layer   **(44)**

Point-to-point configuration   **(56)**

Propagation delay   **(66)**

Radiated   **(59)**

Radio   **(65)**

Refraction index   **(60)**

Repeater   **(71)**

Satellite microwave   **(65)**

Self-clocking   **(52)**

Serial transmission mode   **(54)**

Signaling method   **(46)**

Simple signal modulation   **(50)**

Simplex   **(58)**

Sheath   **(60)**

Shielded twisted pair (STP)   **(61)**

Software key   **(65)**

Standard ASCII   **(54)**

Statistical time-division multiplexing (STDM)   **(74)**

Symbol rate   **(50)**

Terrestrial microwave   **(65)**

Thicknet   **(62)**

Thinnet   **(62)**

Time-division multiplexing (TDM)   **(73)**

Transition coding   **(52)**

Transmission medium   **(44)**

Transmission mode   **(53)**

Twisted-wire pair   **(61)**

Unicode   **(55)**

Unipolar   **(52)**

Unshielded twisted pair (UTP)   **(61)**

Uplink   **(66)**

Wavelength division multiplexing (WDM)   **(75)**

Wired   **(59)**

Wireless   **(59)**

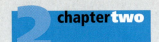

Chapter Questions

Short Answer

1. In general, what purpose does the physical layer serve?

2. Describe at least three ways in which digital signaling differs from analog.

3. How does a point-to-point circuit differ from a multipoint one?

4. What, if any, advantages does radiated media have over conducted media?

5. What is the purpose of multiplexing? Describe one variation of multiplexing.

Multiple Choice

For each of the following questions select one best answer.

1. Which of the following is not a type of cable?
   a. Twisted pair **b.** Coaxial **c.** Microwave **d.** Fiber-optic

2. Which layer does the physical layer communicate with directly?
   a. Application **b.** Data link **c.** Network **d.** Transport

3. Binary bits can be expressed or represented
   a. electronically. **b.** optically. **c.** Either a or b **d.** Neither a nor b

4. How many physical layer components are there?
   a. 1 **b.** 2 **c.** 3 **d.** 4

5. Which simple modulation technique uses the height of an analog wave?
   a. Amplitude **b.** Frequency **c.** Phase **d.** b or c

6. Which simple modulation technique uses the number of waves per second of an analog wave?
   a. Amplitude **b.** Frequency **c.** Phase **d.** a or c

7. Which type of modulation can be used in satellite transmission?
   a. Amplitude **b.** Frequency **c.** Phase **d.** b or c

8. Frequency is measured in which of the following?
   a. Seconds **b.** Bps **c.** Hertz **d.** Amps

9. Period is measured in which of the following?
   a. Seconds **b.** Bps **c.** Hertz **d.** Amps

10. Which type of modulation is most susceptible to noise?
    a. AM **b.** FM **c.** PM **d.** a or b

11. Which term describes the number of bits encoded in a single signal?
    a. Bit rate **b.** Bit speed **c.** Symbol rate **d.** Symbol speed

12. If four amplitudes are defined, how many bits could each amplitude represent?
    a. 1 **b.** 2 **c.** 3 **d.** 4

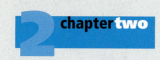

13. Bit rate is measured in which of the following?

  a. Bytes per second **b.** Periods per second
  c. Bits per second **d.** a or c

14. How many bits are contained in an Extended ASCII byte?

  a. 4 **b.** 6 **c.** 7 **d.** 8

15. Which of the following includes at least one transition bit per interval?

  a. Unipolar **b.** Bipolar **c.** Biphase **d.** Triphase

16. How many unique characters can be represented in Extended ASCII?

  a. 7 **b.** 8 **c.** 256 **d.** 64,000

17. Which type of circuit configuration is used to connect most devices in a network?

  a. Point-to-point **b.** Multipoint **c.** Dedicated **d.** Parallel

18. How many types of data flow are there?

  a. 1 **b.** 2 **c.** 3 **d.** 4

19. Which of the following can send and receive data simultaneously?

  a. Simplex **b.** Half-duplex **c.** Full-duplex **d.** Duplex

20. What is another term for conducted media?

  a. Radiated **b.** Wireless **c.** Wired **d.** Infrared

21. A fiber-optic cable's core is measured in

  a. inches. **b.** microns. **c.** centimeters. **d.** AWG.

22. Which of the following encases a cable's elements and keeps them together?

  a. Sheath **b.** Conductor **c.** Cladding **d.** Insulation

23. Which term describes the error of when a signal arrives in a transmission but the signal is not in its original form?

  a. Attenuation **b.** Crosstalk **c.** Distortion **d.** Frequency

24. Which type of connector is typically used with UTP cabling?

  a. RJ11 **b.** RJ45 **c.** RJ58 **d.** RJ 54

25. What is the highest grade of UTP cable?

  a. Cat 1 **b.** Cat 3 **c.** Cat 5 **d.** Cat 7

26. A standard coaxial cable has how many layers?

  a. 3 **b.** 5 **c.** 7 **d.** 8

27. Which wireless medium cannot penetrate walls?

  a. Infrared **b.** Radio **c.** Microwave **d.** Satellite

28. Which of the following is the transmission from a satellite to its Earth-based station?

  a. Uplink **b.** Downlink **c.** Bilink **d.** Geolink

29. Which type of hub requires a power supply?

  a. Powered **b.** Active **c.** Passive **d.** Charged

30. Which of the following converts digital signals to analog and then analog back to digital?

  a. Modem **b.** Multiplexer **c.** Codec **d.** Repeater

31. Which of the following converts analog signals to digital and then digital back to analog?

    a. Modem **b.** Multiplexer **c.** Codec **d.** Repeater

32. Which of the following combines slower-speed circuits into a high-speed link?

    a. Modem **b.** Multiplexer **c.** Codec **d.** Repeater

33. Which of the following is a multiplexing technique that uses guardbands?

    a. FDM **b.** TDM **c.** STDM **d.** WDM

34. Which of the following is a multiplexing technique that allocates specific time slots of the high-speed circuit to each slower-circuit device?

    a. FDM **b.** TDM **c.** STDM **d.** WDM

35. Which of the following is a fiber-optic-based form of multiplexing that is similar to copper-based FDM?

    a. BDM **b.** TDM **c.** STDM **d.** WDM

36. Which of the following is addressed by the physical layer?

    a. Cables **b.** Framing data bits **c.** Connectors **d.** a and c

37. Which of the following is an accurate statement?

    a. To be effective is to be efficient
    b. To be efficient is to be effective
    c. A technology can be effective but not efficient.
    d. If a technology is efficient, it will also be effective.

38. Which type of circuit configuration is not found at the physical layer?

    a. Point-to-multipoint **b.** Point-to-point
    c. Multipoint **d.** Multidrop

39. What binary bits are used to encode digital data?

    a. 0s **b.** 1s **c.** 0s and 1s **d.** 0 through 9

40. In what way can an analog wave be modulated?

    a. Amplitude **b.** Frequency **c.** Phase **d.** All the above

41. Which of the following is amplitude measured in?

    a. Hertz **b.** Volts **c.** Digits **d.** a or b

42. Which of the following is the completion of one full pattern of a wave?

    a. Cycle **b.** Round **c.** Pattern **d.** Period

43. Which of the following describes the relationship between frequency and period?

    a. They are the divisive inverse of each other.
    b. They are the additive inverse of each other.
    c. They are the subtractive inverse of each other.
    d. The are the multiplicative inverse of each other.

44. Which modulation is the most susceptible to noise?

    a. Phase **b.** Frequency **c.** Amplitude
    d. All experience similar amounts of noise.

45. The bit rate and symbol rate

    a. are never the same. **b.** are always the same.
    c. may be the same. **d.** have nothing to do with each other.

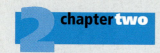

46. Which of the following defines the length of time it takes for a single bit to be transmitted?

   a. Bit duration **b.** Bit time **c.** Bit interval **d.** Bit rate

47. Which of the following is true of bipolar encoding?

   a. It has a direct current component.
   b. It does not have a direct current component.
   c. It has an alternating current component.
   d. a and c

48. Which digital encoding scheme is used in Ethernet networks?

   a. Bipolar **b.** Differential **c.** Manchester **d.** Differential biphase

49. Which is the most secure type of medium?

   a. Twisted-wire pair **b.** Microwave
   c. Coaxial cable **d.** Fiber-optic cable

50. Which of the following is the insulation on a fiber-optic cable?

   a. Sheathing **b.** Cladding **c.** Braiding **d.** Housing

True or False

For each of the following select either True or False.

1. The physical layer does not directly talk or communicate with the data link layer.

2. A frame is an unformatted sequence of bits.

3. A signaling method defines a set of rules for representing how 0s and 1s are defined electromagnetically.

4. Analog is a discrete form of measurement.

5. For frequency, a period is measured in seconds.

6. Digital signaling is usually more expensive than analog.

7. Serial transmission mode is faster than parallel transmission mode.

8. EBCDIC and Extended ASCII both use eight-bit bytes.

9. A circuit is the link used by data in its transmission from one device to another.

10. In a simplex data flow, the circuit supports data flow in both directions, but not at the same time.

11. A signal is transported over a cable's insulation.

12. Whereas copper cable has a conductor, fiber-optic cable does not.

13. Attenuation occurs when one cable or circuit interferes with the transmission of another cable or circuit.

14. UTP is more susceptible to noise than either coaxial or fiber-optic cabling.

15. Fiber-optic cables do not experience electromagnetic interferences.

16. Single-mode fiber-optic is more likely to experience signal distortion than multimode.

17. All radiated media have low security.

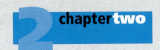

18. Unlike terrestrial microwave, satellite does not have to use line-of-sight devices.

19. Transmission from the earth station to the satellite is referred to as the downlink.

20. Statistical time-division multiplexing is more efficient that time-division multiplexing.

Exercises

Research in Brief

For one or more of the questions below, provide a one- to two-page report based on your findings.

1. What factors would you consider when recommending a data communications medium for a network? Explain why these factors affect your recommendation and what advantages and disadvantages different media have.

2. Describe the measures you could take when using Cat-5 UTP to prevent crosstalk, attenuation, distortion, or other physical problems that might occur when using this type of cabling medium.

3. Search the Internet to find at least three vendors of fiber-optic hardware components. Compare and report back on price, service, warranty, or other related topics for at least three different types of hardware: cable, NICs, tool kits, etc.

4. Wireless is rapidly becoming a preferred physical media. Three standards for wireless include 802.11a, 802.11b, and 802.11g. What standards-setting body (or bodies) is involved with these specifications? How do the standards differ? How are they similar? What implementation issues might there be with wireless media?

Case Study

Sheehan Marketing and Public Relations

Congratulations, you have just been hired by Sheehan Marketing and Public Relations (SMPR) as their new networking technologist. Your first order of business will be to evaluate the current status of SMPR's networks. SMPR has three offices, one in Los Angeles (LA), which is the corporate headquarters, one in Chicago, and another in New York City. You are aware that there are plans to open two additional offices in Miami and Nashville.

You have asked Karla, the LA office LAN administrator, for help in your analysis. However, Karla has told you that she is very busy and not able to provide you with much support. She also indicates that there is little written documentation as to how the various offices are set up. Following is her brief description of the LA office. Later you will visit the

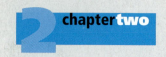
Chicago and New York offices to determine how they are configured. For now, Karla tells you they have a similar, though smaller, set up: Chicago has 10 computers, and New York has 15.

Los Angeles

Los Angeles is the corporate office, and also oldest. It has 24 computers, 19 of them have licensed versions of Windows 95; the 5 newest machines have licensed versions of Windows 2000 Workstation. Karla has configured the computers to run as a peer-to-peer network, so depending on the particular computer, it may function as either a server or a client. Karla admits that it has become complicated for her to keep all the machines current with the various user privileges that are shared across the network. For example, there are three laser printers, each connected to a separate computer. Fifteen other machines have been set up to share these printers, so there are 18 machines with rights to use the printers. The other six computers also need to be configured for printer sharing.

All of the computers have various data, files, and resources that are shared across the network. All computers have licensed copies of Microsoft Office, but different versions. Again, Karla isn't exactly sure which versions are on which machines. Also, individual users have installed many of their own programs on their local computers. The resources (data, files, software) have not been documented in writing as to what is installed where or whether everything is correctly licensed. Karla simply "knows" where things are.

The computers are cabled with Cat-3 UTP Ethernet. The LA facility is composed of a separate room for the president, a reception area for the secretary, and a large open floor space for the rest of the staff. The total office is approximately 1,000 square feet. Three passive hubs connect all the computers together. The hubs are in the general office space. Wires connecting the computers to the hubs run along the perimeters of the wall and, in a few cases, cross floor space where staff frequently walk.

Over the past 2 years, SMPR has acquired more clients who are involved in video and audio work. Currently, because these files do not transport well across the network, when someone needs access to a client's video or audio file, the person must physically access the file on the computer on which it is stored. Staff are finding it difficult to work cohesively as a team because only one person at a time can access a particular file. Also, the different branch offices need to be able to access resources remotely. Currently, two computers in the LA office have a 33 Kbps modem. The Chicago and New York offices each have a similar capacity modem. President Sheehan has heard of devices called multiplexers and wonders if SMPR could use this type of technology for connecting the LA, New York, and Chicago offices.

Case Questions

Using the information just provided, answer the following questions.

1. Interpersonal relations can be an important factor in whether you can successfully do your job or not. How would you describe the situation regarding Karla? How do you plan to proceed in working with her? It can be difficult to work with users who are accustomed to "running their own computers"—installing what they want when they want on their local machines—how do you plan to address this? Is this a problem? If so, why?

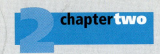
2. Karla has asked you to explain to her how a modem that supported a bit interval of 18 microseconds would affect bandwidth in terms of bps. Using the formula presented in this chapter under the topic heading "Bandwidth," demonstrate to Karla the bps achieved using an 18-microsecond bit interval. (For those who are adventurous and read the Topic in Foucs, if the current modem is operating at 33.3 Kbps, what bit interval is it using?)

3. Focusing on the physical part of the LA network, research and prepare a report on the costs of upgrading a 24-computer network with Cat-5 UTP, NICs capable of 10/100 Mbps, and 3 active hubs. Include in your report the cost of a standard tool kit for yourself. Are there any problems with how the wiring is currently set up? If so, what do you plan to recommend? Don't forget to include in the report any labor costs for installing the new Cat-5 wiring. Assume you can hire a wiring technician for $35 an hour.

4. Do you have any concerns with the level of documentation at SMPR? If so, what steps would you take to improve the situation and why?

5. Prepare a one-page report for President Sheehan that explains to him what a multiplexer is and how multiplexers are used. In your report, indicate whether you think SMPR could use multiplexing, and if so, how and where.

Web References

www.iso.org

www.cablesdirect.com

www.itu.int

www.nuhorizons.com/products/Clock.html

www.unicode.org

www.eia.org

www.linktionary.com/c/cabling.html

www.serverworldmagazine.com/monthly/2003/03/kvm.shtml

www.firewall.cx/cabling_10baseT.php

www.windowsitlibrary.com/Content/405/02/1.html

www.corning.com/opticalfiber/discovery_center/tutorials/fiber_101/

www.fiber-optics.info/glossary-a.htm

www.fiber-optics.info/default.htm

www.arcelect.com/Telebyte_Fiber_frame_page.htm

www.andrew.com/products

www.microstar-antennas.com

www.photoconnect.net/imgIndustryTelecoms/index.php

www.antenna-tower.com

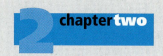

www.satdx.com

www.windows.ucar.edu/cgi-bin/tour_def/space_missions/
sputnik.html

www.amsat.org

www.metoffice.com/satpics/latest_VIS.html

noaasis.noaa.gov/NOAASIS

www.3com.com/corpinfo/en_US/pressbox/resources/hubs.html

www.lashen.com/vendors/ideal/default.asp

www.cables-and-networks.com/kits/cabling-tool-vogo.html

www.tecratools.com

www.flmicro.com/Products/toolkits.htm

www.belkin.com/

Bandwidth

Earlier in this chapter, bandwidth was compared with the capacity of a river to carry, or move, water. The larger the river, the more water it can potentially carry. Bandwidth in terms of data communications is somewhat similar in concept, except that instead of carrying water on a river, data is carried on a circuit. In data communications, bandwidth can be expressed in both an analog and a digital from. Whether analog of digital, bandwidth will have a direct affect on the utilization of a circuit. Utilization is critical, because if a circuit has too much data flowing over it, such that the circuit reaches maximum capacity, data can be lost, distorted, or both.

Throughput also affects utilization. In fact, bandwidth and throughput together define utilization. Throughput is the number of bits being carried by the circuit at any given time. Generally, a circuit will have an average throughput that can be statistically determined using network monitoring tools. Bandwidth, on the other hand, is the total number of bits the circuit can carry. The two terms, throughput and bandwidth, are similar but not the same.

If we divide throughput by bandwidth, the result is utilization expressed as a percentage. The formula would look like this:

$$\text{utilization} = (\text{throughput} / \text{bandwidth}) * 100$$

As an example, assume a circuit can support a bandwidth of 100 Mbps, and, on average, throughput is 25 Mbps. Using the formula, utilization = (25 / 100) * 100, we get a utilization of 25 percent. That may be efficient or inefficient depending on the kind of circuit that is being evaluated. Throughput is also referred to as the *true rate of information transfer*, or TRIT. A more complicated way of looking at TRIT would be the following equation:

$$\text{TRIT} = E_f * E_l * C$$

Here, E_f is the efficiency of the frame, which is much overhead it has. E_l is the efficiency of the link, which is how much of the link is not utilized. C is the capacity of the circuit, which is how much data the circuit can carry.

Getting back to the topic of bandwidth, for analog communications, bandwidth is measured in frequencies; digital, in bits per second, or bps. First, let's consider analog bandwidth.

Analog bandwidth is measured in frequencies. The bandwidth of an analog signal is calculated by subtracting the lowest frequency from the highest frequency in a defined range of frequencies. The defined range of frequencies making up a bandwidth is called the *spectrum*. For analog, this is a frequency spectrum. The frequency spectrum, then, for an analog signal is the group of frequencies, or range of frequencies, that make up a specific bandwidth. A given bandwidth and its frequency spectrum can be graphically demonstrated. Look at Figure 2.23 as you read over the following example.

Assume that a given analog signal can be defined by the following frequencies measured in Hertz (Hz): 200, 400, 600, 800, 1,000, and 1,200. These six frequency values then, in this example, are the frequency

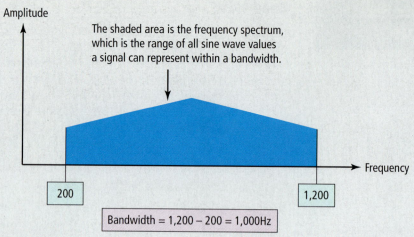

Amplitude

The shaded area is the frequency spectrum, which is the range of all sine wave values a signal can represent within a bandwidth.

Frequency

200

1,200

Bandwidth = 1,200 − 200 = 1,000Hz

Figure 2.23
Bandwidth and Frequency Spectrum

spectrum. Also assume, again just for this example, that each of these six frequencies has a maximum amplitude of no more than 5 volts. (You may recall from earlier in this chapter that amplitude modulation can be measured in volts. When using volts as the measurement in a frequency amplitude modulation, the highest value a volt can take in amplitude must be specified.) With this information, what then is the bandwidth of this frequency spectrum? Bandwidth is determined by subtracting the lowest frequency, 200 Hz, from the highest frequency, 1,200 Hz, giving a resulting bandwidth of 1,000 Hz. Bandwidth then is the measurement of the width of a range of frequencies, not the individual frequencies themselves. In this example, the width of frequencies is 1,000 Hz. What if in our example the highest frequency in the spectrum had been 10,000 Hz? Then the bandwidth would have been 9,800 Hz, a much wider range than 1,000 Hz. With a wider range of frequencies, more data can potentially be carried over a given circuit, just as a wider river can potentially carry more water.

Consider the human voice. Ordinary speech can be adequately captured and transmitted for standard telephone conversation in a frequency range of 300 to 3,400 Hz. Consequently, telephone providers allow for a bandwidth of 4,000 Hz for analog voice communication. Why 4,000 Hz instead of 3,100 Hz (3,400 minus 300)? Because 4,000 Hz allows for guardbands to used at the end of each frequency range. A guardband, as you may recall, serves as a buffer that, in this example, is used to prevent crosstalk from adjacent voice communications.

Unlike analog, digital bandwidth is typically expressed in bits per second (bps). Digital bandwidth is determined from the bit interval and the bit rate. The bit interval is the time needed to send a single bit. The bit rate is the number of bit intervals per second, or bps. These two terms were introduced in our discussion earlier in the chapter on digital signaling. In that discussion, you learned that the bit interval and the bit rate are the multiplicative inverse of each other. So, the bit rate is (1 / bit interval), and the bit interval is (1 / bit rate). Assuming a digital signal with a bit interval of 60 microseconds, what would be its bandwidth? The formula is expressed as:

$$bps = 1 / (60 * 10^{-6})$$

or approximately 16.6 Kbps (thousands of bits per second). If it were a 30-microsecond bit interval, the bps would be approximately 33.3 Kbps. For a 10-microsecond bit interval, the bps becomes 100 Kbps. In this example, rather than having, as we would with analog, a wider frequency range for bandwidth, we have a wider or wider bit range for bandwidth—16.6 Kbps as compared with 100 Kbps. If speed were essential for the digital transmission of the data, which of the two values would you prefer for getting the bits delivered from point A to point B?

If on the other hand we knew the bit rate how would we determine the bit interval? Assume a digital signal with a bit rate of 4000 bps. Knowing that the rate is the inverse of the interval we can now caluculate what the interval is: bit interval = 1 / bit rate, or 1 / 4000, giving .000250, which equals $250 * 10^{-6}$.

We have seen that bandwidth is critical because it affects the utilization of a communication circuit, as well as the amount and type of data that can be supported. A bandwidth that is too narrow may not be able to support such data as sound or video; these types of data require a bigger circuit or "river" to flow along. A bandwidth that is too wide, and therefore underutilized, is not cost-effective. As with many of the topics presented in this chapter, business needs must be considered and balanced with technological requirements.

3 chapter three

Data Link Layer Fundamentals

Learning Objectives

After studying this chapter, you should be able to:

- Identify the components that make up the IEEE 802 implementation.
- Understand the purpose of Logical Link Control (LLC).
- Identify the types of delivery service provided by LLC.
- Define a protocol data unit (PDU).
- Understand the concept of flow control at the data link layer.
- Describe stop-and-wait flow control.
- Describe sliding windows flow control.
- Describe line discipline.
- Identify three types of error detection.
- Identify two types of error correction.
- Explain asynchronous and synchronous data link protocols.
- Understand the purpose of Media Access Control (MAC).
- Describe Ethernet 802.3 as a MAC method.
- Describe token ring as a MAC method.
- Understand the purpose of a Network Interface Card (NIC).
- Describe how a bridge or switch might be used.

As you learned in the last chapter, the lowest-level layer, the physical layer, assigns no meaning to the data bits of the message that it transmits. The physical layer is only concerned with getting the sender's message bits from the originating source device to the final destination device. It is at the data link layer, the second lowest-level layer, where meaning and organization are associated with the bits being transmitted. The data link layer frames message data bits so that they can be passed to the next higher layer, the network layer. A message can be composed of one or many frames. The data link layer not only frames the data bits, but also controls how the frames are moved from one networked device to another.

The Data Link Layer

One of the key functions of the data link layer is to frame binary bits received from the physical layer. A **frame** then is the structure given to binary bits at the data link layer. A frame may have to pass through many intermediary devices and networks on its path from the originating source to the final destination device. Think of it as a relay in which one runner passes the baton, in this case a frame, to the next runner, in this case the next device. While moving the frames between each sending and receiving device in the relay, the data link layer ensures that one device does not overwhelm the other with too much data at one time. **Flow control** is used so that the sending device does not overwhelm the receiving device in a communication. Imagine a single clerk in a store with 20 customers to serve. Without flow control, in this case a single-file line that the customers must wait in, the clerk could be overwhelmed with customer demands. Flow control is important for many human as well as data communications applications.

An associated type of control is line discipline. **Line discipline** controls which device can communicate when. It is like a professor in a class specifying which student can speak in what order to give an opinion or observation. If everyone spoke at once, not much would be accomplished. Instead the professor enforces line discipline so that an orderly discussion can occur. The data link layer performs error control as well. The goal of **error control** is to enable a receiving device to recognize, and potentially correct for, a transmission error.

This chapter also introduces the topic of addressing. Physical addressing is an important function of the data link layer. It may seem odd that physical addressing takes place at the data link layer rather than the physical layer, but that is how it is done. In later chapters, you will learn that other forms of addressing are equally critical. This chapter will identify the devices and components associated with the data link layer. In addition, the chapter will present an entire alphabet soup of new acronyms and terms you will need to know. This should not be a big surprise; think of the great party trivia conversations you can have. More seriously, you will probably find that the data link layer is a fascinating, challenging layer with many important activities.

Components of the Data Link Layer

In 1985, the IEEE developed **Project 802**, an implementation specification for the data link layer used by both the OSI and the TCP/IP networking models. (The IEEE was introduced in Chapter 1. Visit this body's Web site

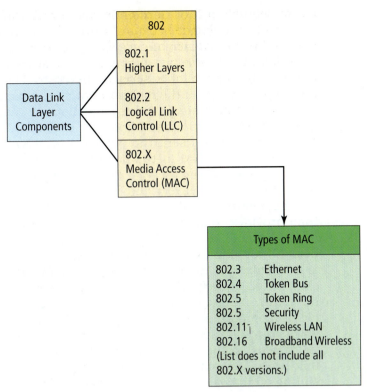

Figure 3.1
Components of the 802 Standard for the Data Link Layer

at: **www.ieee.org**.) The IEEE divided the data link layer into two parts: Logical Link Control and Media Access Control. In the IEEE 802 implementation, the **Logical Link Control (LLC)** sits above the Media Access Control (MAC). The data link layer in effect contains its own miniature stack. The 802 specification is modular, which is one of its strengths. Figure 3.1 shows how the components of the **802** specification fit together. Each module under the 802 umbrella has a number that identifies that module's specific functionality for specific types of MAC: **802.1** for internetworking; **802.2** for LLC; and **802.3** (CSMA/CD for Carrier Sense Multiple Access/Collision Detection), **802.4** (token bus), and **802.5** (token ring). We review the last three MAC protocols listed later in the chapter, in addition to Fiber Distributed Data Interface (FDDI).

Keep in mind as you read through the chapter that the data link layer sits between the physical and network layers. The data link layer not only passes data down to the physical layer for transmission, but must also pass data up to the network layer in a form the network layer will recognize and accept. Together, LLC and MAC make this possible. Let's see how.

Logical Link Control

LLC, also designated as 802.2, provides three types of frame delivery service: Type 1, Type 2, and Type 3. A **delivery service** is a method of getting a frame from point A to point B. Type 1 is a connectionless service that does not provide acknowledgment. In this case, an **acknowledgment** means that the receiver responds back to the sender regarding a communication. If acknowledgment is not provided, the receiver does not tell the sender whether a frame arrived or not. **Connectionless** means that, first, no predefined path or permanent circuit is established between sender and receiver. Second, because there is no acknowledgment, the sender has no direct or immediate way of knowing whether a frame has reached its destination. These two characteristics mean that Type 1 delivery is the fastest but least reliable service offered by LLC. Type 1 service is like putting a postcard in the mail without a return address. You do not know what route the postcard takes. You hope it gets there, but there is no guarantee. And, you cannot know for sure that it has arrived unless you call the person you sent the postcard to, which defeats the purpose of sending the postcard in the first place. Even so, Type 1 delivery is the most popular delivery service because higher-level layer protocols often provide their own delivery and error checking.

The opposite of Type 1, Type 2 is a connection-oriented delivery service that provides acknowledgment. In a **connection-oriented** service, a transmission circuit must be established between the sender and receiver before they can begin to communicate. Also, the receiver eventually acknowledges to the sender whether the frame was received. The circuit established between the sender and receiver does not have to be permanent, and often it is not. However, the circuit is maintained long enough for the communication to take place. With a connection-oriented service, flow control is especially important, but not the kind of flow control that takes place at the physical layer. Two of the most common forms of data link layer flow control that are managed by LLC are **stop-and-wait** and **sliding windows**.

A connection-oriented service is similar to a registered letter that has a guarantee of delivery and that also requires the receiver to sign for receipt, thereby acknowledging that he or she has received your letter. Sending a registered letter is more expensive then sending a postcard. The same is true with regards to Type 1 and Type 2 delivery services.

A Type 3 delivery service is connectionless but offers acknowledgment, thereby providing some of the advantages of both Type 1 and Type 2 services. Even so, Type 3 is the least often used of the three types of delivery service.

To accomplish its work, LLC uses a unit of data called a **protocol data unit (PDU)**. A good Web site that describes PDUs and other protocols can be found at **www.protocols.com**. A PDU can contain up to four elements: (1) a destination service access point (DSAP), (2) a source service access point (SSAP), (3) a control field, and (4) a data or information field.

The DSAP is an 8-bit field that identifies the higher-level protocol using the LLC's services. Remember, the frame has been passed down to the data link layer from a higher-level layer in the TCP/IP layer stack. That higher-level layer uses a specific type of protocol. The first bit of the eight-bit DSAP field indicates whether the frame is meant for an individual host or a group of hosts. A host is any device that can communicate with and is connected to a TCP/IP network. The SSAP is also an eight-bit field that indicates the local user of the LLC service. The SSAP's first bit indicates whether the protocol data unit communication is a command or a response type of frame.

The control field, the third element of a PDU, is a one- or two-byte field that indicates the type of PDU. PDU frames are one of the following: information (I), supervisory (S), or unnumbered (U). Only Type 2 connection-oriented delivery services use I and S frames. All three delivery types use U frames. Information frames are used to transmit connection-oriented data. Supervisory frames are used to supervise and manage the information frames. Unnumbered frames are used for connectionless data and to terminate the logical link between hosts using Type 2 services.

A Logical Link Control (LLC) Protocol Data Unit			
DSAP Address Field	SSAP Address Field	Control Field	User Message Data

DSAP Destination Service Access Point
SSAP Source Service Access Point

A Media Access Control (MAC) Protocol Data Unit				
MAC Control	Destination Address	Source Address	LLC PDU	CRC (Cyclical Redundancy Checking)

Figure 3.2
Elements of a Protocol Data Unit (PDU)

The fourth protocol data unit element, the data field, is of variable length and contains the data or information received from the network layer protocol. The length of the data field will be determined by the media access method used; for example, token or contention. We explore both later when we discuss MAC in more detail. Of the three types of PDU frames, supervisory frames do not have a data field. Figure 3.2 illustrates the components of a PDU.

Flow Control

With a Type 2 connection-oriented delivery service, a sender and receiver must agree on establishing their communication before transmission can begin. Part of their agreement is that the sender will not overwhelm the receiver with the data being transmitted. A faster sending device, without flow control, could overwhelm a slower receiving device. How might this happen? A receiving device typically has a temporary and limited amount of storage memory, called a buffer, available to it for acceptance of incoming data. If a slower receiving device has more data coming in from a faster sending device than it can hold in its buffer, transmission overload results on the receiver's end. Data loss can be expected.

In order to ensure that the sender does not overwhelm the receiver (causing transmission overload), flow control is required. Flow control, which is managed by LLC, restricts the amount of data a sender can send until the sender receives an acknowledgment from the receiver that the receiver is ready for data. In the previous example, if the receiver's buffer is filled, the receiver alerts the sender of this condition. The sender then halts transmission until given the go ahead by the receiver to continue. Two common flow control methods at the data link layer are stop-and-wait and sliding windows. Let's take a closer look at each.

Stop-and-Wait Flow Control

With stop-and-wait flow control, each individual frame that the sender transmits requires an individual acknowledgment back from the receiver that that specific frame has been received. Only after each individual

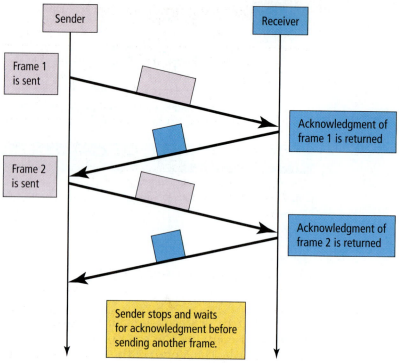

Figure 3.3
Stop-and-Wait Flow Control

frame has been acknowledged can the sender transmit the next sequential frame. A message could be composed of 1,000 frames. With stop-and-wait flow control, the sender would ultimately get back, assuming no transmission problems occurred, 1,000 acknowledgements from the receiver, or one for each of the 1,000 frames sent. Therefore, the sender sends frame 1 and then stops and waits for acknowledgment from the receiver that frame 1 has been received and accepted. Then the sender sends frame 2 and again stops and waits for an acknowledgment from the receiver that frame 2 has been received and accepted. Then the sender sends frame 3, and so on. Figure 3.3 illustrates this process.

Stop-and-wait flow control has one major advantage: It is very straightforward and simple. For messages that are composed of a few, large frames, stop-and-wait flow control can be very efficient over a short link. But this is not a typical situation. Also, the more, and the smaller, frames there are, the more inefficient stop-and-wait becomes as a flow control mechanism. Furthermore, the longer the link between the sending and receiving devices, the more serious the inefficiency becomes in gaining full utilization of the circuit. It does, after all, take time for acknowledgments to travel back and forth across a link. The longer the link, the more time required. So, except under certain limited circumstances, stop-and-wait flow control is not a first choice. Sliding windows is the more popular flow control method.

Sliding Windows Flow Control

If one acknowledgement could be used for multiple frames, instead of one acknowledgment per frame, the result would be more efficient utilization of the communication circuit. This is the idea behind sliding windows. With sliding windows, several frames can be sent before an acknowledgment is required. This method is, of course, more complicated than stop-and-wait, but it is much more efficient.

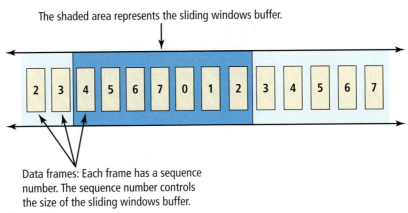

The shaded area represents the sliding windows buffer.

Data frames: Each frame has a sequence number. The sequence number controls the size of the sliding windows buffer.

Figure 3.4
Sliding Window

Earlier you read that the receiver has a memory buffer into which frames are received in order to be processed. The sender also has a memory buffer holding the frames to be sent. These memory buffers on the sender's and receiver's ends are, in effect, the sliding windows. *Window* refers to the memory buffer storage area that is used to hold frame data. The window on either the sender's or receiver's end can slide to become wider or more narrow based on the communication. The acknowledgment going back and forth between sender and receiver controls the communication and causes the windows to adjust their size, sliding open or closed. Before a sender's **sliding windows buffer** can expand, the sender must receive an acknowledgment back from the receiver. Before a receiver's sliding windows buffer can expand, the receiver must send an acknowledgment. Figure 3.4 illustrates the sliding windows concept.

The sliding windows method uses a sequencing number scheme to control the number of frames being transmitted and received based on the acknowledgments going back and forth. This sequencing number scheme controls the size of the sender and receiver's sliding windows buffer. The sender and receiver must both use the same sequencing number scheme to stay in sync with each other. The sequencing number is a field that is part of the frame being sent and received. The **sequencing number field** must have a specific bit size. The bit size of the field must be the same for sender and receiver. The number of bits used to define the field depends on network needs as well as the size of the sender's and receiver's buffers.

Topic in Focus

For those who want to know more about how sliding windows works, see the "Topic in Focus: The Secrets of Sliding Windows" at the end of this chapter.

Line Discipline

Another type of circuit control the data link layer performs is line discipline. The concept is straightforward. Line discipline controls the give and take (i.e., who talks when) between two devices that are communicating.

Assume that a point-to-point, half-duplex circuit connects two devices. From Chapter 2, you know that a device using a half-duplex circuit can send or receive, but not both at the same time. With this example, because there is a point-to-point circuit, only one device at a time can use the half-duplex line to either send or receive. What determines which device can send or receive and when? If both devices attempt to send or receive at the same time, their communications would fail because the transmissions would collide. This is similar to having two cars on a one-way road driving in the opposite direction; an accident is going to happen. A half-duplex line can only be used by one device at a time. Line discipline is required to enforce rules of communication, controlling who can communicate when.

Line discipline is associated with two types of network environments. One is a point-to-point connection between two devices using either a half-duplex or full-duplex line. Whether half- or full-duplex, before communication can occur, a session must be established between the two devices. If half-duplex, the devices have an additional requirement in that they must take turns using the line. The form of line discipline used in this scenario is called **enquiry/acknowledgment (ENQ/ACK)**. Let's consider how this might work.

The sending device, device A, initiates a communication by transmitting an enquiry frame to the receiving device, device B. Device A then waits to hear from device B if it is available and accepting communications. Device B, if available and ready for communication, transmits an acknowledgment frame to the sender, device A. At that point a session is established and device A begins its communication with B. When finished, device A transmits an end of transmission (EOT) frame, terminating the session. If device B were not available for communication, it would transmit an NAK (negative acknowledgment) frame to device A. Device A will have to try again later. If device B, because it is disconnected or down, does not send an acknowledgment frame to A, after a specified time device A will issue another enquiry to device B. After three failed enquiry attempts, A assumes that B is completely unavailable and terminates communication entirely until a later time.

The second type of network environment requiring line discipline occurs when multiple devices on a multipoint line communicate through a central controlling communication device. This is fairly common with terminals connected to a mainframe computer. The terminals do not communicate directly with each other. Instead, they must pass their communications through the mainframe. The mainframe, or other similar central controlling device, controls the multipoint circuit and determines when and if devices can communicate. The central controlling device does this through a process called *polling*.

With **polling**, the controlling device is the key initiator of all communication processes, even when the controlling device has nothing to communicate. This may sound odd. What this means is that all the other devices wait for the central controlling device to "poll" them to see if they having something to communicate. The controlling device is often called the *primary device;* the multipoint attached devices are referred to as *secondary devices.* The secondary devices wait for the primary device to contact them. If a secondary device has a communication need, it makes this known to the primary device, which then carries out the communication.

Error Control

Besides flow control duties, the data link layer also performs various types of error control. We do not live in a perfect world. Neither do data communication systems. For that reason, errors will find their way into any data communications environment. Error control is essential. Error control at the data link layer has two elements: detection and correction. If an error can be detected, it can potentially be corrected. Let's first consider error detection and then how such errors might be corrected.

Error Detection

In data communications, **error detection** and correction requires that additional overhead be attached to the core message data being transmitted. The overhead takes the form of added data elements, above and beyond the core message data itself. The added overhead, referred to as redundant data, is a necessary burden used to ensure data accuracy.

Users of communications technologies rely on the accuracy of their data to make informed decisions. Businesses rely on data accuracy to give them a competitive advantage. Whereas human error can be challenging, and in some cases impossible, to control for, error-detection techniques are available that can be used to ensure that within a communications system the data sent are the data received. Common error-detection techniques include parity checking, longitudinal redundancy checking, checksum checking, and cyclical redundancy checking.

Parity Checking
Parity checking is a very simple but not very accurate method of error detection. Parity checking is also sometimes referred to as *vertical redundancy checking.* Other newer and more complicated techniques offer much higher rates of error detection. With parity checking an extra parity bit is added to a byte. For example, an additional eighth parity bit is added to a seven-bit standard ASCII byte creating an eight-bit unit. The parity bit added is either a 0 or a 1 depending on the type of parity used, even or odd. **Even parity** is usually used with synchronous transmissions and **odd parity** with asynchronous transmissions, both of which will be addressed later in the chapter.

Whether even or odd, both the sender and receiver must agree to use the same parity type. In even parity, the number of 1 bits transmitted in the eight-bit unit must always add to an even number. For odd parity, the number of 1 bits transmitted in the eight-bit unit must always add to an odd number.

The Ethical Perspective

Error Detection and Correction: Who is Responsible?

Businesses rely on the accuracy of their data as a competitive advantage. Consumers also require business data communications systems to be truthful and accurate regarding the data captured and stored about them. However, if the data should, for whatever reason, be inaccurate due to technical error or human error, and a business has discovered this within its own system, should that business be ethically or legally bound to inform its customers of this issue?

Some businesses claim that such disclosures could be so damaging, even if the errors were slight, that the future of their business would be at stake. And yet, the data captured and utilized by a business involve real people who may be affected by such errors. In your view, to what degree must a business disclose any errors that its data communications systems may create? What would be your opinion from a business owner's perspective versus your opinion as a customer? Is there a conflict of interest? Should there be legal ramifications for data that are in error? If so, how moderate or severe should these ramifications be? Should customers be informed of data errors in a system even if over the long term no real harm will result to them?

Assume that two devices are set for even parity. On the sending end is a seven-bit ASCII uppercase character, "A," whose binary value is 1000001. The parity bit is set to 0 or 1 depending on the number of 1 bits in the core ASCII character. Currently, ASCII character A has two binary 1s. Therefore, the parity, or eighth, bit should be set to 0 in order to keep the number of binary 1s an even number. The following eight bits are transmitted: 10000010. The last bit is the parity bit; it is set to 0 to maintain even parity. On the receiving end, the receiver adds the number of binary 1s in the eight-bit unit and determines if the total is even or odd. If even, the receiver assumes the data are good; if odd, the receiver assumes that a transmission error has occurred. The problem with parity checking is that it is only good for single-bit transmission errors.

Using this same example with even parity, if 10000010 is what is sent, but 10000110 is what is received, the receiver will recognize that an error has occurred because the number of 1 bits is odd. But if 10000010 is sent and 10011010 is what is received, the receiver does not recognize an error because the number of binary 1s adds up to an even number. To the receiver, the data are good, although you can see that it is not. With parity checking, the probability of detecting an error is about 50 percent, not very good when you consider you could get the same odds with the toss of a coin.

Longitudinal Redundancy Checking   Simple parity relies on a single bit to detect errors in a single byte. In contrast, **longitudinal redundancy checking (LRC)** generates an entire additional byte, called a **block check character (BCC)**, based on all the bytes in a message. All the bytes that make up the message are the "block." (Be aware that longitudinal redundancy checking works with either Standard or Extended ASCII. You might also find the following Web site of data communications terms, including longitudinal redundancy checking, to be useful: **www.nickara.com/glossary_v0.htm**.) On the sending end, the block check character is calculated and attached to the end of the block of data being sent. Parity is still used, again either even or odd, but in a more complex manner.

Using longitudinal redundancy checking, the bytes in the message that make up the block are evaluated in a row/column manner. Using parity, based on the row/column evaluation, a block check character is calculated. The receiver performs the same block check character calculation on the block of data received and compares its generated block check character with the one sent. If they are not the same, a transmission error is recognized. Evaluating the block of data in a row and column manner generates the block check character. This is difficult to visualize, so let's take a look at a concrete example.

In this example, the word "BYTE" is the data block that needs a block check character. This example will use even parity. The word "BYTE" is a block of four characters. Each character occupies one byte, so the block has four bytes. First, each character is converted into its Extended ASCII binary equivalent. The data block is now expressed as a stream of bits: 01000010 01011001 01010100 01000101. For purposes of longitudinal redundancy checking, let's place these binary values in a table of rows and columns (Table 3.1).

Each character, or byte, has its own row. There are eight columns, one for each bit in the byte. Note that the last row is reserved for the block check character, which has yet to be calculated. To perform the calculation, each column of binary bits is evaluated lengthwise, top to bottom, for even parity. (The term "longitudinal," by the way, literally means "lengthwise.")

Table 3.1 Longitudinal Redundancy Checking Example

Character	Col 1	Col 2	Col 3	Col 4	Col 5	Col 6	Col 7	Col 8
B	0	1	0	0	0	0	1	0
Y	0	1	0	1	1	0	0	1
T	0	1	0	1	0	1	0	0
E	0	1	0	0	0	1	0	1
BCC								

Even parity requires that the number of 1 bits, if present, add up to an even value. Column 1 does not have any 1 bits. Therefore, the first bit value of the block check character byte is set to 0. Column 2 has four binary 1s. Consequently, the second bit value of the block check character is also set to 0. Table 3.2 shows all the bit values of the block check character byte filled in according to the rule for even parity.

Once calculated, the block check character is now attached to the end of the core message data block. The data block stream is now: 01000010 01011001 01010100 01000101 00001010. When the receiver gets the transmitted data block, the receiver's data link layer will perform its own block check character calculation on the core message data. The receiver will then compare its own calculated block check character with the block check character that was transmitted. If they are the same, the data are assumed to be good. If they are not the same, the data transmitted are assumed to be bad. When longitudinal redundancy checking is used in addition to simple parity, the probability of detecting transmission errors increases to 98 percent. Not perfect, but much better than the 50 percent detection capability of simple parity checking.

Checksum Checking   **Checksum checking (CC)** works by computing a running total based on the byte values transmitted in a message block and then applying a calculation to compute the checksum value. A common technique is for checksum to add the decimal value of each byte in the message block to obtain a total. The total is then divided by 255. The remainder becomes the checksum value, which is attached to end of the message block being transmitted. The receiver also performs a checksum computation on the core message block received and compares its computed checksum with the checksum sent. If the two values are the

Table 3.2 Block Check Character Byte Filled in According to Even Parity

Character	Col 1	Col 2	Col 3	Col 4	Col 5	Col 6	Col 7	Col 8
B	0	1	0	0	0	0	1	0
Y	0	1	0	1	1	0	0	1
T	0	1	0	1	0	1	0	0
E	0	1	0	0	0	1	0	1
BCC	0	0	0	0	1	0	1	0

same, the receiver assumes the transmission was error free. Checksum has a 99.6 percent probability of detecting errors in a transmission.

Cyclical Redundancy Checking   If longitudinal redundancy checking is good, and checksum checking is better, then cyclical redundancy checking (CRC) is the best. Cyclical redundancy checking has a 99.9 percent or higher probability of detecting errors in a transmission. The most powerful of the error-detection techniques we have considered, **cyclical redundancy checking** is based on binary division. Cyclical redundancy checking adds an 8-, 16-, 24-, or 32-bit calculated value to the end of the core message block.

The core message data are treated like one long binary number. This binary number is then divided by another unique, fixed prime binary number. The remainder generated is the cyclical redundancy checking value attached to the end of the message block. The receiver, as you probably can guess by now, makes a similar calculation and comparison. The same fixed prime binary number is used by the receiver when it divides the transmitted message's binary number value. If the receiver's computed cyclical redundancy checking value is the same as the sender's cyclical redundancy checking value, the transmission is assumed to be successful and error free.

Error Correction Methods

Once detected, transmission errors need to be corrected. The most common correction technique is also the least complicated. The data are simply retransmitted. If errors are to be corrected by **retransmission**, a technique called **acknowledgment repeat request (ARQ)** is used. An acknowledgment repeat request takes one of two forms: stop-and-wait acknowledgement repeat request or continuous acknowledgment repeat request. Of the two, stop-and-wait is simpler but less efficient than continuous acknowledgment repeat request.

If using stop-and-wait acknowledgement repeat request, the sending device does not send its next sequential frame until it has been advised by the receiving device that the current frame has been received and accepted. This method of error correction uses stop-and-wait flow control. Continuous acknowledgement repeat request uses sliding windows flow control. With continuous acknowledgement repeat requests, the sender does not wait for individual frame acknowledgment. Instead, a continuous stream of frames is sent. The sender will, however, expect acknowledgment from the receiver that all frames were successfully received.

If frames were damaged or not received, the sender will get a negative acknowledgment from the receiver. In that case, the sender retransmits the damaged or missing frames. As with sliding windows, the sender must keep a copy of all frames sent until those frames have been acknowledged. Continuous acknowledgement repeat request also requires a full-duplex circuit.

Error Correcting Codes

Another means of correcting for error is for the receiver to correct the error on its end through the use of **error-correcting codes (ECC)**. This method, sometimes called **forward error correction (FEC)**, requires redundant data to be carried in the message block in the form of error-correcting codes. Similar in concept to error-detection codes, error-correcting codes require more redundant data bits because they are more complicated. The advantage of error-correcting codes is that they can eliminate the need to retransmit erroneous data. The receiver, by evaluating the error-correction data, can determine, and if needed fix, a transmission error. The disadvantage is the overhead of carrying extra data bits for achieving error correction.

The amount of redundant data needed by the error correcting codes varies by the technique used. The most common techniques correct for one-, two-, or three-bit errors in a byte. This means, for example, that every 7-bit character byte might need an additional 3 to 4 bits for error correction, translating into a 10- or 11-bit character. The overhead required for higher bit-error correction is generally considered too great to be efficient.

Data Link Protocols

Communicating devices express their communication as a stream of bits transmitted over a medium. As discussed earlier, this stream may include not only the core data message bits, but also bits used for such purposes as error detection or correction. Recall that ultimately the bits represent characters of data. How do communicating devices determine where one character of data begins and ends within this bit stream? The answer is that the data link protocols delineate the data in the bit stream. **Delineate** means to mark out. Data link protocols are used to mark out in the bit stream where characters begin and end, whether one character at a time or within groups of characters. This delineation is essential in order to give meaning to the bits transmitted. The two types of data link protocols that delineate data in a bit stream are asynchronous and synchronous.

Asynchronous Protocols

Asynchronous data link protocols are used almost exclusively today by modems or terminals connecting to a mainframe. Popular asynchronous protocols include XModem, YModem, ZModem, and Kermit. (See **www.faqs.org/faqs** to find out more about these asynchronous protocols.) In general, asynchronous protocols are simple and relatively inexpensive to implement. However, they are not very efficient. Here is why. An **asynchronous protocol** requires that every data byte include a start and a stop bit before and after it. This means that each character's byte begins with a start bit and ends with a stop bit. Start bits are always 0, and stop bits are always 1. This is illustrated in Figure 3.5.

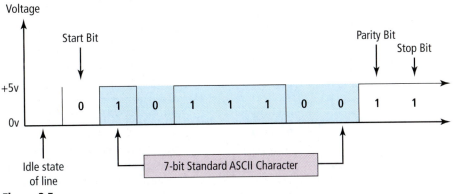

Figure 3.5
Synchronous Transmission

Asynchronous communications are generally less efficient than synchronous ones, but they are more resistant to disruption. Each character in an asynchronous transmission is transmitted independently of all the other characters. And, because the communication is asynchronous, the sender can transmit whenever it is convenient, with no need to coordinate with the receiver. However, because each character in a transmission must be evaluated independently, asynchronous protocols are much slower than synchronous ones.

Synchronous Protocols

Synchronous protocols evaluate groups of characters instead of one byte or character at a time. Because these protocols are synchronous, the sender and receiver must use timing to control their transmissions with each other. To establish the timing, a transmission will start with a series of initial synchronization bits. These synchronization bits put the sender and receiver in sync with each other with regards to the transmission they are sharing. Both the sender and receiver must also be aware of the coding scheme being used, such as EBCDIC or Standard or Extended ASCII. Therefore, after they have processed the initial synchronization data, the sender and receiver can each count off the number of bits that define a byte based on the coding scheme used—EBCDIC or ASCII. In this way, an entire string of data characters can be sent as a group without requiring the individual start and stop flags needed in asynchronous communications. For LANs, BNs, MANs, and WANs, the superior speeds of synchronous transmission make it the preferred protocol choice. Figure 3.6 illustrates a very simple synchronous transmission.

Synchronous protocols are either byte or bit oriented. Byte-oriented protocols are sometimes referred to as being *character oriented*. Of the two, bit-oriented protocols are more flexible because they do not require that frames use eight-bit byte units. Byte-oriented protocols evaluate a frame as a series of characters. Bit-oriented protocols evaluate a frame as a series of bits. Two common examples of byte-oriented protocols are Ethernet 802.3 and Point-to-Point (PPP). Telephone dial-up users connecting to an Internet Service Provider (ISP) most frequently use PPP. The most popular bit-oriented protocol is **High-level Data Link Control (HDLC)**, which has several variants. Additional information on HDLC can be found at **www.webopedia.com/TERM/H/HDLC.html**.

One byte-oriented protocol is **Ethernet.** Ethernet 802.3 is popular primarily because it is used extensively in LANs. Ethernet uses a contention-based form of MAC that is discussed later in greater detail. An Ethernet 802.3 frame has four components. The first component is an eight-byte preamble that marks the beginning of the frame and also enables the

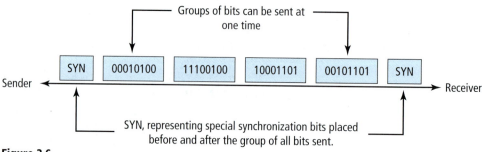

Figure 3.6
Very Simplified Synchronous Transmission

sender and receiver to synchronize their transmission. Following the preamble is the second component, a 14-byte header. This header contains a length field that specifies the length of the message portion of the frame. The length field, therefore, delineates where the message is inside of the frame and is a key reason why Ethernet 802.3 is a byte-oriented protocol. The header is followed by the third component, the message data. After the message data is the fourth component, a four-byte trailer. The trailer contains a cyclical redundancy checking value for error detection.

The bit-oriented HLDC protocol is a formal standard that is defined by the ISO. HLDC, unlike Ethernet, uses a controlled-access form of MAC. A variety of link access protocols have been developed based on HLDC, including LAPB, LAPD, and LAPM, among others. LAPB, Link Access Protocol-Balanced, is used to connect a device to a packet-switching network, a technology addressed later in the text. LAPD, Link Access Protocol-D Channel, is used in ISDN communications. LAPM, Link Access Protocol-Modem, is used in modem communications, allowing HDLC features to be applied to modems.

HDLC supports point-to-point or multipoint circuits over either half- or full-duplex communications. In addition, HLDC supports all three kinds of Type 2 frames: information (I), supervisory (S), and unnumbered (U). A HLDC frame may contain up to six fields: start flag, address, control, information, check sequence, and ending. A HLDC communication has three stages. First, a sender must request session setup by issuing one of six set-mode commands. Next, after initialization has been accepted, a logical connection is established between sender and receiver. Both sides can now exchange I frames. S frames are used for flow and error control. Finally, the session is terminated. Frames exchanged might include RR (Receive Ready) and RNR (Receive Not Ready), among others.

HLDC makes use of an eight-bit control field flag that is composed of six binary 1s enclosed within two binary 0s, as follows: 01111110. It is possible that a message data element might also have six or more binary 1s. To accommodate for this, a technique called *bit stuffing* is performed. Bit stuffing ensures that message bit data are not mistaken for control bit data. Bit stuffing inserts an extra binary 0 after the fifth binary 1 in a series of a message data values. This means that if a binary message has the bit configuration string 01111111100, an extra 0 bit would be inserted, or stuffed, so that the message data would not be mistaken for a control field. The result looks like this: 011111011100. The receiver recognizes the stuffed bit and discards it. This is just one of the many types of technical tricks used to ensure proper data communications.

Media Access Control

Line discipline was discussed earlier in the chapter. Line discipline determines for particular types of data communications circuits how devices get access to the transmission media in order to communicate. Within a LAN, devices share a common circuit using a multipoint configuration. **Media Access Control (MAC)** protocols, the second half of the data link layer, are used to determine how these devices share this common circuit. MAC protocols fall into one of two categories: contention or controlled access. For contention, Ethernet 802.3 is the most common implementation. For controlled access, a form of "token" passing is used, such as token ring or Fiber Distributed Data Interface (FDDI). The MAC sublayer is LAN dependent, meaning that the MAC frame has a specific structure if used with an Ethernet, token ring, or FDDI LAN.

Ethernet 802.3

Ethernet's contention-based MAC protocol is referred to as **CSMA/CD**, which stands for Carrier Sense Multiple Access with Collision Detection. The term **contention** is used because devices contend for use of the circuit. Devices sharing a common line have to take turns to communicate over it. Carrier sense occurs when devices "listen" to the line to see if it is currently being used or if it is free. If the line is free, meaning that no voltage is detected, that device can then use the line to transmit. Multiple access refers to the multiple devices connected to the common circuit, and, if the line is available, any one of these device can use the line. It can happen, however, that two or more devices listening to the line simultaneously discover that the line is free. These devices will then begin to transmit. When this happens, collision detection informs the devices by putting a jamming signal on the line. The jamming signal takes the form of a very high-voltage signal. Devices know when they "hear" the jamming signal that their communications did not succeed. Figure 3.7 shows a simple Ethernet 802.3 LAN.

Only one device at a time can transmit over the circuit. If collision detection occurs, each device that wants to communicate waits a randomly determined interval and then tries for the line once again. It is likely that one device out of all the others will select a shorter amount of time to attempt retransmission. That device, in effect, wins the line and uses it to transmit. As the other devices eventually begin to listen in on the line, they discover that it is occupied and understand that they will have to try retransmitting later.

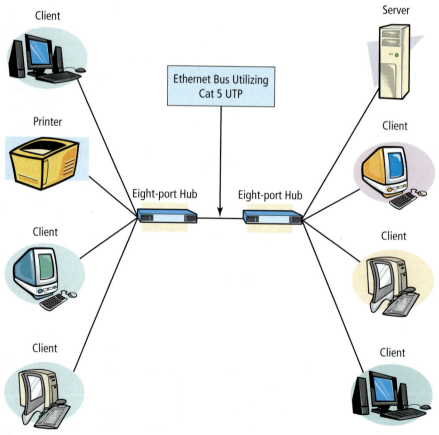

Figure 3.7
Simple 803.3 Ethernet LAN

It is possible on a shared circuit with many devices or on a circuit with a high volume of traffic that collisions will happen repeatedly. In this case, network performance begins to degrade, because no device is able to communicate. Chapter 4 will discuss how different LAN topologies can help to alleviate excessive collisions. It is also possible on a busy 802.3 LAN that one or more devices, because of bad timing, may never, or very infrequently, get access to the circuit, which can be very frustrating to the user of that device. Contention is not a fair-access protocol. However, on a network where there a few devices or where traffic is light, CSMA/CD is very efficient because each device on the circuit would likely get immediate access to the circuit whenever it is needed.

The IEEE 802.3 MAC frame contains seven fields: preamble, start frame delimiter (SFD), destination address (DA), source address (SA), length/type of protocol data unit, 802.2 frame (logical link control), and cyclical redundancy checking. Figure 3.8 shows a standard 802.3 frame. Notice the source and destination address fields. These are the physical addresses associated with the data link layer. These physical addresses are bit patterns physically encoded on each device's network interface card.

A **Network Interface Card (NIC)** (pronounced *nick*) is usually an expansion card plugged into a device's motherboard circuitry. NICs can also take the form of PC cards used in laptop computers or other types of mobile devices. Every NIC has a unique physical address that distinguishes it from every other NIC. If the ultimate receiver of a transmission is on a different logical network, the DA within the frame will be the address of the router connecting the current LAN to the next. The SA within the frame can also be the physical address of the sender or the address of the most recent router to receive and forward the frame.

Do not confuse the frame and its address contents with the encoded addresses on a device's NIC. As a frame is passed from one network to another and is handed off from one device to another, the addresses in the frame are changed to reflect this. Remember the comparison made earlier in the chapter of how the passing of frames from source to destination is like a relay? The addresses on a NIC are physical and part of the NIC. Furthermore, all LAN-connected devices, regardless of the type of MAC, have a NIC. The addresses in a frame are logical and can be modified to reflect a frame's journey from the original sender to the ultimate receiver.

Other types of addressing schemes, such as network layer addressing, are also important in data communications. In addition, Ethernet continues to evolve. Some of the active work groups developing standards related to Ethernet 802.3 can be found at **grouper.ieee.org/groups/802/3/**. Data link layer addressing is just one piece of the puzzle, but all of the pieces tie together to create a communications system.

SFD Or Preamble	DA	SA	Length	User Data	FCS

SFD, or starting frame delimiter, indicates that the frame is about to begin.
DA, or destination address, of where the frame is to be sent.
SA, or source address, of the frame's sender.
Length indicates the number of bytes in the user data.
User Data indicates information content data from the originating user.
FCS, or frame check sequence, is a value used to check for errors in the transmission.
Figure 3.8
Standard 802.3 Frame

Token Ring

Of the MAC controlled-access forms, **token ring**, or 802.5, is the most common within the 802 structure. However, 802.5 is not very popular nor widely implemented. Even so, a brief description of this protocol is described in case you encounter it.

Token ring makes use of a "token" for media access control. A **token** is a specially designated frame that is passed from one LAN device to another. In order to transmit, a device on the LAN must have, or control, the token. A token can be free or busy. If the token is busy, the device that wants to use it must wait until the token is freed. An advantage of 802.5 is that every host eventually does get access to the network within a given length of time, usually within a few hundred microseconds or milliseconds. This characteristic makes controlled-access MAC more efficient in networks that experience heavy traffic. This type of MAC is called fair-access MAC. With token ring, a time limit is placed on any host that needs to use the ring to transmit; therefore, no one host can tie up the ring. Figure 3.9 illustrates a simple token ring LAN.

In a standard token ring, a free token frame circles the ring in one direction only. A host that needs to transmit can intercept the free token frame. The sending host attaches its message and then puts the busy token with the message back onto the ring for transmittal. The message and busy token circle the ring, continuing in the same direction. As the busy token and its attached message pass each host on the ring, the message is evaluated to see if it is addressed to that host. If yes, the message is processed. If no, the message is simply ignored. As you might imagine, the token is a very important element in this type of MAC. No token means no communication. Occasionally a token can be damaged or lost. When that occurs, a new token must be generated.

Generating a lost or damaged token is the job of a device on the ring designated as the **active monitor**. One or more standby or **passive monitors** may also be assigned if, for some reason, the active monitor fails. Should this happen, the passive monitor becomes the new active monitor. The active monitor keeps track of the token. If necessary, the

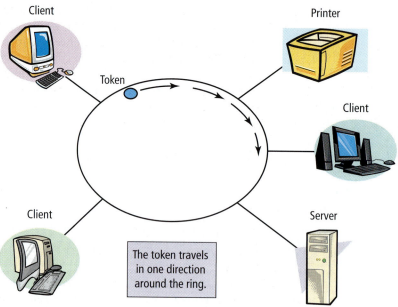

Figure 3.9
Simple 802.5 Token Ring LAN

SD	AC	FC	Destination Address	Source Address	PDU	CRC	ED	FS

SD, start delimiter flag
AC, access control
FC, frame control
PDU, protocol data unit
CRC, cyclical redundancy check
ED, end delimiter flag
FS, frame status

Figure 3.10
Data/Command Frame
Of the three types of frames in a token ring, the data/command frame is the only type that carries a PDU.

active monitor can regenerate another free token and place it back on the ring.

Token ring uses three types of frames: data/command, token, and abort. Of the three, only the data/command frame can carry a PDU and be addressed to a specific destination. The data/command frame has nine fields: start delimiter flag (SD), access control (AC), frame control (FC), destination address (DA), source address (SA), logical link control protocol data unit (PDU), cyclical redundancy checking (CRC), end delimiter flag (ED), and frame status (FS). As was described with 802.3 Ethernet, the destination and source address are associated with the physical addresses of NICs. The token frame uses only three fields: SD, AC, and ED. The abort frame has only two fields: SD and ED. Figure 3.10 is an example of a data/command frame.

A token bus (802.4) MAC specification also exists, but is seldom used. By far, the majority of LANs use some version of Ethernet.

Fiber Distributed Data Interface (FDDI)
Fiber Distributed Data Interface (FDDI) is an ANSI and ITU-T standard, not an IEEE standard. Because FDDI is not an IEEE standard, it does not have an 802 dot value associated with it. Even so, FDDI is another form of MAC. In practice, FDDI MAC layer framing is almost identical to that for token ring. A copper version of FDDI called Copper Distributed Data Interface (CDDI) is also available. A key difference between FDDI and standard token ring is that FDDI uses two dual rotating rings. Data transmission is mostly confined to the primary ring. The secondary ring is used should some portion of the primary ring fail. Use of the secondary ring makes FDDI very reliable, because data circuits can be reestablished and service maintained. Additionally, FDDI provides very high bandwidth. Note in Figure 3.11 the use of the two dual rotating rings.

Data Link Layer Devices

Physical devices are frequently associated with a particular OSI or TCP/IP layer. However, as technology has advanced, devices that once were strictly associated with one layer have become configurable for multiple layers. This is especially true with the two most typical data link layer devices: bridges and switches. Both can be configured or programmed to operate with more than one layer of a networking model, usually the data

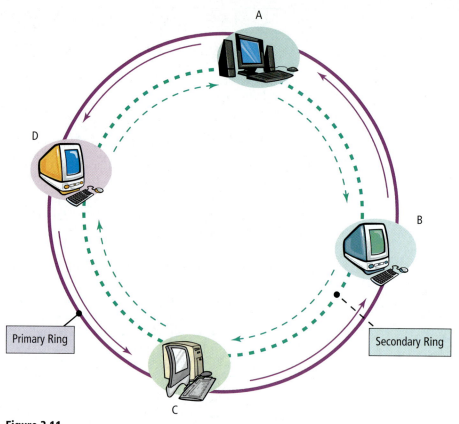

Figure 3.11
FDDI—Dual Rotating Rings
*Should a link in the primary ring fail, the secondary ring can provide connectivity.
The secondary ring serves as a "self-healing" mechanism for FDDI.*

link and network layers. Of course, the right kind of bridge or switch is needed to be multilayer conversant. Generally, devices that can be configured for more than one layer are not only more intelligent devices, but also more complex and expensive. Once again, cost may be a deciding factor in what type to use.

For these reasons, and keeping in mind that devices are no longer as functionally specific to a layer as they used to be, it is still appropriate that a chapter on data link layer services introduce bridges and switches. In Chapter 4, the types and job duties of bridges and switches are revisited along with other LAN devices. First, however, we discuss another data link layer device, the network interface card.

Network Interface Cards

Although a component rather than a device, a NIC is an extremely important part of the network. A NIC is a critical data link layer component that provides the physical address required by networked devices in order to identify and communicate with each other. Also referred to as a LAN adapter, LAN card, network adapter, or network board, these cards allow a device to connect to and access a network. No two NICs should have the same manufactured physical address. If they do, problems will result. A NIC's address identifies its manufacturer. Each NIC has a unique serial

Figure 3.12
Network Interface Card (NIC) from 3Com
The 3Com(R) 10/100 Secure Server NIC is custom-designed for servers that demand high performance and end-to-end security. Its onboard security processor works with Windows 2000 or XP to offload key processing tasks, reducing the load imposed on the CPU.

number that is assigned according to guidelines specified by the IEEE. Figure 3.12 shows a standard NIC. Chapter 4 provides further information on how NICs are used.

Designed for servers that require high performance, the 3Com 10/100 Secure Server NIC also provides for end-to-end security. An onboard security processor that works with Windows 2000 and XP operating systems allows the NIC to offload selected processing tasks and so reduce the workload placed on the server's CPU **(www.3com.com)**.

Bridges

Bridges provide a means of dividing larger LANs into smaller segments. Figure 3.13 shows a wireless bridge from LinkSys (**www.linksys.com**). A bridge connects segments of a network. Larger LANs are broken into smaller segments in order to reduce the amount of traffic experienced on each side of the LAN connected by the bridge. Bridges have multiple ports into which devices are plugged. Devices are recognized as being on one or the other side of the bridge. A bridge reduces traffic by serving as a traffic cop. A bridge works as follows.

A frame sent out on a multipoint circuit, without special intervention, will go to all devices on that multipoint circuit whether addressed to those devices or not. In a large LAN with moderate to heavy communications, a lot of traffic is generated that ends up being ignored by many, if not most, devices. Even so, this ignored traffic takes up valuable bandwidth capacity. When a bridge is used to connect segments of the network, the bridge acts as a filter. Frames that enter the bridge are evaluated, or filtered, by their destination address. The bridge can determine whether the destination device is on one side or the other of the bridge. Based on that knowledge, the bridge either passes the frame through the bridge to the other network segment or disallows it from crossing over. This filtering reduces traffic on both sides of the bridge.

Consider Figure 3.14. Assume that host node A wants to communicate with host node B. The bridge will intercept A's communication and,

Figure 3.13
LinkSys Wireless-G Ethernet Bridge, Model WET54G

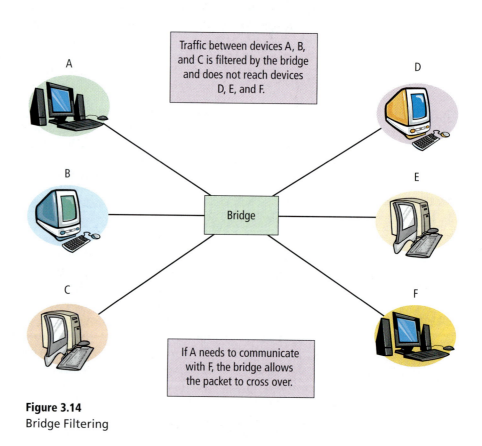

Traffic between devices A, B, and C is filtered by the bridge and does not reach devices D, E, and F.

If A needs to communicate with F, the bridge allows the packet to cross over.

Figure 3.14
Bridge Filtering

recognizing where B is located, not pass A's transmission over to the other segment of the network. In this way, host nodes D, E, and F are not bothered with A's traffic. If A had wanted to communicate with F, the bridge, knowing F's location, would pass A's transmission over to the other network segment.

On a multipoint circuit, all host devices on the circuit intercept the frame or packet transmitted. If the frame or packet is not addressed to the host, the host simply ignores it, but traffic still results. Sometimes people use the terms *frame* and *packet* interchangeably. Others consider a packet to be the unit of storage used at the network layer and reserve the term frame for a data link layer unit. In this text, frame is used as a data link layer unit and packet as a network layer unit to clearly differentiate the processes discussed. In conversations with networking colleagues, you may have to ask them exactly what they mean when they use the term packet. See **www.practicallynetworked.com** to learn about wireless bridges.

Switches

Switches are similar to bridges but have additional functionality that gives them greater efficiency. Like bridges, they have multiple ports into which devices are plugged. Figure 3.15 shows a standard switch. Generally, switches connect two or more LAN segments that use the same data link and network protocols; for example, if LAN segment A is Ethernet and TCP/IP and is connected to LAN B using a switch, LAN B must also be Ethernet and TCP/IP. In this example, Ethernet is the data link protocol and TCP/IP the network protocol.

Switches are most often used to direct traffic over multiple Ethernet networks. Usually having multiple processors, switches also have memory storage buffers that can store frame and/or addressing table information. One important aspect of switches is that each device connected to a

Figure 3.15
Cisco Catalyst 2926 Series XL Switch (rear view)

switch port uses that connection as a point-to-point circuit. This means that even with an Ethernet contention-based protocol, devices connected to a switch do not compete for their connection to the switch. Each device has an independent or point-to-point connection to the switch.

One common type of switch is called store-and-forward. A store-and-forward switch will store all the frames that make up a packet before sending them out as a group. In addition, this type of switch will check each packet for errors before releasing it. Checking for errors in a high-traffic volume network can be time-consuming, resulting in network degradation. Another choice might be to use a cross-point, sometimes called a cut-through, switch. A cross-point switch directs packets without checking for errors. As such, this switch will be much faster than a store-and-forward one. It will be necessary, however, for higher-layer protocols to perform error checking. Cisco is famous for its switching technology. Find out more about switching by visiting the Cisco Web site at **www.cisco.com**.

The data link layer frames message data bits so that they can be passed to the next higher layer, the network layer. A message can be composed of one or many frames. The data link layer not only frames the data bits, but also controls how the frames are moved from one computer or network device to another. A frame may pass through many intermediary devices and networks on its path from the originating source and the final destination device. The data link layer performs error control and physical addressing as well. A key goal of error control is to enable a receiving device to recognize, and potentially correct for, a transmission error.

The IEEE has divided the data link layer into two parts: Logical Link Control (LLC) and Media Access Control (MAC). In the IEEE 802 implementation, the LLC sits above the MAC. LLC, also designated as 802.2, provides three types of frame delivery service: Type 1, Type 2, and Type 3. Type 1 is a connectionless service that does not provide acknowledgment. Type 2 is a connection-oriented delivery service that provides acknowledgment. Type 3 is a connectionless service that provides acknowledgment. Type 1 is the most often used type of delivery service. The three types of frames supported are information (I), supervisory (S), and unnumbered (U). Only Type 2 uses the I and S frames. All service types use U frames.

The two types of data link flow control are stop-and-wait and sliding windows. Stop-and-wait is simple but inefficient. Sliding windows is more complex and more efficient. With stop-and-wait flow control, each individual frame the sender transmits requires an acknowledgment from the receiver that the frame has been received. With sliding windows, several frames can be sent and be in transit before an acknowledgment is required.

Another type of circuit control performed at the data link layer is line discipline. Line discipline is associated with two types of network environments. One is a point-to-point connection between communicating devices using either a half-duplex or full-duplex line. The second occurs when multiple devices on a multipoint line communicate through a central controlling communication device. The central controlling device is often a mainframe with terminals connected to it.

Error control at the data link layer has two elements: detection and correction. Common error-detection techniques include parity checking, longitudinal redundancy checking, checksum checking, and cyclical redundancy checking. Parity checking is a very simple but not very accurate method of error detection. Parity checking is also sometimes referred to as vertical redundancy checking. Longitudinal redundancy checking (LRC) generates an entire additional byte called a block check character (BCC) based on all the bytes in a message. When longitudinal redundancy checking is used with simple parity, the probability of detecting transmission errors increases to 98 percent. Checksum checking (CC) works by computing a running total based on the byte values transmitted in a message block and then applying a calculation to compute the checksum value. Cyclical redundancy checking (CRC), the most powerful of the error-detection techniques, has a 99.9 percent or higher probability of detecting errors in a transmission. CRC is based on binary division.

The most common correction technique is also the least complicated: The data are simply retransmitted. Another means of correcting for errors is for the receiver to correct the error on its end. This method, sometimes called forward error correction, requires redundant data to be carried in the message block in the form of error-correcting codes.

Two types of data link protocols delineate data in a bit stream: asynchronous and synchronous protocols. Asynchronous data link protocols are used almost exclusively by modems or terminals connecting to a mainframe. Popular asynchronous protocols include XModem, YModem, ZModem, and Kermit. Synchronous protocols evaluate groups of characters rather than one byte or character at a time. Because these protocols are synchronous, the sender and receiver must use timing to control their transmissions with each other.

Synchronous protocols are either byte or bit oriented. Byte-oriented protocols are sometimes referred to as character oriented. Of the two, bit-oriented protocols are more flexible because they do not require that frames use eight-bit bytes. Byte-oriented protocols evaluate a frame as a series of characters. Bit-oriented protocols evaluate a frame as a series of bits. Ethernet is an example of a byte-oriented protocol. High-level Data Link Control (HDLC) is a bit-oriented protocol.

Within a LAN, devices share a common circuit through a multipoint configuration. Media Access Control (MAC) protocols are used to determine how devices share a common circuit. MAC protocols fall into one of two categories: contention or controlled access. With contention-based MAC, Ethernet 802.3 is the more common implementation. With controlled access, a form of token passing is used, such as token ring or FDDI (Fiber Distributed Data Interface). The MAC sublayer is LAN dependent, meaning that if Ethernet, token ring, or FDDI are used on a LAN, the MAC frame will have a specific structure. FDDI is an ANSI and ITU-T standard, not an IEEE standard. Because of this, FDDI FDDI does not have an 802 dot value associated with it.

Although a component rather than a device, a NIC is a critical data link layer hardware element that provides the physical address that networked devices require in order to identify and communicate with each other. A NIC's address identifies its manufacturer, has a unique serial number, and is assigned according to guidelines specified by the IEEE.

Bridges provide a means of dividing larger LANs into smaller segments. A bridge connects segments of a network. A larger LAN is divided into smaller segments in order to reduce the amount of traffic experienced on each side of the LAN connected by the bridge. Switches are similar to bridges but have additional functionality, giving them greater efficiency. Like bridges, switches have multiple ports into which devices are plugged. Generally, switches connect two or more LAN segments that use the same data link and network protocols. A store-and-forward switch will store all of the frames that make up a packet before sending them out as a group. In addition, this type of switch will check each packet for errors before releasing it. A cross-point switch sends packets without checking for errors.

802 **(93)**
802.1 **(93)**
802.2 **(93)**
802.3 **(93)**
802.4 **(93)**
802.5 **(93)**
Acknowledgment **(93)**
Acknowledgment repeat request (ARQ) **(102)**
Active monitor **(108)**
Asynchronous protocol **(103)**
Block check character (BCC) **(100)**
Bridge **(111)**
Checksum checking (CC) **(101)**
Connectionless **(93)**
Connection oriented **(94)**
Contention **(106)**
CSMA/CD **(106)**
Cyclical redundancy checking (CRC) **(102)**
Delineate **(103)**
Delivery service **(93)**
Enquiry/acknowledge (ENQ/ACK) **(98)**
Error control **(92)**
Error-correcting codes (ECC) **(102)**
Error detection **(99)**
Ethernet **(104)**
Even parity **(99)**

Fiber Distributed Data Interface (FDDI) **(109)**
Flow control **(92)**
Forward error correction (FEC) **(102)**
Frame **(92)**
High-level Data Link Control (HDLC) **(104)**
Line discipline **(92)**
Logical Link Control (LLC) **(93)**
Longitudinal redundancy checking (LRC) **(100)**
Media Access Control (MAC) **(105)**
Network Interface Card (NIC) **(107)**
Odd parity **(99)**
Parity checking **(99)**
Passive monitor **(108)**
Polling **(98)**
Project 802 **(92)**
Protocol data unit (PDU) **(94)**
Retransmission **(102)**
Sequencing number field **(97)**
Sliding windows **(94)**
Sliding windows buffer **(97)**
Stop-and-wait **(94)**
Switch **(113)**
Synchronous protocols **(104)**
Token **(108)**
Token ring **(108)**

Short Answer

1. In general, what are the functions of the data link layer?
2. Why is flow control necessary?
3. How do asynchronous and synchronous data link protocols differ?
4. Briefly describe MAC and why it is used.

Multiple Choice

For each of the following select one best answer.

1. Which layer is immediately below the data link layer?
   a. Physical   **b.** Network   **c.** Transport   **d.** Application

2. Which layer is immediately above the data link layer?
   a. Physical   **b.** Network   **c.** Transport   **d.** Application

3. How many devices are between a sending and receiving host?
   a. 1   **b.** 2   **c.** No more than 10   **d.** Any number

4. What does flow control determine?
   a. When a device can transmit
   b. Whether a device is connection oriented or connectionless
   c. Both a or b
   d. Neither a or b

5. At which layer does physical addressing occur?
   a. Physical   **b.** Data link   **c.** Network   **d.** Application

6. Which group developed Project 802?
   a. ISO   **b.** ANSI   **c.** IEEE   **d.** None of the above

7. In what year was Project 802 introduced?
   a. 1965   **b.** 1975   **c.** 1985   **d.** 1995

8. How many layers did Project 802 specify?
   a. 2   **b.** 3   **c.** 5   **d.** 7

9. What is the 802 specification for Logical Link Control?
   a. 802.1   **b.** 802.2   **c.** 802.3   **d.** 802.4

10. Which of the following is a connectionless service provided by Logical Link Control?
    a. Type 1   **b.** Type 2   **c.** Type 3   **d.** a or c

11. Which of the following is a connection-oriented service provided by Logical Link Control?
    a. Type 1   **b.** Type 2   **c.** Type 3   **d.** a or c

12. What is the maximum number of fields contained by a PDU?
    a. 2   **b.** 4   **c.** 6   **d.** 8

13. Which of the following determines the type of PDU?

    a. DSAP **b.** SSAP **c.** Control field **d.** Data field

14. Which type of LLC delivery service will contain an I or S frame?

    a. Type 1 **b.** Type 2 **c.** Type 3 **d.** Type 4

15. Which of the following is used to ensure that the sender does not overwhelm the receiver?

    a. Data control **b.** Send control
    c. Receive control **d.** Flow control

16. How many acknowledgments would a 100-frame message require, assuming no transmission errors, when using stop-and-wait flow control?

    a. 1 **b.** 10 **c.** 100 **d.** 1,000

17. Which of the following describes stop-and-wait flow control?

    a. It is simple. **b.** It is complex.
    c. It is best with small frames. **d.** It is best over long distances.

18. For a message of 50 frames using stop-and-wait flow control, how many acknowledgments would be returned to the sender?

    a. None **b.** 1 **c.** 50 **d.** Depends on the medium

19. What must a sender do before a sender's sliding windows buffer can expand?

    a. Send an acknowledgment **b.** Receive an acknowledgment
    c. Either a or b **d.** Neither a nor b

20. What must a sender do before a receiver's sliding windows buffer can expand?

    a. Send an acknowledgment **b.** Receive an acknowledgment
    c. Either a or b **d.** Neither a nor b

21. A point-to-point circuit can be

    a. half-duplex. **b.** full-duplex. **c.** Either a or b **d.** Neither a nor b

22. Controlled access line discipline is used with which type of circuit?

    a. Point-to-point **b.** Multipoint **c.** Either a or b **d.** Neither a nor b

23. Error control is composed of how many defining characteristics?

    a. 1 **b.** 2 **c.** 3 **d.** 4

24. Which of the following is the simplest error-detection method?

    a. Parity **b.** Longitudinal redundancy checking
    c. Checksum checking **d.** Cyclic redundancy checking

25. Which of the following is the most powerful error-detection method?

    a. Parity **b.** Longitudinal redundancy checking
    c. Checksum checking **d.** Cyclic redundancy checking

26. Which type of error detection uses binary division?

    a. Parity **b.** Longitudinal redundancy checking
    c. Checksum checking **d.** Cyclic redundancy checking

27. Which of the following is also called forward error correction?

    a. Simplex **b.** Retransmission
    c. Detection-error coding **d.** Error-correction coding

28. Which data link protocol uses start and stop bits?

    a. Asynchronous **b.** Synchronous **c.** Full duplex **d.** Simplex

29. Which data link protocol evaluates groups of bytes at the same time?

    a. Asynchronous **b.** Synchronous **c.** Full duplex **d.** Simplex

30. Which of the following is true of Ethernet 802.3?

    a. It is bit oriented. **b.** It is byte oriented.
    c. a or b **d.** Neither a nor b

31. Which of the following is true of HDLC?

    a. It is bit oriented. **b.** It is byte oriented.
    c. a or b **d.** Neither a nor b

32. Bit stuffing inserts an extra binary 0 after how many sequential binary 1s?

    a. 1 **b.** 3 **c.** 5 **d.** 7

33. Ethernet is what type of MAC?

    a. Contention **b.** Controlled access
    c. Fair access **d.** None of the above

34. Ethernet is most efficient with which of the following?

    a. High traffic **b.** Low traffic
    c. Any type of traffic **d.** Traffic is not a factor

35. Token ring is what type of MAC?

    a. Contention **b.** Controlled access
    c. Unfair access **d.** None of the above

36. The designation 802.3 specifies which of the following?

    a. Ethernet **b.** Token ring **c.** FDDI **d.** None of the above

37. The designation 802.5 specifies which of the following?

    a. Ethernet **b.** Token ring **c.** FDDI **d.** None of the above

38. Which device can recreate a token?

    a. A monitor **b.** A fast monitor
    c. A token monitor **d.** An active monitor

39. A networked device must have which of the following?

    a. A NIC **b.** A bridge **c.** A switch **d.** A repeater

40. Which of the following filters network traffic but does not provide a point-to-point link to itself?

    a. A NIC **b.** A bridge **c.** A switch **d.** A repeater

41. Which of the following is true of the data link layer?

    a. It performs error control. **b.** It performs flow control.
    c. It handles line discipline. **d.** All of the above

42. The LLC is positioned

    a. below the MAC. **b.** above the MAC.
    c. within the MAC. **d.** It has no relationship with the MAC.

43. Synchronous protocols are

    a. bit oriented. **b.** byte oriented.
    c. bit or byte oriented. **d.** none of the above

44. Asynchronous protocols are
  a. bit oriented.   **b.** byte oriented.
  c. bit or byte oriented.   **d.** none of the above.

45. Which type of frame is used to transmit connection-oriented data?
  a. C   **b.** I   **c.** S   **d.** U

46. Which type of delivery service uses I and S frames?
  a. Type 1   **b.** Type 2   **c.** Type 3   **d.** All of the above

47. How many bit errors in a single byte can be detected with simple parity?
  a. 1   **b.** 2   **c.** 4   **d.** 8

48. In data communications, which of the following is used to control who can communicate when?
  a. Line control   **b.** Line discipline
  c. Data control   **d.** Data discipline

49. Logical Link Control provides how many types of frame delivery service?
  a. 1   **b.** 2   **c.** 3   **d.** 4

50. Which type of delivery service requires an acknowledgment?
  a. Type A   **b.** Type 2   **c.** Type 5   **d.** Type R

True or False

For each of the following select either True or False.

1. The physical layer assigns no meaning to the data bits it transmits.

2. Although able to frame data bits, the data link layer cannot perform error control.

3. LLC sits on top of MAC.

4. LLC uses a data unit called a PDU.

5. A PDU always has four fields.

6. A faster sending device must transmit at a speed that the slower receiving device can accept.

7. MAC manages flow control.

8. Sliding windows can have one acknowledgment for several frames.

9. Stop-and-wait flow control works well for large frames transmitting over a short link.

10. A receiving device can transmit an acknowledgment to a sending device.

11. Polling is a term that describes one type of line discipline.

12. Parity checking is both complex and efficient.

13. A sender and receiver must both use the same type of parity.

14. Longitudinal redundancy checking makes use of a byte called a block check character.

15. Checksum checking uses binary division.

16. The most common error correction technique, retransmission, is also the least complicated.

17. Asynchronous protocols are generally complex and expensive to implement.

18. Synchronous protocols are always bit oriented.

19. It is possible for a transmission error to be corrected at the receiving end.

20. Simple parity can detect at least two-bit byte errors.

Exercises

Research in Brief

For one or more of the questions below, provide a one- to two-page report based on your findings.

1. Visit at least two Web sites of vendors who provide NICs. How does one download or access updated drivers from each site? Compare the usability of each site. Was there an area for frequently asked questions (FAQs)? If so, was it useful and easy to navigate? If not, why not?

2. Research the following data link protocols and explain how they are used, how they are different, and how they are similar: XModem, YModem, ZModem, and Kermit.

3. Briefly describe how Ethernet and token ring function. What are their advantages and disadvantages?

4. Contrast stop-and-wait flow control with sliding windows.

Case Study

Sheehan Marketing and Public Relations

After continued evaluation of SMPR's LA office, you decide to recommend that bridges be replaced with switches. Prepare a report for the president that explains what this might cost and what the advantages are. Provide examples of switches from at least three vendors that show the price and functionality of each switch. Make a recommendation, explaining your reasoning, as to which switch vendor to select. Your reasoning might include cost, warranty, support, vendor reputation, and so on. Also, SMPR's president wants to know why it was necessary to upgrade the old 10-Mbps NICs with new 10/100-Mbps NICs. In your report, include a rationale for this change.

Over the last month, you have arranged for Karla to receive formal training in basic networking analysis and troubleshooting. In a memo to SMPR's president, explain why you believe this cost was justified.

chapter three

In addition, you attended a seminar, which cost $500, on fine-tuning Ethernet networks. Include in your memo why you believe a networking technologist should attend professional seminars.

SMPR's president would also like you to prepare a simple description, no more than one page, for the rest of the staff on how Ethernet functions. He has asked you to use nontechnical jargon so that your description will be easy to understand.

Web References

www.ieee.org

www.protocols.com

www.nickara.com/glossary_v0.htm

www.faqs.org/faqs

www.webopedia.com/TERM/H/HDLC.html

www.linksys.com

www.practicallynetworked.com

www.cisco.com

The Secrets of Sliding Windows

Sliding windows is a form of flow control. Allowing for a single acknowledgment for multiple frames, sliding windows makes more efficient utilization of a communication circuit. Sliding windows requires the use of a sequencing number field that is part of the frame that is being sent and received. The sequencing number field has to be defined with a specific bit size. The bit size of the field must be the same for both the sender and the receiver. The number of bits used to define the field depends on network needs as well as the sender's and receiver's buffer size.

Because the sequence number field will be a specific bit size, the range of values that it can take within that size is limited. As an example, the range of values that a two-bit binary field can contain is from 0 to 3 in decimal. The range of values that a three-bit binary field can contain is from 0 to 7 in decimal. This concept is critical because the bit size of the sequence number field determines the maximum number of frames that a window can contain. The following description uses a three-bit sequencing number field.

Chapter 5 discusses binary numbering in much greater detail and shows how to convert between binary and decimal. For now, trust that the range of a three-bit binary field is from 0 to 7 in decimal. This allows for eight unique values: 0, 1, 2, 3, 4, 5, 6, and 7. The maximum size of a sliding window buffer is $n - 1$. Here, n is the number of unique numeric values that can be assigned, determined by the sequence number field bit size. Given a three-bit sequence field, n equals 8. The maximum window size then becomes: $8 - 1 = 7$. With this example, the maximum number of frames that a sliding window's buffer can hold is seven. As such, frames in our transmission example will be numbered sequentially from 0 to 7. Frames are always numbered in sequence, and the sequence numbers are reused in a circular fashion.

Because this example uses sliding windows as its flow control mechanism, the sender can send none, some, or all of the frames it holds in its sliding windows buffer. The sender does not have to wait for individual frame acknowledgments from the receiver. Each frame the sender transmits has a number attached to it. The numbers are used in sequential order, are continuously reused as transmission proceeds, and are based on the sequence number field. When the receiver sends an acknowledgment, the acknowledgment will contain the sequence number of the next frame that is expected. Let's see how this works.

The following discussion uses several figures to illustrate the sliding windows process. At the beginning of the transmission, both the sender and receiver have a sliding windows buffer space that allows for seven frames, based on a three-bit sequence number field. Look at Figure 3.16. The figure shows a sender and a receiver. From the left, the frames zero through six represent the sender's and receiver's views of their sliding windows buffer space. The sender is holding seven frames, and the receiver is capable of accepting seven frames.

As the sender's frames are transmitted, the sender's sliding windows buffer shrinks from the left edge, going left to right, starting with frame F0. Only when the sender gets an acknowledgment from the receiver can the sender's sliding windows buffer expand from the right edge, left to right.

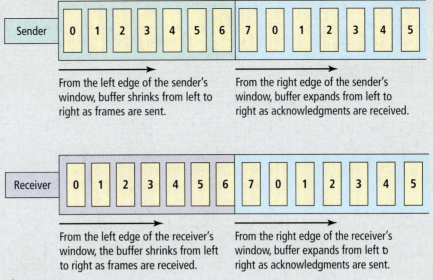

From the left edge of the sender's window, buffer shrinks from left to right as frames are sent.

From the right edge of the sender's window, buffer expands from left to right as acknowledgments are received.

From the left edge of the receiver's window, the buffer shrinks from left to right as frames are received.

From the right edge of the receiver's window, buffer expands from left to right as acknowledgments are sent.

Figure 3.16

Sliding Windows Buffer Space

The sender's and receiver's sliding windows buffer space is numbered 0 through 6 from left of the image.

How many frames the sender's window shrinks or expands depends on the acknowledgment sent back from the receiver. From the receiver's perspective, the sliding windows buffer also shrinks from the left edge, going left to right, as frames are received. Based on the last frame processed, the receiver sends an acknowledgment to the sender, and the receiver's sliding window expands from the right edge, left to right. Before the receiver's sliding windows buffer can expand, it must send an acknowledgment.

Assume the sender initially transmits four frames: F0, F1, F2, and F3. The sender's sliding window shrinks by four frames from the left edge. Figure 3.17 shows the sender's now shrunken sliding window. (The sender, by the way, also keeps a copy of the frames that have been transmitted in a different memory buffer location, just in case one or more of the transmitted frames has to be retransmitted. Not until the frames have been successfully acknowledged does the sender completely drop them.) At this point, the sender has not received an acknowledgment from the receiver for

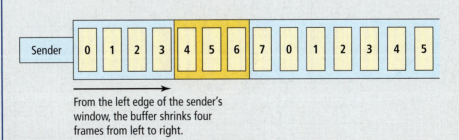

From the left edge of the sender's window, the buffer shrinks four frames from left to right.

Figure 3.17

Shrinking Sliding Windows Buffer—Four Frames

Sender's shrinking sliding windows buffer after sending four frames. No acknowledgments have yet been received from receiver.

the four frames that have been sent. Even so, the sender could send the remaining three frames held in its sliding windows buffer, beginning with frame F4, without having to wait for an acknowledgment. This is the benefit of sliding windows.

However—and this is important—the sender's sliding windows buffer does not expand, and will not expand, until acknowledgment is received from the receiver. Sending frames that remain in the sliding windows buffer and expanding the sliding windows buffer are two separate events. The sender's sliding windows buffer can shrink without waiting for the receiver's acknowledgment. However, the sender's sliding window buffer cannot expand without acknowledgments from the receiver.

In the meantime, assume that the receiver begins to receive the sender's first four frames. As the frames arrive, they occupy available sequential frame slots in the receiver's sliding windows buffer. Once occupied, these slots are not available for other incoming frames. The receiver's sliding windows buffer shrinks accordingly by four frames from the left edge, from left to right, to reflect that these slots are no longer available. The result is that the receiver's sliding windows buffer now has only three frames' worth of space available for use. The receiver's sliding windows buffer does not expand, and will not expand, until the receiver sends an acknowledgment to the sender. Figure 3.18 shows the receiver's and the sender's sliding windows buffer preacknowledgment status.

Now assume that the receiver finally transmits a Ready to Receive 4 (RR4) acknowledgment to the sender. This acknowledgement tells the sender, "I have received frames F0 through F3 and am ready for the next sequential frame." Based on sending this acknowledgment, the receiver's sliding windows buffer now expands by four, from the right edge, left to right, as shown in Figure 3.19.

In time, the sender gets the RR4 acknowledgment from the receiver. The sender, based on this acknowledgment, knows that frames F0 through F3 have been received. The sender's sliding windows buffer in response now

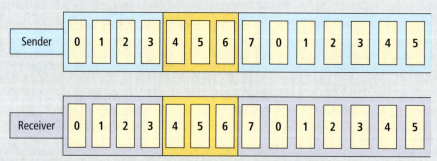

Figure 3.18
Pre-Acknowledgment Buffer Status of Sender and Receiver
Sender has sent four frames. Receiver has received four frames. At this point, no acknowledgment from the receiver has yet been sent.

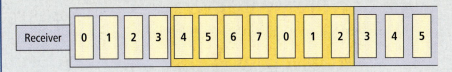

From the right edge of the receiver's window, the buffer expands by four frames, from left to right, as RR4 acknowledgment is sent. Frames 0 through 3 have been successfully processed.

Figure 3.19
RR4 Acknowledgment
Receiver's expanding sliding windows buffer after sending acknowledgment Ready to Receive 4 (RR4) to the sender.

expands, from the right edge, left to right, by four frames. Figure 3.20 shows the sender and receiver's post-acknowledgment sliding windows buffer status.

A receiving device can also send a Receive Not Ready (RNR) frame, which tells the sending device to stop transmitting until further notice. A RNR closes the sliding windows, and a Receive Ready (RR) frame will have to be sent by the receiver to reopen them. The frame sequence numbers in sliding windows are reused in a circular manner. Thus, sliding windows is a continuous cycle, controlled by acknowledgments between the sender and receiver, of memory buffers shrinking and expanding, shrinking and expanding, and so on.

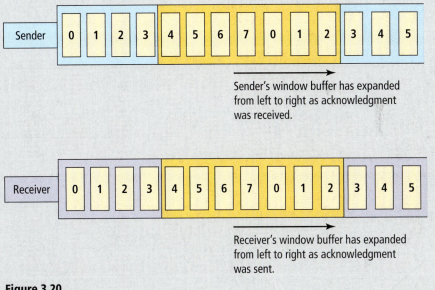

Sender's window buffer has expanded from left to right as acknowledgment was received.

Receiver's window buffer has expanded from left to right as acknowledgment was sent.

Figure 3.20
Post-Acknowledgment Status of Sliding Windows Buffers of Sender and Receiver

4 chapterfour

Components of a Local Area Network

Learning Objectives

After studying this chapter, you should be able to:

- Identify two major LAN components.
- Explain what is meant by topology.
- Describe three major topologies: star, ring, and bus.
- Understand the purpose of a NIC.
- Identify factors that affect NIC selection.
- Identify factors that affect server configuration.
- Understand the use of client devices.
- Describe a client/server network model.
- Describe a peer-to-peer network model.
- Understand the difference between hubs and switches.
- Identify three forms of Ethernet: standard, switched, and Fast.
- Identify two types of Fast Ethernet: 100Base-X and 100Base-FX.
- Explain the purpose of a network/server operating system (NOS/SOS).
- Identify the four major types of server operating systems: Microsoft, Linux, Unix, and Novell.
- Know the purpose of an application server.
- Understand two types of licensing: metered and site.
- Identify key LAN design considerations.

Chapter 2 described the physical layer and how it provides the necessary connectivity to transmit data bits. Chapter 3 explored how the data link layer passes these data bits in frames from one device to another. This chapter takes a slightly different direction, addressing network components rather than layers. Chapter 5 picks up the discussion of layers, reviewing the upper-level layers of the TCP/IP model.

As you read in Chapter 1, networks can be classified into a number of different categories. The focus of this chapter is on LANs. Later chapters focus on BNs, MANs, and WANs. This approach will demonstrate how a small, relatively simple LAN can grow into a larger, more complex system. Each type of network, whether small or large, has its own issues and topics of concern. It is not unusual for a networking professional to specialize in one of these areas, or even a subset of an area. Regardless of your intended area of specialization, it is to your benefit to know something about each type of network.

LAN Components

LAN components are either physical or logical. Physical components include NICs, client devices, servers, printers, cables, hubs, switches, and routers, to name just a few. These items can be seen and touched; they require installation, configuration, and maintenance. Logical components typically include device drivers, network operating systems, and desktop operating systems, as well as software that can be used to monitor, troubleshoot, and evaluate the performance of a LAN. The term **troubleshoot** refers to the ability to find a problem and evaluate it so that corrective action can be taken. Troubleshooting tools may be software based, but they can also be as simple as determining if a documented chain of procedures for accomplishing steps in a process was correctly followed. Logical components, like physical components, also need to be installed, configured, and maintained.

A LAN's physical and logical components are equally important. In fact, physical components could not work without their logical counterparts, and vice versa. Physical components are frequently referred to as **hardware**, as in Figure 4.1. Logical components are usually software, but may also include procedures that define how a particular task should be accomplished. **Software** is a set of programmed instructions that tell a device how to perform its functions. Software is executed, or run, electronically, using some type of computer processor. Figure 4.2 shows a suite of Microsoft Windows 2000 networking software.

Whether physical or logical, successfully working with both types of components is dependent on the quality of their **documentation**. Is the documentation current? Is it accurate? Comprehensive? Readily available? Easily understandable? Writing good documentation is an art, and skilled technical writers are well paid. Regardless of the field of data or telecommunications in which you may find yourself, at times the quality of your documentation will be the only thing between you and disaster.

An additional element in a LAN that also has physical and logical characteristics is the LAN's topology. A **topology** refers to how the pieces of a network are connected. A topology has a physical layout, which may be wired or wireless, as well as a logical mechanism that determines how devices access the physical layout. In fact, based on your reading of Chapter 3, you are already familiar with two ways that devices get access,

Figure 4.1
Hardware Circuit Boards (Integrated Circuits, Resistors, Capacitors)

Ethernet and token ring. Ethernet and token ring are protocols. A third topology is the star topology, which is most often used in mini- and mainframe computer networks.

Topologies

Topologies determine not only how devices are connected to each other, but also how they access the media they use for communication. A topology is both physical and logical. However, a network's logical

Figure 4.2
Microsoft Windows 2000 Server Software

layout may differ from its physical layout. What you physically see may not represent what is logically happening in the LAN. Classic Ethernet is a **bus topology**. Ethernet and variations of it are by far the most commonly deployed topology in LANs today. There is some controversy with the advent of switching technology as to whether an Ethernet LAN that uses switches can still be called a bus. We discuss this in more detail later in this chapter. First, two other types of topologies are explored: star and ring.

Star Topology

A traditional **star topology** is configured such that a central controlling device has other networked devices connected to it by point-to-point circuits. Each connected device typically has two point-to-point circuits, one for sending and one for receiving. The central controlling device is often a mini- or mainframe computer. Devices connected to the mini- or mainframe are usually referred to as **terminals**. For terminals to communicate with each other or with the mini- or mainframe, they must work through the central controlling device. This type of topology can be useful in certain WAN situations whereby applications in outlying offices must communicate with a central office. Figure 4.3 demonstrates a standard physical and logical star topology.

An advantage of the star topology is that it centralizes key network resources, such as data and applications. This centralization simplifies network management. When something goes wrong or needs to be maintained or implemented, only one location needs to be evaluated or modified. Security can also be more tightly controlled, because there

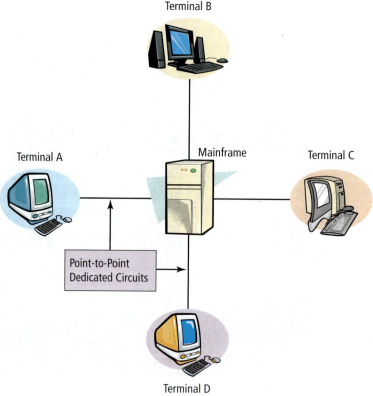

Figure 4.3
Standard Star Topology

is only one point of access. However, one point of access also results in a single point of failure, so if the mini- or mainframe crashes, so does the network. Were this to happen, users of the network would not be able to access the network's resources or **login** to the network for authentication. (A network login generally requires two pieces of identifying information, what is called a user id, probably related to your name or job function, and a password.) To address this single point of failure, redundant systems may be required. Redundant systems result in additional costs and complexity. In addition, with such a topology, cabling costs can be high, because each terminal requires its own connecting cable to the mini- or mainframe. The larger the network, the more costly the cabling becomes. Note that it is possible to have a network with a physical star topology but with a different logical topology, usually a bus.

Ring Topology

IBM introduced the ring topology. (An interesting history of the ring topology can be found at **www.networking.ibm.com/tra/whitepapers/TR00. pdf**.) A **ring topology** uses a single cable such that the cable ends meet and form a closed loop. IBM also introduced the token ring protocol, which is associated with the ring topology. This might seem confusing, but a topology and a protocol are not the same thing. Think of a topology as how devices are to be physically connected and the protocol as that which controls or manages the connection. You may recall from Chapter 3 that the token ring protocol is the 802.5 protocol. The IEEE has a work group on the 802.5 protocol. To find out more visit **grouper.ieee.org/groups/802/5/www8025org**. Physically, a network using a ring topology looks somewhat like a star, because each networked device is connected directly to a central **Media Access Unit (MAU)**. MAUs connect the devices to the ring. Logically, however, the cables connected through the MAUs function as a true ring. As described in Chapter 3, a token circulates around the ring in one direction. Depending on whether the token is free or busy, a device can use the token to issue a communication on the ring. Sometimes referred to as the **fair access** topology, devices on the ring at some point are guaranteed access to the token should they need it. Figure 4.4 illustrates a ring topology using MAUs.

The ring topology performs well in networks that have many devices that need to use the circuit and in environments where communication traffic is heavy. When using the 802.5 protocol in a ring topology, no one device can monopolize the resources of the ring. This structure creates a more balanced, or fair access, topology. Even so, the ring topology accounts for only a small percentage of LAN installations, primarily due to its cost and the complexity of installation. Cost often drives a business to choose a less capable technology over a more sophisticated, expensive one.

Bus Topology

The bus topology, like the ring, views its circuit as a single cable. Unlike the ring, the cable does not form a closed loop. Devices connect to the central cable, using it as a communications pipeline. The protocol most often associated with the bus topology is Ethernet. The IEEE has formalized the bus protocol as Ethernet 802.3 (**grouper.ieee.org/groups/802/3/**). A classic bus topology uses a broadcast mechanism. When a device puts its data packet on the bus, the packet is **broadcast**, or sent, to all of the devices on the bus. All devices evaluate the packet to determine whether it is addressed to them or not. Devices ignore packets not addressed to them and process

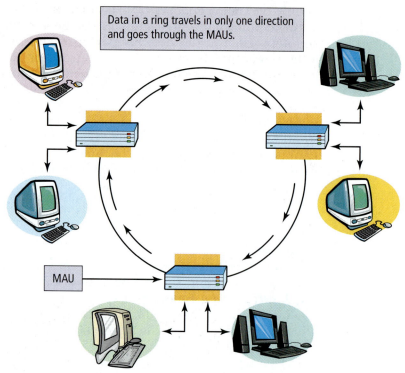

Figure 4.4
Standard Ring Topology with Media Access Units (MAUs)

those that are. In addition, only one device at a time can use the bus for communication.

The bus topology, using the 802.3 protocol, is a **contention-based topology**. Devices contend for access to the communication circuit by means of CSMA/CD, which was described in Chapter 3. It is theoretically possible in an 802.3 network with heavy traffic that some devices will never gain access to the communication circuit. In addition, overall network performance can rapidly degrade when too many devices attempt to use the shared circuit at one time. However, an 802.3 LAN is relatively easy to install and configure and uses relatively inexpensive cabling. Cost has made 802.3 the king of choice in current LAN topologies. Figure 4.5 shows an example of a traditional bus topology using broadcasting.

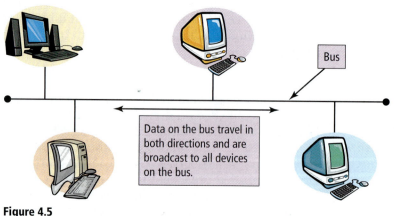

Figure 4.5
Standard Bus Using a Broadcast

Later in this chapter, you will learn how Ethernet has been modified to significantly improve performance and provide improved balance of access to all connected devices. Switching technology has transformed how Ethernet is configured.

Regardless of the topology, a variety of physical hardware elements are used to make the LAN operational. The next section reviews some of these elements.

Physical Elements: Hardware

A LAN might use many different types of physical components, or hardware. It is not possible to describe them all in this text. Instead, this text identifies some of the most common LAN hardware elements, explaining their purpose and operation. Many of these elements were introduced in earlier chapters.

Network Interface Cards

An essential hardware component that each device on a LAN must have in order to communicate is a **Network Interface Card**, or **NIC** (pronounced *nick*). A NIC, like the one shown in Figure 4.6, is also known as an **adapter card**. As you learned in Chapter 3, each NIC has a physical MAC layer address as well as its own unique address. A physical address is an address that is specific, unique, and assigned to one and only one NIC. A NIC's physical address is, in fact, part of the card's physical manufacture. Therefore, if two or more NICs have the same **physical address**, communication problems will occur. It is possible in the manufacturing process that two NICs could erroneously be assigned the same physical address. In such an event, one of the two NICs would have to be replaced. In a TCP/IP network, any device, regardless of its type, that is connected to the network is referred to as a **host**. A host might be a client machine, a server, a printer, or any other type of device connected to the network. That host, however, must have a NIC that allows it to communicate on the network.

Many NICs are internal to the host, meaning that on a typical microcomputer, the NIC is plugged into one of the expansion slots available on

Figure 4.6
3Com Gigabit Ethernet NIC

Figure 4.7
Intel Motherboard Showing PCI Slots
Motherboard, Intel D845GEBV2, 2 DDR 333 (PC2700)
DIMM socket, for socket 478 Pentium 4 or Celeron,
on-board sound, 6-PCI, 1 AGP, 10/100 LAN.

the computer's motherboard. (See Figure 4.7, which shows an Intel motherboard with expansion slots that could accommodate an NIC.) NICs can also be external, possibly connected to a computer's serial or parallel port. Laptops and other types of portable devices often make use of PC cards that plug into a slot. Regardless of the kind of NIC, its most important job is to frame the data that pass through it. The quality and capabilities of a NIC can have a direct effect on the performance of a LAN.

Choosing the most appropriate NIC requires some thought. Depending on the type of host, the capabilities of the NIC can be critical. For example, a file server that services many clients should have a NIC that is fast and has sufficient throughput so that the device it is connected to, in this case a file server, does not become a bottleneck, slowing the network down. So what factors should one consider when selecting a NIC?

First, what is the NIC's **bus width**? A bus is like a multilane highway, providing the circuitry paths along which data bits flow. The wider the bus, the more data bits the bus can transmit at one time. A 32-bit bus can handle four times the data bits of an 8-bit bus. For a high-end server, you would likely want a wide bus, perhaps 64-bit, whereas for a low-end device, a 16-bit bus may be sufficient. Second, how much memory, and of what type, does the NIC support? This memory is also called the NIC's buffer, or **cache**. A NIC's cache is used to temporarily hold data to be processed and assists in speeding up the performance of the LAN. Typically, the larger the cache, the better the performance of the NIC.

Two other NIC memory-related questions need to be addressed. First, does the NIC support direct memory access? **Direct memory access (DMA)** is the capability of the NIC to directly use the host device's memory. Second, does the NIC support **bus mastering**? This is a technique that incorporates a CPU (central processing unit) on the NIC. Through bus mastering, a NIC can process incoming data without having to wait for the host's CPU to do the job.

A NIC's bus width and memory capabilities have a direct impact on its throughput capability. **Throughput** for a NIC is a measure of how many bits it can process within 1 second. An Ethernet NIC can have a throughput of 10 or 100 Mbps. Generally, the higher the throughput, the higher the cost of the NIC. Not all network devices require the highest level of throughput. Part of your analysis as a network administrator will be to determine what is cost-effective in terms of the NIC that you deploy in your organization. A NIC might cost $20 or $1,000, depending on its capabilities. In an organization with 5,000 hosts, you can see that cost becomes a major consideration.

An Ethernet bus is by far the most commonly used topology in LANs today due to its ease of installation and relatively low cost. Consequently, most NICs use Ethernet physical addressing. (NIC addresses, by the way, are assigned and allocated in blocks to card manufacturers by the IEEE.) An Ethernet NIC address consists of 48 bits composed of 12 hexadecimal digits. **Hexadecimal**, or hex, is the Base-16 numbering system. Hex uses the values 0 through 9 and the capital letters A through F. In hex, A is 10, B is 11, C is 12, D is 13, E is 14, and F is 15. For conversion then, a decimal 10 is a hex A, 11 a hex B, and so on, for a maximum up to 15, or F. Ethernet **MAC addresses** are usually expressed in hex octets. An **octet** is equivalent to eight bits. An Ethernet MAC NIC address might then look like this: 08:00:5A:28:E4:F8.

The first six hex digits specify the NIC's manufacturer, the last six hex digits specify the interface serial number. Note the use of the word "digit," keeping in mind that in hex, the capital letter A is the hex-digit equivalent of the decimal 10; E is 14, and F is 15. NIC manufacturers are allocated specific numeric ranges. In our example, 08:00:5A identifies that the NIC was manufactured by IBM. The 48-bit Ethernet MAC numbering scheme allows for almost 300,000,000,000,000 unique addresses. As more devices, such as household appliances, become network aware and require a MAC address, this huge quantity of Ethernet NIC addresses will be quite useful.

NICs, like most hardware devices, also have a logical component, in this case a **device driver**. Device drivers are software programs that control the NIC and allow it to work in association with the host device's network operating system. When purchasing a NIC, it is important to determine if that NIC's driver is compatible with the network operating system in use. It should never be assumed that a given NIC will function in all types of networks. Many NICs do support multiple protocols and can be configured to support differing network environments. However, you should always first consult the NIC's documentation to determine if multiple protocols are supported.

Media

Chapter 2 presented several forms of physical layer media that can be used in a data communications network. **Media** is plural, providing for several types. **Medium** is singular, referring to one specific type. An essential physical component of a LAN is the physical medium over which data are transmitted over the network. Today, the most common LAN medium is unshielded twisted-wire pair (UTP). UTP, illustrated in Figure 4.8, is inexpensive and very flexible and can be made to fit into tight places. Newer buildings typically have UTP automatically installed.

Available in several categories, UTP Category 5, or Cat 5, has become the most common medium found in LANs because of its low cost, ease of

Figure 4.8
CAT 5 Twisted-Wire Pair

installation, and high transmission capacity. As Ethernet has evolved, the type and quality of cabling used to configure an Ethernet network has also evolved. Cat 5 has over time mostly replaced Cat 3 as the UTP cable of choice. In due course, it is likely that Cat 5 will gradually be replaced with Cat 6, a higher-quality UTP. A good, brief, graphical overview of UTP cabling history is available on the IEEE Web site at **grouper.ieee.org/ groups/802/3/10GBT/public/jan03/cobb_1_0103.pdf**.

The UTP cable category classification determines the maximum number of bits that the cable can transmit. A higher cable category number represents a larger cable size. A larger cable size results in less resistance to the signal being carried on the cable. Reduced resistance translates into higher transmission speeds.

Cat 5 is used in segments no longer 100 meters. Segments are connected by RJ-45 connectors. Typical Cat 5 speeds range from 10 to 100 Mbps. An enhanced version of Cat 5 is available if Gigabit Ethernet is being considered. For most LANs, Gigabit Ethernet provides more transmission capacity than is needed, and, consequently, it is not very cost-effective. BNs, which demand much greater throughput capacity, can more adequately take advantage of a gigabit connection.

Network wiring usually runs from all connected devices to a communications **wiring closet**. Wiring closets should be physically secured and locked to prevent unauthorized access. Keep in mind that the length of a cable segment must include the full path from the networked device to the communications closet. In many cases, the signal in the closet is regenerated before it is sent to other areas of the network. When a signal is **regenerated**, it is in effect reissued or re-created at its original strength in order to send the signal to other parts of the network or enterprise.

Servers

Servers are critical to the enterprise. Because of their importance, an entire chapter (Chapter 8) is devoted to servers. **Servers** are computers that fulfill specific, specialized functions. Servers allow LAN resources to be made available for multiple users to share and utilize. LAN resources can include, among other things, printers, applications, data, informa-

Figure 4.9
Network Server from IBM
iSeries 830

chapter **four**

tion, files, databases, security services, directory services, modems, Web hosting, and e-mail—basically anything that a group of users would need to have access to. Figure 4.9 shows an IBM iSeries 830 network server. IBM also makes blade servers. Blade servers are designed to fit into existing servers. Because of their modularity, blade servers are small and cost-efficient. Because blade servers are usually smaller, they also consume less power. A chassis is the housing unit that the blade server plugs into. (A good Web site to look up unfamiliar technology terms is **www.webopedia.com**.)

Because servers can share resources, they provide significant cost savings to a business. For example, rather than purchasing individual printers for each user, users can access a pool of common printers managed by a print server. Or, for applications that are widely used, it is cheaper to buy a networkable version of an application and share it across the LAN using an **application server** instead of buying individual user licenses. Keep in mind that for such sharing to work, the resource must be capable of being accessed or distributed across a network.

Not all devices or applications are network compatible. In addition, for a resource that is mission critical—meaning that the resource must be available when the user requires it—redundant servers may be needed to manage that resource. A single server that manages an essential resource is also a potential single source for failure. If that server fails or crashes, for whatever reason, the resource it manages also becomes unavailable. This can be particularly troublesome for servers that authenticate users to the network. If that server fails, no one can login to the network. In such cases, redundant servers are essential. However, redundancy, while providing fault tolerance and improved security, is also an added expense.

The type of server chosen and its capabilities will be based on the tasks the server is expected to perform. Some resource-intensive services, such as managing and making databases available, require relatively powerful servers. In contrast, a print server that manages 10 or fewer printers can be an inexpensive low-end device. Servers also require controlling and managing software. Such software is called a **network operating system (NOS)** or **server operating system (SOS)**. Depending on the scale of the LAN, the choice of server operating system will be important. Some server operating systems are designed for very small LANs having 20 or fewer networked devices. Larger, more complicated LANs that have hundreds of users require more sophisticated server operating systems.

A server's processor, or CPU, can be critical. For resource-intensive types of applications, a server should have a fast processor, and may in fact require multiple processors. Servers that run multiple processors also require a server operating system that supports multiprocessing. The number of processors a server operating system can support depends on the server operating system. Documentation again becomes critical. The more work a server is expected to perform, the more traffic it is likely to encounter, and, consequently, the more important it becomes that the server have adequate processor capability to perform its duties.

Hard drives can affect server performance. Different hard drives have different access speeds. Where speed of access and transmittal are essential to the server's duties, fast hard drives are a must. As with processors, servers are often configured with multiple hard drives. For servers that store or provide business-critical data and applications, duplicate hard drives can provide necessary fault tolerance. Once again, the server operating system must be evaluated to determine the number of hard drives it can support for a given server.

For servers with multiple hard drives, a decision must also be made as to whether each hard drive should have its own disk controller. Disk controllers manage the hard drive and work with the primary device's processor to make data on the hard drive available. Two hard drives can share the same controller. This is called **disk mirroring**. What is written to the primary, or controlling, drive is written, or mirrored, to the secondary drive. However, should the controller fail, both hard drives become unavailable, and so do any data they contain. Servers with multiple hard drives also can be configured so that each hard drive has its own controller. Such a configuration is called **disk duplexing**. With multiple controllers, should one of the server's hard drive controllers fail, the other will likely still be available. Figure 4.10 conceptually illustrates this point.

Servers with multiple hard drives and multiple hard drive controllers will of course be more costly. Usually, when multiple hard drives with independent controllers are used, the drives are mirrors of each other. This form of mirroring provides a degree of fault tolerance. **Fault tolerance** is achieved because all work performed on the primary drive is duplicated on the redundant secondary device. (Mirroring and a concept referred to as Redundant Array of Inexpensive Devices (RAID) are described in greater detail in the "Topic in Focus" at the end of Chapter 10.) Business needs should decide the degree of fault tolerance required, which will determine how many hard drives and hard drive controllers a server should have.

Server **primary memory**, called **Random Access Memory (RAM)**, is also an important consideration. The quantity of RAM and its speed

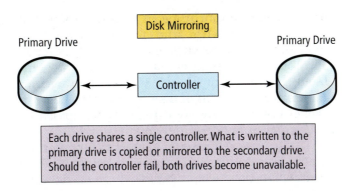

Each drive shares a single controller. What is written to the primary drive is copied or mirrored to the secondary drive. Should the controller fail, both drives become unavailable.

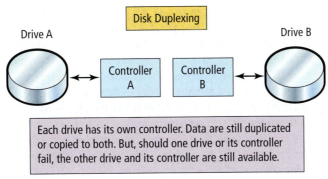

Each drive has its own controller. Data are still duplicated or copied to both. But, should one drive or its controller fail, the other drive and its controller are still available.

Figure 4.10
Hard Drives with Single and Multiple Controllers

should be matched with the purpose for which the server is being configured. The more RAM, and the faster its processing speed, the more expensive the server becomes. Even so, adding memory is one of the most cost-effective enhancements that can be made to a server to improve its performance. In order to perform their work, servers hold the data they are processing in RAM. Data in RAM are directly accessible to the server's processors. RAM is much faster than hard drive storage. The more data a server can hold in RAM, the faster that data will be processed. When servers must constantly go to a hard drive to bring data into RAM to make the data available to the server's processor, performance degrades, ultimately slowing down the network.

Associated with a server's primary memory, but physically a separate component, is a faster access memory called cache. There are two types of cache: level 1 and level 2. **Level 1 cache**, the faster of the two, is an ultra-fast storage location housed directly on the chip that holds the computer's processor. Because level 1 cache is on the same chip as the processor, the processor has pretty much instantaneous access to any data held in level 1 cache. This makes for very, very fast access. **Level 2 cache** is close to, but not on, the chip that houses the processor. Retrieving data from level 2 cache is faster than retrieving data from RAM but slower than retrieving data from level 1 cache. Cache is highly desirable, but also expensive. Business needs have to be weighed against cost to determine what quantities of cache are most effective. High levels of cache on a print server would be unnecessary and wasteful but essential on a heavily used database server.

Earlier you learned that all devices connected to a LAN must have a NIC. However, all of the NICs do not have to be of the same type or have the same capacity. As with memory and hard drives, the server's NIC is of particular importance. It is not unusual for client devices to have lower-capacity NICs and for moderate to heavily used servers to have high-capacity NICs. Client machines might have NICs that support 10 Mbps, whereas selected servers will have more expensive NICs capable of 100 Mbps or higher. The NIC can become a bottleneck on servers that experience a lot of traffic. In such a case, it would be wise to provide those servers with more expensive, higher-capacity NICs so that network performance is adequately maintained.

Software is required for servers to function and perform all of their many duties. Servers depend ultimately on their server operating system to tell them what, how, when, and where to carry out their jobs. Consequently, a server's operating system is extremely important. The scale of a LAN, the types of duties it is expected to support, and the types of services it will provide guide the decision as to which server operating system is most appropriate. A few popular server operating systems are described in greater detail later in the chapter.

Servers have become the modern-day workhorses of the networked world. Much of what we experience as common convenience—sending e-mail, making online reservations, surfing the Web, accessing applications a thousand miles away—depend on server technology. Over the last decade a new phenomenon has emerged—the **server farm**. In this type of installation, such as that shown in Figure 4.11, entire buildings are dedicated to housing and running not dozens of servers, but hundreds. One server farm, for example, run by Sun Microsystems, contains 600 multiprocessor UltraSPARC systems, 2,000 UltraSPARC CPUs, 500 gigabytes of RAM, and 11 terabytes of disk space. Midrange systems, such as IBM's eServers, specifically the iSeries (**www-1.ibm.com/businesscenter/us/products/servers/**), provide another alternative.

A typical scenario might find users remotely submitting jobs to load-sharing software rather than to individual systems. The load-sharing software matches a job to the servers or workstations most capable of

Figure 4.11

What a typical, and unglamorous, server farm might look like.

handling it and schedules the job for execution. An advantage of server farms is that they are able to run 24 hours a day, 7 days a week using processing power that would otherwise sit idle. Server farms are not without controversy, however, because they demand significant amounts of electrical power. During the West Coast energy crunch during the summer of 2002, many network administrators were in crisis mode as they struggled to keep power running to the numerous server farms installed from San Francisco to San Diego. Without power, the largest server farm is just a building housing expensive, but useless, equipment.

Clients

Servers have become an essential LAN tool, but they are essential only because they provide access to resources required by users. Without users, there would be no need for servers, or even for the LAN itself. Users connect to the LAN and to server resources using **client** devices. LAN clients, then, are another hardware component of the LAN architecture. Although client devices are usually associated with human users, this is not always the case. A LAN client can also be another machine, such as a printer. In a TCP/IP LAN, networked devices, like clients, are referred to as hosts. Each host has a physical address identified by its NIC as well as a logical network address. A client's logical network address in TCP/IP is based on a 32-bit binary number that has to be configured in order for that client to connect to the LAN.

Today, clients encompass a wide array of devices. For example, a cell phone or a Personal Digital Assistant (PDA) such as a PalmPilot or Blackberry could be a network client. Figure 4.12 shows a Dell Pocket PC that could function as a network client. The most common client device, though, is a microcomputer, or desktop, of some type. Based on the needs of the user, the client computer may be a standard, moderately scaled device or a very powerful computer. Powerful user computers capable of performing complex and sophisticated applications are usually referred to as **workstations**.

Whether the client is a PDA, a simple $500 desktop, or a $10,000 workstation, it uses some type of user-oriented desktop operating system.

Figure 4.12
A Dell Pocket PC that could function as a network client.

Modern desktop operating systems are often already network aware. This means that the client operating system software contains the necessary functionalities that allow that client to recognize and be easily configured for common network layer protocols.

TCP/IP incorporates protocols at the network layer as well as at the transport and application layers. Chapter 5 describes in some detail how clients are configured for network layer addressing using TCP/IP. Clients login to the network in order to access its resources. Typical login components include a user ID and a password. As part of the login process, clients are validated and authenticated. Assuming they pass this process, the clients are then able to use those resources for which they have been previously configured. This type of LAN, one that uses dedicated servers and independent clients, is called the **client/server model**.

Another type of model used in very small networks, those with 15 machines or fewer, is the **peer-to-peer model**. With a peer-to-peer LAN, a specialized server operating system is not required. Instead, the networking capabilities provided in client operating systems are used. In this type of network, a device can, depending on how it is set up, function as a client, as a server, or both. The term peer means "equal," so in a peer-to-peer network, computers are equal in what they may be configured to do. If a user's computer is attached to a printer, the user can use the desktop operating system's networking ability to share that printer with other users. To do so, the administrator would have to set up an account for each user who wants to access the printer over the network. For a few users, this is not too complicated.

However, if a network grows beyond a certain point, again approximately 15 user stations, then setting up and maintaining user accounts on a peer-to-peer network begins to get complicated and unmanageable. Very likely, other users on the smaller LAN will also have resources that they need to share. User accounts have to be set up on each of these machines as well. If the network grows, and the number of resources to share also increases, the peer-to-peer model no longer functions very well. At that point, the administrator would likely move to a client/server model, which provides greater control for larger groups of users.

Switches and Routers

As a LAN grows, it may be necessary to begin to segment it in order to keep performance at adequate levels. A key indicator of performance is the response time to a request. When there are too many users on the same segment of a LAN, traffic can cause the network to slow to an unacceptable pace. In that case, different types of hardware devices can be used to segment the network. Two devices in particular have become very prominent in LAN architectures: switches and routers. As you learned in Chapter 3, **switches** are often associated with the data link layer, or layer 2. Routers are associated with the network layer, or layer 3. Certain switches called multilayer switches can function at either layer 2 or layer 3.

Multilayer switches are more complicated, sophisticated, intelligent, and expensive than single-layer switches. The choice of going with multilayer switches, then, should be evaluated based on a cost-benefit analysis. One option is to use multilayer switches only in select circumstances and to use layer 2 switches in all other cases. Switches in general cost far less than routers. As switching capabilities continue to improve, especially with layer 2 switches becoming more intelligent, switches are increasingly being implemented where routers were once used. Figure 4.13 shows a Cisco layer 3 8500 series switch.

Figure 4.13
Layer 3 Ethernet Switch from Cisco—8500 Series

Routers are now more commonly being deployed as devices at the edge of the network. Much more expensive than switches, routers are also more complicated to configure and manage. However, routers perform functions that switches cannot, which is why they are still very important. For an organization that has many networks, routers are required for the networks to be able to communicate with each other. Every network has its own logical identifier. If a host on network A wants to send a packet to a host on network B, a layer 2 switch will not be able to route the packet to its correct destination. A layer 2 switch recognizes only its own network. A router, however, recognizes different networks by their addresses. Routers use tables that contain addresses of networks that they can reach and addresses of other routers that they may need to send a packet to in order for that packet to reach its final destination. A router's address table may be manually or dynamically updated based on the router type. Figure 4.14 shows a standard Cisco router.

Because a router uses addressing tables, it does not broadcast packets. A broadcast sends a packet to all hosts on a network. Through addressing, a router determines exactly where to send the packet. Based on the network layer address attached to the packet, a router recognizes the next step the packet should take on its journey. Because packets are not broadcast, traffic is reduced. A router can also connect networks that use different topologies or architectures; for example, it can connect a token ring with an Ethernet network. Hubs and switches connect networks of the same architecture. Routers act like hosts on a network, but unlike an ordinary host, a router has addresses on, and links to, multiple networks at the same time. Put simply, routers accept packets from one logical network and pass them forward to a second connected logical network. In Chapter 6, backbone networks and routers are explored in more detail. As you read earlier, a backbone network connects the many networks of a single enterprise.

Types of Ethernet

Ethernet is the most common LAN architecture. Over time, Ethernet has evolved into several flavors. There is some controversy as to whether some of these new flavors are, in fact, still Ethernet. For example,

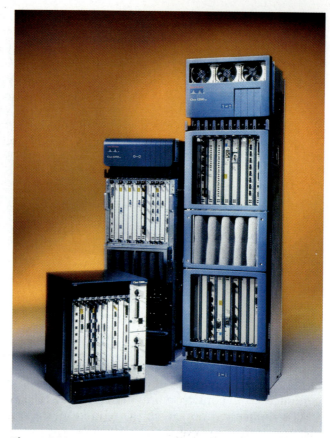

Figure 4.14
Cisco Internet Router

standard 10-Mbps Ethernet LANs use traditional hubs and bridges, maintaining the classic bus architecture. Then there are Ethernet LANs, including standard, Fast, and Gigabit Ethernet, that use switches rather than hubs. Most new Ethernet LANs are more likely to use switches than hubs. This makes for a significant difference in how an Ethernet circuit is shared.

Switches, because of how they function, make contention and collision, the defining characteristics of an Ethernet bus, no longer a factor. The question then becomes, if an Ethernet network is no longer limited or defined by the need for collision detection, is it still an Ethernet network, or is it something else? We defer that decision to the various standards-setting bodies, particularly the IEEE, and present here that switched Ethernet is still Ethernet. The point is that newer forms of Ethernet differ from the older, traditional bus topology and result in faster, more efficient transmission capacity. Following is an overview of some of the forms that Ethernet can take.

Standard Ethernet Understanding standard Ethernet emphasizes the benefits gained from newer Ethernet forms. **Standard Ethernet** is a bus topology that uses hubs to extend the network. On a bus, when a host transmits, all other hosts on the shared circuit receive the transmission, whether it is addressed to them or not. With a bus, only one host at a time can use the circuit. Hubs broadcast all frames that go through them. Filtering is not performed. As far as all the devices connected to a hub are concerned, they are on the same, shared, single circuit. The hub is simply

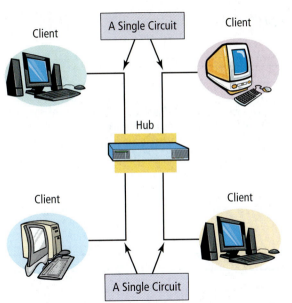

Figure 4.15
Ethernet LAN Utilizing a Hub
Here the LAN is a physical star but a logical bus. Keep in mind that although four cables connect the clients to the hub, the clients share only one circuit.

a means of extending the diameter, or distance, of the LAN. Figure 4.15 illustrates a traditional Ethernet LAN that uses hubs.

By evaluating the destination address, receiving hosts are able to determine if the packet is for them or not. The bus topology uses CSMA/CD as its MAC mechanism. In bus networks that have many hosts on the same circuit or where traffic is heavy, contention and collision of packets is a real problem. Ultimately, network performance degrades to the point where no communication, or work, is being performed. For the end user, this is a frustrating situation. As the network administrator, your phone will begin to ring—often, noisily, and from many annoyed users.

Common standard Ethernet LANs transmit at 10 Mbps using two pairs of either Category 3, 4, or 5 UTP. This type of Ethernet LAN is referred to as **10BaseT**. The "10" stands for 10 Mbps, the "Base" represents baseband, and the "T" is for twisted-wire pair. 10BaseT LANs use Manchester encoding, which was introduced in Chapter 2. The maximum end-to-end LAN diameter of 10BaseT Ethernet is 2,500 meters. The 2,500-meter limitation is based on physics. CSMA/CD requires that a transmitting device be able to sense a collision before an entire frame is sent out onto the transmission medium, in this example, the UTP cable. For standard hub-wired 10BaseT, before the last bit of the frame is sent, the sender must be able to determine if a collision has occurred. If all bits of the entire frame are sent and the sending device has not detected a collision, it assumes that all is well. If the LAN's total diameter were too long, which for 10BaseT is more than 2,500 meters, the sender would not have enough time to be able to determine that a collision has occurred. Here's why.

The smallest Ethernet frame possible is 64 bytes, or 512 bits. Let's assume a frame of 64 bytes needs to be transmitted. At 10 Mbps, sending 512 bits takes 51.2 microseconds. According to CSMA/CD, before the last bit of the 512 bits is sent from the sending host, the first bit must have reached the farthest end of the LAN's diameter. Because this example uses a standard bus having a broadcast mechanism, all devices on the shared, single circuit must get the frame, even those at the far end of the network.

In this way, if a collision occurs at the far end of the network, before the sender has sent that last bit, there will be time for the sender to get back

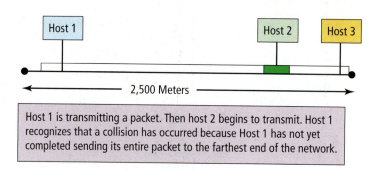

Host 1 is transmitting a packet. Then host 2 begins to transmit. Host 1 recognizes that a collision has occurred because Host 1 has not yet completed sending its entire packet to the farthest end of the network.

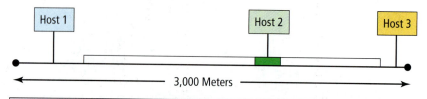

Host 1 has transmitted its entire packet and clears that packet from its buffer. Then host 2 begins to transmit. Host 1, because its packet has been entirely sent, is unaware that a collision has occurred between its packet and the packet that host 2 is tranmitting. The segment length is too long for host 1 to have been made aware of the collision.

Figure 4.16
Transmission of a Packet

a signal that indicates that a collision has occurred. Without that collision signal, the sender assumes that all is well once that last bit is sent. Once all bits of a frame are sent, the sender clears that frame from its buffer, making retransmission of the frame, in the event of a collision, impossible.

If the segment length is too long, the sender could send the last bit of its frame and not be aware that a collision had occurred at the other end of the network because the collision signal had not returned in time. For this reason, a standard 10BaseT Ethernet LAN can have an end-to-end diameter of no more than 2,500 meters. Figure 4.16 illustrates this concept.

In addition, 10BaseT LANs are also limited to NICs that transmit at no higher than 10 Mbps. NICs of this type cannot sense or process data at higher speeds. NICs that can sense and respond to different transmission speeds are said to be **autosensing**. Autosensing NICs are used with Fast or Gigabit Ethernet networks that may need to be backward compatible with legacy Ethernet networks. **Legacy** technologies are older technologies that are still in use and must still be supported. With the advent of newer applications, such as computer aided drafting and manufacturing (CAD/CAM), a 10-Mbps NIC limitation is a significant drawback for distributing data over a network. Also, 10BaseT LANs do not perform well in networks that experience moderate-to-heavy traffic. Speed and access are two primary reasons why standard Ethernet has been modified in ways that improve its performance. One very popular technique is to replace Ethernet hubs with Ethernet switches.

Switched Ethernet   Hubs can extend the diameter, or distance, of a LAN. They do not, however, create independent, dedicated circuits for the devices that are attached to them. This means that if eight devices are connected to a hub, they still only share one circuit, not eight. In a bus topology, contention for the circuit is not improved by using a hub.

Switches, however, are different. Switches, like hubs, have ports that host devices plug into. **Switched Ethernet** LANs use switches in place of hubs. Depending on the switch, switch ports can be configured for different speeds. Each device that connects to a switch has a dedicated circuit to that switch. Because the circuit between the host and switch is dedicated, there is no competition, or contention, for use of that circuit. When a device needs to transmit or receive, its circuit to the switch is always available. Like hubs, switches can also extend the diameter of the LAN, with the added benefit of not broadcasting the data frames that pass through them because switches are capable of recognizing addresses.

Another major difference between hubs and switches is that whereas hubs cannot overcome the maximum distance limitation that a 10BaseT LAN can span (2,500 meters), switches can. Because switches eliminate collisions, collision detection between the two farthest hosts in the network is not a factor. A host can send its entire frame without having to wait for the first bit of the frame to get to the farthest host on the network. The sending host only needs to use its dedicated circuit to the switch, send its entire frame to the switch, and have the switch handle it from there. Thus, switched Ethernet does not have a maximum-distance limitation. A switched Ethernet LAN might be 2,500 or 25,000 meters. Naturally, good network planning and design should determine how big the eventual LAN should be. Simply because you can create a 25,000 meter LAN does not mean you should!

Be aware, however, that although switched Ethernet does not have a maximum-distance limitation for the entire network, there is a distance limitation between each pair of switches. When using UTP, the distance limitation between switches is 100 meters. However, there is no limit to the number of switches deployed between the farthest two hosts. When using fiber, the limitation is much higher, from 1 to 5 kilometers between switches. Fiber, though, is a technology usually implemented for BNs, MANs, or WANs, not the typical LAN.

Whether UTP or fiber, switches are configured in a hierarchy, with no loops among the switches. If loops were allowed, a frame could circle a network endlessly. Because a hierarchy is used, frames can take only one possible path among the hosts. Ethernet switches use address-forwarding tables that are relatively simple. Depending on the switch and how it is used, the forwarding table can be manually or automatically maintained. The larger the network, the more efficient automatic table addressing becomes. Switches have the capability of learning which port is associated or assigned to each connected device's MAC address. Each MAC address of a device connected to a switch has only one switch port number assigned to it. When a frame needs to be transmitted, the switch reads the MAC destination address of the frame to be sent. Then the switch, using its forward addressing table, looks up the MAC port address for the frame. Finally, the switch forwards the frame to that assigned port, and only that assigned port. Figure 4.17 demonstrates a possible switched Ethernet LAN.

Automatic table addressing makes for efficient, and fast, switch-path decisions. In addition, as already mentioned, switches of different capacities can be configured in a hierarchy. The result is that a central or backbone root switch may support gigabit capacity. Switches connected to servers, directly below the root switch, could be 100 Mbps, and those farther below, connected to clients, only 10 Mbps. Not everyone, or every connection, needs a gigabit or even a 100-Mbps switch. Businesses can leverage their switching cost based on the transmission capacity needed at different levels of the hierarchy. Figure 4.18 illustrates a switching hierarchy.

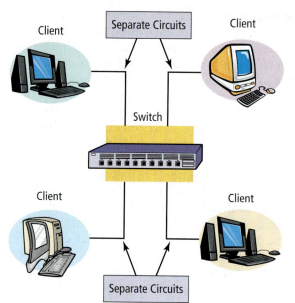

Figure 4.17

Ethernet LAN Utilizing a Switch

A key difference between a switch and a hub is that each client's connection to the switch is its own dedicated circuit. In this example, four circuits, not one, connect to the switch.

Switches vary significantly in capability and price. Some switches are strictly layer 2 devices. Others, costing more, can also operate at layer 3 of the OSI and TCP/IP networking models. The performance of a busy, standard 10BaseT Ethernet LAN that is structured using hubs and bridges can be dramatically improved through the use of switching technology. Traditionally, hubs, bridges, and routers were used to segment a network. Today, growth in switching technology has exploded. A factor that has made such technology particularly attractive is that

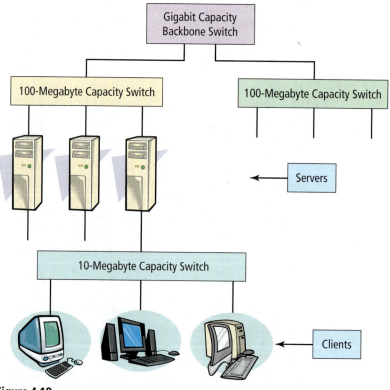

Figure 4.18
Ethernet Switching Hierarchy

when moving to a switched environment, the existing network cabling, NICs, server operating system, topology, protocols, and other infrastructure elements may require no change at all. The hub, bridge, or router is simply swapped out for a switch. Switches, of course, cost more than hubs, but for most organizations the performance gain has outweighed the added expense. Also, switches will require more configuration and monitoring then simple hubs or bridges. Costing far less than routers, switches have caused routers to be pushed to the edge of the network.

Switched Ethernet has also resulted in a discussion as to whether this form of Ethernet is still Ethernet. Because the connections between switches and connecting devices are point-to-point, collisions are no longer a concern. And yet, collisions and their detection are defining characteristics of the bus Ethernet protocol. The question becomes, if switched Ethernet eliminates collisions and the need for their detection, is this still Ethernet, or something else? For many of us, this controversy is not as relevant as the result of having networks configured with improved performance but without significant cost increase.

Fast Ethernet Using switches is one way to improve Ethernet performance. Another way of increasing data rate, without changing the minimum size of the Ethernet frame, is to decrease the roundtrip time it takes for a collision signal to get back to a sender. To decrease roundtrip time, the length of the Ethernet LAN diameter is shortened from 2,500 to 250 meters. This decrease in LAN diameter does not require a change in frame format, or access method, so the Ethernet standard remains intact. **Fast Ethernet** is based on LAN diameters of 250 meters when hubs are used. When used with switches, as with standard Ethernet, the LAN diameter is only limited by the network design. The IEEE has designated two categories of Fast Ethernet: 100BaseX and 100BaseT4. Of the two, 100BaseX has been the clear market winner

There are two types of **100BaseX**: **100BaseTX** and **100BaseFX**. As with the 10BaseT label, important Fast Ethernet characteristics can be determined from the standard's name. For 100BaseTX, "100" represents 100-Mbps capacity; "Base" is, again, baseband; and "TX" designates, at a minimum, two pair of either Cat 5 UTP or STP cables that connect a host to a hub. One wire pair carries frames from the host to the hub. The second wire pair carries frames from the hub to the host. The maximum segment length of a 100BaseTX cable, as with 10BaseT, remains 100 meters. An important difference between the two is that 10BaseT can use less expensive Cat 3 or 4 level cable. 100BaseTX, though, must use, as a minimum, the more expensive Cat 5 cable. For Gigabit Ethernet using UTP, enhanced Cat 5 cable or better should be used, which is an additional expense. For optimal Gigabit Ethernet, fiber-optic cabling is recommended, an even higher additional expense.

100BaseFX is fiber-optic-based Fast Ethernet; it is more likely found in BNs. Significantly, the maximum segment length of fiber Fast Ethernet is 412 meters to 2 kilometers, depending on the type of fiber medium used. Gigabit Ethernet is examined more closely in Chapter 6 during the discussion of BNs. Fast Ethernet also includes 100BaseT4, another IEEE standard. Designed to avoid the need for rewiring to achieve a higher data rate capacity, 100BaseT4 has proven unsuccessful in the networking market. 100BaseT4 requires four pairs of Cat 3 UTP. Most modern buildings already have this wiring available. Even so, 100BaseT4 has been mostly ignored.

NICs for Fast Ethernet are sometimes called 10/100-Mbps adapters. These types of NICs, unlike those for a standard 10BaseT Ethernet LAN, often have the ability to perform autosensing. Autosensing enables Fast Ethernet NICs to automatically sense, and adjust, to speed capabilities of 10 or 100 Mbps. In an enterprise that has a mix of 10- and 100-Mbps devices, the faster device must communicate at the slower device's capacity. If a 100-Mbps host device with an autosensing NIC senses that it is communicating with a 10-Mbps hub, the faster host device will slow down to accommodate the hub's slower speed. Slower NICs cannot speed their capacity to match the faster device. A good Web site for additional information on Fast Ethernet is **www.ethermanage.com/ethernet/ ethernet.html**. This Web site also has a graphic showing the first hand drawing of standard Ethernet by Dr. Robert M. Metcalfe in 1976.

Network/Server Operating Systems

Today, most LANs are of the client/server model and use some form of server software. Server software makes up the bulk of a network operating system (NOS). The NOS controls and manages the servers. Because of this server focus, some networking professionals refer to a NOS as a server operating systems (SOS). The TCP/IP protocol suite has become the platform of choice for many common SOSs.

Older, legacy network operating systems had an additional client component that had to be installed on each client in order for that client to connect to the network. Today, most modern client operating systems automatically provide networking capability, especially for TCP/IP, thus the client element may no longer be required. The server operating system controls the means by which client hosts connect to the LAN in order to access server resources. Depending on the NOS, many types of server resources can be managed. One essential aspect of a NOS is its ability to authenticate and validate users who are attempting to login to the network. Login usually requires the user to have both a user ID and a password. How complex the user ID and password are, how frequently user passwords must be changed, and how user IDs and passwords are created, maintained, and distributed are based on network administration policies. The more important security is, the tighter and more defined network administration policies are, or at least should be. The following discussion identifies some of the more common server operating systems that you will likely encounter in a real-world setting. A detailed look at multiple server operating systems would require a separate text, and likely a separate course. However, the "Topic in Focus: A Closer Look at Microsoft Server 2003" at the end of this chapter provides a more complete overview of one of the market-leading server operating systems.

Microsoft

Microsoft (**www.microsoft.com**) has been the giant of the server software market since the mid-1990s. At the time of this writing, Microsoft's server operating systems accounted for 49 percent of the total market share (**news.com.com/2100-1001-959049.html**). Microsoft's primary server operating system has transitioned from a product called Windows NT (for New Technology) Server to its latest product, Windows 2003 Server. Windows NT Server installations, as well as Server 2000, are still common. Microsoft's server products make use of graphical user interfaces that are similar in look and feel to Microsoft's most popular desktop operating systems, such as Windows 95, 98, NT Workstation, 2000 Professional, and the latest, XP. Although it dominates the small to midrange departmental server market, Microsoft has positioned Windows 2003 Server as appropriate for large-scale enterprises.

As with the other types of software that Microsoft markets, its server products come in several versions. Windows 2003 Server has Standard, Enterprise, Data Center, and Web editions. The varying editions come with different capabilities and are targeted at different types of organizations. Each edition has its own pricing scale. See the "Topic in Focus" for a comparison of these editions.

Linux

A server operating system that has received a lot of notice recently is Linux. Linux has several factors that make it appealing. Foremost, Linux is free; however, this does not necessarily mean that businesses don't usually end up paying something to use it. Free versions of Linux typically do not come with documentation or technical support. For those reasons, most businesses are willing to pay $50 to $100 for packaged versions of Linux. Another Linux advantage is that it runs on common Intel, or Intel-compatible, microprocessors. Based on Unix, Linux shares that operating system's reputation for reliability and stability. The disadvantages are that it is difficult to learn and use, and because it is relatively new, finding qualified technical staff proficient in the product can be challenging. Extensive retraining may be required. As of this writing, Linux accounts for 25 percent of the server operating system market, fairly impressive for a new guy on the block.

As just mentioned, although Linux server software can be found for free, many business choose to purchase the software. To address this market, several vendors have Linux-based server solutions. Vendors offering such solutions include Caldera (**www.caldera.com**), Red Hat (**www.redhat.com**, Figure 4.19), and SuSe (**www.suse.com**). An interesting research paper might be to compare and contrast the advantages, disadvantages, capabilities, and price of various Linux server solutions.

Figure 4.19
Red Hat is a popular Linux SOS choice.

Unix

Unix has been around for a very long time. It was first introduced by AT&T's Bell Labs in 1969, so it is a well-established and proven technology. Unix's major advantages are its stability and high functionality; it performs well in complex server environments. However, Unix is also intricate and difficult to learn. Unix comes in several versions, one popular one being Sun Microsystems's Solaris (**www.sun.com**). Used to power the Internet, Unix is also the server operating system of choice for large-scale servers. It makes up 12 percent of the server market.

Novell

Novell's NetWare server operating system (**www.novell.com**) once dominated the server market, but has since been eclipsed by Microsoft and Linux. Novell's NetWare is primarily known for its excellent file and print services as well as for its directory service management capabilities. In fact, Novell's directory service capability is one reason why many businesses still choose to run NetWare servers. It is probably the best product of this type on the market. Today, NetWare accounts for 12 percent of the server market. The remaining 2 percent of the server market is taken by Apple's MAC line of server software, primarily MAC OS X (**www.mac.com**).

Application Servers

Something to keep in mind is that server operating systems are not applications in the sense of user tools such as word processors and spreadsheets. Rather, a server operating system is used to interface with user applications and make those applications available to the user. It is fairly common for application software to be installed and managed on application servers. Cost savings usually result when a business is able to put a networkable version of an application on a server and then have the server manage and distribute the application across the network. In this way, the business does not need to buy individual user licenses for each client, but instead achieves economies of scale by purchasing either a metered or site license for application products.

Licensing

A **metered license** is one whereby the server is programmed to count how many users are currently using a given product. When a certain number has been reached, a number determined by the metered-license agreement, the server prevents new users from accessing the product. Once the metered value has been reached, a current user has to log out of the application for a new user to access it. An analysis should be performed to determine what the most effective metered value should be. If it is too small, users will become frustrated because they will not be able to access the application. If the value is too large, the business will be paying for licenses that it is not using. A balance has to be determined.

In contrast, a **site license** covers the entire site so that anyone validated by the network can access the application as needed. Typically, a site license costs more than a metered license, but it is still less than purchasing an individual license for everybody. The size of the site will of course depend on the business; for example, a business may have as few

The Ethical Perspective

A License to Steal?

Software piracy is an illegal, multi-billion-dollar worldwide business. Many organizations that develop, market, and sell software are concerned about the extent to which software piracy goes unreported, unpunished, and uncontrolled. In an attempt to coordinate the fight against software piracy, the Software and Information Industry Association (SIIA; **www.spa.org**) has become an advocate for antipiracy legislation. According to SIIA, U.S. and Canadian businesses alone lost more than $12 billion to software piracy in 1999. On their Web site, SIIA provides a toll-free telephone number and online link for reporting corporate and Internet software piracy violations.

As a data communications administrator, one of your jobs might be to manage, monitor, and control the software licensing for your organization. Such management is critical, because a business can be found legally responsible, and heavily fined, should unlicensed software be found running on the corporation's enterprise network. Organizational policy may dictate that no user is allowed to install software, of any type, on business equipment, but rather that all software must be installed, and properly documented as licensed, by network administration staff.

Some users find such restrictions frustrating and, in their opinion, unnecessary. If you were the administrator in charge of corporate software licensing, what policies would you advocate? What steps would you take to ensure that policies were being followed? What would be your ethical argument to your user community as to why they should follow software installation procedures? What steps would you take to deliver this argument in a way that would not cause your users to resent you, but rather to understand and help you? What is your opinion about Web sites such as that offered by SIIA that allow for anonymous reporting of corporate software piracy?

as 50 or as many as 10,000 users. Metered and site licensing are similar in that they are both used to determine how many copies of a software program an organization is legally authorized to use.

LAN Design Considerations

Having identified the physical and hardware components of a LAN, the question becomes one of how to put these elements together when designing the network. No two businesses are exactly alike, so network needs will vary. Several factors can guide the design of a LAN. The factors listed in this section are not the only ones, of course, but they are likely ones that most network designers would address when designing a LAN. Figure 4.20 illustrates that LAN design is a cyclical process, meaning that once a LAN is implemented it must continually be evaluated and improved.

Perhaps one of the most important items to consider is the budget. Businesses want the best technology, the fastest throughput, and the highest level of security, but many may not be able to afford them. Realistic budget data are needed in order to determine the type of network that can

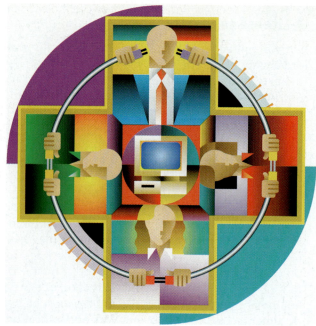

Figure 4.20

A successful network design often allows a user to connect to his or her network from wherever he or she may be, locally or remotely.

be configured. The budget will affect the number and type of servers that are installed, the quality of the NICs used on all host devices, the number of clients and servers, the server operating system, software licensing, the type of cabling, staffing for installation and maintenance, and whether hubs or switches are used.

The list could go on, but you probably get the point. You cannot know what you can build until you know how much you can afford. A budget gives you a baseline from which the best alternative solutions can be pursued. Part of this decision process may involve the solicitation of **request for purchase (RFP)** proposals from various networking vendors. It is good to have competing bids, but you need to be very clear as to what it is you are requesting bids for. Good systems analysis skills are essential.

The design of the LAN will have to address the types of applications that the LAN is expected to support. Applications such as CAD/CAM or digital/video editing are resource and bandwidth intensive and require an infrastructure that can support such needs. However, if the business primarily makes use of low-end, text-driven types of data applications, then bandwidth and throughput requirements will be far less demanding. For the applications used, how, where, and when are they to be distributed? Do users expect 24/7 remote and local access or is the business run along the lines of a more traditional 9-to-5, five-days-a-week operation?

In addition, you should ask yourself the following questions: What type of facility is the network to be installed in? Is there appropriate air conditioning and/or air filtration for sensitive equipment, if such equipment is required? Are server rooms and wiring closets expected? If so, are they available? If required but not currently available, is there space for their construction? Does the facility accommodate the types of cabling your network may demand? Will walls, floors, or ceilings be affected by wiring needs? If your approach is wireless, are there wall or other obstructions that have to addressed that may prevent line-of-sight access? Is the facility on a factory floor where powerful electrical and/or magnetic equipment may be used? If so, the installation of your network must take that into consideration.

The LAN design should also address the scale of the network. Is the network for a small business of 10 employees or will it need to support 1,000? Scale will also impact your level of staffing. Very small networks may have only one person who performs all tasks: installation, configuration, maintenance, troubleshooting, user and technical support, and so on. Larger networks will likely require dedicated staff with specific and identified responsibilities. Is there sufficient staff to support the network proposed? If not, is such staff available for hire? If so, at what cost? Also, for future reference, how do you plan to keep your technical and user staff trained as your network evolves with changing technologies?

As more businesses of all sizes have begun to depend on networking technologies, and as access to these technologies has become more prevalent, the importance of network security has also increased significantly. How does your LAN design account for securing the network? What procedures determine who has access to the network? Are critical pieces of equipment, such as servers, switches, and routers, protected and secured from unauthorized access? What policies are in place that protect against intrusion into the network by unauthorized individuals? Does your LAN design need to make use of such technologies as firewalls, encryption, or multiple layers of login authentication? What areas of the network are most vulnerable? What applications and data are critical to the business, such that if they were lost, stolen, or corrupted, lasting damage would result? In that event, does your LAN design include backup and recovery procedures? Have those procedures been tested? As you can see, many questions will need to be answered.

All of the steps in the design and implementation of the LAN should be well documented. Once the LAN is in place, continuing the documentation process will be crucial. Assume you work for a large organization. The organization has 20 database servers in different locations of the enterprise. You have been put in charge of upgrading all database servers with a software patch critical to their functioning. Without that patch, the servers might fail or be vulnerable to outside attack. How are you going to discover where these database servers are? If your documentation is well maintained, it should tell you exactly the type, location, and address of all of servers in the enterprise.

Documentation needs to be current, accurate, and reliable. Your documentation should be able to tell you such things as what types of NICs you are using and where; the names, locations, and addresses of all your hubs, switches, routers, and servers; the status of your licensing for the server operating system and client applications; where and what types of printers you have; how users are granted or denied login user IDs and passwords; when and how backups are performed; who is responsible for administration of each part of the network; and so on. Good LAN design is an art, and with the rise of pervasive computing, increasingly important.

LAN components are either physical or logical. Physical components include NICs, client devices, servers, printers, cables, hubs, switches, and routers, just to name a few. Logical components may include device drivers, network operating systems, and desktop operating systems, as well as software that can be used to monitor, troubleshoot, and evaluate the performance of a LAN. Device drivers are associated with peripheral devices, network operating systems with servers, and desktop operating systems with clients. Logical components, like physical components, also need to be installed, configured, and maintained. Whether physical or logical, successfully working with both types of components is critically dependent on the quality of their documentation.

An additional element in a LAN that has both physical and logical characteristics is the LAN's topology. Topologies determine not only how devices are connected to each other, but also how devices get access to the media they use for communication. Three types of topologies are the star, ring, and bus. Of the three, the bus is the most commonly used. The IEEE has formalized the bus topology as Ethernet 802.3. A classic bus topology uses a broadcast mechanism when packets are placed on the bus. The bus topology is a contention-based topology. Devices contend for access to the communication circuit using CSMA/CD. An 802.3 LAN is relatively easy to install and configure and uses inexpensive cabling. Use of switching technology has especially transformed how Ethernet is configured. In fact, because of how switches function, some consider the newer forms of switched Ethernet to no longer be a true bus topology, but an alternative form that requires its own designation.

A LAN may use many types of physical components, or hardware. An essential hardware component that each device on a LAN must have in order to communicate is a NIC, which provides a physical layer MAC address. These cards are also called adapters. Factors to consider when choosing a NIC include its bus width and memory capabilities. An Ethernet NIC address consists of 48 bits composed of 12 hexadecimal digits. Hexadecimal, or hex, is the Base-16 numbering system. Ethernet MAC addresses are usually expressed in hex octets. An octet is equivalent to eight bits. The first six digits specify the NIC's manufacturer, the last six digits the interface serial number.

Another essential physical component of a LAN is the physical medium over which data are transmitted over the network. The most common form of LAN medium installed today is unshielded twisted-wire pair, or UTP. A UTP's cable category classification determines the maximum number of bits that it can transmit. A higher cable category number represents a larger cable size. A larger cable size results in less resistance to the signal being carried on the cable. Reduced resistance translates into higher transmission speeds. Category 5 UTP is the most popular.

Server and client devices also make up part of the physical LAN. Servers are computers that fulfill specific, specialized functions. Servers allow LAN resources to be made available for multiple users to share and utilize. LAN resources can include, among other things, printers, applications, data, information, files, databases, security services, directory services, modems, Web hosting, e-mail, or almost anything that a group of users would need to have access to. When configuring a server, several factors should be considered, including the server's processor, hard drive speed, primary memory, and cache. A server also has a network, or server, operating system. Users connect to the LAN and to server resources through client devices. In a TCP/IP LAN, client devices are referred to as hosts. Popular server operating systems include those from Microsoft, Linux, Unix, and Novell.

As a LAN grows, it may be necessary to segment it in order to maximize performance. Two popular LAN segmentation devices are switches and routers. Switches are often associated with the data link layer, or layer 2. Routers are associated with the network layer, or layer 3. Today, the use of switches has pushed routers to the edge of the network.

Most LANs use a form of Ethernet. Standard Ethernet uses the classic bus topology with hubs. Standard Ethernet is referred to as 10BaseT. Switched Ethernet eliminates the contention/collision characters of the hub-based Ethernet LAN. Fast Ethernet has two categories: 100BaseX and 100BaseFX. There are also two types of 100BaseX: 100BaseTX and 100BaseT4. Of the two, 100BaseTX is the most popular and requires the use of Category 5 cable at a minimum. 100BaseFX is more commonly found in BNs.

Finally, a number of issues must be considered when designing a LAN. Design considerations include the budget, the types of applications the LAN should support, the scale of the LAN, the facility the LAN is to be housed in, security needs, and staffing requirements. All elements of the LAN should be well document. Documentation should also be a continuing process as the LAN evolves.

10BaseT **(147)**

100BaseFX **(151)**

100BaseTX **(151)**

100BaseX **(151)**

Adapter card **(135)**

Application server **(139)**

Autosensing **(148)**

Broadcast **(133)**

Bus mastering **(136)**

Bus topology **(132)**

Bus width **(136)**

Cache **(136)**

Client **(143)**

Client/server model **(144)**

Contention-based topology **(134)**

Device driver **(137)**

Direct memory access (DMA) **(136)**

Disk duplexing **(140)**

Disk mirroring **(140)**

Documentation **(130)**

Fair access **(133)**

Fast Ethernet **(151)**

Fault tolerance **(140)**

Hardware **(130)**

Hexadecimal **(137)**

Host **(135)**

Legacy **(148)**

Level 1 cache **(141)**

Level 2 cache **(141)**

Login **(133)**

MAC address **(137)**

Media **(137)**

Media Access Unit (MAU) **(133)**

Medium **(137)**

Metered license **(154)**

Network Interface Card (NIC) **(135)**

Network operating system (NOS) **(140)**

Octet **(137)**

Peer-to-peer model **(144)**

Physical address **(135)**

Primary memory **(140)**

Random Access Memory (RAM) **(140)**

Regenerated **(138)**

Request for purchase (RFP) **(156)**

Ring topology **(133)**

Router **(145)**

Server **(138)**

Server farm **(142)**

Server operating system (SOS) **(140)**

Site license **(154)**

Software **(131)**

Standard Ethernet **(146)**

Star topology **(132)**

Switches **(144)**

Switched Ethernet **(149)**

Terminal **(132)**

Throughput **(137)**

Topology **(130)**

Troubleshoot **(130)**

Wiring closet **(138)**

Workstation **(143)**

Chapter Questions

Short Answer

1. What is the purpose of a NIC? What are three factors that might influence your selection of a NIC?

2. Briefly describe how a server differs from a client.

3. What differences, if any, are there between how switches function versus hubs?

4. How do metered and site licensing differ? Are they in any way the same?

Multiple Choice

For each of the following select one best answer.

1. LAN components are of what type?
   a. Physical   **b.** Logical   **c.** a and b   **d.** Neither a nor b

2. Which of the following is not a physical LAN component?
   a. NIC   **b.** Printer   **c.** NIC Driver   **d.** Switch

3. What does the term troubleshoot mean?
   a. To cause a problem   **b.** To evaluate the cause of a problem
   c. To correct a problem   **d.** b and c

4. What can troubleshooting tools be based on?
   a. Software   **b.** Documentation   **c.** a or b   **d.** Neither a nor b

5. A topology has what type of characteristics?
   a. Physical only   **b.** Logical only
   c. Physical or logical, but not both   **d.** Physical and logical

6. Which type of topology centralizes network management?
   a. Star   **b.** Ring   **c.** Bus   **d.** None of the above

7. Which type of topology broadcasts packets?
   a. Star   **b.** Ring   **c.** Bus   **d.** None of the above

8. Which topology makes use of tokens?
   a. Star   **b.** Ring   **c.** Bus   **d.** None of the above

9. Which of the following is also known as the 802.3 protocol?
   a. Star   **b.** Ring   **c.** Bus   **d.** None of the above

10. Which of the following is also known as the 802.5 protocol?
   a. Star   **b.** Ring   **c.** Bus   **d.** None of the above

11. Which protocol uses a contention-based topology?
   a. 802.2   **b.** 802.3   **c.** 802.4   **d.** 802.5

12. How many bits are in the address of an Ethernet NIC?
   a. 16   **b.** 32   **c.** 48   **d.** 64

13. Ethernet NIC addresses are expressed in what type of numbering system?

  a. Binary   **b.** Decimal   **c.** Hexadecimal   **d.** Nexadecimal

14. The decimal value 13 is what value in Base-16?

  a. A   **b.** B   **c.** C   **d.** D

15. What is the highest letter value that a Base-16 number can be expressed with?

  a. E   **b.** F   **c.** H   **d.** Z

16. Which of the following is the capability of a NIC to use the host device's memory?

  a. DMA   **b.** AMD   **c.** MEM   **d.** ADM

17. Which term describes a NIC that incorporates its own CPU?

  a. Mastering   **b.** NIC mastering
  c. Bus mastering   **d.** CPU mastering

18. Which digits of an Ethernet NIC address specify the manufacturer?

  a. The first six   **b.** The last six   **c.** All of them   **d.** The last four

19. What does the UTP cable category determine about a NIC's ability to transmit a number of bits?

  a. The minimum number of bits that can be sent
  b. The average number of bits that can be sent
  c. The maximum number of bits that can be sent
  d. The frequency at which bits can be sent

20. A larger UTP cable size in relation to the signal sent results in

  a. more resistance.   **b.** less resistance.
  c. no effect.   **d.** average resistance.

21. Which of the following is the fastest form of memory?

  a. RAM   **b.** ROM   **c.** Level 1 cache   **d.** Level 2 cache

22. Which term describes the housing of hundreds of servers in a single facility?

  a. Server maximum   **b.** Server range
  c. Server city   **d.** Server farm

23. Which term is used to refer to any device connected to a TCP/IP network?

  a. Client   **b.** Server   **c.** Switch   **d.** Host

24. Which of the following is a network model where a device may be a client, a server, or both?

  a. Client/server   **b.** Peer-to-peer   **c.** a or b   **d.** Neither a nor b

25. Standard switches perform at what layer of a network model?

  a. Layer 1   **b.** Layer 2   **c.** Layer 3   **d.** Layer 4

26. Standard routers perform at what level of a network model?

  a. Layer 1   **b.** Layer 2   **c.** Layer 3   **d.** Layer 4

27. Which device will broadcast all the packets it receives at all times?

  a. Server   **b.** Router   **c.** Switch   **d.** Hub

28. Fast Ethernet can use what category of UTP cable?

  a. 3, 4, or 5   **b.** 4 or 5   **c.** 5   **d.** Any category

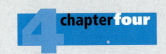

29. What is the diameter limitation for a standard Ethernet LAN using hubs?

    a. 100 feet **b.** 100 meters **c.** 250 meters **d.** 2,500 meters

30. What is the diameter limitation for a Fast Ethernet LAN using hubs?

    a. 100 feet **b.** 100 meters **c.** 250 meters **d.** 2,500 meters

31. What is the distance limitation between switches?

    a. 100 feet **b.** 100 meters **c.** 250 meters **d.** 2,500 meters

32. What is the size of the smallest possible Ethernet frame?

    a. 64 bits **b.** 64 bytes **c.** 620 bits **d.** 640 bytes

33. Which of the following refers to software that is used to manage a server?

    a. Server control system **b.** Server manager system
    c. Server operating system **d.** Server software system

34. Which of the following is a type of license that is usually based on the number of users currently using the application?

    a. Numbered **b.** Metered **c.** Site **d.** Limited

35. Which of the following is a type of license that can cover an entire organization regardless of how many users are accessing that application?

    a. Maximum **b.** Metered **c.** Site **d.** Unlimited

36. Which of the following should be considered when designing a LAN?

    a. The budget **b.** The facility **c.** Scale **d.** All the above

37. Which of the following is not a software component?

    a. NIC adapter **b.** NIC driver **c.** SOS **d.** NOS

38. Which of the following generally costs the most?

    a. Hub **b.** Router **c.** Switch **d.** Repeater

39. Which of the following is used to create a dedicated circuit between a host and a connecting port?

    a. Hub **b.** Switch **c.** Client **d.** Router

40. When using a switch, a connected device will have how many assigned port addresses?

    a. 1 **b.** 2 **c.** It depends on the switch **d.** Many

41. Which term describes a NICs ability to process bits?

    a. Output **b.** Efficiency **c.** Throughput **d.** Capacity

42. Which device does not broadcast packets?

    a. Hub **b.** Switch **c.** Router **d.** b and c

43. Using a traditional bus with hubs, how many devices can use a circuit simultaneously?

    a. Many **b.** 1 **c.** 2 **d.** It depends on the hub

44. What is another term for server primary memory?

    a. Cache **b.** Level 1 cache **c.** Level 2 cache **d.** RAM

45. Which topology forms a closed loop?

    a. Star **b.** Bus **c.** Ring **d.** b or c

46. The Base-16 numbering system is also called

    a. binary.   **b.** decimal.   **c.** hexadecimal.   **d.** nexadecimal.

47. Which standards body assigns blocks of NIC addresses?

    a. IOS   **b.** IEC   **c.** ANSI   **d.** IEEE

48. How many categories of Fast Ethernet have been designated?

    a. 1   **b.** 2   **c.** 3   **d.** 4

49. Which of the following has the fastest access speed?

    a. Hard drive   **b.** RAM   **c.** Level 1 cache   **d.** Level 2 cache

50. A NIC might use which of the following?

    a. DMA   **b.** Bus mastering   **c.** a or b, but not both   **d.** a and/or b

True or False

For each of the following select either True or False.

1. Unlike physical components, logical components do not need to be installed or configured.

2. The logical components of a LAN are only defined by software.

3. A bus topology is sometimes referred to as the fair access topology.

4. In general, a ring topology is more expensive than a bus topology.

5. A NIC is responsible for framing data that passes through it.

6. High-end servers should have a narrower NIC bus.

7. The first six digits of an Ethernet physical address are used for the serial number.

8. A large cable size results in less resistance to the signal being carried.

9. Mirrored hard drives provide better fault tolerance, but at a higher cost.

10. TCP/IP incorporates protocols only at the network layer.

11. Routers have displaced switches in many places in modern networks.

12. A router can connect networks that use different architectures.

13. Fast Ethernet can use switches.

14. Fast Ethernet LANs that use switches can be more than 250 meters in diameter.

15. A switch's addressing table can only be modified manually.

16. 100BaseTX can use either Cat 3, 4, or 5 UTP.

17. 10BaseT NICs are capable of autosensing.

18. Switches are often used in a hierarchy from fastest to slowest from top to bottom.

19. A problem with changing from Ethernet hubs to switches is that the topology must also change.

20. Modern client desktop operating systems often include networking capabilities.

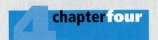

Exercises

Research in Brief

For one or more of the questions below, provide a one- to two-page report based on your findings.

1. Research and contrast Linux-based software for servers and Windows 2003 Server. How are they similar? How are they different? What are their relative advantages and disadvantages?

2. Explain whether the choice of NICs can affect the performance of a network for both clients and servers. When choosing NICs for clients and servers, what characteristics should you consider and why? Use a Fast Ethernet network with a Gigabit Ethernet backbone as your basis for NIC selection.

3. Visit the Web site for the IEEE (**www.ieee.org**). Search the site and report back on three current topics related to LANs.

4. Investigate how server farms are being used today. What types of computers are used in server farms? What is their cost? How are they connected? In what industries are server farms more prevalent?

Case Study

Sheehan Marketing and Public Relations

You have visited all three of SMPR's locations: Los Angeles, Chicago, and New York. Based on your analysis, you see a real need for SMPR to move from a peer-to-peer network infrastructure to a client/server network infrastructure. President Sheehan has asked you to prepare a report identifying the advantages and disadvantages of using either a Linux- or a Microsoft-based solution for both client and server machines. He wants your report to include such information as cost, service, ease of use, staff training, and any other areas you think might be relevant.

Part of your analysis should be recommendations on what might need to be done with the current hardware being used by SMPR. All of the offices have computers that are at least 5 years old running on Windows 95. The only new computers are five Pentium 4 machines in the LA office that are running Windows 2000 Workstation. President Sheehan wants to know what issues might be involved in upgrading SMPR's technology.

In addition, President Sheehan would like to know, in general, how servers differ from ordinary computers and what benefits SMPR might get from using a server technology. Would security be improved? Would staff be better able to share resources? Would the use of servers make managing the three regional office networks easier? And if so, how? Your report is due in a week and is expected to include a narrative description, a cost analysis of the two proposed solutions (Linux or Windows), and a final recommendation.

www.networking.ibm.com/tra/whitepapers/TR00.pdf

grouper.ieee.org/groups/802/5/www8025org

www.webopedia.com

www.ethermanage.com/ethernet/ethernet.html

www.microsoft.com

www.caldera.com

www.redhat.com

www.suse.com

www.sun.com

www.novell.com

www.mac.com

www.spa.org

www.ieee.org

A Closer Look at Microsoft Server 2003

In this chapter, you learned that network operating systems are often referred to as server operating systems. Servers play a critical role in managing resources that must be shared across a network or enterprise. Although there are a variety of server operating systems from which to choose, the market leader is Microsoft. Because of Microsoft's dominance in the server operating system market, Windows Server 2003 is the focus of our "Topic in Focus" discussion. This discussion will be a broad overview, as mastering this sophisticated software product would require a class and textbook of its own.

Microsoft is famous, or infamous depending on your perspective, for offering multiple versions of its various products. Windows 2003 Server follows this approach. The 2003 Server family has four editions, Standard, Enterprise, Datacenter, and Web. Each is geared toward a particular market, offering different capabilities and having different requirements for installation and configuration. Let's explore how these versions differ.

Standard Edition

Server 2003 Standard Edition is targeted at small organizations and departments. Standard Edition supports four-way symmetric multiprocessing, or SMP. SMP provides for multiple central processing units, CPUs, to be available for completing individual tasks simultaneously. The use of additional CPUs improves a server's performance and allows it to handle increased workloads. Devices using SMP share common memory and disk input/output resources. A server running Standard Edition can have up to four gigabytes of RAM. Advanced networking features in Standard Edition include Internet Authentication Service (IAS), Network Bridging, and Internet Connection Sharing (ICS).

IAS is Microsoft's implementation of Remote Authentication Dial-In User Service. This service performs centralized connection authentication, authorization, and accounting for many types of network access. The Network Bridging component of Standard Edition allows a computer running a version of the Windows Server 2003 family to bridge multiple networks to create a single subnet. (Subnets and IP addressing are presented in the next chapter, Chapter 5.) ICS is a technique for connecting multiple computers in a LAN to the Internet using a single connection and a single IP address. Standard Edition shares with the other editions the ability to use various Microsoft .Net application services, file and print services, and management services. The Standard and Enterprise Editions also include an Internet connection firewall.

Enterprise Edition

Targeted at medium to large businesses, Enterprise Edition Server 2003 offers capabilities suitable for inventory and customer service systems, as well as database and e-commerce applications. Enterprise Edition includes all of the features of Standard Edition. In addition, Enterprise Edition provides for eight-way SMP and up to 32 gigabytes of memory. Both Enterprise and Datacenter Editions support eight-node clustering. Both SMP and clustering are scalability features that allow a business to gear up, or down, depending on resource needs. As an example, four Enterprise Edition 2003 servers might be configured to form a cluster in which they share external storage devices. An advantage to clients that use the cluster is that to the clients the cluster appears as one virtual server. Servers in a cluster can perform workload balancing, which increases their efficiency.

Enterprise Edition, like Datacenter Edition, also has a 64-bit version. When using the 64-bit version of Enterprise Edition, the maximum amount of memory supported increases to 64 gigabytes. The 64-bit addition is optimized for memory-intensive and computational-intensive processes. Applications such as mechanical design, graphics, and database access are better suited for 64-bit capability. Network administrators like that Enterprise Edition allows for hot-added memory. This means, for servers that have hardware that support this feature, memory can be added to the server without having to power down and then reboot or restart the server. This, in turn, means little or no downtime, definitely a plus from the user's perspective.

Datacenter Edition

For businesses that require the greatest degree of availability, scalability, and reliability, Microsoft recommends Datacenter Edition. This edition is also suitable for organizations that have very high-volume, real-time transaction processing requirements. Datacenter Edition allows for 32-way SMP. Like Enterprise Edition, Datacenter Edition has both a 32- and 64-bit version. However, unlike Enterprise Edition, Datacenter Edition can accommodate up to 128 gigabytes of memory. Datacenter Edition is only available through Microsoft's Windows Datacenter Program. Qualified server vendors participate with Microsoft in offering an original equipment manufacturer (OEM) installed version of the Datacenter Server. Server vendors include IBM, Dell, and Hewlett-Packard, among others. A complete list can be found on Microsoft's Web site for Datacenter Server 2003 (**www.microsoft.com/windowsserver2003/evaluation/overview/datacenter.mspx**).

Web Edition

Web Edition Server 2003 is intended for building, hosting, and managing Web applications and services. Supporting only two-way SMP and having only two gigabytes of memory, Web Edition is designed specifically for Web server services. Many of the features available in the other editions of Server 2003 are not included in Web Edition. But then, the intent of how Web Edition is to be used is also very different from the other editions. Like Datacenter Edition, Web Edition is not available through traditional retail stores, but through designated Microsoft partners. The list of providers can be found at **www.microsoft.com/serviceproviders**. Interestingly, all of the features found in Web Edition are included in the other Server 2003 editions.

Table 4.1 provides an overview of Server 2003 Edition requirements. It should be noted that the minimums identified are not likely to be deployed in the real world. It would be wise to assume that much higher-end resources are going to be used.

The following Web sites provide additional information on Microsoft Server 2003.

Server 2003 Homepage: **www.microsoft.com/windowsserver2003**

Server 2003 Deployment Guide:
www.microsoft.com/technet/treeview/default.asp?url = /technet/prodtechnol/windowsserver2003/Default.asp

Table 4.1 Server 2003 Edition Resource Requirements

Edition	Approximate Cost	Minimum CPU	Minimum RAM	Minimum Storage
Standard	$999	133 Mhz	128 MB	1.5 GB
Enterprise (32-bit)	$3,999	133 Mhz	128 MB	1.5 GB
Datacenter	OEM	400 Mhz	512 MB	1.5 GB
Web	$397	133 Mhz	128 MB	1.5 GB

Standard Edition Sever 2003 Overview:
www.microsoft.com/windowsserver2003/evaluation/overview/standard.mspx/

Enterprise Edition Server 2003 Homepage:
www.microsoft.com/windowsserver2003/evaluation/overview/enterprise.mspx/

Datacenter Edition Server 2003 Overview:
www.microsoft.com/windowsserver2003/evaluation/overview/datacenter.mspx/

Web Edition Server 2003 Overview:
www.microsoft.com/windowsserver2003/evaluation/overview/web.mspx/

Server 2003 Technical Overviews:
www.microsoft.com/windowsserver2003/techinfo/overview/default.mspx

chapter**five**

Network, Transport, and Application Layer Services

Learning Objectives

After studying this chapter, you should be able to:

- Differentiate among network, transport, and application layer services.
- Describe the key elements of network services.
- Describe the key elements of transport services.
- Describe the key elements of application layer services.
- Understand IP address formats.
- Convert binary numbers to decimal and back again.
- Identify IP address classes.
- Understand how an IP address class can indicate the number of hosts on a network.
- Discuss IP addressing guidelines.
- Define a subnet mask.
- Understand subnet addressing.
- Know the purpose of ANDing.
- Know the advantages of the subnetwork architecture.
- Describe supernetting.

In Chapter 4, you learned that a LAN is composed of both logical and physical components. These components work together so that resources can be shared and network devices can communicate. A business may, of course, have more than one LAN and want its multiple LANs to be able to communicate and share resources. For such communication and sharing to occur, network devices require two critical pieces of information.

First, a sending device needs to know the network address of the receiving device. Second, the sending device must also know the specific, individual address of the receiving device within the receiving device's network. Addressing is critical to any network, regardless of the type of network model used. Chapter 5 explores how addressing is accomplished in the TCP/IP model.

Mid- and High-Range Services

Originally designed as a collection of protocol suites to support very large networks—and what could be larger than the Internet—TCP/IP has emerged as the network model of choice for LANs as well as WANs. Figure 5.1 shows a graphic of Internet, TCP/IP, byte traffic. (Visit **www.isoc.org/internet/ history** for an interesting history of the Internet.) The network and transport layers perform mid-level services for TCP/IP. Upper-level services are provided at the application layer. Each of these layers makes use of protocols to fulfill its functionalities. In an earlier chapter, a protocol was defined as a set of rules or procedures that specify how something works. By defining standards, protocols enable communication to occur, whether between people or between machines. In communications between people, the protocols or languages used can be very sophisticated and complex, far more so than the relatively straightforward protocols that enable machines to talk to each other.

This chapter explores the various protocols used by mid- and upper-level services in the TCP/IP model. Figure 5.2 shows the layers of the TCP/IP model. This chapter also presents the network layer Internetworking Protocol (IP) and explores how it is used to implement communications not only within a LAN, but also between LANs and

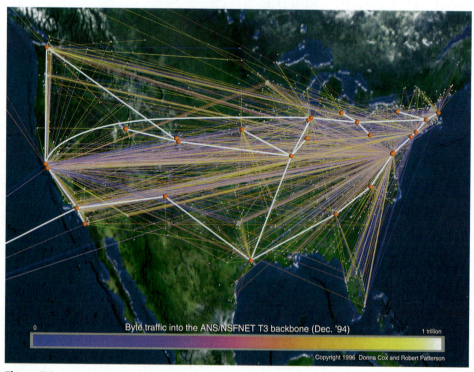

Byte traffic into the ANS/NSFNET T3 backbone (Dec. '94)

0   1 trillion

Copyright 1996 Donna Cox and Robert Patterson

Figure 5.1
Map Showing Internet Byte Traffic in the United States

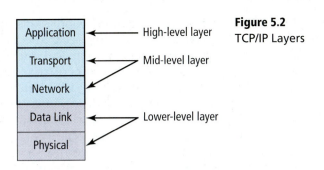

Figure 5.2
TCP/IP Layers

WANs. You will discover that the process is very logical and that the rules, based on the IP portion of the TCP/IP protocol suite, create a communication infrastructure that enables LANs and other networked devices to recognize and talk to each other. From bottom to top, this chapter will examine network, transport, and application layer services. IP addressing will be examined later in the chapter.

Throughout this discussion, remember that the collection of all networks owned by a single organization is commonly referred to as the **enterprise**. An organization's enterprise might include dozens of LANs, BNs, MANs, and WANs. The scale of the enterprise depends on the business. The larger the scale, the more important addressing becomes.

Network Layer Services

Sitting just above the data link layer, which was described in Chapter 3, and below the transport layer is the TCP/IP **network layer**. At the heart of the network layer is IP, the Internetworking Protocol, which in turn is supported by four other protocols: Address Resolution Protocol (ARP), Reverse Address Resolution Protocol (RARP), Internet Control Message Protocol (ICMP), and Internet Group Message Protocol (IGMP). Think of IP as being in charge of a team of dedicated assistants whose only concern is getting the job done. Figure 5.3 shows how these protocols fit into the overall architecture of the TCP/IP model. Each of these four protocols helps IP at the network layer by performing the specific duties that they are assigned.

Address Resolution Protocol

The **Address Resolution Protocol (ARP)** is used to relate a logical IP address with a physical address. Much of this chapter concentrates on what is meant by a logical IP address. For now, understand that each host device in a TCP/IP network is assigned a logical **IP address**. Because an IP address is a **logical address**, it can be changed or modified. Each IP address in turn will be associated with a particular physical address. The **physical address** is the MAC layer address that comes from the host device's NIC. The MAC address is physical in that it cannot be modified. (You may also recall from Chapter 4 that each NIC address is unique.)

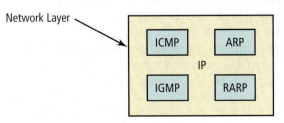

Figure 5.3
IP Protocol Suite at the Network Layer

In a TCP/IP environment, logical IP addresses must be associated with their physical MAC address counterparts. The process of associating a specific logical address to a specific physical address is called "*resolving*" the address. ARP is the TCP/IP protocol that resolves logical TCP/IP addresses to physical MAC addresses. ARP, like a detective, tracks down and finds the matching physical address for a known logical IP address. When two TCP/IP devices need to communicate, both the logical and physical addresses of each device are required. When the sending device knows the logical IP address of the receiving device but not the receiving device's physical address, ARP is used to determine the device's physical address. ARP is the dedicated IP assistant that resolves addresses. Here is how ARP works.

First, recall from Chapter 3 that communicating devices at the data link layer use physical, or MAC, addresses. Also remember that both the sender and receiver have multiple layers in their protocol stacks. The different layers have different requirements. Consequently, a logical IP address, which is required at the network layer, must still be associated with a physical address, which is required at the data link layer. The data link and network layers work together.

Say that a sending device wants to communicate with a receiving device. Assume that the sending device has the receiving device's logical IP address. The sending device must also have the receiving device's physical address. The sending device, which has IP in its network layer stack, issues an ARP request. As you have already learned, ARP comes bundled with IP at the network layer.

The sender's ARP first checks the sending device's memory storage to see if the requested information, the receiving device's physical MAC address, is already available. The sender may have recently communicated with the receiver and may therefore still have the receiver's physical MAC address information in its memory. If this is true, no further effort is required. ARP immediately resolves the address, matching the physical address with the logical address, and the sender sends its data packet. But what if the sender has never communicated with the receiver? Or, what if any previous communication happened so long ago that the receiver's physical MAC address information has been flushed from the sender's memory buffer? This means that the sender no longer has the receiver's physical address information. Again, ARP comes to the rescue!

The sender's local network layer IP stack broadcasts an ARP data packet. From Chapter 4, you know that a broadcast goes to all of the devices on the local network. Each device on the local network receives and evaluates the broadcast ARP request. If one of the devices has the requested information, that device sends the information to the originating device's ARP. If none of the local devices has the requested information, the originator's ARP request is passed on to the network routers to be sent to other networks in the enterprise. Eventually, if all goes well, the requested information is brought back to the sending device, and the sender's ARP completes its job by resolving the address request. The sender can now forward its packet to the receiver. Figure 5.4 illustrates this process. For even more on ARP, visit **whatis.techtarget.com**.

Reverse Address Resolution Protocol

Reverse Address Resolution Protocol (RARP) does the opposite of ARP. When a sending device knows the physical address of the receiving device but not its logical IP address, RARP is used. RARP is also used when a host device is connected to a network for the first time or when a diskless computer is powered up. When a host device connects to a TCP/IP network for

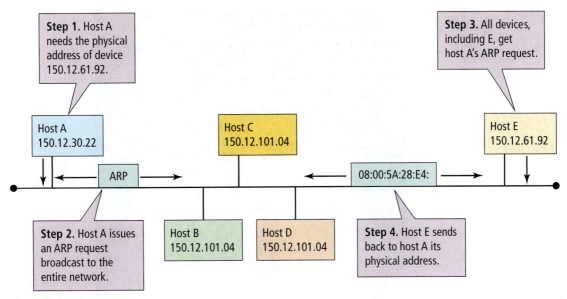

Figure 5.4
How ARP Works

the first time, it must resolve its logical IP address. A device that is networked must, by definition, have a NIC. The NIC, in turn, provides the device's MAC physical address. Therefore, a host will know its own physical layer address.

Diskless computers do not have hard drives or floppy drives. A diskless computer's physical address can be stored in a Read Only Memory (ROM) chip. However, a diskless computer on a TCP/IP network still needs a logical IP address for it to function at the network layer. RARP is used to resolve the diskless computer's logical IP address. When the diskless machine boots, or powers up, an RARP request is initiated and broadcast to the network. Another device on the network that has a table of IP addresses assigned to all devices on the network responds and sends the diskless device its IP address information. The diskless device stores its logical IP address information in its temporary memory. When the diskless device reboots, it must again go through the RARP process.

You may be asking, why would a business use a diskless device? Diskless devices have several advantages. They are particularly useful when security is essential. Without a disk drive, or, more precisely, a drive that a user can write data to, it becomes very difficult to copy data and remove it from the premises. Also, one of the most common ways of spreading a virus throughout an organization is through the use of floppy disk drives. Removing a system wide virus, Figure 5.5, can be very difficult. Without a floppy drive or other local storage device, the network administrator has a much easier job of controlling the spread of malicious programs. Of course, users will likely be less than thrilled at having no secondary storage devices available for storing data. Secondary storage devices include floppy drives, hard drives, and other devices to which data can be saved. Cost can also be a consideration for using diskless client stations, because such stations are typically less expensive than their more fully featured alternatives.

Internet Control Message Protocol

By itself, IP has no error-reporting or error-correcting controls, so if something goes wrong with an IP datagram, IP has no direct way of compensating for the error. A **datagram**, Figure 5.6, is a packet of data used by an IP network. IP also does not directly support management functions, so if a

Figure 5.5
Computer Vaccination
*An important part of a network administrator's duties is
to ensure that networked devices are virus free.*

VERS	HLEN	TOS	Total Length	ID	Flags	Frag Offset	TTL	Protocol	Header Checksum	SA	DA	IP Options	Data or Payload

VERS: Version, for example IPv4.
HLEN: or destination address, of where the frame is to be sent.
TOS: Type of Service, defining how the datagram should be used.
Total Length: Number of octets in the datagram, with a maximum of 65,535 octets.
ID: An identification number that helps in the reassembly of fragmented datagrams.
Flags: Can be used to specify whether a datagram can be fragmented.
Frag Offset: A value specified for each data fragment in a reassembly process.
TTL: Time-to-Live, that determines how long a datagram can exist on a network.
Protocol: A value that identifies the protocol sending the datagram; for example, TCP uses 6 and UDP uses 17.
Header Checksum: Error control information for the header only.
SA: Source Address.
DA: Destination Address.
IP Options: For testing, debugging, and security.
Data: Message being communicated; also referred to as the payload. Padding may be included depending on the size of the payload.

Figure 5.6
IP Datagram

host is trying to determine whether a router is available, no management mechanism is available to assist it. This is where Internet Control Message Protocol comes into play.

Internet Control Message Protocol (ICMP) supports IP by providing two important functions: error reporting and query management. ICMP only reports errors, it does not correct them. For example, if a datagram, for whatever reason, is unable to reach its final destination, then an error has occurred. ICMP can report back to IP that a "destination unreachable" error has occurred for that packet.

ICMP can report five types of errors: (1) destination unreachable; (2) source quench, which notifies a sending host that a datagram has been discarded due to congestion; (3) time exceeded, which is sent when a datagram's time-to-live value has counted down to zero (without this value a lost datagram could circle the network endlessly); (4) parameter error, which is sent when a datagram's header has a problem; and (5) redirection, which is used by routers to inform a sending host that the sending host has directed a datagram to the wrong router.

Internet Group Message Protocol

Internet Group Message Protocol (IGMP) is used by IP primarily when multicasting is required. Two types of communication can occur over a TCP/IP network: unicasting and multicasting. **Unicasting**, Figure 5.7, is the more common and is a communication between one sender and one receiver.

Multicasting, Figure 5.8, occurs when a sender wants to send to many receivers. In a TCP/IP environment, it is possible to set up a multicasting group. A multicast address can only be used as a destination, not as a source address. IGMP helps multicast routers identify the hosts in a network that are part of a multicast group. The multicast router maintains a list of group multicast addresses.

IGMP supports two types of messages: reporting and query. Reporting messages are sent from a host to a router. Query messages are sent from a router to a host. An IGMP packet is very simple and includes a field for group address identification.

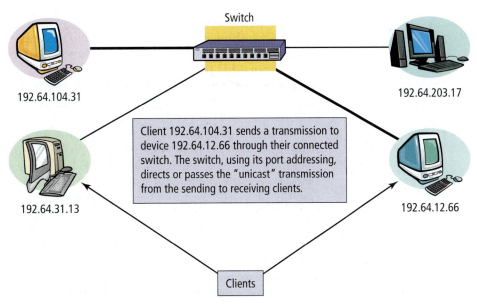

Switch

192.64.104.31

192.64.203.17

192.64.31.13

Client 192.64.104.31 sends a transmission to device 192.64.12.66 through their connected switch. The switch, using its port addressing, directs or passes the "unicast" transmission from the sending to receiving clients.

192.64.12.66

Clients

Figure 5.7
Unicast Transmission

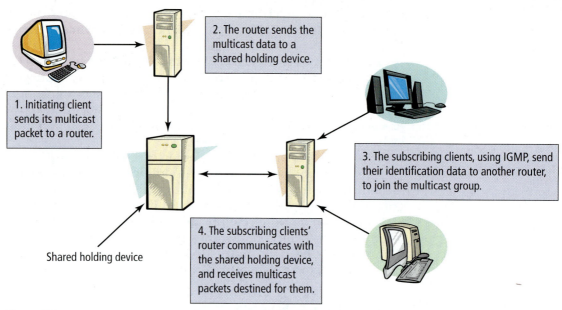

Figure 5.8
Multicast Transmission

Transport Layer Services

As with network layer services, the **transport layer**, which sits above the network layer and below the application layer, also uses protocols. The two key transport layer protocols are the Transmission Control Protocol (TCP) and the User Datagram Protocol (UDP). The two protocols operate in very different ways.

Transmission Control Protocol

Transmission Control Protocol (TCP) is a connection-oriented protocol; it is also called a reliable stream transport layer service. The term **connection oriented** applies because the sender cannot send until the receiver is contacted and agrees to a communication. This agreement establishes the connection. To better understand the concept of a *reliable stream*, keep in mind that there are sending and receiving TCP hosts.

When used, the TCP on the sending host accepts a stream of data from the sending host's application layer and segments this data into packets. The packets are then sent, using reliable services, to a receiving TCP host. The TCP on the receiving host's end takes the incoming packets and delivers them as a steam of data to the receiving host's application layer. The TCP service is said to be reliable because before data transmission can begin between the sender and receiver, a connection must be established. This implies that both the sender and receiver are reliably prepared for and ready to begin communications with each other.

TCP has much more overhead than its counterpart, UDP. TCP provides for packet acknowledgment, error detection and control, and flow control. Generally, the use of TCP as a delivery service is appropriate when larger data streams that cannot fit into a single packet need to be transmitted across the network. Also, for a message for which it is especially important that all the data packets arrive without loss and in the proper sequence, TCP is the delivery method of choice. With TCP, the data packets that make up the message all take the same route to their destination. For noncritical

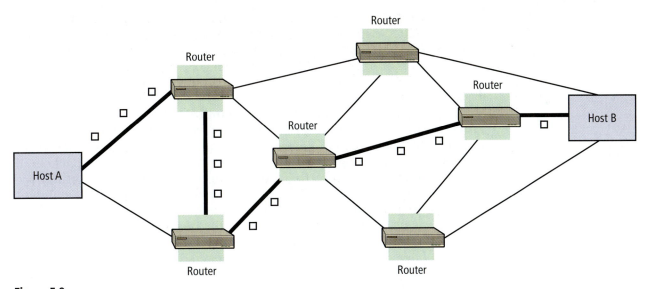

Figure 5.9
TCP Transmission
The packets that make up a message all take the same route from Host A to Host B.

data or for data that can fit within a single packet, UDP is the more appropriate protocol. Figure 5.9 shows an example of a TCP communication.

TCP takes a three-step approach to establishing a reliable communication. First, from the transport layer of the sending device a request packet is transmitted to the receiving device's transport layer asking if a session can be established. Second, if available, the receiving device sends a packet back to the sending device indicating that it is available for communication. Then, in the third and final step, the sending device begins to send its data to the receiving device.

The information sent by the sender includes source and destination values, sequence numbers for data messages that may be broken into smaller segments for transmittal, and a checksum value that is used by the receiver to determine whether a transmission error has occurred. The information sent from the receiver back to the sender includes acknowledgment values for the packets received. The sender's TCP for flow control then uses the receiver's acknowledgment values. TCP uses the sliding windows method of flow control.

In Chapter 3, you learned that checksums can be used for error detection. The chapter also examined the benefits of sliding windows and how it works. You can now see how these two topics relate to the TCP/IP transport layer. The original Request for Comments 1981 document on TCP can be found at **www.faqs.org/rfcs/rfc793.html**. **Request for Comments (RFCs)** are a series of formal documents that, since 1969, present technical and organizational notes about the Internet (originally the ARPANET). See **www.rfc-editor.org** to find out more about this important document series and how it is managed. Any standard that is eventually formally incorporated into the Internet or TCP/IP starts as a Request for Comment. As you might imagine, these comments can be very influential.

User Datagram Protocol

Unlike TCP, **User Datagram Protocol (UDP)** is a connectionless, unreliable delivery service. **Connectionless** means that the sender does not have to first establish a link to the receiver before beginning to transmit data. Unreliable does not mean worse or unacceptable. With UDP, **unreliable** simply means that the sender does not guarantee to the receiver that all of the transmitted data packets will arrive. Also, if a message requires multiple packets, the packets may or may not take the same route to the receiver, and thus may arrive out of sequence. It is up to the receiver to verify that the data expected has in fact been received and to put the packets back in order, if needed.

Depending on the data being transmitted, UDP can be the better choice than TCP. Because UDP does not require the sender and receiver to establish a connection before sending data, time is saved, increasing efficiency. The sending host simple begins to transmit its UDP packets. If a message requires more than one datagram, the sent datagrams are treated independently. This means that the datagrams may take different routes to their ultimate destination and likely will not arrive in sequence. UDP leaves it to higher-level services on the receiving host's end to determine whether all packets have been received, whether any of the packets received have errors, and to place the packets back in order. As a result, at the transport layer, UDP can provide greater efficiency, but at the potential cost of high-layer services having to do more work. Figure 5.10 demonstrates a UDP transmission.

UDP does not provide for packet acknowledgment, error detection and control, or flow control. Because UDP does not support these services, it has far less overhead than TCP. With less overhead, UDP can be more efficient, assuming that all packets arrive with no errors at the receiving host. Also, because UDP packets are independent of each other, they can be routed through different links, unlike a TCP transmission. This means that if a UDP datagram encounters a bad or congested link, it can be routed around the problem area. Under the right circumstances, then, UDP can be the preferred delivery option. You can read the 1980 RFC about UDP at **www.faqs.org/rfcs/rfc793.html**.

Interestingly, the use of UDP has evolved over time. Although still mostly associated with small data files that require few packets, today UDP also is used for streaming audio and video. With a streaming audio or video file, it is usually not essential that every single byte be accounted for, as would be the case with traditional data, especially numeric data.

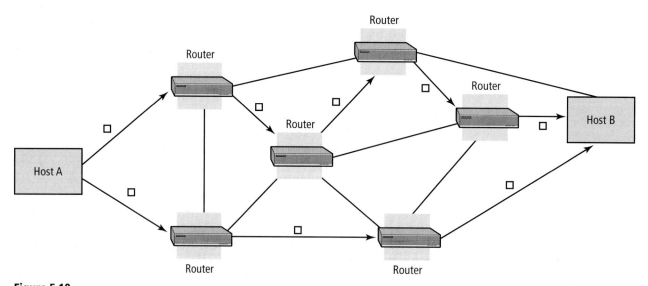

Figure 5.10
UDP Transmission
In a UDP communication, packets from Host A can take varying routes to destination Host B.

Whether using TCP or UDP, the transport layer ultimately passes its data stream up to application layer services. Remember from Chapter 1 that the application layer sits at the top of the TCP/IP model. You should also recall that in the TCP/IP model the application layer includes the session, presentation, and application layer equivalents of the OSI model.

Application Layer Services

Many protocols are defined at the application layer of the TCP/IP model, and covering them all would be another text in itself. The application layer sits at the top of the TCP/IP layer stack, directly above the transport layer. The **application layer** provides the user an interface and a connection to the network. Many application layer protocols follow the client/server approach. In the client/server model, a local host machine runs an application layer program called a *client*. The client application requests a resource from a remote host that is running a server-based application layer program. Server-based applications, assuming that the request is successfully authenticated and/or supported, fulfill requests for services. Note that a host can, if so configured, run both client- and server-based services. It may be a little confusing, but a device running server services is not necessarily a server. A formal server is a more specialized type of device. Chapter 8 looks at servers and how they are used.

The following presents a sampling of some of the more common protocols that you are likely to encounter. With each example, keep in mind that a client component is installed on the local host machine and that a server component is running on the remote device that is providing the service.

Terminal Network

Terminal Network, or **Telnet**, is an application layer program that enables a user to remotely login and use the resources of a remote computer. To be successful, the remote computer must authenticate the user. Authentication is usually accomplished by means of a user ID and a password. Once authenticated, a user can use the processor, file system, drives, and other resources of the remote host.

Telnet was designed for use in time-sharing environments, whereby a large central computer, typically a mainframe, supported multiple users who logged in to the computer to access its resources. Network administrators also use Telnet to monitor, configure, and maintain remote devices.

File Transfer Protocol

Another popular application layer program is File Transfer Protocol. In the TCP/IP environment, **File Transfer Protocol (FTP)** is used to copy files from one host to another. On the client host side, Figure 5.11, FTP has three components: a user interface, a client control process, and a client transfer process. On the server host side, there are two components: a server control process and a server transfer process. Depending on the connection, user authentication may be required. Many FTP servers are set up for *anonymous* users, meaning that anyone with a FTP client can connect to the anonymous FTP server and use that server's resources. Other FTP servers have more stringent login requirements. Many free FTP clients are available over the Internet. One popular version is WS-FTP, which is provided by Ipswitch (**www.ipswitch.com**). More fully featured versions, some of which are also offered by Ipswitch, are available for a fee. When you purchase an FTP client, documentation and technical support are often provided.

Sharing? Or Something Else?

The Internet has come a long way from being a tool used mostly by scientists and researchers to exchange technical information. Now, millions of people shop, play, communicate, and share resources over the Internet. The issue of sharing has become a major ethical issue. Web-based applications, primarily using peer-to-peer sharing protocols, enable a user to exchange and share files with other local computers. Many of these "shared" files are music, video, or other types of artistic- or entertainment-based materials. To the businesses and artists who create these works, the rampant sharing of these materials has resulted in a loss of control over their works, as well as millions of dollars of lost income.

Many users who "share" these works do not reimburse the artist or owner for use of the work. To many, such works should be free, and they see no problem with sharing technologies. The Digital Consumer Organization (**www.digitalconsumer.org**) lobbies on behalf of consumers to ensure that consumers can make copies of electronic content that they buy. However, buying a single version of the content and then sharing that version with many others is very controversial. Some say that this is illegal; others say it is unethical. This type of file sharing, with no reimbursement to the original owner, was a key reason for the passage in 1998 of the Federal Digital Millennium Copyright Act (DMCA; **www.loc.gov/copyright/legislation/dmca.pdf**).

What do you think? Is it ethical to share copyrighted materials without reimbursing the creators or owners? Should there be laws for or against such sharing? How would you argue for or against these sharing technologies? If you were a network administrator, would you define a policy on the sharing of files using corporate computers and networks? How would you enforce such a policy? Should a business be legally responsible for what an employee does, even if the organization has no knowledge of what the employee is doing? As you can see, this is a very complicated issue.

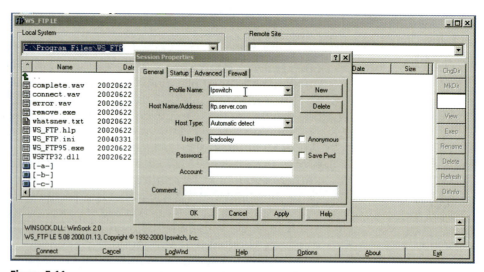

Figure 5.11
FTP Client Screen Shot Using WS-FTP

Simple Mail Transfer Protocol

Simple Mail Transfer Protocol (SMTP) is a popular network protocol for providing e-mail services. SMTP makes use of two components: a user agent and a mail transfer agent. On the client end, the **user agent (UA)** prepares the message and puts it into a form that can be transmitted across a TCP/IP network. The **mail transfer agent (MTA)** transfers the mail across the network or over the Internet. On the server end, SMTP servers receive outgoing mail from clients and transmit mail to destination e-mail servers. Another type of SMTP server maintains the mailboxes from which e-mail clients retrieve their mail. Figure 5.12 shows a simplified diagram of how user agents and mail transfer agents might be configured.

Two common protocols that servers use to maintain e-mail mailboxes are **Post Office Protocol Version 3 (POP3)** and **Internet Message Access Protocol (IMAP)**. One machine may run POP3 or IMAP in addition to SMTP. In that case, the servers are not separate physical devices, but one device running multiple logical server operations. Chapter 8 looks more closely at the different types of servers used to integrate the enterprise. A basic discussion on e-mail and the use of SMTP and POP3 can be found at **www.howstuffworks.com/email.htm**.

Simple Network Management Protocol

Simple Network Management Protocol (SNMP) provides a basic set of tools for managing a TCP/IP network. Because it uses UDP, SNMP is also connectionless. Generally, certain host devices that have a "manager" component control a group of devices, usually routers, that run an "agent" component. SNMP is sufficiently general so that hosts from different manufacturers and on different physical networks can be monitored. The manager receives information from agents and assembles it for presentation to network administrators.

Many networked devices, including routers, switches, and hubs, can serve as agents, reporting back to the manager device regarding the status of the network. Each agent has a **Management Information Base (MIB)** that it builds as it collects network statistics. The agent distributes its MIB to the manager. Based on the data received, a management station can cause an action to take place at an agent or it can change an agent's configuration setting.

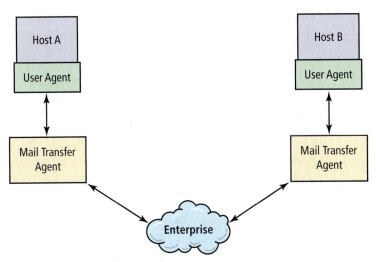

Figure 5.12
User and Mail Transfer Agents

Figure 5.13
HTTP is a Standard Used
Worldwide

Hypertext Transfer Protocol

Hypertext Transfer Protocol (HTTP) is used primarily to access information on the World Wide Web (WWW), as demonstrated in Figure 5.13. HTTP enables data (text, hypertext, video, graphic, audio, or other medium) to be transferred from a server device to client, meaning a Web server to a client browser. After a TCP/IP connection is established, the client browser and the Web server can begin to exchange data. HTTP uses two message types: requests and responses. Every HTTP message has a start line, an optional header, a blank line that identifies the end of the header section, and the body of the message, which is also optional. A formal Internet working group is devoted to HTTP. You can find out more about this interesting group at **ftp.ics.uci.edu/pub/ietf/http**.

Of course, other useful application layer protocols are also available, such as the Domain Name System, or DNS. However, the remainder of the chapter focuses on the network and transport layer services that specify how devices in a TCP/IP network are addressed.

The Layers in Context

Let's place the TCP/IP layers in context. The application layer provides the enterprise network user an interface for connecting to and interacting with the network. Very likely, the user wants to either communicate with another user or with a service offered by another network in the enterprise, for example, a database server. The destination user or service could be on the same or different network as the originating user. When two hosts in a TCP/IP network communicate, it is critical, as with any communication, that they be able to identify each other. This is where the network and transport layers take over.

A key responsibility of the network and transport layers of the TCP/IP model is determining how host devices use addressing to identify each other so that they can communicate. Without this addressing identification, communication would not be possible. Imagine that you send a letter to a friend in another state or country but that you put no forwarding or return address on the envelope. Do you think your letter will arrive? Not likely. A full communication, assuming that you want your friend to write back, requires complete addressing from the source, you, and the destination, your friend. This same addressing principle is true for networked devices. For an application layer service to send and receive data, two communicating hosts must be able to identify each other. They identify each other through addressing. The rest of this chapter examines this critical topic, exploring how addressing is implemented in a TCP/IP network.

The Importance of Addressing Schemes

As you read at the beginning of this chapter, an organization's enterprise may be very large. The larger the enterprise, the more critical addressing within the enterprise becomes. In a TCP/IP network, each device connected to the network can also be referred to as a **host**. Each host device on the network has a unique address that identifies it specifically and uniquely throughout the entire enterprise. Without unique addresses, devices in an enterprise would not be able to be individually identified.

The need for identification requires that each network in the enterprise have a unique logical address. Furthermore, each host device within each network must also have a logical address. If designed correctly, the network and host addresses together enable the unique identification of each device in the enterprise. Such identification is especially crucial in an enterprise that has many networks. In such a scenario, the organization will very likely want the hosts on the different networks to be able to communicate with each other. Figure 5.14 shows a possible enterprise configuration with five network addresses.

In TCP/IP, the combined network and host addresses of each device make up what is called an "IP address." A country's postal service usually organizes postal addresses through an addressing scheme. For example, in the United States, a zip code is used to route mail, whether between cities or across states. TCP/IP networks must also have an addressing scheme. The larger and more complex the enterprise, the more critical the design of the organization's IP addressing scheme becomes. To implement communication over any TCP/IP network, small or large, an IP addressing scheme must be developed. In this addressing scheme, the IP address will contain not only a LAN or network identifier, but a host or device identifier as well. Each host device's IP address reveals two things: the network address the host is on and the address of the host itself within the network.

Let's consider our postal service example again. For a letter to be delivered to you, the sender would need to know your city, street, and house or apartment number and write that information on the outside of the letter's envelope. Think of the letter inside the envelope as the original user application layer data. In the IP address scheme, the enterprise network can be compared with your city, which likely has many streets. The network portion of the IP address compares with your specific street, on which there are likely many houses or apartments. The host portion of the same IP address compares with your house or apartment number, which is specific to you and your household. The result is that you have been identified by your individual address within a street, within a city, and now you can send or receive a letter! A networked host device is within a network, within an enterprise.

Routers connect the networks that make up the enterprise and the Internet. In a very real way, routers are like the post offices that make sure that your letter gets from one post office to another and eventually to your friend's mailbox. Routers, though, instead of delivering letters, deliver a data packet from one network to another. Routers, as discussed in Chapter 4, are primarily used to segment and subdivide network traffic. Network and subnetwork boundaries are created using routers. Routers use internal address tables to discover which networks they can reach. Routers make the Internet and the organization's enterprise appear as one single network.

A later chapter will explore routers in much greater detail. For now, all you need to know is that routers are devices that make use of IP addresses to determine where to send a data packet. In the mail example, the post

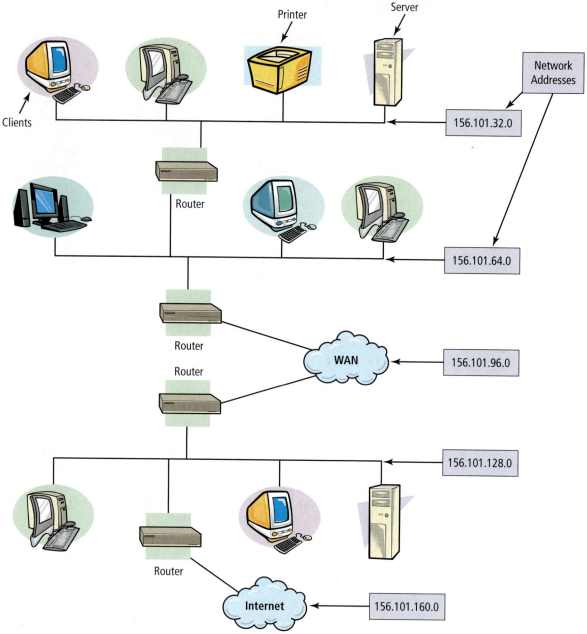

Figure 5.14
Five-Network Enterprise Configuration

office functions in the same way as a router, determining where next to send a letter. Figure 5.15 shows how a router might be used to connect different networks.

The network portion of the IP address must be unique across all the networks of the enterprise as well as across the entire global TCP/IP network if the enterprise is directly connected to the Internet. All hosts on the same network share the same network identifier. If a host device is moved from one network to another, the host's IP address will have to be reassigned and reconfigured. The newly reconfigured IP address will have a new network as well as a new host identifier.

In practice, most businesses that use TCP/IP refer to each separate network in the enterprise as a subnet. Rather than have one very large

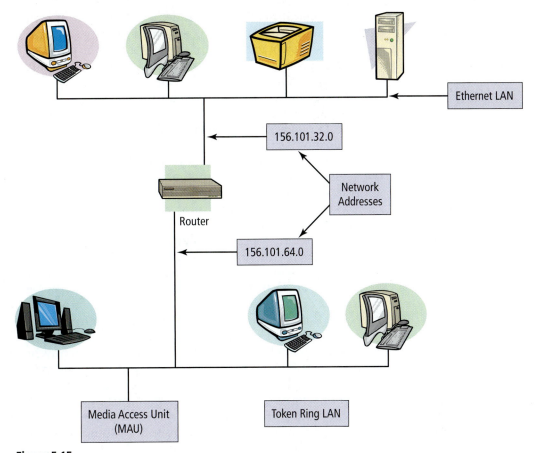

Figure 5.15
Use of a Router Connecting Two Logically Different Networks, Networks 56.101.32.0 and Network 156.101.64.0
This router has two network address assignments and will have two Network Interface Cards as well, one for each network. In this example, network 156.101.32.0 could be an Ethernet network, whereas 156.101.64.0 is a token ring.

network, with hundreds or thousands of hosts, most organizations segment or subdivide a single network address through a process call **subnetting**. With subnetting, a single network identifier is *subdivided* into multiple uniquely identified segments, which is why we call this subdivision a subnet. Subnetting is accomplished by borrowing bits from the host portion of an IP address and reassigning those bits for use as network address identifiers.

In order to subnet, something called a *subnet mask* is used. **Subnet masks** use binary ones to represent the network portion of an address and zeros to represent the host portion. Before describing how subnetting and submasking work, let's examine a few advantages of the subnetwork architecture.

Advantages of the Subnetwork Architecture

Subnetworks offer several advantages. Subnets allow networks with different topologies to be supported. For example, a router can connect an Ethernet subnet with a token ring subnet. Subnets also address the problem of the physical limitations of a network's capacity. An Ethernet network can only accommodate so many devices. Through subnetting, the physical limitations of an Ethernet LAN are overcome. If a network becomes too large, management and configuration may become quite complicated. Subnets allow a greater number of hosts to be provided for and more easily managed over the entire enterprise. Another advantage of subnets is that they can reduce traffic. Reducing traffic improves the overall performance of the network, allowing for faster response.

The construction of a well-structured subnetting enterprise requires careful analysis and good planning. With additional networks comes additional complexity, especially in maintaining an IP addressing scheme that is accurate, reliable, and easy to modify across the enterprise. With more hosts, maintenance and configuration efforts will likely be impacted. Several factors should be considered when designing a subnetwork architecture.

First, how many network address identifiers will be required? Each subnet requires its own unique IP address. When determining the number of network addresses, you should plan for the future growth of the organization. A separate network identifier will be required for every network bordered by a router, including any WAN connections bordered by routers. Once the total number of network addresses has been determined, the number of hosts to be supported per subnet must be considered.

Each device with a NIC will require a unique host IP address. As with network identifiers, future growth in the number of hosts within a subnet must be considered. The decision as to how many hosts should be supported within a subnet will directly affect the subnet mask that must be defined for the enterprise. (The subnet mask is explained in more detail soon.) Performing the necessary planning and analysis right the first time will prevent you from having to reconfigure every host device with a new subnet mask in the future. Figure 5.14 illustrated an enterprise with five subnets. The numbers shown in the figure are unique subnet addresses. Note that both the WAN and Internet networks connected by the router have subnet identifiers.

The subnet mask will determine the number of network address identifiers the organization will have available for use. Once selected, the subnet values need to be well documented so as to verify that they are already in use. In this way, when a new network identifier is required, all of those already in use will be known. Once subnet network identifiers have been selected, host identifiers within each subnet can be appended to the network address. As with network identifiers, host identifiers should be well documented to ensure that no duplicate or invalid addresses are used within a subnet. The network administrator should develop a numbering range scheme that allocates particular ranges of IP addresses to particular types of devices, for example, routers, switches, servers, static and dynamic clients. A useful 1998 article on IP subnetting can be found at **www.ezine.com/EZInternet.SubNet.html**.

As you have read, subnetting is common among businesses that use the TCP/IP networking model. To better understand this concept, let's now turn to IP address configuration and subnet masking.

IP Addressing

IP addresses can be represented in both binary and decimal formats. Network administrators, being people and not machines, generally work with the decimal equivalent of an IP address, because that is much more convenient. However, it is important that network technologists understand both the binary and decimal representations of an IP address and be able to work and convert between the two. To understand how IP addresses are resolved—meaning how a sending host discovers whether a receiving host is on the same logical network or not—you first must understand binary numbering.

Converting Binary Numbers to Decimal and Back Again

Decimal IP addresses are composed of four numbers, each of which is referred to as an **octet**. The term *octet* is used because each decimal number has an eight-bit, or octet, equivalent. With **binary numbering**, a **bit** is represented by either a zero or a one; that's it, no other values are used. A sequence of eight zeros or ones, in any combination, is called a **byte**. Further, each of the four decimal numbers making up the IP addresses is tied, or anchored, to its neighboring decimal number with a dot; hence, the **dotted-decimal notation** of an IP address. Therefore, an IP address is composed of four bytes, each having eight bits. Because computers use binary numbers, a computer will view a dotted-decimal IP address as a 32-bit binary number. The decimal values that a given octet can take range from 0 to 255, for a total range of 256 different values, because 0 is also a value. Table 5.1 shows an example of a dotted-decimal IP address with its binary, or computer, equivalent.

In an eight-bit octet, each bit can have a value of either zero or one. The decimal value for each bit position in the octet can be determined using the equation 2^{n-1}, where n is the position of the binary bit from the right of the octet. A value of one in the octet indicates that the decimal value is to be accumulated into the total; a value of zero indicates that the decimal value equivalent is not accumulated. Consequently, in the octet, only the ones have to be accumulated. For example, the binary octet 00010110 has the following position accumulations, going from right to left in the octet:

$$2^{2-1} + 2^{3-1} + 2^{5-1} \text{ or } 2 + 4 + 16 = 22 = 00010110$$

The maximum value that any octet can take is 255, as demonstrated in Table 5.2.

Every IP address within an enterprise or on the Internet must be unique. Organizations with no plans to connect their networks to the Internet need not be concerned with allocation or duplication of addresses already on the Internet. In effect, such organizations have private IP addresses. A key problem with private IP addresses is that they cannot be routed across the public Internet unless the devices that sit on the boundary of the private and public networks use additional software. Few organizations go to the labor of developing an enterprise network that does not connect to or utilize the Internet.

For this reason, it is critical that an organization use validated and authenticated IP addresses. The **Internet Corporation for Assigned Names and Number (ICANN)** (**www.icann.org**) is the official body

Table 5.1 A Dotted Decimal Number and Its Binary Equivalent

Dotted Decimal	Binary Equivalent
192.01.36.240	11000000.00000001.00100100.11110000

Table 5.2 Binary Octets and Their Corresponding Bit and Decimal Values

Binary Octet	Octet Bit Value	Octet Decimal Value
00000000	0	0
10000000	128	128
11000000	128 + 64	192
11100000	128 + 64 + 32	224
11110000	128 + 64 + 32 + 16	240
11111000	128 + 64 + 32 + 16 + 8	248
11111100	128 + 64 + 32 + 16 + 8 + 4	252
11111110	128 + 64 + 32 + 16 + 8 + 4 + 2	254
11111111	128 + 64 + 32 + 16 + 8 + 4 + 2 + 1	255

responsible for allocating and assigning the IP addresses, domain names, and protocol parameters that enable organizations to connect their networks to the Internet. ICANN, in turn, uses commercial vendors to assist it in the management of its responsibilities.

Duplicate IP addresses are not allowed within an intranet or on the Internet. An **intranet** is an internal TCP/IP network owned by a given organization. Intranets are used by staff within the business and are not meant for outside user access. This means that customers and vendors the business works with usually do not have access to the organization's intranets. The portion of the enterprise that a customer or vendor is given access to is called an **extranet**. An enterprise differs from both an intranet and extranet in that it is the collection of all of the networks owned by an organization, which may include any intranets and extranets. Most hosts within an organization's enterprise that require an IP address do not need public IP addresses, because most hosts function as clients and do not provide services that need to be accessible over the Internet. Today, due to the scarcity of public IPv4 addresses, organizations typically lease their public IP addresses from an Internet Service Provider (ISP).

IP Address Classes

IPv4, at the time of this writing, is the most widely implemented version of TCP/IP. Eventually, IPv4 will be replaced by its new and improved version, IPv6. Even so, IPv4 is the current reality. Under IPv4, IP addresses are divided into five **address classes**, ranging from Class A through Class E. Of these classes, D and E are reserved for special and/or research use, leaving Classes A, B, and C for public use. For Classes A, B, and C, each class reserves a portion of its IP address for network identification and the remaining portion for host identification. Depending on the class, more or less of the IP address is available for more or less of the network or host identifier. Recall that for a communication to occur between a sender and receiver, both a network and host address must be provided. An IP address contains elements of both.

Table 5.3 IP Address Network and Host Portions by Class

Class	IP Address Octets	Network Portion Octets	Host Portion Octets
A	$1^{st}.2^{nd}.3^{rd}.4^{th}$	1st	$2^{nd}.3^{rd}.4^{th}$
B	$1^{st}.2^{nd}.3^{rd}.4^{th}$	$1^{st}.2^{nd}$	$3^{rd}.4^{th}$
C	$1^{st}.2^{nd}.3^{rd}.4^{th}$	$1^{st}.2^{nd}.3^{rd}$	4th

Regardless of the class, each IPv4 address will always have four octets. The octets used for network identification and those used for host identification differentiate the classes from each other. The network portion of an IP address always begins from the left-most octet. A standard Class A IP address uses its first octet from the left for network identification and its last three right-most octets for host identification. A standard Class B address uses its first two left-most octets for network identification and its last two right-most octets for host identification. A standard Class C address uses its first three left-most octets for network identification and its last right-most octet for host identification. Table 5.3 illustrates the portion of an IP address used for network identification and the portion used for the host.

From the left, the first three bits of the first octet will clearly tell into which class an IP address falls. For a Class A address, the first high-order bit (the left-most bit of the left-most byte) of the first octet is always zero. For a Class B address, the first two high-order bits of the first octet are always 10. Finally, the first three high-order bits of the first octet for a Class C address are always 110. Because the first three high-order bits are used to identify the class of an IP address, they also affect the range of values that the first octet can take for each of the class addresses. Furthermore, each class can support only a specific number of networks and hosts. Depending on the class, more networks or hosts can be supported. Table 5.4 shows the number of networks and hosts available for each class.

IP Address Classes and the Number of Hosts on a Network

In a Class A address, the high-order bit of the first octet is always set to zero. That leaves only seven bits in the first octet for use by network addresses. These 7 bits provide a maximum decimal value of 127, or 01111111 in binary. However, network address 127 is reserved for what is referred to as a network adapter loopback function. For that reason, only 126 Class A networks are, or were, in fact, available. All 126 public Class

Table 5.4 Network and Host Values Available for Each Class

Address Class	First Octet in Binary	Decimal Values of First Octet	Number of Network Octets	Number of Host Octets	Networks Available	Hosts Available
Class A	01111111	1–126	1	3	126	16,777,214
Class B	10111111	128–191	2	2	16,384	65,534
Class C	11011111	192–223	3	1	2,097,152	254

A addresses were assigned long ago. (If you want to know what organizations were lucky enough to get those priceless Class A addresses, visit **www.iana.org/assignments/ipv4-address-space**.)

For Class A IP addresses, 24 bits (the last three octets) are available for host address assignment. This allows for $2^{(24-2)}$, or 16,777,214, host addresses. The reason that 2 is subtracted from the 24 is that a host address of all zeros or all ones is not allowed. The use of all zeros in a host address indicates that the communication is for a particular network without specifying a host. All ones in the host address indicates that the communication is for all hosts on a particular network.

As it happens, a network address of all zeros and all ones is also not allowed. All zeros in a network address indicate that the host is on the local network, so the communication will not be routed. All ones in the network address indicate a broadcast whereby all hosts on the network receive the communication. In addition, all zeros and all ones are used in particular combinations in an IP address to define something called a subnet mask.

The first two octets of Class B addresses are for the network identifier. Of the remaining 16 bits, only 14 may be used for host addressing, again because a host of all zeros or all ones is not allowed. Using 14 bits (2^{16-2}) provides for a possible 65,534 hosts per Class B network. Using its first three octets for network identification, Class C addresses use the last eight bits, minus two, 2^{8-2}, for host addressing, giving a decimal value of up to 254 hosts per Class C network.

IP Addressing Guidelines

Connecting a network to the Internet requires an authenticated and validated public IP address. Due to the scarcity of IPv4 addresses, organizations have little choice with regard to the network IDs they are assigned. When planning a TCP/IP enterprise, IP addressing guidelines become critical for effective communication by the networks that make up the enterprise. (An interesting article on IP address design can be found at **www.intel.com/technology/itj/q42000/articles/art_2.htm**.)

Several factors need to be considered when selecting addresses. For example, organizations should choose a class address that reflects not only the current size of the enterprise, but one that will also accommodate future expansion of the network. Each intranet within the organization must be given a unique, accurately documented network address. The larger the enterprise, the more important full and accurate documentation becomes.

Within a specific LAN or intranet, host addressing should be well thought out and planned. Each host within a LAN must have a unique address. Network administrators should be careful not to assign host addresses that are restricted, such as all zeros or all ones. Using particular ranges of host addresses that identify specific types of devices can also be beneficial; for example, having servers fall within one range of host address values and routers within a different range. Table 5.5 provides an example of the use of address ranges to identify host devices. Using the guidelines in Table 5.5, if an address ended in X.X.X.36, what type of device might it be?

Defining a Subnet Mask

Once an organization has been officially assigned a network IP address or a range of IP addresses, it will likely be the case that the address or addresses assigned do not provide enough unique network identifiers to

Table 5.5 Use of Address Ranges to Identify Types of Host Devices

IP Address	Type of Host
120.x.x.10 to 120.x.x.30	DCHP and DNS Servers fall into the range of .10 to .30
120.14.68.10	DHCP Server in the Accounting LAN
120.50.72.11	DHCP Server in the Marketing LAN
. . .	
120.32.01.29	DNS Server in the Corporate LAN
120.x.x.31 to 120.x.x.40	File and Print Servers fall into the range of .31 to .40
120.21.18.31	File Server in the Accounting LAN
120.101.02.32	File Server in the Marketing LAN
. . .	
120.16.122.40	Print Server in the Corporate LAN
120.x.x.41 to 120.x.x.50	Switches fall into the range of .41 to .50
120.12.133.41	Switch in the Accounting LAN
120.84.03.42	Switch in the Marketing LAN
. . .	
120.111.53.48	Switch in the Corporate LAN

support the needs of the organization. Assume that a business has only one authorized ICANN IP address, yet it needs five networks in its enterprise. In order to get five unique network addresses from a single network address, the single network address must be subdivided, or subnetted. For the subnetting to function correctly, an additional element must be defined. That additional element is a *subnet mask.*

A subnet mask acts like a filter. When an IP address is compared with its associated subnet mask, what is revealed or filtered out is the network portion and value of the IP address and the host portion and value of the IP address. This comparison process is done through a technique called **ANDing**. ANDing compares a host's IP address with a subnet mask and derives a result. ANDing an IP address to its subnet mask reveals network and host address values so that a sending host knows whether a receiving host is on the same or on a different network. If a receiver is on a different logical network than the sender, then routing must occur. A subnet mask helps to reveal whether routing is needed. Let's find out how this works by looking at the subnet mask in more depth.

A subnet mask, like an IP address, has 32 bits. The type of subnet mask used is based on the class of the IP address: Class A, B, or C. Each IP address class has a standard, or **default subnet mask**, defined. In the binary representation of the subnet mask, ones indicate the network portions and zeros indicate the host portions of the IP address. Table 5.6 shows the default subnet masks used for Class A, B, and C addresses.

An organization is generally given one IP address to use as its network identifier. Given the current status of IPv4, public IP addresses are particularly expensive and difficult to come by. For this reason, organizations that require multiple networks take their single IPv4 network IP address

Table 5.6 Default Subnet Masks for Class A, B, and C IP Addresses

Class	Subnet Mask in Decimal	Subnet Mask in Binary
A	255.0.0.0	11111111.00000000.00000000.00000000
B	255.255.0.0	11111111.11111111.00000000.00000000
C	255.255.255.0	11111111.11111111.11111111.00000000

and subdivide, or subnet, it. When businesses modify their allocated IP address, they must also modify its associated default subnet mask. Borrowing bits from the subnet's host portion allows for more network addresses to be accommodated. By extending the network portion of the subnet mask into the host portion, additional network or subnet identifiers can be created. However, this means that the default subnet mask will no longer work. Once reconfigured or modified, the same subnet mask must be used throughout the organization's entire enterprise.

Subnet Addressing

Borrowing bits from the host portion of an IP address in order to use those bits as part of a network identifier creates a subnet. Each network in the enterprise requires a unique identifier. If an organization's enterprise is completely private, meaning that it is not connected to the public Internet, then subnetting is not an issue. This is because the organization could use the full range of class addresses defined in the IPv4 TCP/IP protocol suite. However, this is usually not the case for most enterprise networks. For this reason, some degree of subnetting is generally required in order for the organization to use its public IP address to connect to the Internet.

Organizations that connect their enterprise network to the Internet by means of a proxy server or firewall can also independently allocate IP addressing on the private portion of their networks. A proxy server or firewall hides the internal structure of the private potion of the enterprise and provides mapping of incoming and outgoing packets to internal hosts. Figure 5.16 illustrates how a proxy server might be positioned. Proxy servers and firewalls are described in detail in a later chapter. For now, you only need to understand that most organizations use some form of subnetting, because the number of public IP addresses they have available to identify their networks are very limited. Eventually, the transition to IPv6 will eliminate this problem. Potentially, with IPv6, even your house or apartment could have its own public IP address.

Assume that ICANN has assigned an organization a Class B public network address of 156.101.0.0. However, the organization needs at least five network identifiers to support its current enterprise network configuration. Recall that the default subnet mask for a Class B address is 255.255.0.0, identifying the first two octets as network and the last two octets as host. The solution is to borrow high-order bits from the host portion of the standard subnet mask to create additional network identifier values. The number of high-order bits that will be borrowed depends on the number of network identifiers required.

The number of network identifiers available can be determined by a formula: $2^n - 2$, where n is the number of high-order bits borrowed. So, if three bits are borrowed, the formula would be $2^3 - 2$, giving a result of 6, which in this example is one more network identifier than required (remember, five are needed). The reason that two must be subtracted is

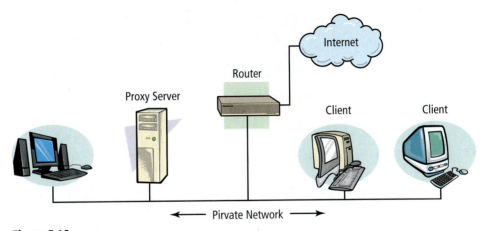

Figure 5.16

Use of a Proxy Server

In this example, the proxy server functions as a layer between individual clients on a private network and the outside world. The proxy allows the clients to be hidden from those outside the network.

that a network identifier cannot be all zeros or all ones, which eliminates two values. If only two bits had been borrowed from the host, the formula $(2^2 - 2)$ shows that there are only two usable network identifiers, too few for the organization's needs.

Borrowing high-order bits from the host requires that the subnet mask be modified to reflect the borrowed bits. Table 5.7 shows a standard Class B subnet mask and a Class B subnet mask with three high-order bits borrowed from the host.

In this example, note that, rather than $16 - 2$ bits available for host addressing, only $13 - 2$ bits are available. The two is subtracted because a host address of all ones or all zeros is not allowed.

With the three bits borrowed from the host to make up network identifiers, the following bit network combinations are available: 000, 001, 010, 011, 100, 101, 110, and 111. There are only eight ways to put a combination of three binary zeroes and ones together. Of these eight, only six can be used because a network identifier of all zeros, 000, or all ones, 111, is not allowed. Also, recall that the three bits borrowed were the *high-order bits* of the host octet, and these high-order bits will have corresponding high-order decimal values. Table 5.8 shows the range of network identifier values in binary and decimal that are available based on the new subnet mask configuration. Note that the high-order three bits in the byte are separated out to illustrate where they are located. Their high-order location determines their equivalent decimal value.

Table 5.7 Class B Subnet Mask with Three Bits Borrowed	
Standard Class B Subnet Mask in Binary	**The Same Standard Class B Subnet Mask in Decimal**
11111111.11111111.00000000.00000000	255.255.0.0
Class B Subnet Mask with Three Bits Borrowed in Binary	**The Same Class B Subnet Mask with Three Bits Borrowed in Decimal**
11111111.11111111.11100000.00000000	255.255.224.0

Table 5.8	Network Identifiers Available with Three High-order Bits Borrowed for Original IP Address of 156.101.0.0	
Binary		**Decimal**
001 00000		32
010 00000		64
011 00000		96
100 00000		128
101 00000		160
110 00000		192

The following unique network identifier addresses are now available for use in the private portion of the enterprise: 156.101.32.0, 156.101.64.0, 156.101.96.0, 156.101.128.0, 156.101.160.0, and 156.101.192.0. Each of these addresses is now a potential subnet. Of course, these additional subnets were gained at the cost of having fewer host identifiers available. The new subnet mask must now also be configured for all hosts in the enterprise. Using this subnet mask, a TCP/IP host, by means of ANDing, can now determine whether the intended recipient of an IP packet is on the same logical network or on a remote network. By comparing a host address to the subnet mask, ANDing can determine whether two hosts are on the same local network. ANDing uses a comparative process and is a very interesting topic. For those who want to know more about ANDing and exactly how it works, please see the "Topic in Focus" at the end of this chapter.

Setting up an IP addressing scheme by means of subnetting and subnet masking is crucial. One of your jobs as a network administrator may be to design just such an addressing scheme or to modify one already in place. Understanding why a business would want to subnet helps a great deal in understanding how to subnet. The reality is that while IPv4 is in wide-scale use, subnetting and subnet masking are going to be required.

Supernetting

Although many organizations choose to subnet their IP address, IP addresses can also be combined or aggregated in a process called *supernetting*. **Supernetting** borrows bits from the network, rather than from the host (i.e., subnetting), in order to create additional networks. An organization might use supernetting when it has several Class C IP addresses, none of which allow a sufficient number of hosts for the desired network. Remember that a Class C address only allows for a maximum of 254 hosts in the network.

Assume you work for an organization that has four Class C addresses at its disposal. Also assume that your organization must have more than 254 hosts in its particular network. Yet, with a Class C address, you are limited to just 254 hosts. Do you give up and tell your boss the company is out of luck? No, instead you recommend supernetting, using supernet masking, and get that big raise and promotion you well deserve.

With supernetting, several IP addresses are in effect combined, or masked, to appear as one network that has a larger number of hosts.

Rather then implementing supernetting with a subnet mask, a supernet mask can be used instead. A supernet mask works in just the opposite way of a subnet mask. Instead of borrowing bits from the host and making the borrowed bits ones, bits are borrowed from the network portion of the mask and made into zeroes.

Supernetting is a function of **Classless Inter-Domain Routing (CIDR)**. The benefit of CIDR is that it reduces the size of the routing tables used by the routers on the Internet backbone. By reducing the size of the routing tables, faster lookup, and, in turn, access, can be achieved. By using a group of Class C addresses, CIDR provides for the aggregation of multiple routes to a particular organization. For example, consider an organization with four Class C addresses. All four addresses would have to be provided for in Internet backbone router tables. By using CIDR aggregation, only one entry in the router table would be required, not four. For one business, this may not seem like much, but what if this were done for 20,000 or more businesses? Suddenly the issue of routing table maintenance has become much more complicated. However, CIDR requires a contiguous set of network identifiers and does not work well with all routers, so caution should be used in its implementation. For a good discussion on CIDR, see **public.pacbell.net/dedicated/cidr.html**.

TCP/IP has become a very popular networking model not only for WANs, but for LANs as well. With TCP/IP, both networks and devices, called hosts, have addresses. The use of these addresses enables communication within a LAN and across an enterprise, which is the collection of all the networks owned by a single organization. These addresses have a specific binary format that has a decimal equivalent. With IPv4, addresses are based on a 32-bit, 4-byte octet. Each octet contains eight bits. When these four bytes, anchored with dots, are converted to decimal, the result is referred to as dotted-decimal notation.

IP addresses are categorized into five specific classes: A, B, C, D, and E. Of the five, Classes D and E are reserved for special use. Classes A, B, and C are used in public networks and for Internet connections. If an IP address will be used for public purposes, it must be officially authorized by ICANN. ICANN is the managing body that controls the allocation of IP addresses, although ICANN works with commercial vendors in fulfilling its responsibilities. Due to their scarcity, most businesses lease IP addresses from ISPs.

The type of IP address class determines the number of networks and hosts that can be supported on a network. Each class uses specific octets to identify the network and host portions of an IP address.

Subnet masks are used to filter the network and host components from an IP address. Each IP class has a standard default subnet mask: ones indicate network components, zeros indicate host components. Standard subnet masks are frequently modified to accommodate subnetting, which is the subdividing of a single IP address into multiple addresses.

Because most organizations require more than one unique network identifier for the enterprise, public IP addresses are often subnetted. With subnetting, an organization can subdivide one network address into multiple network addresses. Such subnetted addresses are used for internal communications within the enterprise. Subnetting uses a common subnet mask for the entire organization. The subnet mask differs from the standard mask in that bits from the host portion of the subnet mask are borrowed to create additional network address identifiers. Based on organizational needs, the number of bits borrowed can vary, which in turn affects the number of network identifiers available. Borrowing bits from the host will result in fewer host addresses being available. These are among the considerations that should be understood when planning a subnetwork architecture.

In contrast to subnetting, supernetting aggregates network addresses. But, like a subnet, a supernet also requires a mask, called a supernet mask. The supernet mask borrows bits from the network, rather than the host.

Address classes **(190)**

Address Resolution Protocol (ARP) **(173)**

ANDing **(193)**

Application layer **(181)**

Binary numbering **(189)**

Bit **(189)**

Byte **(189)**

Classless Inter-Domain Routing (CIDR) **(197)**

Connectionless **(179)**

Connection oriented **(178)**

Datagram **(175)**

Default subnet mask **(193)**

Dotted-decimal notation **(189)**

Enterprise **(173)**

Extranet **(190)**

File Transfer Protocol (FTP) **(181)**

Host **(185)**

Hypertext Transfer Protocol (HTTP) **(184)**

Internet Corporation for Assigned Names and Number (ICANN) **(189)**

Internet Control Message Protocol (ICMP) **(177)**

Internet Group Message Protocol (IGMP) **(177)**

Internet Message Access Protocol (IMAP) **(183)**

Intranet **(190)**

IP address **(173)**

Logical address **(173)**

Mail transfer agent (MTA) **(183)**

Management Information Base (MIB) **(183)**

Multicasting **(177)**

Network layer **(173)**

Octet **(189)**

Physical address **(173)**

Post Office Protocol Version 3 (POP3) **(183)**

Request for Comments (RFCs) **(179)**

Reverse Address Resolution Protocol (RARP) **(174)**

Simple Mail Transfer Protocol (SMTP) **(183)**

Simple Network Management Protocol (SNMP) **(183)**

Subnet mask **(187)**

Subnetting **(187)**

Supernetting **(196)**

Telnet **(181)**

Transmission Control Protocol (TCP) **(178)**

Transport layer **(178)**

Unicasting **(177)**

Unreliable **(179)**

User agent (UA) **(183)**

User Datagram Protocol (UDP) **(179)**

Short Answer

1. What is the function of ARP? Why is it used?
2. How does TCP differ from UDP?
3. Under what circumstances might UDP be preferred over TCP, if ever?
4. What purpose does a subnet mask serve?
5. For the first octet, identify the default decimal range of values for Class A, B, and C addresses.

Multiple Choice

For each of the following select the one best answer.

1. How many octets does an IPv4 address have?
   a. 2 **b.** 4 **c.** 8 **d.** 16

2. How many bits are in an octet?
   a. 2 **b.** 4 **c.** 8 **d.** 16

3. How many octets does a Class A address use for network identification?
   a. 1 **b.** 2 **c.** 3 **d.** 4

4. How many octets does a Class B address use for host identification?
   a. 1 **b.** 2 **c.** 3 **d.** 4

5. Which term describes the subdivision of a single network identifier?
   a. Subletting **b.** Netting **c.** Subnetting **d.** Subleasing

6. Which of the following is the organization that manages the allocation of IP addresses?
   a. ICN **b.** ICAN **c.** ICANN **d.** CANN

7. What is the minimum number of bits that must be borrowed if three additional network identifiers are required?
   a. 1 **b.** 2 **c.** 3 **d.** 4

8. Which of the following compares a subnet mask with an IP address?
   a. BINDing **b.** ANDing **c.** COMPing **d.** SUBing

9. How many different values can a bit have?
   a. 1 **b.** 2 **c.** 4 **d.** 8

10. How many bits are in a byte?
    a. 4 **b.** 8 **c.** 16 **d.** 32

11. Which formula determines the decimal value for each bit position in an octet?
    a. 2^{n-1} **b.** 2^{n-2} **c.** 2^n **d.** $n-1$

12. Which IP address class does 128.16.201.84 fall under?

    a. A **b.** B **c.** C **d.** D

13. Which IP address class does 198.101.16.23 fall under?

    a. A **b.** B **c.** C **d.** D

14. Which octet in a Class C address denotes the host?

    a. First octet **b.** Second octet **c.** Third octet **d.** Fourth octet

15. How many usable networks are available with the Class A set of IP addresses?

    a. 126 **b.** 127 **c.** 255 **d.** 360

16. Which layer is at the top of the TCP/IP model?

    a. Network **b.** Data link **c.** Application **d.** Transport

17. Which TCP/IP layer uses the TCP and UDP protocols?

    a. Network **b.** Data link **c.** Application **d.** Transport

18. Which TCP/IP layer uses the ARP and RARP protocols?

    a. Network **b.** Data link **c.** Application **d.** Transport

19. Which protocol supports IP in error reporting?

    a. ICMP **b.** IMPC **c.** IMGP **d.** IGMP

20. Which protocol supports IP in multicasting?

    a. ICMP **b.** IMPC **c.** IMGP **d.** IGMP

21. Which of the following is a popular protocol for copying files from one host to another?

    a. TFP **b.** PTF **c.** FTP **d.** FPT

22. Which protocol is used to support e-mail servers?

    a. SNPM **b.** SMTP **c.** SPTM **d.** SMPN

23. Which protocol provides simple network management functions?

    a. SNPM **b.** SMTP **c.** SPTM **d.** SMPN

24. Which protocol uses MTAs?

    a. SNPM **b.** SMTP **c.** SPTM **d.** SMPN

25. Which protocol enables remote logins to a computer?

    a. Lognet **b.** Tellog **c.** Nettel **d.** Telnet

26. What type of network can TCP/IP be configured for?

    a. LAN **b.** MAN **c.** WAN **d.** All the above

27. Which TCP/IP layer is below the application layer?

    a. Presentation **b.** Network **c.** Transport **d.** Data link

28. Which TCP/IP layer is above the network layer?

    a. Transport **b.** Application **c.** Data link **d.** Presentation

29. Which TCP/IP layer provides the highest-layer services?

    a. Data link **b.** Network **c.** Application **d.** Transport

30. What is the function of ARP?

    a. It resolves a logical IP address to a physical address.

    b. It resolves a physical address to a logical address.

    c. Neither a nor b

    d. Either a or b

31. What is the function of RARP?

    a. It resolves a logical IP address to a physical address.
    b. It resolves a physical address to a logical address.
    c. Neither a nor b
    d. Either a or b

32. ARP is bundled with which of the following?

    a. Transport services **b.** RARP **c.** Telnet **d.** IP

33. How many types of errors can ICMP detect?

    a. Many **b.** 2 **c.** 5 **d.** It depends

34. Which of the following is true of ICMP?

    a. It reports and correct errors.
    b. It only correct errors.
    c. It reports but does not correct errors.
    d. Depending on the error, it may report or correct errors.

35. Which protocol is used if multicasting is required?

    a. ARP **b.** RARP **c.** ICMP **d.** IGMP

36. Which of the following is a transport layer protocol?

    a. ICMP **b.** UDP **c.** IGMP **d.** RARP

37. Which statement best describes TCP?

    a. It is connectionless and reliable.
    b. It is connection oriented but unreliable.
    c. It is connection oriented and reliable.
    d. It is connectionless and unreliable.

38. Which statement best describes UDP?

    a. It is connectionless and reliable.
    b. It is connection oriented but unreliable.
    c. It is connection oriented and reliable.
    d. It is connectionless and unreliable.

39. Which transport layer protocol is preferred for large messages with many data packets?

    a. ICMP **b.** IGMP **c.** TCP **d.** UDP

40. Which transport layer protocol is preferred for small, noncritical data packets?

    a. ICMP **b.** IGMP **c.** TCP **d.** UDP

41. In a TCP delivery, multiple packets from the same message

    a. always take different routes from sender to receiver.
    b. always take the same route from sender to receiver.
    c. may or may not take the same route from sender to receiver.
    d. Packet delivery is not an issue related to TCP.

42. In a UDP delivery, two packets from two different messages

    a. always take different routes from sender to receiver.
    b. always take the same route from sender to receiver.
    c. may or may not take the same route from sender to receiver.
    d. Packet delivery is not a issue related to UDP.

43. Where might a diskless computer's physical address be stored?

    a. ROM **b.** RAM **c.** Hard drive **d.** Cache

44. What is an advantage of using diskless computers?

  a. Reduced cost   **b.** Increased security
  c. Less susceptibility to malicious programs   **d.** All the above

45. A client using SMTP must be configured with which of the following?

  a. A user alias   **b.** An agent   **c.** A user agent   **d.** A user transfer

46. POP3 is a common type of

  a. ICMP server.   **b.** SNMP server.   **c.** IMAP server.   **d.** SMTP server.

47. Which of the following is true of all hosts on the same logical network?

  a. They all have the same logical network address.
  b. They may or may not have the same logical network address.
  c. They never have the same logical network address.
  d. They do not have a logical network address, only a host address.

48. Which of the following is true of SMTP and POP3 servers?

  a. A single physical device can be both an SMTP and a POP3 server.
  b. A single physical device can never be both an SMTP and a POP3 server.
  c. SMTP and POP3 have nothing to do with servers.
  d. Two physical devices are required to run both services.

49. Which three bits can be used to determine an IP address's class?

  a. Low-order bits of the right-most octet
  b. Low-order bits of the left-most octet
  c. High-order bits of the right-most octet
  d. High-order bits of the left-most octet

50. What type of mask would be used in supernetting?

  a. Subnet   **b.** Supernet   **c.** Either a or b   **d.** Neither a nor b

True or False

For each of the following select either True or False.

1. TCP/IP was originally designed as a network model for small-scale networks.

2. A protocol is a set of rules or procedures that specify how something works.

3. A diskless computer can use RARP to discover its IP address.

4. IGMP is used when multicasting is required.

5. Logical IP addresses can be modified.

6. By itself, IP has several error-correcting controls.

7. In a typical TCP/IP network, multicasting is more common than unicasting.

8. TCP has less overhead than UDP.

9. UDP does not provide for flow control.

10. Many protocols at the application layer function in a client/server model.

11. When using HTTP, the client uses a browser application.

12. An octet contains eight bytes.

13. Dotted-decimal notation refers to the binary notation of an IP address.

14. Each device connected to a TCP/IP network can be referred to as a host.

15. SMTP has three components.

16. SNMP makes use of the MIB of each agent device.

17. Different subnet masks are typically used within the networks of a single enterprise.

18. In decimal notation, the highest numeric value that an octet can contain is 256.

19. Subdividing a single network address is done through a process called subnetting.

20. With supernetting, bits are borrowed from the host portion of the IP address.

Exercises

Research in Brief

For one or more of the questions below, provide a one- to two-page report based on your findings.

1. Why might an organization choose to subnet?

2. Make up a Class B subnet address. Define its standard subnet mask. Then define a modified subnet mask that will allow for a minimum of four additional networks. How many bits were borrowed? What ranges of values in binary and decimal might the new networks take?

3. The Domain Name System (DNS) is a critical application layer protocol that was not explored in this chapter. Research and report back on the elements that define the DNS.

4. How can IP class addresses be differentiated?

Case Study

Sheehan Marketing and Public Relations

The following network IP addresses have been authorized for use by SMPR:

Los Angeles: 195.017.121.0
New York: 201.162.24.0
Chicago: 205.110.37.0

You have decided to develop an IP addressing scheme that will identify different types of devices: clients, servers, switches, printers, routers, and so on. Prepare a memo that outlines your addressing scheme for each branch office. Explain your reasoning for the scheme you have chosen.

You have also determined that the Los Angeles office could benefit by subnetting its single network into two networks. One network will host the organization's financial and business operations, such as payroll, accounts receivable, and the customer database. The second network will be used by the general staff. Provide an analysis that details such factors as the bits borrowed, the network addresses available, subnet masking, and so on.

Finally, over the past few weeks you have been working more closely with Karla. She is confused over how the subnetting process works and has asked you to explain it to her. In your own words, write a narrative description for Karla on the subnetting process that describes why it is used and how it is implemented.

Web References

www.isoc.org/internet/history

whatis.techtarget.com

www.faqs.org/rfcs/rfc793.html

www.rfc-editor.org

www.faqs.org/rfcs/rfc793.html

www.digitalconsumer.org

www.loc.gov/copyright/legislation/dmca.pdf

www.ipswitch.com

www.howstuffworks.com/email.htm

ftp.ics.uci.edu/pub/ietf/http

www.ezine.com/EZInternet.SubNet.html

www.iana.org/assignments/ipv4-address-space

www.intel.com/technology/itj/q42000/articles/art_2.htm

public.pacbell.net/dedicated/cidr.html

How ANDing Works

ANDing is a relatively simple mathematical process that compares a given host's IP address with its subnet mask in binary form. As a host initializes (i.e., when it is turned on), ANDing occurs. The result of the ANDing is stored in the host's memory. Each of the 32 bits of a given IP address is compared with its corresponding bit in the subnet mask. If any two corresponding bits are both one, the result is a one; any other combination of corresponding bits, zero and one, one and zero, or zero and zero, results in a zero.

Stored in the host computer's memory, the ANDed result can be used by the host to determine its own network identifier address. When the same host needs to send an IP packet to another host, the destination host's IP address is ANDed with the subnet mask. This result is then compared with the sending host's previously ANDed result that is still stored in memory. If the network identifier addresses are the same, the two hosts are on the same logical network; if not, the destination host is on a remote network, and the IP packet will need to be routed to its proper network.

The following example assumes a Class C network address of 224.16.128.0. The address is subnetted by borrowing three bits from the host octet, which gives six additional network subnet values:

> 224.16.128.32
>
> 224.16.128.64
>
> 224.16.128.96
>
> 224.16.128.128
>
> 224.16.128.160
>
> 224.16.128.192

So far, only the first three values are used: the network identifiers ending in 32, 64, and 96. A host with an IP address of 224.16.128.33 wants to send an IP packet first to host 224.16.128.60 and then to host 224.16.128.66. Are these hosts all on the same logical network? ANDing will reveal the answer. Table 5.9 contains the results of three ANDing processes: the initial host's ANDing and then the ANDing of the two hosts it wants to communicate with.

What some find confusing is that in IP subnet addressing, the address has both the network ID and the host ID embedded within it. In our example, because of how the subnet mask was set up, the IP address 224.16.128.33 reveals that this address is for network 224.16.128.32 and host 1. Thus, the last octet value of 33 really contains information on two things: the network and the host ID. The same is true, of course, for the other two addresses. For the first receiver, the last octet value of 60 after ANDing reveals network 32 and host 68. For the second receiver, the last octet value of 66 after ANDing reveals network 64 and host 2. At first it may not be clear whether two IP addresses are on the same network. By deriving the network address identifier, ANDing resolves that question.

Table 5.9 Three ANDing Results

	Decimal IP	Network Binary IP	Host Binary	Host Decimal
IP address of sending host	224.16.128.33	10100000.00010000.1000000.001	00001	1
Subnet mask	255.255.255.224	11111111.11111111.11111111.111	00000	
Initial ANDing	224.16.128.32	10100000.00010000.1000000.001	00000	

This is host 1 on network 224.16.128.32.

	Decimal IP	Network Binary IP	Host Binary	Host Decimal
IP address of first receiver	224.16.128.60	10100000.00010000.1000000.001	11100	28
Subnet mask	255.255.255.224	11111111.11111111.11111111.111	00000	
Second ANDing	224.16.128.32	10100000.00010000.10000000.001	00000	

This is host 28 on network 224.16.128.32—a local host.

	Decimal IP	Network Binary IP	Host Binary	Host Decimal
IP address of second receiver	224.16.128.66	10100000.00010000.10000000.010	00010	2
Subnet mask	255.255.255.224	11111111.11111111.11111111.111	00000	
Third ANDing	224.16.128.64	10100000.00010000.1000000.010	00000	

This is host 2 on network 224.16.128.64—a remote host.

Note: For the addresses above, note that the fourth and last octet is, for purposes of illustration, divided into two portions. In the first portion, the three high order bits have been subnetted and given over the network identification. In the second portion, the five low order bits are used for host identification. Here we see an example of how an 8-bit octet, through subnetting, uses some of its bits for network, and some for host identification.

6

chaptersix

Backbone and Metropolitan Area Network Fundamentals

Learning Objectives

After studying this chapter, you should be able to:

- Describe BNs and MANs.
- Understand the term horizontal network.
- Understand the term vertical network.
- Explain what is meant by a backbone protocol.
- Identify two forms of backbone architecture: distributed and collapsed.
- Explain when particular backbone architectures may be appropriate.
- Understand the purpose of backbone fault tolerance.
- Describe simple backbone design considerations.
- Differentiate between wiring closets and data centers.
- Identify basic backbone problems.
- Understand the use of ping as a diagnostic tool.
- Know the purpose of Switched Multimegabit Data Services (SMDS).

In Chapter 5, you learned that each network in an organization's enterprise requires a logical address. The organization will very likely want the various networks in the enterprise to communicate and share resources with each other. To accomplish such sharing and communication, the networks of the enterprise must be connected in some way. This chapter explores how networks in the enterprise are connected to each other. Specifically, this chapter presents BN and MAN technologies, with an emphasis on BNs.

Backbone Networks and Metropolitan Area Networks

A small organization might have only one LAN; larger organizations may have dozens or hundreds of LANs. Organizations with multiple LANs will want these LANs to communicate with each other, not only to share physical resources, such as printers, but data, information, authentication, and software as well. Connecting all of the LANs of an organization entails another type of network, a **backbone network (BN)**. When properly designed, a BN provides a high-speed circuit that serves as the central conduit across which the LANs of an organization can communicate. (A good, concise article on network design best practices can be found at **www.more.net/technical/research/network/bestpractices/netdesign-bestpractices-print.pdf**. Although not specifically about BNs, the topics addressed by the article are still highly relevant.)

Not surprisingly, BNs have their own issues and topics of interest. BNs can be used to connect LANs within a building, across a campus, and, increasingly, across much greater distances. An organization might also utilize a **metropolitan area network (MAN)**. A MAN spans a city and is often used to connect remote BNs. In a very real sense, a MAN is a citywide backbone. In fact, as backbone technologies have evolved, and as the geographic distances they cover have increased, especially with the use of fiber-optics, it is becoming increasing difficult to determine whether a particular network is a BN, a MAN, or even a WAN.

Today, BNs connect networks between floors of a building, across a city, or between states and countries. Because of the importance of BNs to data communications, the emphasis in this chapter is on BNs. However, much of the information presented holds true for a MAN as well. The terms BN and MAN are sometimes used interchangeably, based on the scope of the BN.

Network Segments

Each individual LAN owned by an organization is a **network segment**. A moderate- to large-scale organization might have a network segment on each floor of a multistory building. Because each network segment, or LAN, typically occupies its own floor, this type of network segment is often referred to as a **horizontal network**. For example, assume that a business occupies three floors of a building. On each floor is a separate LAN, or horizontal network segment. In addition, each of these LANs could, and probably would, be connected to each other by a BN. This type of multifloor connection is an example of a **vertical network**. The BN in this instance is the central connecting cable running vertically from floor to floor that enables the horizontal networks to communicate with each other. Figure 6.1 compares a horizontal network with a vertical one.

A BN, as indicated by its name, is a network of its own. Besides connecting the various network segments, the backbone may have its own devices that can be accessed by other network segments. Later in the chapter you will see how this might work.

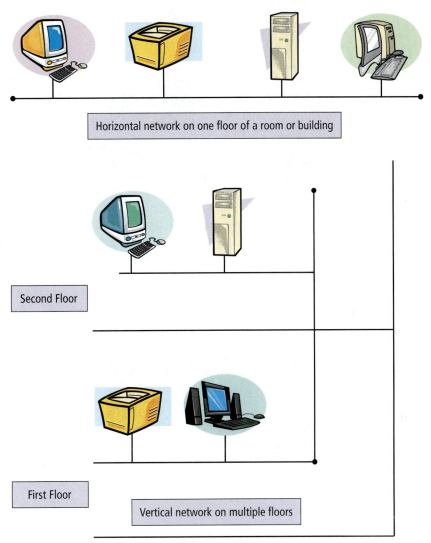

Horizontal network on one floor of a room or building

Second Floor

First Floor

Vertical network on multiple floors

Figure 6.1
Simple Horizontal Network Versus a Vertical Network

This configuration, with LANs on different floors of a building connected vertically, is fairly common. However, it may be the case that the network segments are housed in a large, single-story warehouse such that each network segment is on the same horizontal plane. In this case, the BN that connects the LANs together, rather than being vertical, is also horizontal. The physical facility in which the networks are housed determines how the BN is configured.

Part of configuration analysis includes determining how each network segment connects to the BN. Generally, each network segment is connected to the BN using either a switch or a router. Figure 6.2 shows an example of how a switch and router might be used to connect LANs to a backbone. Switches and routers enable a host on one LAN to communicate with a host on any other LAN that is connected to the backbone. The choice of which connecting device to use—switch or router—depends on how the network is to be used. Because routers are typically far more expensive than switches, part of the BN configuration analysis includes determining whether the right device is in the most effective location. However, one of the first decisions to be made regarding a BN is deciding which type of BN protocol to use.

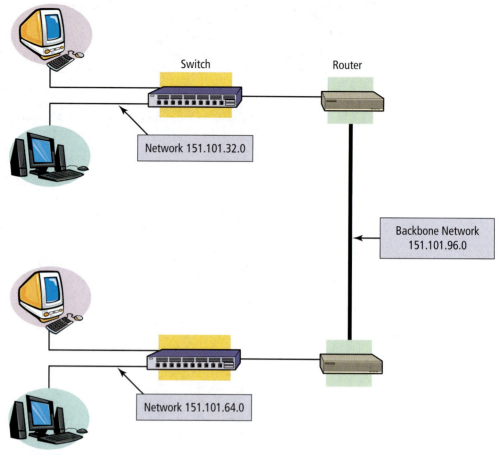

Figure 6.2
Switch and Router Connecting to a BN

Backbone Protocols

Of the many factors that will influence your decision as to which BN protocol to use, one key factor stands out: What are the traffic demands of the network segments to be supported? For example, are the various LANs connected to the backbone in constant communication with each other? Or, do the individual network segments work mostly independently of each other?

In the first case, the BN needs to support high traffic demand. This means that the BN protocol selected should support higher throughput than the protocol used by the LANs. Assume that all of the network segments connected to the backbone use Fast Ethernet and that the network segments communicate extensively with each other. If the backbone is going to adequately support this amount of traffic, it will need a protocol that offers a faster throughput than Fast Ethernet. A logical choice would be to run the BN using Gigabit Ethernet.

In fact, **Gigabit Ethernet** is a very popular choice for BNs. The IEEE's initial standard for Gigabit Ethernet is the 802.3z standard. Gigabit Ethernet allows for a data rate of 1,000 Mbps, or 1 Gbps. A major advantage of all of the officially recognized forms of Gigabit Ethernet is that each form builds on the standards of the preexisting Ethernet protocol. This means that the MAC layer and access method for Gigabit Ethernet are the same as those for standard and Fast Ethernet. Additionally, Gigabit Ethernet supports both half- and full-duplex communications. For those who want to know more about this important technology, see the" "Topic in Focus" at the end of this chapter.

In the second case, assume that most traffic is confined within the individual network segments and rarely traverses the backbone. This means that the backbone has relatively little traffic. In such a case, the backbone does not require a faster, and more expensive, protocol to support the needs of the enterprise. Supposing again that the LAN segments are using Fast Ethernet, there is no reason why Fast Ethernet cannot also be used for the backbone. Using the same protocol for the LANs and the BN results in lower cost and easier configuration, with little, if any, negative impact on organizational communications.

As mentioned earlier, Gigabit Ethernet is one of the most popular protocols for backbones. One of the reasons for its popularity is the wide installation base of standard and Fast Ethernet. For this reason, Gigabit Ethernet has become the leading **backbone protocol**. Other protocols that might be used for a backbone include **Frame Relay (FR)** and **Asynchronous Transfer Mode (ATM)**. Frame Relay and ATM are also frequently associated with WANs. As such, discussion of Frame Relay and ATM will be reserved for Chapter 7, which focuses on WANs.

Backbone Architectures

Like any networking technology, BNs have a **backbone architecture**, or manner in which they are constructed. The two most common BN architectures are distributed and collapsed. Factors that influence a business's decision as to which architecture to use include business needs, the condition of the physical facility (sometimes called the plant or campus), how users need to communicate, and the budget. The larger and more complex the organization, the more critical the decision becomes as to what type of backbone architecture to use. It can be very costly to change an existing backbone architecture once one has been put in place.

Distributed Backbones

The word *distributed* means "in more than one location." A **distributed backbone** is one that runs throughout the entire enterprise. This type of backbone uses a central cable to which the network segments are connected. The central cable, which is the backbone, requires its own protocol, such as Gigabit Ethernet; it is also its own network. The backbone is considered to be distributed because each network segment has its own cabled connection to the backbone. The backbone is distributed to the LANs by connecting the LANs to the backbone.

LANs may be connected to the backbone by either switches or routers. Other devices, such as servers, can also be attached to the backbone. A server connected directly to a backbone is part of that backbone's network; it is not part of one of the LANs connected to the backbone. Shortly you will see why having certain types of servers, or other devices, directly connected to the distributed backbone cable is a good idea. Figure 6.3 illustrates a simple distributed backbone.

A distributed backbone typically has separate routers that connect each logical network to the backbone. Because separate routers are used, internetwork traffic may have to pass through several routers to reach its destination. The more routers a packet has to pass through, and the

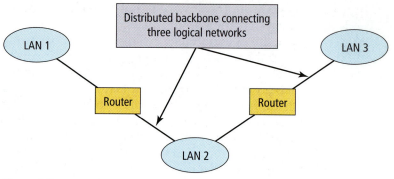

Figure 6.3
Simple Distributed Backbone

greater the internetwork traffic, the more likely communications will be delayed. Additionally, because each network segment has its own cabling and connecting device to the backbone, distributed networks can be costly. Security, maintenance, and monitoring of a distributed backbone are also complicated because connecting resources are distributed.

However, depending on the layout of the enterprise, a distributed backbone may be the only practical solution. For example, it may be that the distance of the network segments from the backbone to which they must be connected is too great for a copper cable to support. In this case, a collapsed backbone, discussed shortly, is not possible, and a distributed one will have to be deployed.

One advantage of a distributed backbone is that it allows resources required by most, if not all, internetworking users to be placed directly on the BN. Assume that an organization has a customer database server located on LAN A that is to be used by all of the other network segments. If for some reason LAN A becomes unavailable, perhaps the room in which LAN A is housed has a power failure, then the customer database server is unavailable to the entire organization. Even if LAN A remains available, because it has the database server, all internetwork traffic for that database server goes to LAN A, which may become overwhelmed by the resulting traffic. The result is that no one gets access to the server.

A better solution would be to put resources required by most network segments on the backbone network itself, as shown in Figure 6.4. In this example, the database server is placed directly on the backbone. Usually, the backbone has a higher bandwidth capacity than the networks connected to it, allowing for a faster and more reliable response. Such a scenario is possible on a distributed backbone, but not on a collapsed one. The following text describes why this is so.

Collapsed Backbones

Essentially, a **collapsed backbone** connects all of the network segments to a central, single router or switch. This central device is, in effect, the backbone. The network segments typically connect to the central backbone device by means of a hub, switch, or router. Because only a single, central backbone device is used, cabling is greatly reduced. Furthermore, additional connecting devices are not required. A collapsed backbone can result in significant cost savings. Also, because the collapsed backbone is a device and does not use a central cable, as does a distributed backbone, a separate protocol for the backbone is not required. This means, for

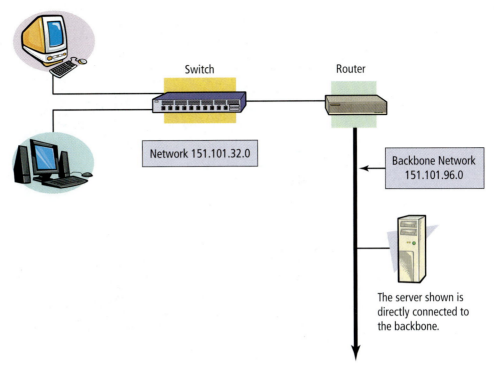

Switch   Router

Network 151.101.32.0

Backbone Network
151.101.96.0

The server shown is
directly connected to
the backbone.

Figure 6.4
Database Server Directly Connected to Backbone

example, that a collection of Fast Ethernet network segments could connect to a Fast Ethernet-based switch or router. A collapsed backbone's central connecting router or switch makes use of something called a *backplane*.

A **backplane** is an internal, high-speed communications bus that is used in place of the connecting cables found in a distributed backbone. A **communication bus** is like a highway that enables components and devices to transmit data between themselves, and thereby communicate. The hubs, switches, and routers of the organization's network segments plug directly into the collapsed backbone's backplane. In a typical configuration, the hubs and switches of a collection of 100Base-TX copper-based network segments are connected to a 100Base-FX switch or router by fiber-optic cabling. The switch or router then routes the traffic between the various network segments. Figure 6.5 shows a simple collapsed backbone.

Because fiber-optic cabling is used to connect network segments to the collapsed backbone's backplane, long distances are possible. With fiber-optic cabling, network segments may be widely scattered across a building or even a campus. Legacy Ethernet networks, however, may not be able to utilize a collapsed backbone architecture. Remember that the term *legacy* describes older technologies that are still in use and that must still be supported. An organization may have several legacy Ethernet 10-Mbps networks that use older media such as Category 3 UTP or Thin Ethernet cabling. These types of media cannot support long cable runs to a distantly located collapsed backbone device. If the legacy network segments are in different buildings, the problem of connecting to a central collapsed backbone only increases. One solution to this problem would be to upgrade legacy networks to current standards. An alternative solution would be to use a distributed backbone. Either option should be evaluated with a cost-benefit analysis. A factor in this analysis should be the future

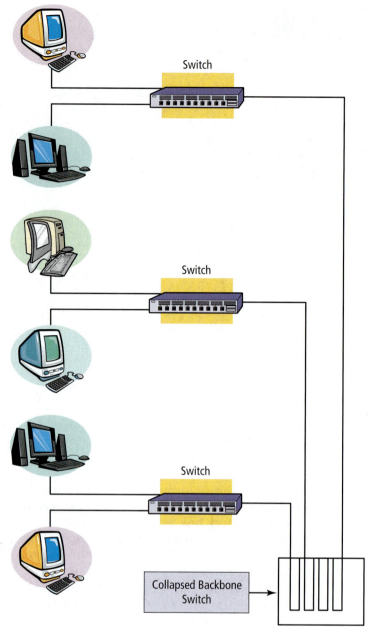

Figure 6.5
Simple Collapsed Backbone

needs of the organization. Keep in mind that the wiring, configuration, and installation of network cabling is one of the most significant costs a business incurs. However, this cost can be depreciated over time. Different options will afford different breakeven time lines.

A major advantage of a collapsed backbone configuration is that inter-network traffic has to pass through only one device, usually a router, on its way to its final destination. However, each hub or switch for each net-work segment must be able to span the distance to the central router, or collapsed backbone. Another benefit is that because a collapsed backbone is centralized, security, monitoring, and maintenance are much easier than with a distributed backbone. For newer networks, or those with few, if any, legacy segments, a collapsed backbone can be a cost-effective and efficient means of providing internetworking connectivity. Table 6.1

Table 6.1 Advantages and Disadvantages of Distributed and Collapsed Backbones

Backbone Architecture	Advantages	Disadvantages
Distributed	Devices can be placed directly on the backbone	Increased cabling costs
	Usually offers a higher bandwidth capacity	Complex to manage due to distribution
	Can support legacy Ethernet networks	Cabling may not support long distances between networks and the backbone
	Well suited for networks that may be widely separated from each other	Internetwork traffic may need to pass through several intermediary devices
Collapsed	Reduced cabling costs	Devices cannot be placed directly on the backbone
	Easier to manage due to centralization	Does not support legacy Ethernet networks
	Fiber-optic cabling allows for long distances between networks and backbone	Not well suited for networks that are widely separated from each other
	Internetwork traffic only needs to pass through one intermediary device	Hubs and switches must be able to span distance to a distant backbone

compares the advantages and disadvantages of distributed and collapsed backbones.

Regardless of the type of backbone architecture selected, backbone fault tolerance must be provided for. Without the backbone, network segments have no means of communicating and sharing resources with each other. The following text considers fault tolerance and how the enterprise can be secured against a potential backbone failure.

Backbone Fault Tolerance

An organization's backbone allows the various segments of the enterprise to communicate and share resources with each other. Should the backbone fail for some reason, internetworking may no longer be possible. In such an event, business could come to a standstill and, depending on the recovery time, irreparable damage may occur. However, if fault tolerance has been built into the backbone, internetworking will likely still be possible. **Fault tolerance** is the capability of a technology to recover in the event of error, failure, or some other unexpected event that disrupts organizational communications and functions. Part of a network administrator's job is to prepare for future network catastrophes. When designing backbone architectures, a network administrator can do several things to ensure adequate fault tolerance.

Many network administrators provide a level of fault tolerance by allowing for redundancy of critical resources in their network design. Duplicating a networked resource creates **redundancy**. Such a resource may be either software or hardware. By duplicating a resource, should one of them fail, the other is probably still going to be available. The more critical the resource, the more redundancy that should be implemented. For example, if a given network segment is particularly critical for internetworking communications, the network administrator may decide to use two routers on that network segment to connect it to the backbone. In that way, should one router fail, the functioning router can still route data to and from that segment. In addition to routers and switches, important servers may also be duplicated. If all of the network segments use e-mail, the network administrator may not only place the e-mail server on the distributed backbone, but also provide two or more such e-mail servers in the event that one should fail. Redundancy is a simple way of providing for fault tolerance; however, it does result in higher costs and maintenance.

For those organizations in which the backbone is particularly critical, meaning that failure of the backbone for any length of time would result in severe damage to users, customers, or the business, a **redundant backbone** is probably required. Should one backbone become unavailable, the other can still be used for internetworking traffic. Furthermore, using a redundant backbone also allows for the load balancing of internetworking traffic. By placing half of the network segments on each backbone, internetworking traffic is shared, or balanced, across the backbones, resulting in improved communications performance. Of course, duplicating the entire backbone is much more expensive than simply duplicating one or more key devices. Figure 6.6 shows what a redundant backbone architecture might look like.

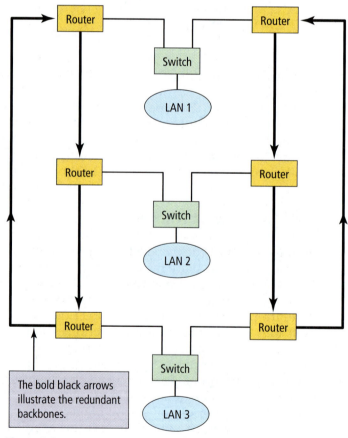

Figure 6.6
Redundant Backbone

Fault tolerance is more than just a technology; it is also the use of good procedures and documentation. Recall that a technology's degree of fault tolerance will determine its ability to survive an error, damage, or some other unforeseen circumstance. As you design and implement your backbone, part of your implementation will be the defining, documenting, and testing of procedures to follow in the event of component failure. Your documentation should include a written history of the network and diagrams of important details such as where routers and switches are located, what their addresses are, where and how the backbone cabling has been deployed, what network segments are supported and their location, the personnel responsible for corrective measures should problems occur, and any other information that will help you in recovering your network and backbone as quickly as possible.

Once the documentation is created, it is equally important that it be maintained and kept as up-to-date as possible. Documentation that does not reflect the current status of the enterprise's environment is not very useful, and it may do more harm than good. Procedures should be in place that describe how the documentation is to be maintained.

Backbone Design Considerations

Backbones connect other network segments. Therefore, when designing network segments, you must also consider how they fit into the design of the backbone. How the network segments are connected to the backbone is critical. When connecting network segments to the backbone, will the cabling be internal; that is, behind the walls, above the ceilings, or beneath the floors? Internal installations usually connect network segments to wall plates and patch panels.

A **patch panel,** as shown in Figure 6.7, is a central wiring point located near the devices to be connected to it. The patch panel shown is similar to those made by Belkin (**www.belkin.com**). The patch panel is not a hub, switch, or router; it provides no communication of its own. It is simply a means of organizing cables so that they can be efficiently maintained. The network designer must know where all of the devices for each network are located and how these devices are going to be cabled to run to their central connecting hub, switch, or router.

Depending on the size of the enterprise, there may be hundreds of identical wires running through walls, ceilings, and floors, which makes planning and documentation essential. Knowing the cable routing path from the network segments to the backbone should never be a matter of guesswork, but rather information that should be able to be retrieved relatively quickly. The internal design must take into consideration such factors as media susceptibility to the external environment, local building code regulations, fire and safety hazards, and data link layer protocol capabilities. Recall that the various forms of Ethernet have collision

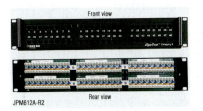

Figure 6.7

Belkin 24-Port Cat-5E Patch Panel

Figure 6.8
Technician Wiring a Patch Panel

domain parameters that have to be accounted for in a backbone design. Figure 6.8 shows a technician wiring a patch panel.

A **collision domain** is bounded by the length of the cable for a particular implementation of an Ethernet network. You may recall from Chapter 4 that a standard Ethernet segment may be up to 2,500 meters, whereas a Fast Ethernet segment can be no more than 250 meters. This length is the collision domain. An enterprise with multiple types of Ethernet networks (standard, Fast, and/or Gigabit) may consequently have networks with differently bounded collision domains. It is important that you know the collision domain of each of the Ethernet networks within an enterprise as you design and build your backbone.

As you might expect, implementing an **internal wiring** design, which encompasses the wiring within ceilings, floors, and walls, can be very complicated. It is not unusual for businesses to contract such work to a facility-wiring specialist. **External wiring**, although unattractive, is far simpler, because the cabling is exposed. However, exposed wires are more susceptible to damage and have fire and safety issues as well.

Internal Wiring Guidelines

The first thing the network administrator should do when designing the internal wiring is to produce a detailed plan that identifies the location of each patch panel and the precise path that each cable will take to connect to it. Once the plan is confirmed, the wiring can begin. From each patch panel location, wires should be pulled through the walls, ceilings, or floors, depending on the facility, to each device that is to be connected to the patch panel. Each wire should be labeled, and documented, as to its final location (i.e., the device to which it is to be connected). When installers pull wire from the patch panel to its ultimate location, they may use a *pull string*, a *telepole*, a *fish tape*, or another cabling tool. One vendor

The Ethical Perspective

Enterprise Wiring and Safety

Wiring a network, especially a large one, isn't just a matter of having things work and look nice. Real-world fire, health, and safety issues are also involved. Several government bodies set building regulations and safety standards. One such body is the U.S. Department of Labor's Occupational Safety and Health Administration, or OSHA (**www.osha.gov**). Many OSHA regulations and standards cover wiring methods, components, and how and where equipment is deployed. Businesses are expected to follow OSHA regulations, as well as those set by local governing bodies, such as those at the state, county, and city levels.

Meeting all of these regulations costs money. Staff must be hired to determine where a business may or may not be in compliance. For areas not in compliance, necessary modifications must be made, again at a cost, to ensure that a business meets the legal requirements. Some businesses may reduce the incurred costs by meeting only the minimum legal requirements. Other businesses may go above and beyond regulatory agency requirements, perhaps as a quality of service feature for employees or clients. Of course, the staff employed should have the proper training to ensure that all wiring, electrical, and other infrastructure work is of good quality. It may surprise you to know that many of the courses on network wiring completed by networking technologists have an ethics component. The ethics component often discusses quality of work, honesty, the technician's ability to follow instructions, integrity, and other interpersonal skills.

Assume that ACME Corporation has requested that you present a bid to do the installation wiring for their entire enterprise network. You have visited several of their facilities and have noted that many of the networks do not comply with current fire and safety regulations. ACME has made it clear that they want the work done for the lowest possible cost. After completing your analysis, you provide your estimate.

Later, one of ACME's managers informally, not in writing, tells you that you can have the job if your bid were lower, perhaps through the use of lower-quality materials. This is a job that you and your employees would really like to have, because it could lead to other jobs. What would you do in this scenario? If you do not accept the job at ACME, should you alert a government agency about ACME's lack of compliance? What if other firms will not hire you should they discover that you reported ACME for lack of compliance? Does this situation involve business ethics?

of these types of tools is PushPullRods (**www.pushpullrods.com**). A tele-pole is a telescoping pole used to pull wire from hard-to-reach places, such as ceilings, floors, and walls.

A **wall plate** should be mounted within reach of each network-connected device, depending on the medium being used. Wires running from the patch panel should be connected to the wall plate. The wall plate serves as the port connector to the patch panel and may have up to four RJ-45 jacks. Wires are connected to both a port in the patch panel and an associated wall plate using a punch-down tool. When connecting the wires to the patch panel and wall plate, the wires are **punched down** into the port slot using a punch-down tool. A standard punch-down tool can be purchased from such vendors as Time Motion

Figure 6.9
Standard Twisted-Wire Pair Patch Cables

Tools (**www.timemotion.com**). This punch-down process establishes a connection between the wires.

Patch cables, like the ones illustrated in Figure 6.9, connect the ports of the patch panel, usually to a network segment's hub. A **patch cable** is simply a length of cable with an RJ-45 connector at each end. The networked device is then connected to the wall plate jack. Finally, after both ends of the wires have been punched down, their connections should be tested to verify that they work. This can be accomplished with testing tools or you could try to connect a computer to the network using its punched-down wire run. An interesting Web site on wiring can be found at **www.epanorama.net/links/wire_telecom.html**.

Wiring Closets

Many network configurations require the use of one or more **wiring closets**. In fact, the patch panel is usually housed in the wiring closet. The wiring closet may also contain servers that provide resources across the enterprise. In a multifloor design, wiring closets are usually placed one above the other. Placing the wiring closets in vertical alignment greatly facilitates their connection. Figure 6.10 shows three wiring closets in vertical alignment. Although wiring closets tend to be relatively small, because they house only the essential equipment to support the backbone, they are usually well lit and tightly secured.

The closet should be environmentally friendly to the equipment it houses; for example, it should have adequate air conditioning, heating, and air filtration, as needed. Specialized electronic circuitry can be particularly susceptible to heat, cold, dust, and humidity. Fortunately, administrative tools running on routers, switches, servers, and other devices have made it increasingly possible for network administrators to monitor and fine-tune their wiring closet equipment without having to physically be in the room itself. This makes remote administration, even from a different city, state, or country, possible. A brief article on good wiring closet design is available at **net-services.ufl.edu/infrastructure/closetdesign.html**.

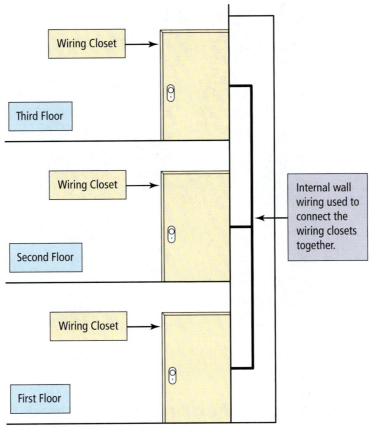

Wiring Closet

Third Floor

Wiring Closet

Second Floor

Wiring Closet

First Floor

Internal wall wiring used to connect the wiring closets together.

Figure 6.10
Vertical Alignment of Wiring Closets
Closets contain essential equipment to connect networks together.

Data Centers

For horizontal backbone architectures that use a distributed environment, wiring closets are fairly common. A collapsed backbone architecture, however, is more likely to make use of what is commonly referred to as a *data center*. Wiring closets tend to be small rooms housing minimal, but essential, backbone networking equipment. In contrast, **data centers** are usually moderately to largely spaced and house all of the necessary networking equipment for the entire enterprise in a central location. As with wiring closets, data centers should be tightly secured and environmentally appropriate for the equipment they house. The data center may contain routers, switches, servers, and even network segment hubs that connect individual devices to their network segment.

For organization and ease of access, equipment in a data center is usually mounted on racks that may reach from floor to ceiling. **Racks** are at least 19 inches wide, and hubs, switches, routers, and servers can be stacked and bolted into them. Figure 6.11 shows a typical rack housing network servers. Other types of racks, available through Server Racks Online (**www.server-rack-online.com**), are also used to house multiple servers. Racks are also used to centralize wiring. Because most, if not all, of the essential networking equipment of the enterprise is centralized in one location, maintaining, servicing, and troubleshooting equipment is much easier than with a distributed environment.

Figure 6.11
Standard Racks Housing Network Servers

Troubleshooting the Gigabit Ethernet Backbone

Gigabit Ethernet is a very popular backbone protocol. Because Gigabit Ethernet is based on standard Ethernet, many of the troubleshooting tips for a Gigabit Ethernet backbone can also be applied to standard and Fast Ethernet networks. Certain types of errors may require specialized diagnostic tools for detection and analysis of network traffic. Other types of errors may be detected using software applications such as Microsoft's Windows Network Monitor or Novell NetWare's Monitor.nlm. Many things can go wrong in a network, and it is not possible in this text to explore all corrective procedures. This section presents just a few of the more common problems a network administrator might encounter in a Gigabit Ethernet environment.

Packet Errors

Packet errors occur for a variety of reasons in an Ethernet network. Several of these errors are related to collisions. Collisions in an Ethernet network are to be expected, and the collisions themselves are not a problem. However, when too many collisions occur, say, 5 percent or more of the total packets, then corrective measures are needed. This scenario is sometimes referred to as an **early collision** problem. Network administrators should monitor the frequency of collisions encountered at regular intervals and especially at peak service times. If too many collisions are occurring, the network segment may need to be split into two collision domains.

One type of collision that can be difficult to detect is a late collision. **Late collisions** can result when data takes too long to cross the network. Recall from Chapter 4 that a standard Ethernet cable segment cannot be more than 2,500 meters long. Late collisions can be caused by excessive cable lengths. Another potential cause is the use of too many repeaters. Late collisions can result in lost packets that require retransmission by higher-level protocols.

Ethernet packets have a minimum length of 64 bytes and a maximum length of 1,518 bytes. Runts occur when a packet is too small. When packets are too large, a giant results. Runts and giants are physically defective packets that can result in network error.

Runts may result from a defective NIC. They are also caused when a transmitting device stops transmission in the middle of a packet due to the detection of a collision. Runts can never be entirely eliminated, because they result from normal collisions, but when the number of runts is greater than the monitored number of collisions, a problem is indicated.

Giants are usually caused by a jabbering NIC. A **jabbering** NIC is one that is transmitting continuously and incorrectly. Unlike runts, giants are not the result of a normal Ethernet operation, and therefore indicate a definite problem. Whereas a bad NIC is the mostly likely cause of a giant, another hardware device may also be faulty or a cable segment may be defective. If a NIC or cable segment is found to be the cause of the problem, the best solution is to remove and discard the failing component and replace it with a new one.

Another type of error that can bring network traffic to a standstill is a broadcast storm. Usually the result of a badly formed broadcast transmission packet from an originating device with a defective NIC, the bad broadcast packet causes the devices that receive it to generate their own broadcasts. By definition, a broadcast packet goes to all of the devices on a shared circuit. When the total broadcast traffic reaches or exceeds a rate of 126 packets per second, a **broadcast storm** results. The major problem with such a storm is that it is self-sustaining, resulting in a flood of garbage packets that eventually consume all network bandwidth, preventing any other valid communications from occurring.

Cable Errors

Cable errors can result from a variety of causes, and, of course, must be corrected once detected. The first step in good cable management is to have documentation that shows which cable belongs to which device and where and how a cable is routed. Once installed behind walls, floors, or ceilings, it can be next to impossible to determine a cable's identity. An inexpensive and essential tool is a good label maker. Other tools are also very helpful. For example, a wide variety of cable-testing tools are available. Simple, inexpensive tools may only check for a cable's continuity and **pin-out**, meaning that individual wires are connected to the right pins. More sophisticated tools can analyze a cable's electrical properties. Such electrical properties include:

- **Near-end cross-talk**. A measure of how much a signal on one wire interferes with signals on an adjacent wire.

- **Attenuation**. A measure of how much of the original signal is lost over the length of a cable segment.

- **Impedance**. A measure of the opposition to changes in the current that arises from the resistance and inductance of the cable. Impedance can result in reflected signals at the point where cables are joined.

- **Attenuation to cross-talk**. A measure that compares signal strength with noise.

- **Capacitance**. A measure of whether electrical field energy is being properly stored in the cable.

Another important measure is **cable length**. The length of a cable can be determined by measuring how long it takes a signal to return on a cable. This is especially helpful if the cable is hidden behind walls or other obstructions. Cable lengths that are too long can result in lost or corrupted data packets.

NIC Errors

Many problems with NICs are the result of improper configuration. However, NICs are physical devices, and they do occasionally fail. One way to test a questionable NIC is to connect the device having the questionable NIC with one that has a NIC known to be good. The cable connecting the two devices should also be one known to function properly. The result is a two-device network. If communications are not occurring, it is likely that we have proven that the device with the questionable NIC does, in fact, have a bad NIC. When troubleshooting a TCP/IP connection, the IP numbers and masks must also be properly configured on each device, as otherwise a bad software configuration could mask a physical or hardware problem.

Vendors of NICs often provide diagnostic software with their products. This software can often be used to verify the NIC's configuration. For example, the software's diagnostic information may report on what interrupt the NIC is using or if there are interrupt conflicts with other devices. An "interrupt" is a specifically assigned address value used by peripheral devices, such as NICs, hard drives, modems, etc., to communicate to a computer's CPU (Central Processing Unit). A peripheral uses its designated interrupt address value to alert the CPU that it needs the services of the CPU. Other types of configuration errors include settings that affect DMA channels, memory location addresses, bus mastering, and packet frame types. (DMA and bus mastering were both discussed in Chapter 4.) However, the software may be limited as to the types of errors it is able to verify. It is a good idea to check the vendor's Web site to see if updates for diagnostic software are available or if problems similar to yours have been reported. Most technology vendors provide a **Frequently Asked Questions (FAQs)** page on their Web site that provides consumers with product information and answers to common questions. FAQs, as the name implies, provide answers to questions that have most frequently been asked by customers, employees, or even students.

Finally, you may want to swap out the NIC, Figure 6.12, that you think is malfunctioning with one that you know is working. If communication can be established, then the suspected NIC is the problem. If communications are still not possible, the problem is likely something other than the NIC.

Connectivity Testing with Ping

The techniques described thus far relate to testing physical, electrical, and mechanical Ethernet problems. A simple software tool used almost universally to detect simple connectivity between two networked devices,

Figure 6.12
Installing a NIC
NICs must be properly installed and configured to prevent errors.

local or remote, is a small program called *ping.* Created by Mick Muuss, **ping** is now a formalized component of the IP protocol. Based on ICMP, ping passes error messages and information about network performance between networked devices.

Put simply, ping is a small utility program that enables one networked device to send a packet requesting a response to another networked device. If the connection is successful, the device receiving the request sends back a packet. The timing of the request and response is measured, which indicates the length of the path between the two devices. A consistent response from multiple, differing pairs of devices provides an indication of the quality of the connection. If a ping does not receive a response, it immediately becomes clear that connectivity has not been established and that a problem exists. If hardware problems have been ruled out, ping can quickly help a network administrator determine if simple connectivity between two devices is or is not occurring.

Although ping can respond to several types of ICMP messages, it relies on two in particular: Echo_Request and Echo_Reply. When a sending host sends an **Echo_Request**, the time at which the packet is sent is included in the packet. The receiving host uses the time sent to calculate the time needed to cross the network and places that information in the **Echo_Reply** response. The receiving host also places a sequence number and a time-to-live value in the packet. The **time-to-live (TTL)** value is like a counter and gives the packet a finite, definite lifetime. This limited lifetime ensures that a lost packet does not endlessly circle the network, using up valuable bandwidth. If a packet has not arrived at its destination by the time its time-to-live value has expired, the packet is dropped from network traffic. If the initial sending host does not eventually receive an Echo_Reply response packet, the sending device presumes that the packet is lost or that the receiving host is not available for some reason.

Most implementations of ping provide for additional options beyond the simple Echo_Request/Echo_Reply responses. Vendors such as Cisco,

Microsoft, and Sun each have ping implementations. Additional information on how ping works can be found at **www.inetdaemon.com/tools/how_ping_works.html** and **livinginternet.com/?i/ia_tools_ping.htm**. The second site in particular is a lot of fun because it allows users to run a ping against various devices in such places as Greece, Australia, Canada, Belgium, and the United States.

Switched Multimegabit Data Services

This chapter has focused on backbones and Gigabit Ethernet. However, you also need to be familiar with a set of services designed specifically for MANs. This set of services is called **Switched Multimegabit Data Services (SMDS)**. SMDS supports the exchange of data between LANs in different parts of a city or between network segments over a large campus. The term *campus* refers to any organization that has several buildings spread over numerous acres that need to be networked in order to share resources. SMDS is a packet-switched datagram service for high-speed MAN traffic. In the next chapter, packet-switched services are described in much greater detail.

Typically, businesses link their LANs to a common carrier's SMDS network through routers. SMDS relies on the **SMDS Interface Protocol (SMDSIP)**. SMDSIP provides for three layers of protocols that define user information frame structuring, addressing, error control, and overall transport.

SMDSIP Level 1 defines the physical interfaces and the type of transmission medium and signaling system used. SMDSIP Level 2 provides an access method, defined in IEEE Project 802.6, that is referred to as a distributed queue dual bus (DQDB). (It is beyond the scope of this text to go into the details of DQDB; however, it is interesting to note that the access method used is not contention or token passing, but one called distributed queues.) SMDSIP Level 3 accepts user data and adds header and trailer information to it for processing by the SMDS network.

An advantage of SMDS is that subscribers pay only when they use the common carrier's network. Also, although SMDS is associated with MAN technology, it can also be considered a type of backbone, and it is also used in WANs. As you can see, it is sometimes difficult to limit a particular technology to a specific network category.

Chapter Summary

A backbone network (BN) is used to connect all of an organization's LANs. When properly designed, BNs provide a high-speed circuit that serves as a central conduit over which all of the organization's LANs can communicate. An organization might also use a metropolitan area network (MAN). MANs span a city and are often used to connect remote BNs. The terms BN and MAN are sometimes used interchangeably, depending on the scope of the backbone.

Each of an organization's individual LANs is a network segment. An organization might have a network segment on each floor of a multistory building. Because each network segment, or LAN, is on its own floor, this type of network segment is often referred to as a horizontal network. The BN links the network segments together. Devices accessible to other network segments may reside directly on the BN.

A BN, like a LAN, has a protocol. One of the most popular backbone protocols is Gigabit Ethernet. A major reason for this is the wide installation base of standard Ethernet. Other protocols that might be used for a backbone include Frame Relay (FR) and Asynchronous Transfer Mode (ATM). FR and ATM are also frequently associated with WANs.

Two common types of backbone architectures are distributed and collapsed. A distributed backbone is one that runs throughout the entire enterprise. This type of backbone uses a central cable to which the network segments, or LANs, are connected. A collapsed backbone connects all of the network segments to a central, single router or switch. This central device is, in effect, the backbone. Because the collapsed backbone uses a single, central backbone device, cabling is greatly reduced.

Fault tolerance is the capability of a technology to recover in the event of error, failure, or some other unexpected event that disrupts smooth organizational communications. Many network administrators provide for backbone fault tolerance by duplicating critical network resources. This duplication is called redundancy. Documentation is also important to network design. Documentation should include such important details as where routers and switches are located, what their addresses are, where and how the backbone cabling has been deployed, what network segments are supported and their location, and the personnel responsible for corrective measures should problems occur.

When designing network segments, consideration should also be given to how the segments fit into the design of the backbone. With internal installations, network segments are connected to wall plates and patch panels. External installations are simpler, but exposed wires are more susceptible to damage and have fire and safety issues. In a usual configuration, especially for horizontal networks housed on multiple floors, organizations use one or more wiring closets that provide a centralized location for network cabling. The wiring closet may also contain servers that provide resources across the enterprise. With a multifloor design, whenever possible, wiring closets are usually placed one above the other.

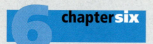

Data centers, which are usually associated with collapsed backbones, are moderately to largely spaced and provide for a centralized location to house all the necessary networking equipment for the entire enterprise. As with wiring closets, data centers should be tightly secured and environmentally appropriate for the equipment they house.

Troubleshooting an Ethernet backbone can involve packet, cable, and connectivity errors. A variety of packet errors can occur in an Ethernet network. Software and hardware tools are available that permit a network technician to identify types of packet errors, and so resolve them. Many are related to collisions. Good documentation is key to solving cable errors. Good documentation will include which cables belong to which devices and where and how the cables are routed. A wide variety of testing tools are available to test cables. NIC cards can also cause networking problems. One means of testing a NIC is to connect a malfunctioning networked device with another networked device known to have components and software configuration in proper working order. Network technicians must often go through a process of elimination when resolving a networked device's communications problem.

Ping is a simple software tool used almost universally to detect simple connectivity between two networked devices, local or remote. With ping, one networked device sends a packet that requires a response to another networked device. When successful, the device receiving the request sends back a packet. Ping can respond to several types of ICMP messages, but it relies on two in particular: Echo_Request and Echo_Reply.

Switched Multimegabit Data Services, or SMDS, is a set of services designed specifically for MANs. SMDS is used to support the exchange of data between LANs in different parts of a city or between network segments over a large campus. SMDS is a packet-switched datagram service for high-speed MAN traffic. SMDS is coordinated through the SMDS Interface Protocol (SMDSIP).

6 chapter six Keywords

Asynchronous Transfer Mode (ATM) **(213)**

Attenuation **(225)**

Attenuation to cross-talk **(226)**

Backbone architecture **(213)**

Backbone network (BN) **(210)**

Backbone protocol **(213)**

Backplane **(215)**

Broadcast storm **(225)**

Cable errors **(225)**

Cable length **(226)**

Capacitance **(226)**

Collapsed backbone **(214)**

Collision domain **(220)**

Communication bus **(215)**

Data center **(223)**

Distributed backbone **(213)**

Early collision **(224)**

Echo_Reply **(227)**

Echo_Request **(227)**

External wiring **(220)**

Fault tolerance **(217)**

Frame Relay (FR) **(213)**

Frequently Asked Questions (FAQs) **(226)**

Giants **(225)**

Gigabit Ethernet **(212)**

Horizontal network **(210)**

Impedance **(225)**

Internal wiring **(220)**

Jabbering **(225)**

Late collision **(224)**

Metropolitan area network (MAN) **(210)**

Near-end cross-talk **(225)**

Network segment **(210)**

Packet errors **(224)**

Patch cable **(222)**

Patch panel **(219)**

Ping **(227)**

Pin-out **(225)**

Punch down **(221)**

Racks **(223)**

Redundancy **(217)**

Redundant backbone **(218)**

Runts **(225)**

SMDS Interface Protocol (SMDSIP) **(228)**

Switched Multimegabit Data Services (SMDS) **(228)**

Time-to-live (TTL) **(227)**

Vertical network **(210)**

Wall plate **(221)**

Wiring closet **(222)**

Chapter Questions

6

Short Answer

1. Why would an organization use a BN?

2. Under what circumstances would you recommend a business implement a collapsed backbone rather than a distributed one?

3. Describe at least one design consideration when designing a backbone.

4. Why is it important to implement fault tolerance on the backbone?

Multiple Choice

For each of the following questions select the one best answer.

1. Which of the following is a high-speed circuit that connects the network segments of an enterprise?
   a. LAN   b. BN   c. MAN   d. WAN

2. A BN can connect LANs across which of the following?
   a. A floor   b. A building   c. A campus   d. All the above

3. Which of the following is specifically associated with citywide data communications?
   a. LANs   b. BNs   c. MANs   d. WANs

4. Which term describes an individual LAN in an enterprise?
   a. Network link   b. Network point   c. Network segment   d. Route

5. Which of the following describes networks that are maintained on separate floors of a multistory building?
   a. Horizontal networks   b. Vertical networks
   c. a or b   d. Neither a nor b

6. Which of the following is true of a BN?
   a. It is its own network.   b. It is not a network.
   c. It is part of a network segment.   d. It is part of a LAN.

7. Which of the following may be directly attached to a BN?
   a. Server   b. Router
   c. A server or a router, but not both
   d. Either a server or a router, or both

8. Which BN Ethernet protocol is preferred when network segments have a large amount of internetworking traffic?
   a. Standard   b. Fast   c. Gigabit   d. Terabit

9. Which of the following is a BN protocol?
   a. ATM   b. FR   c. a and b   d. Neither a nor b

10. Which of the following was the initial IEEE standard for Gigabit Ethernet?
    a. 802.2z   b. 802.3z   c. 802.4z   d. 802.3x

11. What data rate does Gigabit Ethernet support?

    a. 1,000 Mbps   **b.** 1 Gbps   **c.** Neither a nor b   **d.** a and b

12. Which of the following is used by both Gigabit Ethernet and Fast Ethernet?

    a. MAC   **b.** Access method   **c.** Neither a nor b   **d.** a and b

13. Which of the following is supported by Gigabit Ethernet?

    a. Half-duplex   **b.** Full-duplex   **c.** a and b   **d.** Duplex

14. How many common types of backbone architectures are there?

    a. 1   **b.** 2   **c.** 4   **d.** 8

15. Which backbone architecture enables backbone and the network segments to use different protocols?

    a. Aligned   **b.** Distributed   **c.** Concentrated   **d.** Collapsed

16. Which backbone architecture requires that the backbone and the network segments all use the same protocol?

    a. Aligned   **b.** Distributed   **c.** Concentrated   **d.** Collapsed

17. Which backbone architecture requires extensive cabling?

    a. Aligned   **b.** Distributed   **c.** Concentrated   **d.** Collapsed

18. Which of the following is the central connecting device of a collapsed backbone?

    a. Backsplash   **b.** Backplane   **c.** Backplate   **d.** Backplant

19. Which term refers to an older technology that is still in use?

    a. Antique   **b.** Obsolete   **c.** Legend   **d.** Legacy

20. A backbone is

    a. frequently used in large enterprises.
    b. mostly associated with small networks.
    c. cannot connect different logical networks.
    d. only used within a building.

21. In which type of BN architecture does internetwork traffic take only one pass through a device?

    a. Aligned   **b.** Distributed   **c.** Concentrated   **d.** Collapsed

22. Which of the following is the capability of a technology to recover in the event of error or failure?

    a. Fault diversion   **b.** Fault tolerance
    c. Error tolerance   **d.** Tolerance

23. Which backbone technique enables traffic load balancing?

    a. Redundant hubs   **b.** Redundant clients
    c. Redundant backbones   **d.** Fault tolerant hubs

24. Which of the following is a central wiring point located near the devices connected to it?

    a. Patch panel   **b.** Patch port   **c.** Panel patch   **d.** Port patch

25. Which of the following is a length of cable with an RJ-45 connector at each end?

    a. Patch wire   **b.** Wire patch   **c.** Patch cable   **d.** Cable patch

26. Which of the following is commonly used with horizontal networks?

    a. Wiring rooms   **b.** Wiring closets   **c.** Data rooms   **d.** Data centers

27. Which of the following is commonly used with a collapsed backbone?
   a. Wiring rooms   **b.** Wiring closets
   c. Data rooms   **d.** Data centers

28. Which of the following may occur when a packet takes too long to cross the network?
   a. Early collision   **b.** Late collision   **c.** a or b   **d.** Neither a nor b

29. Which of the following is a packet that is less than the Ethernet minimum?
   a. A short   **b.** A run   **c.** A runt   **d.** A pic

30. What is the minimum Ethernet packet size in bytes?
   a. 60   **b.** 62   **c.** 64   **d.** 68

31. Which term refers to a packet that is greater than the Ethernet minimum?
   a. Big   **b.** Large   **c.** Giant   **d.** Oversize

32. What is the maximum Ethernet packet size in bytes?
   a. 1,000   **b.** 1,218   **c.** 1,500   **d.** 1,518

33. A NIC that continuously and incorrectly transmits packets it is said to be
   a. chatting.   **b.** jabbering.   **c.** talking.   **d.** casting.

34. Which of the following is a measure of how much a signal on one wire interferes with signals on an adjacent wire?
   a. Impedance   **b.** Near-end cross-talk
   c. Attenuation   **d.** Capacitance

35. Which of the following is a measure of how much of the original signal is lost over the length of a cable segment?
   a. Impedance   **b.** Near-end cross-talk
   c. Attenuation   **d.** Capacitance

36. Which of the following can result in reflected signals at the point where cables are joined?
   a. Impedance   **b.** Near-end cross-talk
   c. Attenuation   **d.** Capacitance

37. Which of the following is a measure of whether electrical field energy is being properly stored in the cable?
   a. Impedance   **b.** Near-end cross-talk
   c. Attenuation   **d.** Capacitance

38. Which of the following is a location on a Web site where vendors supply answers to common customer questions?
   a. FAQ   **b.** AQFS   **c.** SQAS   **d.** FASQ

39. Which of the following is a small utility program that allows one networked device to send a packet requesting a response to another networked device?
   a. Pong   **b.** Ping   **c.** Gong   **d.** Pang

40. Which of the following is a value that determines how long a lost packet can remain on a network circuit?
   a. Time-to-die   **b.** Time-to-live
   c. Time-to-transmit   **d.** Time-to-send

41. Which of the following is a set of services associated with MANs?

    a. SMDS **b.** SDMS **c.** BN **d.** MDSS

42. The terms BN and MN

    a. always mean the same thing.
    b. sometimes mean the same thing.
    c. never mean the same thing.
    d. have no relationship to each other.

43. Which of the following is used to connect a network to a backbone?

    a. Switches **b.** Routers **c.** Servers **d.** a or b

44. In general, which of the following is easier to manage?

    a. Distributed backbones **b.** Meshed backbones
    c. Collapsed backbones **d.** Expanded backbones

45. When the time-to-live value on a packet expires, the packet is

    a. unaffected. **b.** dropped. **c.** renewed. **d.** retransmitted.

46. Which protocol is ping based on?

    a. ITCP **b.** IMP **c.** ICMP **d.** TCP

47. Which of the following is used by ping?

    a. Echo_Request **b.** Echo_Reply **c.** Neither a nor b **d.** a and/or b

48. Which of the following characterizes the use of ping as a diagnostic tool?

    a. It is complicated. **b.** It is expensive.
    c. It is rarely used. **d.** It is simple.

49. Typically, how do LANs connect to a carrier's SMDS network?

    a. Hubs **b.** Servers **c.** Routers **d.** Bridges

50. Which of the following describes SMDS?

    a. It is packet switched. **b.** It is circuit based.
    c. It is packet neutral. **d.** It is circuit switched.

True or False

For each of the following select either True or False.

1. Only large organizations have more than one LAN.

2. A backbone is not a separate network.

3. Horizontal networks can be connected vertically when they are on separate floors.

4. The physical facility should have little effect on how a backbone is designed.

5. A backbone can have a different protocol than the network segments attached to it.

6. Network traffic may influence backbone protocol decisions.

7. Gigabit Ethernet is a popular choice for enterprise backbones.

8. Network segments that communicate extensively with each other usually do not require a backbone with a faster protocol throughput.

9. A distributed backbone is generally easier to manage and secure than a collapsed backbone.

10. The word distributed means "in more then one location."

11. A distributed backbone is often implemented in conjunction with a collapsed backbone.

12. In a distributed backbone, each network segment has its own cabled connection to the backbone.

13. Generally, a distributed backbone configuration requires less wiring.

14. An advantage of a collapsed backbone is that internetwork traffic has to pass through only one device to reach its final destination.

15. Fault tolerance is the capability of a technology to recover in the event of an error or failure.

16. A patch panel is like a hub or a switch.

17. Collision domain parameters should be considered when wiring the backbone.

18. The first thing to do when implementing the backbone is to "pull" all the wires.

19. A broadcast storm will eventually die out, because it is not self-sustaining.

20. There is only one implementation of ping.

Exercises

Research in Brief

For one or more of the questions below, provide a one- to two-page report based on your findings.

1. This chapter has presented a generalized approach to backbone solutions. However, the importance of Gigabit Ethernet in backbone architectures was emphasized. Many vendors provide the technologies required to implement a Gigabit Ethernet backbone. One such vendor is Cisco. Visit the Cisco Web site at **www.cisco.com**. Research and report back on the ways in which Cisco provides Gigabit Ethernet solutions. What types of hardware do they offer? What are the costs of the different types of hardware? How does Cisco differentiate their Gigabit Ethernet solutions from other vendors?

2. This chapter compared distributed versus collapsed backbones. Select one of these two models and do more research on it. For the model you select, what types of businesses might that model appeal to and why? What types of hardware are associated with the model and at what cost? Recommend at least one vendor who provides the technology to implement the model, explaining why you made the recommendation.

3. Cable testing equipment can be very useful in maintaining, fine-tuning, and troubleshooting a backbone. Investigate different types

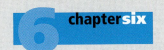

of cable testing equipment and report back on their varying costs and functionalities.

4. Wiring closets are important, especially for distributed backbones. Research the types of equipment you might expect to find in a wiring closet. Also identify and describe how wiring closets should be properly set up for security and to house the equipment they hold.

Case Study

Sheehan Marketing and Public Relations

During your time with SMPR, the business has been very successful. So successful, in fact, that the Los Angeles office has had to move from its 1,000-square-foot office space on one floor to a 2,000-square-foot facility that occupies two floors. You are now in the process of designing the configuration of SMPR's networks for the new location. You need to create a backbone that connects the networks on the first and second floors.

The president of SMPR wants you to create a report for him that describes what a backbone is and why SMPR needs one. He also wants to know the type of backbone you are planning to deploy and why. In your report, he wants you to address the type of facility issues that might be important and that should be addressed prior to the move. You view the move to the new office as an opportunity to put frequently used services, such as e-mail and database servers, on the common backbone. The president of SMPR, however, is not convinced that this would be a good idea and wants to know your rationale for such a plan. He has asked that you be as specific as possible regarding any costs or particular vendors that you may be recommending for the backbone solution.

Web References

www.more.net/technical/research/network/bestpractices/netdesign-bestpractices-print.pdf

www.belkin.com

www.osha.gov

www.pushpullrods.com

www.timemotion.com

www.epanorama.net/links/wire_telecom.html

net-services.ufl.edu/infrastructure/closetdesign.html

www.server-rack-online.com

www.inetdaemon.com/tools/how_ping_works.html

livinginternet.com/?i/ia_tools_ping.htm

Gigabit Ethernet

As organizations began to transition from standard (10 Mbps) Ethernet to Fast (100 Mbps) Ethernet, the IEEE saw the need for a faster backbone protocol. The result was the development of Gigabit Ethernet and the 802.3z standard. Gigabit Ethernet allows for a data rate of 1,000 Mbps, or 1 Gbps. A major advantage of all of the officially recognized forms of Gigabit Ethernet is that they are all built on the standards of the preexisting Ethernet protocol. This means that the MAC layer and access method for Gigabit Ethernet are the same as for standard and Fast Ethernet. Additionally, Gigabit Ethernet is backward compatible with existing media, which makes it easy to upgrade from standard or Fast Ethernet. Finally, Gigabit Ethernet supports both full-duplex and half-duplex operations.

One key difference with Gigabit Ethernet, however, is that the collision domain, or diameter of the network, is reduced. Because of the reduced collision domain, additional planning is required when connecting network segments to the backbone. Network segments must be able to reach the backbone, thus an important consideration is the type of cabling used. It is not unusual for a Gigabit Ethernet backbone to be connected to Fast Ethernet networks. (The Gigabit Ethernet Alliance, a nonprofit organization, provides additional information on Gigabit Ethernet at the following Web site: **www.10gea.org/index.htm**.)

Forms of Gigabit Ethernet

Gigabit Ethernet comes in several forms. The original IEEE 1000Base-X standard (802.3z) allowed for three physical layer cable options: 1000Base-LX and 1000Base-SX, both using fiber-optic, and 1000Base-CX, using copper. Of the three, 1000Base-CX never became a market success, and virtually no products were available for it. A fourth form of Gigabit Ethernet, 1000Base-T, ratified by the IEEE in June of 1999, uses UTP cable. Gigabit Ethernet, besides being used for backbones, is also a popular option for server farm configurations and for networks using applications that have high bandwidth requirements (e.g., graphics programs). Increasingly, MAN service providers are offering Gigabit Ethernet as a lower-cost option to businesses that need metrowide data communications capabilities.

Gigabit Ethernet also has other advantages. Because Gigabit Ethernet is based on standard Ethernet, technical personnel are probably familiar with the technology, so retraining is likely minimal. When upgrading to Gigabit Ethernet, because cabling and adapter cards may not need to be upgraded for most devices, disruption to the network is usually low. Gigabit Ethernet offers full-duplex data flow. Also, Gigabit Ethernet provides for Quality of Service (QoS) services, such as traffic prioritization. QoS also allows data to be transported without packet loss, offering predictable end-to-end delay and real-time delivery of data once a connection is completed.

Resource Reservation Protocol (RSVP), which is the capability to call for a service level from the network to support a particular application, can be implemented using Gigabit Ethernet. Essentially, RSVP enables network bandwidth to be reserved and supported on intermediate devices such as routers. This allows network administrators to fine-tune traffic demand and throughput.

Because it is based on standard Ethernet, Gigabit Ethernet is fully compatible with networks configured for standard and Fast Ethernet hosts, which allows for scalability. A technology is *scalable* when it allows for easy expansion or contraction as growth and transaction volume demand.

Vendors commonly reference the scalability of their hardware and software products as a competitive advantage. Businesses that buy into a technology want that technology to be flexible so that it can, at a reasonable cost, grow or shrink with business needs.

1000Base-LX

As a fiber-based physical layer implementation, 1000Base-LX is used for backbones that span relatively long distances. If using single-mode cable, the maximum segment length is 5,000 meters. This is the longest segment length for any of the forms of Gigabit Ethernet presented in this chapter. [As an interesting side note, 1000Base-LH (for Long Haul) is a form of Gigabit Ethernet not approved by the IEEE that allows for distances of 1 to 100 kilometers, depending on the form of 1000Base-LH used.] A single-mode 1000Base-LX fiber core is 9 microns in diameter. Do you recall microns from Chapter 2? Microns are measured in millionths of a meter. Single-mode cable, because it can span relatively long distances, is best for long-distance applications, for example, connecting networks across a city.

Multimode 1000Base-LX uses segment lengths of 550 meters. Thus, it is better suited for short-distance applications, such as connecting networks across a campus. With multimode, the core diameter is either 50 or 62.5 microns. 1000Base-LX uses long-wavelength laser transmissions that range from 1,270 to 1,355 nanometers. Single-mode fiber is more expensive than multimode, but it spans greater distances.

1000Base-SX

Usually, 1000Base-SX is used for shorter backbones or in horizontal wiring. Unlike 1000Base-LX, 1000Base-SX uses only multimode fiber-optic cable. Segment lengths usually are 220, 275, 500, or 550 meters. Segment lengths of 220 and 275 meters have core diameters of 62.5 microns; 500 and 550 meter lengths have core diameters of 50 microns. 1000Base-SX uses short-wavelength laser transmissions that range from 770 to 860 nanometers. Note that these short-wavelength transmissions are the same as those used in CD and CD-ROM players.

1000Base-T

Not included in the original IEEE Gigabit Ethernet standard (802.3z), the goal of the later 1000Base-T standard (802.3ab) was to provide gigabit speeds on Category 5 UTP cable. Although Category 5 UTP cable is specified in the standard, the standard strongly recommends the use, at a minimum, of Category 5E (Enhanced Category) cable or higher. Generally, when a standard makes a recommendation, especially a strong recommendation, it is wise to follow that recommendation.

To achieve gigabit speeds on Category 5 UTP cable, 1000Base-T changes the way the Ethernet protocol uses the cable. Whereas Fast Ethernet 100Base-TX uses only two of the four pairs of wire available in an UTP cable, 1000Base-T uses all four pairs. This doubles the throughput of 100Base-TX. Even so, doubling the throughput does not produce gigabit speeds. An additional factor is required. The trick is that 1000Base-T uses a different signaling scheme than 1000Base-X to transmit data. The 1000Base-T signaling scheme uses each of the four wire pairs to carry 250 Mbps of data for a total of 1 Gbps. This is an example of a signaling scheme that uses a form of Pulse Amplitude Modulation, or PAM.

7 chapterseven

Wide Area Networking Fundamentals

Learning Objectives

After studying this chapter, you should be able to:

- Understand the need for varying types of WAN connectivity options.
- Explain switching services.
- Describe circuit-switching services.
- Describe packet-switching services.
- Differentiate between X.25, Frame Relay, and Asynchronous Transfer Mode.
- Explain Point-to-Point Protocol.
- Describe trunk carrier services (such as T-1).
- Describe Integrated Service Digital Network (ISDN).
- Describe Digital Subscriber Line (DSL).

In Chapter 6, you learned that an organization's enterprise might include LANs, BNs, and MANs. The scope of an organization's data communications needs may be multistate or global. Large enterprises and home users connecting to the Internet require **wide area network (WAN)** services. WANs facilitate electronic payments, they make information available to clients wherever they may reside, enable employees to access data and software from remote distances, and permit dial-up modems to connect with ISPs. This chapter explores some of the major architectures that make up WAN technologies.

Connecting to a WAN

Depending on the enterprise's needs, WAN connections can be established in several ways. Usually, because of cost, organizations make use of common carrier infrastructures, such as those provided by AT&T, MCI, and

Sprint, to make their WAN connections. Common carriers are essential to the North American telecommunications infrastructure. The Institute for Telecommunication Sciences has an interesting Web site that provides detailed information about the U.S. telecommunications infrastructure (**www.its.bldrdoc.gov**).

The type of carrier service that a business uses will of course have particular expenses and requirements. A WAN connection, for example, may be established by a simple dial-up connection or through elaborate packet-switching or cell relay technologies. Frame Relay (FR) is a popular packet-switching implementation. Asynchronous Transfer Mode (ATM) is the leading cell relay technology. The following common WAN connectivity options will be described in detail in this chapter:

- Switching services
- Circuit-switching services
- Packet-switching services
- X.25
- Frame Relay (FR)
- Asynchronous Transfer Mode (ATM)
- Point-to-Point Protocol (PPP)
- Trunk carrier services (T-1)
- Digital Subscriber Line (DSL)

Switching Services

For data communications, various devices need to communicate with each other, whether across a room or across a continent. For this communication to occur, some type of physical connection must be established. If the devices were in the same room, the creation of a direct point-to-point connection, whereby each device would have a direct physical connection to all of the other devices, might be a realistic solution. This is called a *mesh topology*. However, if the scope is larger than a single room or if there are more than 10 devices, a mesh topology can quickly become impractical and extremely expensive to implement. Figure 7.1 shows how complicated a mesh topology of only six devices can be. The larger the network infrastructure, the more devices there are that need to communicate, and the more links that will be required to connect those devices to each other. An infrastructure with too many links becomes overly complicated and costly to support. The solution to this problem is a technology called *switching*.

In a **switched network**, interlinked devices called switches are used to create temporary connections between two communicating devices. Switches may be hardware, software, or a combination. Switches can be connected to form multiple links, providing for alternative pathways through a networking infrastructure. Communicating devices use switches to create a link without concern as to how the route is established. The advantage of this strategy is that a permanent link is not required between any two communicating devices. Instead, communicating devices use the switching infrastructure as a means of establishing and creating a link when one is needed. This switching infrastructure is often referred to and graphically illustrated as a **cloud**, as shown in Figure 7.2.

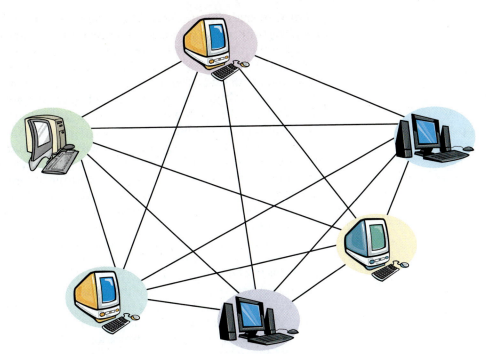

Figure 7.1
Mesh Topology of Six Devices
Even in this simple network of six devices, the cabling within a mesh topology begins to get complicated. Each device has a point-to-point connection to all other devices.

Two common switching technologies are circuit and packet switching. (A Web site that provides white papers on switching technologies can be found at **www.itpapers.com**.) Switches reside in and make up the cloud, whereas external devices connect to the cloud in order to communicate. The external devices that connect to the cloud are often referred to as **edge switches** or **edge routers**, because they are on the "edge," or outer boundary, of the cloud. Once the data arrive at the cloud, the cloud's switching network takes over and assumes control in getting the data from the sender to the receiver.

Circuit Switching

A key characteristic of **circuit switching** is that it creates a direct connection, or path, between two communicating devices. The term **path** is used with circuit switching; the term **link** is used with packet switching. When a circuit is established, no other devices can use that circuit path to

Figure 7.2
Switching Cloud
Whether circuit or packet switching, a business needs only to be concerned with its local connection to the cloud. Within the cloud, the services of the carrier take over.

communicate. In this sense, the circuit is dedicated when it is in use. Probably the most common communication that uses circuit switching occurs when two people share a standard telephone conversation. While their call is in progress, they have a direct, dedicated circuit to each other, and once their call is complete, after one or the other hangs up the phone, the circuit is then terminated. In fact, circuit switching, which is provided by Public Switched Telephone Network (PSTN) providers, was designed for voice communications.

Throughout this chapter, as in previous chapters, new terms will be introduced. In an earlier chapter, Webopedia (**www.webopedia.com**) was noted as a good online source for defining technical terms. Another good reference site is offered by Novell, a vendor of networking software solutions. Novell's online glossary is available at **www.novell.com/info/glossary/glossary.html**.

Circuit-switched paths may be temporary, as with a standard dial-up connection, or permanent, meaning that the circuit is leased and is always available to the user leasing the line. Permanent lines are much more expensive, but they guarantee the user that the line will be available whenever it is required. Whether temporary or permanent, while the circuit is being used, it is dedicated to that particular communication. Although this is well suited for voice communications, circuit-switching networks are not efficient for most types of data communication.

A basic characteristic of data transmissions is that they tend to be *bursty*. **Bursty** means that the data are sent in bursts, not as a continuous stream, like most voice communications. Because the data are sent in bursts, when a business uses a circuit-switched path, much of the bandwidth of the path is not used, which is inefficient. For businesses, inefficiency translates into lost income.

In addition, when two devices establish a path using a circuit-switched connection, their link will be at one constant rate, and the rate will be determined by the slower of the two devices. Faster devices will have to transmit at slower speeds to accommodate slower devices, which again is inefficient for data transmissions. Also, for a circuit-switched service that does not use permanently leased lines, it is possible for calls to be denied due to lack of circuit availability.

Finally, circuit switching treats all requested transmissions in the same manner, meaning that whoever requests an open circuit first can have it. This may sound fair, but in many cases certain data transmissions are likely to be regarded as more critical than others. In such a scenario, it would make sense for there to be a way to prioritize communications so that the most critical data transmissions are assured of getting the circuit first. For these reasons, packet switching is preferred for data communications.

Packet Switching

With **packet switching**, the data are broken into units called **packets**. Individual packets are sent though the packet-switching cloud from the sender to the receiver. Between the sender and the receiver, and within the cloud, are many packet-switching devices. The connection between each packet-switching device is referred to as a *link*, rather than a path. Packet switching significantly improves line efficiency because packet streams from different communications can use the same links between packet-switching nodes. Links are not dedicated to one single communication, but can be used by many communications. In this way, packet-switched

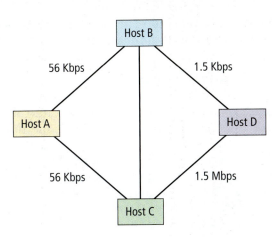

Figure 7.3
Packet Switching with Varied Link Rates
Host A can only transmit at 56 Kbps to either host B or C. But both host B and C can transmit at the faster rate of 1.5 Mbps without regard to host A's slower rate.

services do not use a dedicated path between the sender and the receiver, as with circuit-switched services, but instead have a series of shared links between packet-switching nodes. A simple simulation of the packet-switching process is offered by RAD Data Communications at **www2. rad.com/networks/1998/packet/sim.htm**.

Because links are used, data-rate link conversion between packet-switching nodes can be performed, which is a considerable advantage. This means that the data transmission rate between the originating sender and ultimate receiver is not determined by the slower of the two devices. Instead, link transmission rates between each packet-switching node can be negotiated and used to maximum efficiency. Thus, if the link between packet-switching nodes A and B is slow, A and B will transmit at that rate. However, if the link between B and C is fast, the faster rate of B and C can be used without regard to A and B's slower rate. Figure 7.3 illustrates this point.

With circuit-switched services that do not use expensive leased lines, such as standard dial-up services, it is possible that some communications can be denied access when "all circuits are busy." Maybe you have experienced this when making a phone call, such as when an event of national significance takes place and millions of users are trying to place calls at the same time. An advantage of packet-switched services is that such communications may be delayed, but they will not be denied. Another advantage of packet-switched services is that communications can be prioritized. This means that packets can be tagged for high-priority delivery. Prioritization provides much greater control over organizational communication needs. With circuit-switched services, you saw that there is a distinct difference between temporary dial-up and permanent services. Packet-switched services also vary.

The network implementation determines the size that a packet can take. Regardless of the packet size, a packet contains not only user data, but also control information, such as source and destination addresses, that is used by the packet-switching network. Packets are sent through the cloud, from one packet-switching device to the next. Along the way, the packet is temporarily stored and then routed, depending on the control information contained in the packet. Based on the type of packet-switched service used, how the packets are sent will differ. Packet-switching services are based on datagrams or virtual circuits. As you might guess, the two methods differ greatly as to how packets are delivered through the packet-switching cloud. A datagram approach works well for transmitting a simple e-mail message, for example, but not so well for a file containing critical financial data. For data files in which every bit of every byte is critical, a virtual-circuit approach is preferred.

Datagram Packet Switching

When a packet-switching network makes use of datagrams, a sender's initial message is broken into individual and independent units called **datagrams**. A critical characteristic of this method is that each packet, or datagram, that makes up the message is treated independently. A small message may be contained within one datagram, but a larger message may require several datagrams. Because each datagram is treated independently, each datagram may take a completely different route through the packet-switching cloud. Furthermore, there is no guarantee that all the packets that make up a message will arrive in order at the receiver's end, and in fact it is likely that they will not.

For a message of 10 packets that are sent as datagrams through the packet-switching cloud, packet 7 could arrive first, followed by packets, 3, 6, 5, 4, 2, 1, 10, 8, and finally 9 as illustrated in Figure 7.4. When using a datagram service, the receiver's higher-level layer services must put the packets back in order. The receiver's higher-level layer services must also determine if any packets are missing, and if so, request retransmission of the message.

One advantage of the datagram method is that, as there is no predetermined route, datagrams require little overhead, therefore the routing information does not have to be maintained for the stream of packets that make up a message. A second advantage is that datagrams are flexible in that they can take alternative routes to get to their destination. If a link within a cloud is bad, congested, or unavailable for some reason, a datagram can be routed around it. Because datagrams can be routed through alternative links, should one or more links fail, datagrams are more consistent in terms of delivery. Also, because datagrams

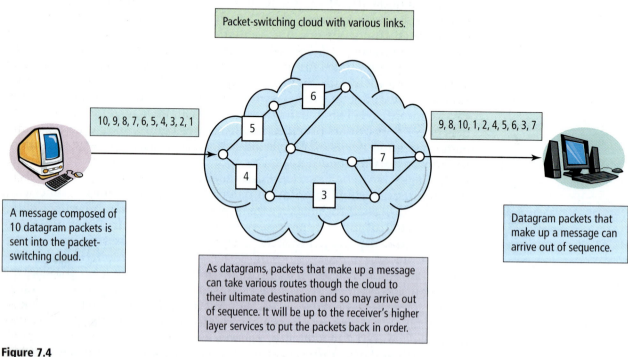

Figure 7.4
Datagram Delivery

do not require any setup procedures between the sender and the receiver, the datagram method of service is faster than virtual-circuit packet services. A disadvantage of datagram delivery, however, is that routing decisions, which require time, must be made at each link that a datagram traverses through.

Virtual-Circuit Packet Switching

Datagram circuits are one type of packet-switched service. The other major type of packet-switched service is the virtual circuit. **Virtual circuits (VCs)** come in two forms: switched and permanent. Both switched and permanent virtual circuits set up a single route of links between the sender and the receiver. Keep in mind that the links are shared by multiple communications, meaning that multiple senders and receivers can use the same link. However, because a single route of links is established, both forms require a setup procedure before communication can begin. Any time setup procedures are required, time is involved, which is one of the disadvantages of VCs as compared with datagrams. Datagrams do not require any special setup between senders and receivers.

Switched virtual circuits (SVCs) are similar to standard dial-up, circuit-switched connections in that the route of links a circuit takes is only established temporarily for the duration of the communication. After a communication concludes, SVCs are dissolved, as with a circuit-switched, dial-up connection. Because SVCs are temporary, a setup procedure is required for every established communication.

In contrast, permanent virtual circuits are more like a leased-line, circuit-switched connection. **Permanent virtual circuits (PVCs)** are continuous, and, once defined, they do not require an additional setup procedure because they are permanent. The user of a PVC is guaranteed use of that circuit. All the communications that use a PVC take the same route each time. Whether using an SVC or a PVC, all of the packets that make up a single message are sent in sequence along the same route of links. This is very different from a datagram service in which each packet can take an independent route between the sender and the receiver.

Virtual circuits are less flexible than datagrams in that if a problem occurs along the route, the packets cannot simply be routed around the problem area. Instead, a new virtual circuit must be established. Recall that with a datagram, if a link is bad or congested, the datagram can simply take a different route. In order to use a single route, virtual circuits also require that packets carry, besides sequence numbers, additional identification information. This identification information includes the address of the virtual circuit being used as well as the address of the specific communication on the virtual circuit. An address for the specific communication is required because multiple communications share the virtual circuit links and the packet-switching cloud needs a way to differentiate one communication from another. Figure 7.5 illustrates this concept.

Three popular forms of packet-switched services are X.25, Frame Relay, and Asynchronous Transfer Mode. X.25 is the oldest, and Asynchronous Transfer Mode is the most recent. Asynchronous Transfer Mode is also called a cell relay packet-switching service.

X.25

In 1976, the **X.25** packet-switching model was accepted by the ITU-T (the International Telecommunications Union-Telecommunication Standards Sector introduced in Chapter 1). The X.25 model uses data terminal equipment (DTE) and data circuit-terminating equipment (DCE) to transfer packets through the X.25 cloud. (DTE and DCE were discussed in Chapter 2.)

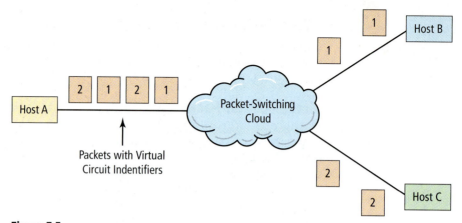

Figure 7.5
Virtual Circuit with Identifiers
A logical virtual circuit connection between one device and another is established. Packets that make up a message are tagged with virtual circuit identification numbers. These numbers in turn identify the series of links that packets will take to get from one packet-switching device to another. In this example, host A is sending packets to host B using virtual circuit number 1. Host A will use virtual circuit number 2 in sending packets to host C.

X.25 uses virtual circuits and statistical time-division multiplexing (also presented in Chapter 2) to transfer packets. Like the OSI and TCP/IP models, X.25 is also a layered design. X.25 defines three layers, from bottom to top: physical, frame, and packet. The physical layer matches the physical layers of the OSI and TCP/IP models. The frame layer functions at the data link layer of these models. The packet layer functions at the network layer of these models.

The physical layer of X.25 uses a protocol called X.21, which is similar to other physical layer protocols. The frame layer, which provides data link control, uses a bit-oriented protocol called **Link Access Procedure-Balanced (LAPB)**, which is a subset of HDLC. The X.25 frame layer uses three types of frames: I, S, and U. (HDLC and the frame types I, S, and U were presented in Chapter 3.) In an X.25 network, frames convert the data into packets. I-frames encapsulate the data sent down from the packet layer. S-frames are used for error and flow control. U-frames are used to set up and dissolve links between DTEs and DCEs. The X.25 packet layer's job is to create VCs for use between communicating devices.

One way that X.25 differs from FR and ATM is that an X.25 network creates virtual circuits at the network layer rather than the data link layer. In the X.25 implementation, two types of packets are used at the packet layer: control and data packets. Also, X.25 uses two types of flow and error control. At the frame layer, flow and error control are performed between the link that connects a DTE device to a DCE device. At the packet layer, flow and error control are for the end-to-end connection between the originating sending device and the eventual receiving device, which may have many links in between them. What this means is that flow and error control are only performed by the sender and receiver, the end-to-end devices, and not all of the other intermediary devices between them. These are two very different types of flow and error control. The amount of error checking provided by X.25 was once an advantage due to the lower quality transmission media that were used in the past. With today's better quality media, it is now a disadvantage. Much of the bandwidth capacity of an X.25 network is taken up by traffic related to error control.

The Ethical Perspective

WAN Technology, Employees, and Privacy

Many businesses rely on WAN technologies to provide services to various groups of users. The WAN infrastructure enables project data to be shared among staff members, product information to be made available to customers, and partnering vendors to more efficiently exchange financial data. Within these three groups, employees, customers, and vendors, much discussion is taking place, particularly as to what defines appropriate use of the corporate WAN. For example, is sending an e-mail on company time to a family member using company networking technology an ethical use of that technology? Or, if an employee is accused of harassing another employee using the same corporate e-mail system, is the business also at fault should legal damages be sought by the harassed employee?

WANs, and particularly the Internet, have transformed the boundaries between private and business communications. Today, it is not unusual for businesses and universities to have written policies on ethical behavior regarding the WAN. The San Joaquin County Office of Education in California has a detailed employee Internet ethics and acceptable user policy that guides employee behavior (**www.sjcoe.net/InformationTechnology/Employee.pdf**).

Businesses also expect employees to be responsible in their use, management, and protection of corporate information resources. *Darwin* magazine reported in its May 2003 edition (**www.darwinmag.com/read/050103/pda.html**) of a sales representative who lost his Personal Digital Assistant (PDA) device and did not report the loss to his manager. The PDA had been purchased for the employee by the business. The PDA was later found by a couple of teenagers. Using information stored on the sales representative's PDA, the teenagers were able to electronically break into the business's databases. They succeeded in corrupting and damaging data that ultimately resulted in lost sales and jeopardized customer confidence.

Once the break-in was discovered, the sales representative was dismissed for not having reported his loss of the PDA. The business blamed the representative for not doing enough to protect the privacy of its customer and financial data. Do you think the representative should have been dismissed? Do you think the representative had an ethical duty to report the loss of his PDA? Finally, do you think that policies such as those defined by the San Joaquin County Office of Education should bind employees to an ethical agreement? What would you include in or leave out of such a policy?

For delivery purposes, X.25 packets use **virtual circuit identifiers (VCIs)** and **logical channel numbers (LCNs)**. The VCI identifies the route between the sender and the receiver, whereas the LCN identifies who the sender and receiver are. Recall that multiple communications from different senders and receivers can be carried on the same virtual circuit. As a packet-switching technology, X.25 is a mature and proven implementation. However, new types of data communications needs, specifically those related to graphics, multimedia, and voice, have shown that X.25 is inadequate because of its limited data rate capacity.

A simple tutorial on X.25 is available from Sangoma Technologies at **www.sangoma.com/x25.htm**. Alternative solutions have since been developed. The following text explores two other packet-switching implementations, Frame Relay and Asynchronous Transfer Mode.

Frame Relay

As a packet-switching alternative, **Frame Relay (FR)** has proven to be very popular due to its relatively high-speed transmission capability, flexibility, and cost. Unlike X.25, Frame Relay does much of its work at the data link layer of the OSI and TCP/IP models. Like X.25, Frame Relay uses variable-length data packets. For delivery purposes, a **Data Link Connection Identifier (DLCI)** identifies the virtual circuit between the sender and the receiver. (A useful tutorial on Frame Relay is available at the Frame Relay Forum Web site: **www.frforum.com/basicsguide.html**.)

With Frame Relay, a **subscriber** negotiates a **committed information rate (CIR)** from a carrier that guarantees a specific level of bandwidth. Based on the subscriber's needs, the carrier can also dynamically provide, usually at an additional cost, more bandwidth for those occasions when network demand exceeds normal usage. This temporary need for higher bandwidth is referred to as a *burst*. The user negotiates with the carrier a price for a **committed burst rate (CBR)**, which specifies a maximum bandwidth that will be available during such temporary increases in traffic.

When connecting to a Frame Relay cloud, the user site makes use of a Frame Relay Access Device. The **Frame Relay Access Device (FRAD)** is the interface between the local user site and the Frame Relay cloud. Whereas Frame Relay does much of its work at the data link layer, the FRAD functions at the network layer. On the sending end, a FRAD takes data from the local network and repackages it for transport through the cloud. On the receiving end, another FRAD does just the opposite, repackaging the data into a form required by the local network. A FRAD can assemble and disassemble frames from other protocols, such as SNA, X.25, IP, ATM, and so on. The FRAD provides no routing services, but simply forwards data packets from the local network to an edge switch at a carrier's local **point of presence (POP)**. A point of presence is an access point to a WAN infrastructure that is provided by a common carrier.

A leased line is the most common way that Frame Relay users connect to their carrier's point of presence. Because the cost of a leased line is usually directly related to the length of the line, an important consideration is the location(s) of a carrier's point of presence. Businesses choosing Frame Relay as a WAN solution should evaluate how many POPs a carrier has and their location when selecting a solution provider.

Another important consideration is the number of virtual circuits that run from the FRAD's leased line to other business network sites. For example, if a business has six remote sites that need to be connected through a Frame Relay WAN, the leased lines at each of the six sites should be capable of handling the virtual circuit traffic demands coming from the five other locations. If a leased line cannot adequately support all of the traffic coming through, an additional leased line might be required. Alternative solutions could be, again, based on business needs, purchasing Fractional T-1 services (covered later in this chapter) or even a standard dial-up modem connection.

Frame Relay uses only two layers, the physical and data link layers, thereby making it inherently more efficient than X.25. At the physical layer, Frame Relay supports any protocol defined by ANSI (the standards-setting body identified in Chapter 1). At the data link layer Frame Relay uses a simplified form of HDLC called core **Link Access Procedure-Function (LAPF)**. LAPF provides only a minimum level of data link control functions. This means that Frame Relay has far less overhead than X.25. Another significant difference between Frame Relay and X.25 is that in a Frame Relay network, virtually no flow and error control are provided for between links or by end-to-end routing. Instead, Frame Relay leaves it up

Figure 7.6
Traffic officers may be needed when traffic congestion occurs. Data infrastructures also need ways for managing data congestion.

to higher-level services to provide these functions. However, because Frame Relay does not support flow control, traffic congestion can be a real problem.

Congestion Control in Frame Relay   **Congestion control** has two basic characteristics: avoidance and recovery. Figure 7.6 uses the image of a traffic officer to demonstrate the concept of congestion control. Frame Relay has a fairly primitive mechanism that it uses to address these two elements. Frame Relay makes use of two bits in a frame to notify the sender and/or receiver of congestion on the network. Frame Relay uses a **backward-explicit congestion notification (BECN)** bit signal to alert the sender of network congestion. A **forward-explicit congestion notification (FECN)** bit signal is used to alert the receiver of network congestion. If either of these signals is detected, the network should initiate congestion-avoidance procedures. **Congestion avoidance** implies that the sender or the receiver will begin to reduce, or throttle down, its transmission in recognition of the network's congested status. Here is a practical comparison. Imagine that you are driving on a superhighway with a speed limit of 70 miles per hour. Also imagine that initially there is little traffic, so it is possible to drive the maximum speed limit. Now assume you begin to encounter very heavy traffic, such that you are required to throttle down your speed to 5 miles an hour. You are performing a type of congestion avoidance.

In a Frame Relay network, if for some reason congestion-avoidance procedures are not initiated, then congestion-recovery procedures are started. With **congestion recovery**, a "discard eligibility" bit signal is used on frames that are considered less important. If a frame's discard eligibility bit is turned on, then that frame can be discarded in the event of network congestion. Again, it will be up to higher-level network services to request retransmission of any frames discarded due to network congestion. In the superhighway example, congestion recovery would be similar to highway patrol officers directing cars off of the superhighway until traffic had a chance to clear up and return to normal.

Various vendors provide Frame Relay solutions. One such vender is Cisco. (See Cisco's Frame Relay glossary at **www.cisco.com/warp/public/74/87.html**.) Compared with X.25, Frame Relay provides better transmission capacity and flexibility at a reduced cost. Still, Frame Relay is not a perfect solution. For the integration of voice, data, and video, Frame Relay has proven to be inadequate. A proposed WAN solution, which has yet to be widely deployed due to its cost and complexity, is Asynchronous Transfer Mode.

Asynchronous Transfer Mode

The promise of **Asynchronous Transfer Mode (ATM)** is that it is a universal, integrated carrier of voice, data, video, and any other resource-intensive type of data. These are the advantages. However, two significant disadvantages of ATM are its high cost and high level of complexity. These two disadvantages have delayed the widespread acceptance of ATM as a WAN connectivity solution. Like Frame Relay, ATM operates at two levels: the physical and data link layers. Unlike Frame Relay and X.25, ATM uses fixed-length packets called **cells** to transmit data. ATM cells are fixed at 53 bytes. These 53 bytes are divided into 5 bytes of header and 48 bytes of data, as shown in Figure 7.7. The 5 bytes of header may not sound like a lot, but these 5 bytes account for almost 10 percent of the total cell, a relatively large amount of cell consumption. In comparison, a full-sized Ethernet frame has less than 2 percent of its frame taken up by control information.

Because ATM cells are fixed, it is much easier to measure and regulate their bandwidth usage over a connection. The fixed cell length also makes ATM easier to manage and predict than variable-length delivery systems such as X.25 and Frame Relay. Another feature that makes ATM so appealing is that a quality-of-service feature has been built into the protocol, making it easy to implement prioritization of data transmission. Communications considered critical can be flagged and have priority access to circuit capacity. As a protocol, ATM has been more successful as a backbone technology, primarily due to its cost and complexity. With desktop LAN speeds of 25.6 Mbps, ATM is at a disadvantage compared with Fast Ethernet, with its speeds of up to 100 Mbps. As a backbone, however, ATM can run up to 2.46 Gbps.

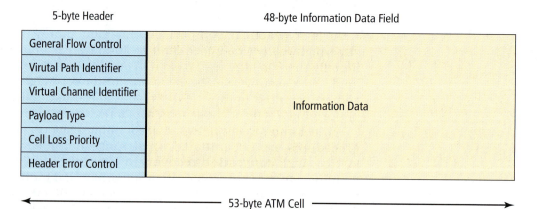

Figure 7.7
Simple ATM Cell

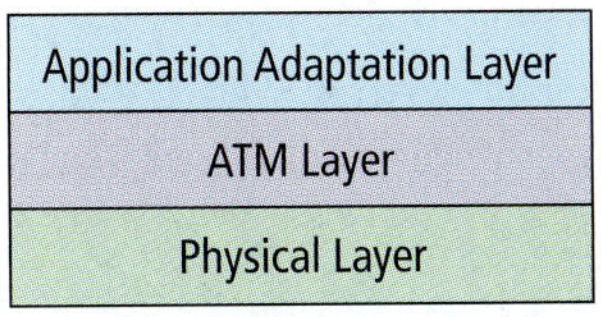

| Application Adaptation Layer |
| ATM Layer |
| Physical Layer |

Figure 7.8
ATM layers

ATM is a Point-to-Point Protocol solution. For this reason, ATM networks do not use routers, but rather switches. However, ATM switches, as well as NICs, are typically far more expensive than those found in a comparable Ethernet network. ATM, by definition, is a connection-oriented protocol that does not have broadcasting capabilities. Consequently, without complicated software interfaces, protocols such as Ethernet and token ring cannot directly detect an ATM network. The fact that setting up and maintaining an ATM network is so complicated also means that finding qualified staff can be challenging, and if found, likely expensive.

Although it functions at the physical and data link layers, ATM defines three layers, as shown in Figure 7.8. From the bottom to top, these layers are the physical, Asynchronous Transfer Mode (ATM), and Application Adaptation layers. At the physical layer, the transmission medium can be twisted-wire pair, coaxial cable, or fiber-optic. The ATM layer is responsible for delivery, traffic control, and switching and multiplexing services. For delivery, the ATM layer makes use of a **virtual path identifier (VPI)** and a **virtual channel identifier (VCI)** between the sender and the receiver. A VPI and a VCI are carried in each cell and are important for identifying the destination device. The Application Adaptation layer permits existing networks to connect to ATM services.

Application Adaptation is responsible at the sender's end for disassembling upper-layer data into ATM's fixed 53-byte cells and at the receiver's end for reassembling the data back into its original format. A significant advantage of ATM is that it can easily handle all data types, including voice, data, audio, and video. However, for organizations that do not have high-bandwidth applications, such as videoconferencing, Gigabit Ethernet is probably a more cost-effective and more easily managed backbone solution. A group of individuals and organizations specifically interested in ATM make up The ATM Forum. The organization's Web site, **www.atmforum.com**, offers information on the latest ATM developments.

Other WAN solutions in addition to X.25, Frame Relay, and ATM are also possible. Three in particular that are widely available and implemented are Point-to-Point Protocol, trunk carrier services, and Digital Subscriber Line.

Point-to-Point Protocol

Point-to-Point Protocol (PPP) is a data link layer standard developed by the IETF. PPP creates a physical link serial connection between two communicating devices. Currently, PPP is the most common protocol used by standard dial-up analog modems to connect to the Internet or to connect one remote computer with another, hence the name "point-to-point." Prior to PPP, the dial-up protocol of choice was **Serial Line Internet Protocol (SLIP)**. PPP has pretty much completely replaced SLIP. A key advantage of SLIP was its simplicity; ironically, this simplicity was also a major disadvantage.

As a serial link protocol, SLIP is very easy to implement and has negligible overhead. However, SLIP only supports IP packets, it does not allow for the dynamic allocation of IP addresses, it does not support user authentication, and it has no error correction and detection capabilities.

Figure 7.9
Typical External Modem

Thus, SLIP has some serious limitations. Also, SLIP does not support multiprotocol networking, which is very common today. PPP was developed as a response to SLIP's shortcomings. Public Switched Telephone Network (PSTN) providers offer both SLIP and PPP.

PPP is used with external modems, Figure 7.9, internal modems, Figure 7.10, and other direct end-to-end connections. It does not require a MAC protocol. Functioning at only the two lower-level layers, the physical and data link layers, PPP is used in conjunction with other higher-level layer services. For users who connect to ISPs with PPP, it is up to the ISP to implement access control measures to protect its network from unauthorized users.

PPP supports multiplexing and several authentication protocols; in doing so, PPP actually uses several other protocols. For example, for authentication, PPP frequently uses Password Authentication Protocol (PAP) and Challenge Handshake Authentication Protocol (CHAP). (A description of

Figure 7.10
Typical Internal Modem

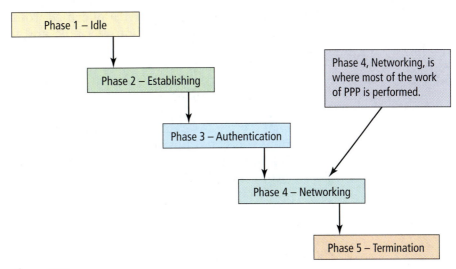

Figure 7.11
Five Phases of the Point-to-Point Protocol

how CHAP works can be found at **www.ietf.org/rfc/rfc1994.txt**.) Both PAP and CHAP are defined by TCP/IP standards, but PPP can also use authentication protocols supplied by private vendors.

Between two end-to-end devices connecting through PPP, five states, or phases, are possible. Figure 7.11 illustrates the sequence of these phases. In the first phase, prior to a connection being established, the two devices are in an *idle state*, meaning that there is no activity on the line. At some point, one of the two devices begins a communication, initiating phase two, the *establishing state*. While in the establishing state, the two devices negotiate and must agree on their communication. Examples of this negotiation include the type of authentication and the network layer protocols that will be used. Once communications are successfully negotiated, the *authentication state* may be entered. This third phase is optional, but if used, it requires that the requesting device be authenticated and approved by the receiving device. If the third phase is initiated and the communication is successfully authenticated, the fourth phase, or the *networking state*, is entered. If the third phase is not required, the fourth phase is immediately entered into. The networking state is where the bulk of PPP's work is done. At this point, the two devices begin exchanging user control and data packets. Eventually, one of the devices initiates the final and fifth phase, the *termination state*. This final state ensures a controlled end of communications between the two end-to-end devices.

PPP relies on the **Logical Control Protocol (LCP)** to establish, maintain, and terminate communications. LCP uses a variety of configuration, monitoring, debugging, and termination packets. Once communications have been established, and the networking state has been entered, PPP next uses the **Network Control Protocol (NCP)**. In the networking state, PPP uses NCP to encapsulate data coming from various network layer protocols, including IP.

In terms of transmission capacity, modems using PPP have a theoretical maximum throughput of 56 Kbps. However, in the United States, the maximum throughput permitted by the Federal Communications Commission (FCC) is 53 Kbps. Even so, due to line conditions and a variety of factors, it is very unusual for a typical analog modem user to achieve 53 Kbps of bandwidth. The major attractions of a PPP WAN link are affordability and ease of implementation. The low-cost hardware and the extensive competitive service offerings from many vendors continue to make PPP dial-up connections a viable and much used WAN technology. A more detailed discussion of PPP can be found at **www.faqs.org/rfcs/rfc1661.html**.

Trunk Carrier Services

Although PPP connections are inexpensive, widely offered, and easy to implement, they also suffer from seriously limited bandwidth capacity. For many users and businesses, higher-capacity WAN links are required. Like PPP links, other options supplied by PSTN providers also include various forms of leased lines. The most commonly used forms are referred to as T-1, T-3, and Fractional T-1 services, although there are others. The "T" in these names stands for **trunk carrier service**. Organizations that lease these lines are referred to as subscribers. T-1 lines are among the most common trunk lines for businesses and universities due to their lower cost. A simple description of how a T-1 line works can be found at **www.howstuffworks.com/question372.htm**.

Leased lines provide, at a significant cost, a dedicated and permanent connection between two sites linked by a telephone network. The line is dedicated in that it is available 24 hours a day, 7 days a week, to the subscriber. The line is permanent in that it is not necessary to dial in to establish a connection. However, it is also not possible to call a different location without changing the line's hardware installation. Of course, a service provider will be happy to do whatever the business wants—for a price. Realistically, when an organization sets up its leased line connections, it needs to plan wisely and accurately as to how the installation is to be implemented.

The cost of a leased line includes an initial installation fee, the hardware costs for connecting devices, and an ongoing monthly subscription fee. For this cost, the subscriber gets a guaranteed, specified bandwidth and quality of service, both determined by how much the subscriber is willing to pay. Within the quality of service, the provider stipulates a guaranteed percent of service availability and error-free communications. For example, the provider may guarantee that its infrastructure will be available 99.7 percent of the time and error-free 99.8 percent of the time. These types of quality of service percentages are negotiated.

The subscriber uses the leased line for communications between two connecting points. The two points may be separated by a state or a continent. For the subscriber, the PSTN provider installs a dedicated link between each of the subscriber's two communicating end points and the PSTN's own local point of presence. A point of presence is the provider's local connecting point or facility for establishing local physical links to subscribers.

Once the subscriber's communications reach the provider's point of presence, the provider's switching facilities take over and supply the rest of the communication link. Thus, a leased, permanent line does not literally mean that the provider gives the subscriber a single physical wire connecting two end points. Instead, the provider's switching facilities, or cloud, are being leased.

The subscriber does not need to be concerned with what happens to communications once they reach the provider's point of presence. From the point of presence, the cloud takes care of end-to-end communications. The advantage to subscribers is that they do not need to concern themselves with how the cloud is configured or maintained. The disadvantage is that subscribers have no control over how the cloud implements and secures communications.

Table 7.1 Characteristics of the Trunk-Carrier Levels

Trunk-Carrier Level	DS Level	Bandwidth Capacity	Number of 64-Kbps Channels
DS-0	DS-0	64 Kbps	1
T-1	DS-1	1.54 Mbps	24
T-2	DS-2	6.31 Mbps	96 (4 T-1's)
T-3	DS-3	44.74 Mbps	672 (28 T-1's)
T-4	DS-4	274.18 Mbps	4,032 (168 T-1's)

Leased lines can be analog or digital; most leased WAN connections are digital. Digital leased lines have a range of bandwidth capacities that are referred to as **digital signal (DS) speeds**. The digital signal speeds are used to categorize the various trunk-carrier levels: T-1, T-2, T-3, and T-4. A given trunk-carrier level is capable of supporting a given number of 64-Kbps, voice-grade communication channels. The higher the trunk-carrier-level designation, the greater the number of communication channels possible, and the higher the bandwidth capacity. Table 7.1 identifies the various trunk-carrier levels and their associated characteristics.

Within a trunk-carrier level, each 64-Kbps channel can be used for voice or data traffic. One potential problem with leasing a trunk carrier is that the organization's voice and data demands may not fully utilize the amount of bandwidth available. Although costs vary, in general, as of the writing of this text, the monthly charge for a T-1 line that spans a city could be as much as $2,000 a month, whereas one that spans a country could cost $20,000 a month. Organizations that do not require a dedicated, always available T-1 connection may instead lease a *Fractional* T-1 connection. **Fractional T-1** lines are shared by multiple subscribers and provide a more cost-effective solution for businesses whose data communication needs do not require the capacity of a private T-1 connection. However, a dedicated T-1 line might be cost-effective for an organization that has hundreds of users who need frequent, reliable, and secure access to such resources as Web and e-mail services.

Channel and Data Service Units To establish a T-1 connection, each end of a digital leased line requires two devices that are usually combined into one unit: a channel service unit and a data service unit. The **channel service unit (CSU)** is the end point of the digital link; it keeps the link open and active even when the communication device connected to it—a bridge, router, or Private Branch Exchange—is not using the link. A **Private Branch Exchange (PBX)** is an on-site switching facility that connects the telephones of a site and provides access to a PSTN. For large organizations, T-1 lines are commonly used to support PBX operations. Figure 7.12 graphically illustrates how these components are used in a T-1 connection.

The job of the **data service unit (DSU)** is to convert signals from the connecting device, again, usually a bridge, router, or PBX, into the type of digital signal, usually bipolar, required by the leased line. The CSU/DSU can be configured to provide channeled or unchanneled services. A **channeled service** breaks up the leased line into multiple channels for multiple uses. Multiple channels require that a multiplexer be placed

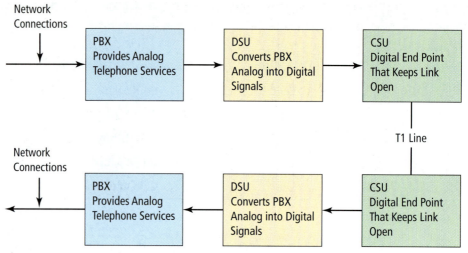

Figure 7.12
Use of a PBX, DSU, and CSU

between the CSU/DSU and the connection to the local network. Recall that with multiplexing, multiple devices can share a single high-speed circuit. An **unchanneled service** simply uses the leased line as a single-channel pipeline for transmitting communications. As of this writing, a basic CSU/DSU unit, which is required at each end of the leased line, costs approximately $1,000.

At one time, T-1 lines were just about the only game in town for organizations requiring reliable, secure, and relatively high-capacity bandwidth WAN connections. Today, other solutions are available that offer cost-effective WAN services. One such solution, which is popular in Europe but that has never found a wide market in the United States, is **Integrated Service Digital Network (ISDN)**. Those who want to know more about ISDN should see the "Topic in Focus" at the end of this chapter. Another WAN solution is Digital Subscriber Line.

Digital Subscriber Line

Whereas ISDN has not proven very successful in the Unites States as a WAN connectivity solution, **Digital Subscriber Line (DSL)** has become a popular choice in the U.S. market. Two factors have made DSL a popular choice: its relatively low cost and high transmission speeds. Like ISDN, DSL can support simultaneous voice and data communications based on the type of DSL service selected. Because there are different types of DSL services, DSL is not a single service type, but rather an umbrella of service types. DSL is technically referred to as xDSL, with the "x" used to indicate the type of DSL service provided, as shown in the following list:

- Asymmetrical Digital Subscriber Line—ADSL

- Asymmetrical Digital Subscriber Line Lite—ADSL Lite

- High-bit-rate Digital Subscriber Line—HDSL

- ISDN Digital Subscriber Line—IDSL

- Rate-Adaptive Digital Subscriber Line—RADSL

- Symmetric Digital Subscriber Line—SDSL

- Very-high-bit-rate Digital Subscriber Line—VDSL

Table 7.2 DSL Service Options

Type of xDSL Service	Segment Length	Simultaneous Voice Support	Bandwidth
ADSL	10,000 to 18,000 feet	Yes	1.544 to 8.448 Mbps downstream; 640 Kbps to 1.544 Mbps upstream
ADSL Lite	8,000 feet	Yes	Up to 1 Mbps downstream; up to 51k Kbps upstream
HDSL	12,000 to 15,000 feet	No	1.544 Mbps to 2.048 Mbps
IDSL	18,000 feet	No	Up to 144 Kbps
RADSL	10,000 to 18,000 feet	Yes	1.544 to 8.448 Mbps downstream; 640 Kbps to 1.544 Mbps upstream
SDSL	10,000 feet	Yes	1.544 Mbps to 2.048 Mbps
VDSL	1,000 to 4,500 feet	Yes	12.96 to 51.84 Mbps downstream; 1.6 to 2.3 Mbps upstream

Table 7.2 provides a snapshot view of the various DSL service options and lists some of their characteristics. The characteristics of each DSL service option are described in greater detail in the following sections.

Notice in Table 7.2 that shorter segment lengths are associated with higher bandwidth capacity, and that not all forms of DSL simultaneously support voice and data communications. Notice also that depending on the type of DSL service selected, the terms *downstream* and *upstream* are used. Let's take a moment to describe what these terms mean and how they might affect a subscriber's decision as to what DSL service to choose.

Symmetric and Asymmetric DSL Services When a user of a DSL service pulls data, meaning that the data are coming from a remote location to the local device, the term **downstream** is used. When a user pushes data from the local device to a remote device, the term **upstream** is used. When the DSL downstream and upstream bandwidth capacities, or speeds, are equivalent, the type of service is symmetric. When the two rates vary, with the downstream speed generally being greater than the upstream speed, the service is asymmetric. For most users, especially those at home using DSL as an Internet connectivity solution, most traffic is generated downstream, pulling data rather than pushing data upstream.

For this reason, **Asymmetric Digital Subscriber Line (ADSL)** is among the most popular of the DSL services offered. (A somewhat technical overview by the International Engineering Consortium on how ADSL is provided can be found at **www.iec.org/online/tutorials/adsl/topic01.html**.) International telephone providers have aggressively positioned ASDL as a solution to the **last-mile problem**. The last-mile problem refers to the difficulty of connecting residential users who want high-speed Internet access to a communication provider's high-speed infrastructure. Typically, the residential user is about a mile away from the provider's point of presence, hence the term, *last-mile problem*.

Recent consumer complaints, specifically about home ADSL service quality, have caused some to question whether telephone providers are promising more capability than they can adequately handle. As a last-mile solution, DSL works as follows.

The typical telephone line that connects a home or business to a telephone provider's local point of presence uses only a small amount of the line's bandwidth for voice communications. Standard voice communications do not require much in terms of transmission capacity. This leaves much of the bandwidth available for other services, such as DSL. Standard voice telephone bandwidth frequencies are in the range of 0 to 4,000 Hz (hertz). DSL uses frequencies above this range, up to 1.1 MHz, to carry data traffic. Critical, however, to the ability of DSL to work is the distance of the user from the telephone provider's local point of presence. Users beyond 18,000 feet of a local provider's point of presence are not able to use DSL. The greater the distance the user's local site is from the point of presence, the slower the transmission rate.

Asymmetric services are less costly than symmetric services. As it happens, when data travel upstream from the user's machine to the telephone provider's local point of presence, the wiring at the point of presence is more susceptible to near-end cross-talk, which can result in signal loss. Because signal loss is more likely to occur upstream than downstream, asymmetric services compensate by using slower upstream speeds than downstream speeds. Because most DSL users are more interested in downstream data, offering ADSL has worked out well for service providers. For businesses that require faster or equivalent upstream and downstream rates, services such as HDSL are available, but cost more because the lines used must be configured to support faster upstream rates.

ADSL provides far greater transmission capacity than ISDN, which is another reason why it has proven the more popular of the two technologies. In addition, as opposed to ISDN, ADSL offers an "always on" connection, assuming that the devices using the connection are turned on. The data portion of the ADSL circuit functions in many ways like a leased line, but at far less cost. Because the connection is always on, there is no need, as there would be for an ISDN connection, for a session-setup procedure.

Devices that are always on and connected to the Internet are useful in that content is always available to customers, employees, or other service users. Of course, devices that are always on and connected to the Internet are also much more vulnerable to security attacks and attempts by unauthorized users to break in. Chapter 10 explores how to secure the enterprise against this type of unauthorized access.

ADSL Devices   ADSL requires two pieces of hardware at the user's location. One component is called the ADSL Terminal Unit-Remote, or ATU-R. This device is also commonly referred to as the ASDL modem, as shown in Figure 7.13. It usually connects to the user's communicating device using a standard 10Base-T Ethernet port. The ATU-R breaks the user's data into packets and sends them on to the second required component, the **remote splitter**. The splitter is "remote" in that it is not at the provider's location, but is remotely located at the user's site. The remote splitter separates voice signals from data signals on the user's local loop. Recall that with ADSL the same line can be used for both voice and data. The **local loop** is simply the physical connection between the user and the telephone provider's local point of presence.

On the provider's end of the local loop is a **local splitter**, which performs the same function as the user's splitter. The provider also has an ADSL Terminal Unit-Central, or ATU-C, which reverses the process of

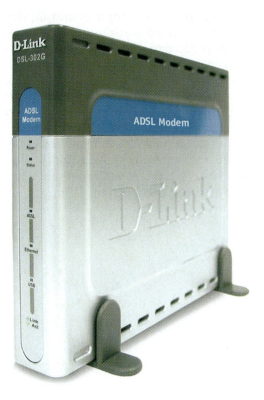

Figure 7.13
Typical DSL Modem

the ATU-R. Many ADSL providers use ATM switching to implement ADSL services. One problem with standard ADSL installations is the difficulty encountered by many users in configuring the remote splitter. To eliminate the issue of user remote-splitter installation, another form of ADSL has been promoted: Universal Asymmetric Digital Subscriber Line, or **G.lite**.

The advantage of G.lite is that it eliminates the need for a remote splitter at the user's location. Instead, passive filtering is used by the ATU-R to separate voice from data signals. A disadvantage is that G.lite only supports fixed downstream and upstream data rates. Downstream traffic will be no more than 1.5 Mbps, whereas upstream traffic has a maximum rate of 512 Kbps. Maximum rates, though, are the exception, and G.lite users typically have slower-than-maximum rate connections. Another problem with G.lite is that it is not as effective as a remote splitter in separating voice from data traffic, which can either cause data rate speeds to decrease or produce noise on the channel carrying a voice communication.

DSL services have been positioned not only as a consumer solution for high-speed Internet access, but as a cost-effective business solution as well. Unlike the typical consumer, a business owner will very likely require e-mail and Web hosting, an electronic payment system, online catalogs and product information, or other customer-focused services. For these reason, business DSL services generally cost more. The following Web site offers a centralized portal for comparing DSL vendors: **www.dslchoices.com**.

A business also needs to consider whether to lease a static or a dynamic IP address. **Static IP addresses** are fixed and unchanging. **Dynamic IP addresses** may change each time a connection is established.

You may recall from Chapter 5 that all devices connected to the Internet must have an IP address. Static IP addresses usually cost more, but have several advantages. For example, for a corporate Web server that is accessed by employees and customers, a static IP address is desirable. Also, with a static IP address, the business will be able to associate and register an Internet domain name for that address. Static addresses also work well when the business needs to frequently transfer files. However, static IP addresses also pose a greater security risk, due to the fact that they are unchanging. Dynamically assigned IP addresses are like a moving target and are less susceptible to hackers. An organization should evaluate with its DSL provider whether a static or dynamic IP address is better for its business needs.

Chapter Summary

WAN connections can be established in several ways. For example, a WAN connection might be created by means of a simple dial-up modem used by a home user or by use of elaborate packet-switching or cell relay technologies. Frame Relay (FR) is a popular packet-switching technology. Asynchronous Transfer Mode (ATM) is the leading example of a cell relay technology.

A switched network is one in which a series of interlinked devices, called switches, are used to create temporary connections between two communicating devices. Switches can be hardware, software, or a combination of both. Switches can be connected to multiple links, providing for multiple pathways through a networking infrastructure. This switching infrastructure is often referred to and graphically illustrated as a cloud. Two common switching technologies are circuit and packet switching. A key characteristic of a circuit-switching service is that it creates a direct connection, or path, between two communicating devices. The term *path* is used for circuit switching; *link* is used for packet switching. Circuit-switched paths may be temporary, such as a standard dial-up connection, or permanent, meaning that the circuit is leased and is always available to the user leasing the line.

With a packet-switched network, rather than treating the data or communication as one flowing, continuous stream, similar to a voice transmission, the data are broken into units called *packets.* Packet switching significantly improves line efficiency because packet streams from differing communications can use the same links between packet-switching nodes. Packet-switching services may be datagram or virtual-circuit based. When a packet-switching network uses datagrams, a sender's initial message is broken into individual, independent units called datagrams. Virtual circuits (VCs) are either switched virtual circuits (SVCs) or permanent virtual circuits (PVCs).

X.25 is a packet-switching model that was developed by the ITU-T in 1976. Like the OSI and TCP/IP models, X.25 is also a layered design. It has three layers: physical, frame, and packet. X.25 packets use virtual circuit identifiers (VCIs) and logical channel numbers (LCNs). Unlike X.25, FR does much of its work at the data link layer of the OSI and TCP/IP models. FR uses a Data Link Connection Identifier (DLCI) that identifies virtual circuits. When connecting to a FR cloud, the user site makes use of a Frame Relay Access Device (FRAD). The FRAD is the interface between the local user site and the FR cloud. A leased line is the most common way users of FR connect to their carrier's POP. FR networks do not provide for flow or error control.

Like FR, ATM operates at two levels, the physical and data link layers. Unlike FR and X.25, ATM uses fixed-length packets, called cells, to transmit data. As a protocol, ATM has been more successful as a backbone technology, primarily due to its cost and complexity. ATM is a point-to-point solution. For this reason, ATM networks do not use routers, but instead use switches. For delivery, the ATM layer makes use of a virtual path identifier (VPI) and a virtual channel identifier (VCI) between the sender and the receiver.

Point-to-Point Protocol, or PPP, is a data link layer standard developed by the IETF. PPP creates a physical link serial connection between two communicating devices. PPP is used with modems and other direct end-to-end connections and does not require MAC. PPP relies on Logical Control Protocol (LCP) to establish, maintain, and terminate communications. Once communications have been established and the networking state has been entered, PPP next uses Network Control Protocols (NCPs).

Like PPP links, other options supplied by PSTN providers include various forms of leased lines. The most commonly used forms are referred to as T-1, T-3, and Fractional T-1 services. Leased lines provide a dedicated and permanent connection between two sites linked by a telephone network. Leased lines can be analog or digital; most leased WAN connections are digital. To establish a T-1 connection, each end of a digital leased line requires two devices that are usually combined into one unit: a channel service unit (CSU) and a data service unit (DSU).

Another connectivity option that has been widely accepted is Digital Subscriber Line, or DSL. Two factors have made DSL a popular choice: its relatively low cost and high transmission speeds. DSL is not a single service type, but rather an umbrella of service types. Not all forms of DSL support simultaneous voice and data communications. When a user of a DSL service pulls data, the term *downstream* is used. When a user pushes data from the local device to a remote device, the term *upstream* is used. When DSL downstream and upstream bandwidth capacities, or speeds, are equivalent, the type of service is symmetric. When the two rates vary, with the downstream speed generally being greater than the upstream speed, the service is asymmetric. Asymmetric services are less costly than symmetric services.

Asymmetrical Digital Subscriber Line (ADSL) **(259)**

Asynchronous Transfer Mode (ATM) **(252)**

Backward-explicit congestion notification (BECN) **(251)**

Bursty **(244)**

Cell **(252)**

Channeled service **(257)**

Channel service unit (CSU) **(257)**

Circuit switching **(243)**

Cloud **(242)**

Committed burst rate (CBR) **(250)**

Committed information rate (CIR) **(250)**

Congestion avoidance **(251)**

Congestion control **(251)**

Congestion recovery **(251)**

Datagram **(246)**

Data Link Connection Identifier (DLCI) **(250)**

Data service unit (DSU) **(257)**

Digital signal (DS) speeds **(257)**

Digital Subscriber Line (DSL) **(258)**

Downstream **(259)**

Dynamic IP address **(261)**

Edge router **(243)**

Edge switch **(243)**

Forward-explicit congestion notification (FECN) **(251)**

Fractional T-1 **(257)**

Frame Relay (FR) **(250)**

Frame Relay Access Device (FRAD) **(250)**

G.lite **(261)**

Integrated Service Digital Network (ISDN) **(258)**

Last-mile problem **(259)**

Link **(243)**

Link Access Procedure-Balanced (LAPB) **(248)**

Link Access Procedure-Function (LAPF) **(250)**

Local loop **(260)**

Local splitter **(260)**

Logical channel number (LCN) **(249)**

Logical Control Protocol (LCP) **(255)**

Network Control Protocol (NCP) **(255)**

Packet **(244)**

Packet switching **(244)**

Path **(243)**

Permanent virtual circuit (PVC) **(247)**

Point of presence (POP) **(250)**

Point-to-Point Protocol (PPP) **(253)**

Private Branch Exchange (PBX) **(257)**

Remote splitter **(260)**

Subscriber **(250)**

Serial Line Internet Protocol (SLIP) **(253)**

Static IP address **(261)**

Switched network **(242)**

Switched virtual circuit (SVC) **(247)**

Trunk carrier service **(256)**

Unchanneled service **(258)**

Upstream **(259)**

Virtual channel identifier (VCI) **(253)**

Virtual circuit (VC) **(247)**

Virtual circuit identifier (VCI) **(249)**

Virtual path identifier (VPI) **(253)**

Wide area network (WAN) **(241)**

X.25 **(247)**

Chapter Questions

Short Answer

1. Describe two ways in which circuit switching differs from packing switching.

2. What is meant by a switching "cloud"?

3. State two ways that Frame Relay differs from X.25.

4. What do upstream and downstream mean with regards to DSL?

Multiple Choice

For each question below select one best answer.

1. Which of the following is a topology in which all of the devices are directly connected to each other?
   a. Mosh **b.** Mesh **c.** Mixed **d.** Crossed

2. Switches can be
   a. hardware. **b.** software. **c.** a and/or b **d.** Neither a nor b

3. Which term refers to a switching network infrastructure?
   a. Storm **b.** Space **c.** Cloud **d.** Object

4. Which of the following is an external device that connects to the outer boundary of a switching network?
   a. Edge hub **b.** Edge switch **c.** Edge router **d.** b or c

5. Which type of switching network creates a path between two communicating devices?
   a. Circuit **b.** Packet **c.** a or b **d.** Neither a nor b

6. Which type of switching network creates a series of links between two communicating devices?
   a. Circuit **b.** Packet **c.** a or b **d.** Neither a nor b

7. Data transmissions tend to be
   a. static. **b.** continuous. **c.** fixed. **d.** bursty.

8. Voice transmissions tend to be
   a. static. **b.** continuous. **c.** fixed. **d.** bursty.

9. At what rate do devices using a circuit-switched connection communicate at?
   a. Constant **b.** Variable **c.** Temporary **d.** Permanent

10. In a circuit-switched connection, which device determines the rate of transmission?
    a. The faster device **b.** The slower device
    c. It depends on the line **d.** None of the above

11. Which type of switching service is preferred for data communications?
    a. Data switched **b.** Circuit switched **c.** Packet switched **d.** a or b

12. Which switching service can be used to transmit data?
    a. Data switched **b.** Circuit switched
    c. Packet switched **d.** b or c

13. Data link rate conversion is associated with which type of network?
    a. Data switched **b.** Circuit switched
    c. Packet switched **d.** Link switched

14. Which type of network might deny communications when all circuits are busy?
    a. Data switched **b.** Circuit switched
    c. Packet switched **d.** Link switched

15. Which of the following treats packets independently?
    a. Cellgrams **b.** Packetgrams **c.** Datagrams **d.** Virtualgrams

16. Which of the following allows the flexible routing of a packet around a congested link?
    a. SVC **b.** PVC **c.** VC **d.** Datagram

17. Which of the following is a temporary route used in a packet-switched network?
    a. SVC **b.** PVC **c.** VC **d.** TVC

18. Which of the following is a permanent route used in a packet-switched network?
    a. SVC **b.** PVC **c.** VC **d.** TVC

19. How many types of virtual circuits are there?
    a. 2 **b.** 4 **c.** 6 **d.** 8

20. Which of the following requires a setup procedure?
    a. SVC **b.** PVC **c.** RVC **d.** TVC

21. Which of the following is a cell relay packet-switching service?
    a. PPP **b.** X.25 **c.** FR **d.** ATM

22. Which of the following operates at three layers of the OSI and TCP/IP models?
    a. PTP **b.** X.25 **c.** FR **d.** ATM

23. Which of the following is a bit-oriented protocol used by X.25?
    a. LAPD **b.** LABP **c.** LAPB **d.** LAPF

24. Which of the following is a bit-oriented protocol used by FR?
    a. LAPD **b.** LABP **c.** LAPB **d.** LAPF

25. At what layer does X.25 create VCs?
    a. Physical **b.** Data link **c.** Network **d.** Transport

26. At what layer does FR create VCs?
    a. Physical **b.** Data link **c.** Network **d.** Transport

27. ATM operates at how many layers of the OSI model?
    a. 1 **b.** 2 **c.** 3 **d.** 4

28. Which of the following uses virtual circuit identifiers?
    a. PPP **b.** X.25 **c.** FR **d.** ATM

29. Which of the following uses virtual channel identifiers?

    a. PPP **b.** X.25 **c.** FR **d.** ATM

30. Which of the following uses fixed-length packets called cells?

    a. ATM **b.** X.25 **c.** FR **d.** ISDN

31. Which of the following uses data link connection identifiers?

    a. PPP **b.** X.25 **c.** FR **d.** ATM

32. Which of the following is an interface between a local site and an FR cloud?

    a. IRAD **b.** CRAD **c.** DRAD **d.** FRAD

33. Which of the following provides flow and error control at two layers?

    a. PPP **b.** ATM **c.** X.25 **d.** FR

34. Congestion control has what basic characteristic?

    a. avoidance **b.** recovery **c.** a or b **d.** a and b

35. How many bits does FR use in a frame for congestion control?

    a. 2 **b.** 6 **c.** 12 **d.** 64

36. Which solution was designed for the integration of voice, data, video, and audio?

    a. ATM **b.** X.25 **c.** FR **d.** ISDN

37. Approximately what percentage of an ATM packet is taken up by control information?

    a. 2 **b.** 4 **c.** 5 **d.** 10

38. For a maximum-sized Ethernet packet, approximately what percent of the packet is taken up by control information?

    a. 2 **b.** 4 **c.** 5 **d.** 10

39. What is the approximate desktop LAN speed of ATM?

    a. 10 Mbps **b.** 25 Mbps **c.** 100 Mbps **d.** 2.5 Gbps

40. Which standards group developed PPP?

    a. IEEE **b.** ANSI **c.** ITFE **d.** IETF

41. During which state is most of PPP's work done?

    a. Authentication **b.** Establishing **c.** Networking **d.** Idle

42. Which protocol does PPP use to terminate communications?

    a. LCP **b.** LPC **c.** PCL **d.** None of the above

43. What is the theoretical maximum throughput of PPP?

    a. 28 Kbps **b.** 56 Kbps **c.** 64 Kbps **d.** 128 Kbps

44. What does the "T" in T-1 stand for?

    a. Timed **b.** Termed **c.** True **d.** Trunk

45. Leased lines can be

    a. analog. **b.** digital. **c.** a or b **d.** None of the above

46. Which term refers to when a user of a DSL service pulls data?

    a. Sending **b.** Downstream **c.** Pushing **d.** Upstream

47. Which term refers to when a user of a DSL service pushes data?

    a. Pulling **b.** Downstream **c.** Receiving **d.** Upstream

48. When the two rates provided by a DSL connection vary, the connection is said to be

    a. symmetric. **b.** timed. **c.** asymmetric. **d.** doubled.

49. When the two rates provided by a DSL connection are the same, it is said to be

    a. symmetric. **b.** timed. **c.** asymmetric. **d.** doubled.

50. Standard voice telephone bandwidth frequencies are not above what hertz frequency?

    a. 2,000 **b.** 4,000 **c.** 12,000 **d.** 64,000

True or False

For each of the following select either True or False.

1. Standard dial-up telephone connections can be used to create a WAN link.

2. Frame Relay was developed before X.25.

3. Switches can be connected to multiple links.

4. An edge switch is usually placed at the center of a switching infrastructure.

5. Circuit switching uses temporary circuits only.

6. Circuit switching treats all requested transmissions in the same manner.

7. Packet-switching links can use data rate link conversions.

8. Datagrams have relatively little overhead.

9. Packets for a specific message using a virtual circuit take the same route.

10. The user of a permanent virtual circuit must share the circuit and is not guaranteed use of the circuit if the circuit is busy.

11. X.25 provides for relatively little flow control.

12. Frame Relay does much of its work at the data link layer.

13. A FRAD provides routing services for packets.

14. Frame Relay provides for significant flow and error control.

15. Packets in an ATM network are called cells.

16. PPP was developed by ANSI.

17. PPP does not support authentication protocols.

18. The user of a T-1 service is responsible for how the cloud is configured.

19. Symmetric DSL services provide the same downstream and upstream data rates.

20. Most users of DSL services are more interested in downstream data.

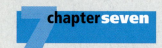

Exercises

Research in Brief

For one or more of the questions below, provide a one- to two-page report based on your findings.

1. Many different vendors offer DSL services. Investigate three providers in your area who offer DSL. Identify what types of DSL service they offer, at what cost, and at what service level. Report on the type of equipment they provide and if there are any issues involving home installation.

2. This chapter has presented material on Frame Relay as a WAN connectivity solution. Visit the Frame Relay forum Web site at **www.frforum.com**. What types of information does the site provide? Sample and evaluate one or more of the tutorials on the site. How does this site promote the use of Frame Relay?

3. Investigate in greater detail how datagram packet switching differs from virtual circuit packet switching. Identify situations when one or the other may be more appropriate. Explain the relative advantages and disadvantages of each technology.

4. X.25 is a mature WAN connectivity solution. Research and report back on the history and development of X.25. What bodies were involved in its evolution? What benefits does an X.25 network provide? What issues with X.25 have caused other WAN connectivity solutions to be pursued, if any?

Case Study

Sheehan Marketing and Public Relations

Two additional branches, one in Miami and the other in Nashville, have finally joined the three original SMPR offices. The growth of SMPR means that more networking staff must be hired. You are working closely with President Sheehan and with Karla to plan for SMPR's WAN and staffing needs.

President Sheehan has asked you to present and prepare a report identifying the different WAN connectivity options that can be used to connect the five branch offices. He wants to know the relative advantages and disadvantages of each and which one you recommend SMPR use and why. Because of the nature of SMPR's business, very large audio and video files need to be shared by project teams who may be located at two or more remote branches. Video conferencing is not required. President Sheehan wants fast and reliable bandwidth capacity to support the type of data that SMPR's clients provide. Furthermore, he wants your solution to provide for any multiplexing that might be required across the sites. He also wants to know the costs that such a solution would entail.

You have been approved to hire three additional networking staff. Working with Human Resources, you have been asked to provide job descriptions for two intermediate networking technicians and one senior

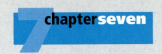
networking administrator. The Vice President of Human Resources is unfamiliar with the skills required for these types of positions. He has asked you to research classified advertisements, professional organizations, and local employment agencies to develop accurate job descriptions with salary profiles.

Privately, you have some concerns that Karla may be anxious about the new hires. Over the past year, you have developed an excellent working relationship with Karla and have assisted her in getting the technical training that she needed. In fact, she has become a valuable asset, and you worry that she may be looking for another position. Do you plan to share this concern with either President Sheehan or the Vice President of Human Resources? Why or why not? Would this news put Karla in an awkward position? How would you deal with Karla's unease with the new staffing positions?

Web References

www.its.bldrdoc.gov

www.itpapers.com

www.novell.com/info/glossary/glossary.html

www2.rad.com/networks/1998/packet/sim.htm

www.sjcoe.net/InformationTechnology/Employee.pdf

www.darwinmag.com/read/050103/pda.html

www.sangoma.com/x25.htm

www.frforum.com/basicsguide.html

www.cisco.com/warp/public/74/87.html

www.atmforum.com

www.ietf.org/rfc/rfc1994.txt

www.faqs.org/rfcs/rfc1661.html

www.howstuffworks.com/question372.htm

www.iec.org/online/tutorials/adsl/topic01.html

www.dslchoices.com

www.frforum.com

A Closer Look at ISDN

Integrated Service Digital Network, or ISDN, is a WAN connectivity solution that, although popular in Europe, have never found a wide audience in the United States. Like PPP, ISDN is a digital point-to-point telephone system service. ISDN makes use of existing copper PSTN cable from a home or business to carry data at relatively high transmission rates. However, basic-rate ISDN requires that the telephone service provider's point of presence (POP) be no more than 18,000 feet from the point of installation. ISDN is included in a list of technologies, such as DSL, that are designed to solve the last-mile problem. The last-mile problem refers to the difficulty of providing a high-speed link from a user's home or business to the nearest POP of a telephone service provider. The distance that this high-speed link typically needs to cover is about 1 mile. Once the local link reaches the POP, the cloud takes over.

ISDN Hardware

Unlike a leased T-carrier line, an ISDN link is not permanent. ISDN uses dial-up devices to make a connection to the service provider's telephone network infrastructure. One benefit of ISDN is that the existing telephone copper wiring already installed in most homes and businesses does not have to be modified, as long as the 18,000-foot limit from the nearest POP is not exceeded. ISDN requires that each end of the communication link have a special hardware device called an NT1, or Network Terminator-1 unit. (This hardware is also sometimes referred to as an ISDN modem, as shown in Figure 7.14.) The telephone service provider connects the NT1 to what is referred to as a U interface. This U interface, using one twisted pair of wires, converts signals from the NT1 and passes these signals to an S/T interface. The S/T interface is used by ISDN terminal equipment for communications. ISDN terminal equipment devices use the ISDN connection. An S/T interface may use six to eight wires, depending on how it is installed. The extra wires can be used to provide emergency power to a telephone in the event of a local power failure.

Some devices can connect directly to the S/T interface. These are referred to as Terminal Equipment-1 (TE-1) devices. TE-1 devices are ISDN-ready. Other devices, such as standard analog telephones and fax machines, require an intermediary connector called a terminal adapter (TA). The analog device connects to the TA, which then connects to the S/T interface. Devices that require a TA are called Terminal Equipment-2 (TE-2) hardware. Up to seven

Figure 7.14
Typical ISDN Modem

devices, either TE-1 or TE-2, can be connected to an NT1 unit. The NT1 unit and the S/T interface are often combined into a single device, such as an expansion card for a personal computer. Often these devices, or the combined single device, are inaccurately referred to as an ISDN modem. Modems convert digital computer signals to analog and back. ISDN equipment does not perform this type of conversion, because the data it receives are already digital.

ISDN devices are dial-up devices. However, they do not have standard dial-up telephone numbers. Instead, they dial and establish a digital connection by dialing another ISDN number. It is possible, though, to buy ISDN telephones that permit a user to dial standard analog telephone numbers. Because ISDN is a dial-up service, the subscriber in most cases pays only for the bandwidth used. Typically, subscribers pay additional per-minute charges beyond the installation and monthly subscription fees. For the home user, these per-minute costs can make ISDN an expensive option. For a business, though, an ISDN line can be much more cost-effective than having a leased line. Bear in mind that with a leased line, the subscriber pays for bandwidth even when it is not being used. Also, because ISDN is a dial-up service, the two communicating devices must perform a session-establishment procedure before communications can occur. This means that the sender and the receiver perform a session-setup "handshake" before they can begin to communicate.

Types of ISDN Services

The two general types of ISDN services are Basic Rate Interface (BRI) and Primary Rate Interface (PRI). Of the two, BRI is marketed mostly as a home-user solution for connecting to the Internet, whereas PRI is more often aimed at the business community. Both use what are called B channels and D channels. B channels are used to carry voice and data traffic. D channels are used to carry control information only. With BRI, the user gets two 64-Kbps B channels and one 16-Kbps D channel. One of the B channels is usually used for voice communications, whereas the second is used for data. However, it is possible to combine both B channels into a single 128-Kbps connection. The channels can be used to connect to the Internet or to establish a private network.

PRI provides up to 23 B channels and one 64-Kbps D channel. The total bandwidth of a PRI line can equal a T-1 connection. As with BRI, PRI B channels can be combined to form bandwidths of varying capacity based on business needs.

8 chaptereight

Servers in the Enterprise

Learning Objectives	After studying this chapter, you should be able to:
	• Differentiate between clients and servers.
	• Describe five physical components that can affect server performance.
	• Identify the major types of servers.
	• Understand the basic functionalities of the major types of servers.
	• Describe how well-known ports are used in a TCP/IP environment.
	• Explain server clustering and its advantages.
	• Understand the concept of system area networks (SANs).

Up to now, you have learned about different data communications networking models, including LANs, BNs, MANs, and WANs. Part Four of this text begins to consider ways in which these models can be integrated, supported, and secured. Various hardware devices and their associated software are critical to the seamless integration of these networking models.

Servers and Clients

Servers have become a critical component at all levels of the enterprise. This chapter explores how and why servers differ from clients. The chapter also presents several types of commonly used servers. How servers were used in the past and how they are used today are in some ways the same, but in other ways quite different. Let's begin by defining servers and clients.

At its simplest level, a **server** is a device that provides services and resources to other devices, called clients. A **client** is a device that requests

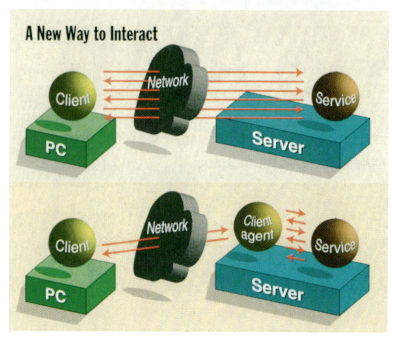

Figure 8.1
Client/Server Concept
In a client/server network, the client and server devices each have a role to play.

services and resources from servers. In the distant past, the late 1980s, the distinction between servers and clients was very clear. Servers were **dedicated**; they only provided resources to clients, they were never used as clients themselves. Similarly, clients never functioned as servers, meaning that clients did not share resources or services with other clients. Servers and clients had specific, limited roles, as conceptualized in Figure 8.1. Servers and clients also had distinctly different types of operating systems.

This all changed with the introduction of network-aware client desktop operating systems. Desktop operating systems that are **network aware** are capable of sharing the local resources (e.g., printers or files on a hard drive of the devices on which they run). One of the earliest examples of this type of network-aware desktop operating system was Microsoft's Windows for Workgroups, introduced in 1992. Desktop operating systems that are network aware can be fairly easily configured to run in a peer-to-peer networking model. You may recall from an earlier chapter that a *peer-to-peer network* allows a device to function as both a server or a client based on how that device is configured.

Virtually all modern desktop operating systems, such as Windows XP in Figure 8.2, are able to run in a peer-to-peer network. For very small networks, this works well; however, for medium- to large-scale networks, the peer-to-peer model is inefficient and difficult to manage. Also, for very small networks, it is possible to run server services on standard desktop computers. However, more robust and demanding networks require specialized servers running specialized software.

Today, servers normally run some type of **Server Operating System (SOS)** such as those illustrated in Figure 8.3 that provides services and resources to clients. In the past, an SOS was also referred to as a **Network Operating System (NOS)**. Although servers using modern SOSs can function as clients, this is not common. Instead, most servers are, for all practical purposes, dedicated machines that do not perform such client-based

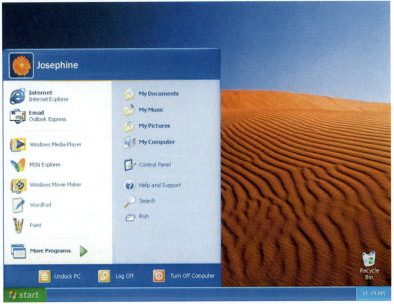

Figure 8.2
Windows XP is one of Microsoft's newest client desktop operating systems.

Figure 8.3
This suite of Microsoft products features software designed for clients as well as servers.

tasks as word processing, payroll, or inventory analysis. Typically, servers are physically secured in such a way that only certain authorized personnel can access them. Because of how servers are used, they have specific physical considerations that make them different from clients.

Server Characteristics

Because servers are not used in the same way that client machines are used, servers differ physically from clients. For example, servers do not normally need to offer audio features. Therefore, servers are not usually provided with speakers or advanced audio/sound features. Considering that servers are frequently locked away in secured rooms or closets, it makes sense that a high-end sound system would not be deemed very significant or cost-effective. Other physical characteristics, however, are significant. This section considers five physical features that differentiate a server from a client: the physical case, the memory, the processor, the drive interface, and NIC support.

The Physical Case

Client machines are placed on top of or very near a user's physical desk; the user usually likes to have as much room on or near his or her desk for items such as papers, pens, manuals, photos, file cabinets, or other work-related materials. Because other items occupy the space on or near a user's work area, the footprint of client machines is usually kept to a minimum. This means that the physical case that houses the components that make up the user's computer is also kept to a minimum. If you have ever opened up a standard desktop computer, you know that inside the case there is generally not a lot of room. Circuitry and components are positioned very tightly in order to make the case, and its footprint, as small as practically possible. With a server, however, small footprints are not as critical an issue.

In most enterprises, servers are not left in public or open areas where they are vulnerable to unauthorized access. Instead, whenever possible, servers are placed in secured rooms or closets. Because servers are isolated and infrequently accessed by the staff, footprint considerations are not as critical as with a client machine. The result is that servers generally have larger and more rugged physical cases than do client machines. A **server case** is frequently referred to as a **chassis**. Larger physical cases also make it easier to upgrade a server because there is more space for expansion bays and slots and because there is more room to work within the case. (A good Web site for comparing prices for server cases from various vendors is **shopper.zdnet.com**.)

Larger cases also allow for more components to be installed within the server. With more components, more electrical power is required. This means that servers, because of the quantity of components within a case, also tend to have larger, more robust power supplies. A server might have not only a stronger power supply, but also redundant power supplies, depending on how critical the server is in the event of a power failure. Because power surges can also negatively affect a computer's circuitry, a server might also have an internal surge protector. Of course, such redundant and additional features have additional and nonredundant costs!

The Memory and Processor

At the time of this writing, standard client machines typically come configured with 128 to 512 MB of memory called **random access memory (RAM)**. RAM modules, or **sticks**, plug into slots housed on a computer's motherboard. A **motherboard** is the key circuitry component that all internal devices connect to within a computer's case. Servers generally accommodate much higher RAM capacities than clients, supporting anywhere from a very low end of 128 MB to 4 GB or more. Furthermore, although a server's motherboard may not have more RAM slots than a typical desktop computer, the server's RAM slots are usually able to support much higher-capacity sticks of RAM. Figure 8.4 shows a standard RAM chip.

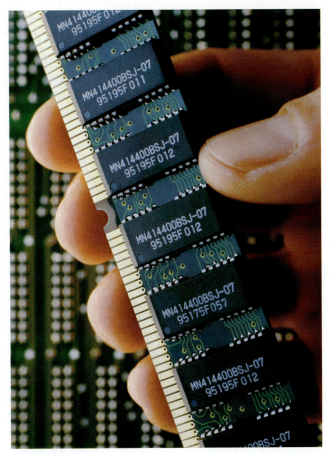

Figure 8.4
Various RAM chips might be used in either a server or client device.

Another key difference between a server's motherboard and a client's is the number of processor slots on the motherboard. A processor is also referred to as a **Central Processing Unit (CPU)**. The CPU is the workhorse of the computer and is critical to the processing of instructions and data. A standard client machine may have one, or at the most two, CPU slots on its motherboard. However, a server might have 4, 8, 16, 32, or more CPUs. Of course, the more CPUs that are supported and used, the higher the cost of the server. Also, servers with multiple CPUs require SOSs that support this functionality. If a server has eight CPUs but its SOS only supports four, then half of that server's processing power will go unused.

Examples of SOSs that support varying CPU levels are Microsoft's Windows 2000 and 2003 Server products (**www.microsoft.com**). Windows 2000 Server, for example, supports four **symmetric multiprocessing (SMP)** CPUs and up to 4 GB of RAM. (A brief and straightforward article on SMP can be found at **www.nwfusion.com/news/tech/2001/1029tech.html**.) Operating systems, such as Windows 2000, that can simultaneously control two or more physical CPUs are said to be SMP capable. The processors being controlled are given equal access to input/output devices. Windows 2000 Advanced Server can support up to 8 SMP CPUs. Windows 2000 Datacenter Server can support up to 32 SMP CPUs. Today, SMP CPUs for LAN servers are fairly common. The advantage of using multiple CPUs within a server is that processing tasks can be shared by the CPUs. SMP CPUs share a common memory pool and input/output (I/O) bus. A **bus** is the circuitry on the motherboard that allows data to be moved from one location of the computer to another. A motherboard has several types of buses. It is beyond the scope of this text to explore the different kinds of buses, but a brief explanation of buses is provided at **www.webopedia.com/TERM/B/bus.html**. Manufacturers producing processors that support SMP include Intel, SPARC, Alpha, and PowerPC.

One problem with servers using multiple SMP CPUs is that although the CPUs share a common memory pool, they do not share cache memory. **Cache memory** is a very high-speed memory, faster than ordinary RAM, that is used for recently or frequently accessed data and instructions. Each CPU has its own cache. Data or instructions needed by one CPU might be stored in the cache of a different CPU. Motherboards that provide for multiple SMP CPUs are hardwired to allow CPUs to reference each other's cache, but this referencing results in additional processing overhead. Beyond eight CPUs, the overhead needed to support cache referencing, as well as memory and I/O bus sharing, can result in contention problems that will cause server responsiveness to degrade. Also, for a server running multiple CPUs, should one of the CPUs fail, it may be necessary to stop, repair, or remove the failing CPU and then restart the server. Bringing down a server, even for a short period of time, is something network administrators try to avoid.

The Drive Interface

Servers typically need to support more drives than a standard desktop machine. These drives may include tape drives, CD-ROMs, hard drives, and floppy drives, among others. Because servers provide resources to potentially hundreds, if not thousands, of users concurrently, they have to support varied and highly capable drive systems. Two common **drive interfaces** are **IDE**, for **Integrated Drive Electronics**, and **SCSI**, pronounced "skuzzy," for **Small Computer System Interface**. (For additional information on SCSI, see **www.scsilibrary.com**.) In general, IDE drives are used for user desktop workstations, and SCSI is used for servers or high-performance computers. IDE is more often used in client devices for a number of reasons, cost being the most significant. An enterprise will generally have many more clients than servers, and because IDE drives are fairly inexpensive, it makes economic sense to configure most clients with IDE technology.

An IDE drive interface has a maximum transfer rate of 100 Mbps. An IDE controller is integrated into an IDE drive. The IDE controller communicates with and assists the CPU when IDE resources are accessed. An IDE controller has two channels. Each IDE channel can support two devices per channel, allowing for a maximum of four internal devices. When two devices use one IDE channel, one device is configured as the *master* and the other as the *slave*. Additionally, if both a master and a slave are using the same IDE channel, only one of the two devices can use the channel at one time. For client machines, this is usually not much of an issue. However, for servers that provide data resources to many clients, IDE drives can be far too slow.

Furthermore, because IDE is limited in the number of devices that it can support, and because IDE devices have to share a common channel, IDE is not a good choice for data-intensive services. Rather, SCSI is commonly found in servers that support large numbers of clients. SCSI has a maximum transfer rate of 160 Mbps and can support up to 15 internal and/or external devices. SCSI devices also require, like IDE devices, a controller. A SCSI controller is commonly referred to as a *host adapter*. The SCSI host adapter may be part of the server's motherboard or

Figure 8.5
Standard SCSI Cable

it may be an expansion card that plugs into an available motherboard slot, with the latter being more common. SCSI devices also use their own specific types of cables, like the one illustrated in Figure 8.5.

A significant difference between IDE and SCSI is that a SCSI host adapter uses a *parallel bus* to communicate with the devices attached to it. Each device on the parallel bus has its own unique SCSI identifier number. The SCSI devices plug into each other in a daisy-chain manner, forming what looks and functions like a mini-network of SCSI devices. SCSI devices, because of their parallel bus, can work independently of each other and are not restricted to a shared channel as IDE devices are. Especially for frequently accessed hard drives shared across a network, SCSI provides much better performance. SCSI also supports device types that IDE cannot. The downside to all of this is that SCSI is a more complicated and much more expensive technology than IDE. However, the benefits of SCSI as a server technology sufficiently outweigh its cost and complexity, making SCSI the drive interface of choice for servers. Figure 8.6 compares how IDE and SCSI devices are connected.

NICs

Drives, and hard drives in particular, can be a critical bottleneck in a network when demand from clients exceeds the ability of the server to respond in a timely manner. Because of this, servers commonly use SCSI devices. Another component that can result in a network performance bottleneck is the server's NIC. Whether a client or server, all devices connected to the network must have a NIC. Before data can enter or exit a networked machine, the data must pass through that device's NIC. The speed, or throughput, at which the NIC is capable of passing data

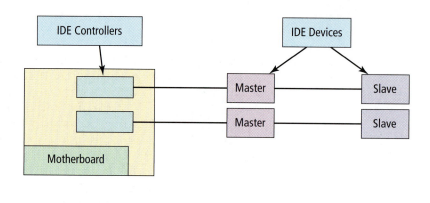

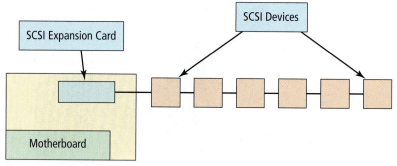

Figure 8.6
Conceptual IDE and SCSI Device Connections

becomes a significant factor in how responsive that NIC-connected device can be. For a server that has a lot of traffic passing to and through it, having a fast NIC is a necessity.

All of the devices in the network do not have to have NICs of the same throughput capacity. Faster and more capable NICs cost more. In a network, the NICs used by clients do not have to be of the same capability as those used by the servers. Using less expensive and less capable NICs for clients helps keep network costs down. For example, clients may use standard Ethernet NICs, whereas servers on the backbone may use Fast or Gigabit Ethernet NICs. Additionally, because NICs can support either half- or full-duplex communications, it may be worth the cost to purchase server NICs that are capable of full-duplex communications. Servers that experience significant throughput traffic should have full-duplex NICs.

Server NICs can also support **direct memory access (DMA)**, which allows the server to move data directly from the NIC's memory buffer to server RAM without the direct intervention of the server's processor. A server NIC might also use bus mastering. **Bus mastering** enables the NIC to take temporary control of the bus into which it is plugged into to move data directly into the server's system RAM. In addition, NICs may have their own RAM, called **buffers**. With larger buffers, the NIC can store data that it cannot immediately process. The NIC can then process the data later, with later being mere fractions of a second, thereby preventing the NIC from becoming a bottleneck. Finally, NICs can incorporate their own processors. By having a processor on the NIC, the NIC puts less work on the server's processor, thereby improving network performance.

As physical and logical devices, servers are regularly monitored to ensure that they are running correctly and at optimal performance. Many monitoring tools are available to network administrators to help them keep their servers running in top form. See the "Topic in Focus" at the end of this chapter for information on just a few such tools.

Types of Servers

Now that you have learned how servers differ physically from clients, let's examine a few of the different types of servers that an enterprise might use. If a resource can be networked, a server can probably be configured to manage it. Networked resources may include data, software, hardware, information, e-mail, or directory services or anything else that needs to be shared and managed. Depending on what the server does, how many users it services, and the complexity of the resource or resources that it manages, the server will need to be more or less capable. Also keep in mind that a single physical device can run more than one logical server. Servers are logical as well as physical. One physical device may be an e-mail server, a file server, and a Web server, all at the same time. However, if one device runs too many types of server services, network performance begins to degrade. As performance degrades, thought should be given to dividing out server services to other physical server devices.

File and Application Servers

Files and applications are two commonly accessed resources needed by multiple users in an enterprise. Keeping duplicate copies of frequently used files on each user's local hard drive very quickly proves unmanageable and confusing. Who has the most current version of the file? When was the file last updated and by whom? If a file is copied across multiple locations, how can it be secured? How many copies of the file have been distributed? As you can see, such a system would be quite problematic. **File servers** that control, manage, and make commonly used files available by request are a better solution for networked environments.

File servers control access to file and disk resources. These servers also are usually configured to authenticate users before they can access a file resource, thereby providing a level of security. Not only can users be authenticated, but access to files can be synchronized. Synchronization of access can be critical when two or more users are attempting to modify the same file. In such a scenario, without controls, it is possible for one user's changes to overwrite those made by a different user. A well-run file server ensures that file or data locking occurs so that files do not become corrupted.

A file server must be fast and reliable and have sufficient storage to accommodate users' needs. File server services are often implemented through software that runs on a physical device. One potential problem with file servers is that when users log in to the server to request a file, the server must send the entire file across the network to the user's local machine. If the file is small, the traffic and time needed to send it across the network is not likely to be significant. But for very large files, the traffic generated by sending copies across the network may result in a file server bottleneck. Fast hard drive access is essential and is one reason, as discussed earlier, why SCSI drives are a popular choice for servers.

Like frequently used files, applications can also benefit from server management. Businesses usually find that they save money by using site or metered licensing for commonly used applications rather than giving users their own individual licensed copy. Maintaining one version of an application that everyone uses is much simpler than trying to maintain multiple versions across multiple workstations. Also, when applications are stored and accessed from a central **application server**, upgrading the application becomes much easier.

Applications that are controlled and run from a server have two parts. One part, called the front end, runs on the client machine. The **front end** allows the user from his or her local machine to request and give commands necessary to the application server. The second part, the **back end**, runs on the application server, and, depending on the application, much of the work can be performed there. To the user, it appears as if the application is running on his or her local machine. This front-end/back-end structure typifies a **client/server architecture**. Be aware that not all applications can be networked, which may be a business factor when selecting applications.

Database Servers

Database servers provide management access control software that makes database records available to users across the network. Based on a user's request for data, the database server retrieves the data record, processes the data according to the user's request, and sends the result of the process to the requesting user. This means that, unlike a file server, much of the work is done on the database server, not on the user's local device. Like application servers, database servers have a front end on the client and a back end on the server.

For very large databases, servers can be configured to manage a portion of the database, which results in a distributed database environment. Databases can be distributed in a number of different ways. For example, one database server may host customer accounts A through M, whereas a second server, in a different physical location, hosts accounts N through Z. Another distribution could be by geographical location or by functionality. However the database is distributed, to the user it appears as if the database is at one physical location. Figure 8.7 illustrates the distributed database concept.

Database servers can also be configured so that they replicate the database across several locations. In such a situation, as the master version of the database is modified, the modifications are replicated to copies of the database that are maintained in other locations. In this discussion, replication means that a master or original version of the database is copied and/or updated to other database servers. Replication of databases can be very handy when user groups are scattered across remote distances. For example, a business with a branch office in Los Angeles and another in Chicago could benefit from replicated database technology. If there were two database servers, one in Chicago and one in Los Angeles, each user

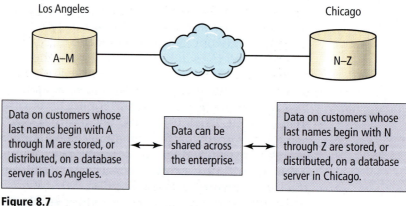

Figure 8.7
Distributed Database

group would have faster access to the database because a copy of the database is geographically close to them and their applications.

Web, E-mail, and FTP Servers

Many organizations rely on Web-based services to support their clients and staff. A business may want to make an online catalog available to customers or allow staff to remotely log in to project files hosted on a Web server. Simply put, Web servers run software that enables clients to make requests for services. For Web services to function, the client must also have a component called a **browser** in order to make requests. Two popular client-based browsers are Microsoft's Internet Explorer and Netscape's Navigator.

A **Web server** runs application layer TCP/IP protocols. One such protocol is **Hypertext Transfer Protocol (HTTP)**. Another commonly used protocol is **File Transfer Protocol (FTP)**. (These protocols were presented in Chapter 5.) Web pages hosted on a Web server are expressed, or programmed, in **Hypertext Markup Language (HTML)**. HTML is referred to as a "tag based" programming language, because it uses "tags" to indicate what function or operation to perform when displaying a Web page. Web servers, based on what they need to do, do not necessarily have to be powerful machines. However, the more clients that are expected to access the Web server, the more capable the Web server needs to be. Another option, typical with e-mail servers, is to have more than one server of a particular type available for client access. For organizations that support moderate-to large-scale e-mail, FTP, or Web site hosting, multiple Web servers are usually configured to provide the needed resources.

A Web server is a program. Windows- and UNIX-based Web servers are by far the most common, although that may change with the advent of Linux. For Windows, Microsoft provides a free copy of Internet Information Server (IIS) with its server products. In the UNIX world, the Apache server is highly popular. It even has its own user group at **httpd.apache.org**. Apache is an open-source technology that supports not only UNIX, but Windows and Macintosh platforms as well.

Regardless of its origination, a Web server program running on its host computer "listens" for incoming client browser TCP requests. Requests come to the Web server over *ports*. **Ports** are logical designations that represent a particular type of requested service. Port values, referred to as **well-known ports**, are assigned by the Internet Assigned Numbers Authority, or IANA (see **www.iana.org/assignments/port-numbers**). The most common port used by client browsers when requesting a HTTP service is port 80. Port 80 is the standard port for an HTTP server. (Port 80, in fact, is one of the most targeted ports assaulted by hackers attempting to break into a network. Why? Because port 80 is used extensively in HTTP for access by a Web client browser. Chapter 10 explores port security in more detail.)

Different types of service requests are made using different logical port designators. Many such application layer service requests have been standardized to use particular logical, well-known ports. Although Web-based services use many well-known port identifiers, depending on the network, nonstandard ports also can be specified. However, if a client uses something other than the standard port for a particular service, the nonstandard port number must be specified in the request.

A client request is accomplished through what is known as a **Uniform Resource Locator (URL)**. For most users of a Web server, a URL takes the form of a World Wide Web (WWW) address, for example, **http://www.woodbury.edu**.

A URL may have four parts. First, a protocol is specified. In the example address, the protocol is HTTP. For a FTP server, the protocol is ftp://. Second, either the server's IP address or the server's Domain Name System (DNS) name is provided. Third, a port number may be provided. If the port number is the standard logical port for the requested service, then the number does not have to be provided. For example, an HTTP request using standard logical port 80 would not have to include 80 in the request URL. Finally, the directory and/or file being requested needs to be specified. Thus, a URL has the following format:

protocol://server-identifier:port-identifier/directory/file.htm.

For the address provided in the example, a complete URL would look like **http://www.woodbury.edu:80/index.html**. In this example, it is not necessary to specify port 80 because that is the default well-known port for this URL request. However, if the URL were not available at standard port 80, the nonstandard port would have to be included in the URL request.

You may recall from Chapter 5 that **Simple Mail Transfer Protocol (SMTP)** is another application layer protocol used by TCP/IP. When TCP is used as the transport protocol, SMTP uses well-known port 25 at the server. SMTP servers receive outgoing e-mail from clients and transmit e-mail to destination **e-mail servers**. Another type of e-mail server works with SMTP to maintain the mailboxes from which clients access their e-mail. The two most common installations of this type of server are **Post Office Protocol Version 3 (POP3)** and **Internet Message Access Protocol (IMAP)**, both of which were presented in Chapter 5. POP3 and IMAP often run on the same physical device as the SMTP server. More sophisticated e-mail server products are available, such as Microsoft's Exchange Server, Novell's GroupWise, IBM's Lotus Domino, and InterShield's Mail-Server.

A POP3 server provides basic mailbox services. A client needs a service such as a POP3 server because clients, in general, are not always connected to the Internet or to the network that provides their e-mail. Because clients are not always connected, they are not always available to receive incoming e-mail from an SMTP server. This is where POP3 comes in. A POP3 server is, or at least should be, always connected to the network so that it is always available to receive e-mail from an SMTP server. The POP3 server can temporarily store the client's e-mail in a **mailbox** so that the client can eventually access and download his or her mail. POP3 uses well-known port 110.

Between a POP3 client and a POP3 server, three phases or stages are possible. In the first stage, authorization, the POP3 client creates a TCP connection with a POP3 server. The client must identify itself to the server before the server will allow the client access to the mailbox. If the server grants authorization, the two connecting systems enter the second, or transaction, stage. In this stage, the client can transmit commands to the server that enable the server to retrieve messages from the client's mailbox. At some point the client will have completed its download of messages from the server. When this occurs, the client issues a quit command to the server and the two devices enter the final stage—update. In update, the server can begin to delete all messages that have been marked for deletion from the client's mailbox. After completing the update stage, the server releases its lock on the client's mailbox and terminates its connection with the client.

POP3 provides for only temporary storage of a client's e-mail. IMAP, however, stores e-mail on its server for as long as required, even permanently.

IMAP is a more sophisticated mailbox service protocol and offers more ways for clients to access and control their e-mail. IMAP allows clients to create folders in their mailboxes in order to file their messages. Also, IMAP allows clients to view their mail in a list format by header only, so that clients can more easily select which messages they want to download. Finally, IMAP allows for search capabilities not provided by POP3, so a client can search messages based on the header, subject, or body of the message itself. The benefits of IMAP, though, come at a cost. IMAP requires much more in terms of network and system resources. The choice between POP3 and IMAP may depend on how critically important the organization views its e-mail capabilities.

FTP is also a widely used application layer service that requires an FTP server and client. FTP servers enable authenticated clients to transfer files from one host machine to another. As a service, FTP is fairly basic, having just a few file-management commands. Unlike HTTP, which uses a single well-known port, FTP uses two ports to perform its job. Well-known port 21 is used by an FTP client to create a connection to an FTP server. If successful, this connection remains intact and open for the duration of the communication. Using the port 21 connection, the FTP client and server can exchange command and reply information. For the file transfer itself, the FTP server creates a second connection over well-known port 20. After the file has been transferred, the port 20 connection is terminated. Table 8.1 summarizes some of the most commonly used well-known ports.

Keep in mind that whether using Web, e-mail, or FTP services, both a server and a client must be involved for the service to be successful. Many free programs are available for each of these services for both the client and the server. Many other programs are available for a fee. Fee-based programs usually have more features, a better user interface, and documentation and/or support.

Table 8.1 Common Well-Known Ports

Port	Service
8	Ping requests
20	FTP file transfer
21	FTP client/server command exchange
25	E-mail
67	DHCP server
68	DHCP client
80	HTTP Web page transfers
135	Microsoft Distributed Computing Environment locator service for Remote Service Management
139	Windows file and print services
445	Microsoft transport service for Server Message Block over TCP
1433	Microsoft SQL Server
3128	Proxy services
8080	HTTP and proxy servers

Using Web Server Technology to Track Employees

Web servers enable a business to have a global presence. Using Web servers, a business can market, sell, and track products and services to customers who are geographically distant from the business. Web servers, however, can also be used by a business to track and observe its own employees.

Many employees may not be aware that Web servers are configured to maintain activity logs. These activity logs are like electronic diaries that keep track of every activity an employee performs while using Web-based services. As an example, the following list identifies just a few of the types of information that a Web server can record and track:

• The name, domain, and Internet address of the host computer from which the employee accesses a Web site.

• The date, time, and duration that an employee spends at a particular Web site.

• The specific Web page accessed within a Web site; the number of times a particular page was accessed; and whether any data, text, audio, or graphic files were downloaded.

Most businesses require employees to log in to their workstations using a unique user ID and password. Yet, it is possible that an employee could step away from his or her desk, perhaps for a coffee or tea break, without logging out of his or her workstation. Someone else could then in the employee's absence use that workstation in a manner that violates company policies. For example, a business policy on sexual harassment may state that employee workstations may not be used to view pornographic Web sites and that employees who violate this policy will be terminated.

If such a scenario were to occur, do you think that the business has an ethical duty to verify that the employee being dismissed was in fact the policy-violating employee? What if the innocent employee claims that he or she had no knowledge of the policy violation and did not even know about such a policy because the policy had not been openly and visibly published for all employees to read? How do you think such a situation should be handled?

A product by Spector Professional (**www.spectorsoft.com**) can invisibly record a user's e-mail, chat, Instant Message sessions, Web sites visited, and keystrokes entered and then place this information in a hidden location on a user's computer. A manager could then later review this recorded data. Do you think this type of recording would engender a sense of trust among employees? Do you think a business and/or manager is ethically correct in installing such recording software on a worker's computer? Are there arguments for and against this type of employer tracking of employee activities?

Laura Harman offers some insightful comments regarding the monitoring of employees in the workplace; you can read her comments at **www.elronsoftware.com/pdf/ethicswp.pdf**. On its Web site (**www.ethix.org**), the Institute for Business, Technology, and Ethics (IBTE) provides 10 principles for an ethically run business. What do you think are the ethical boundaries a business should follow in tracking its employees?

Domain Name System Servers

Another type of server of particular importance in a TCP/IP environment is a **Domain Name System (DNS) server**. Figure 8.8 shows a Microsoft Windows DNS server being configured. To understand this type of server, you must first understand what is meant by DNS. Recall that in the TCP/IP model, there are several types of addresses. For example, the data link layer has a MAC physical address. The network layer has a logical IP addresses, with its 32-bit, or dotted-decimal, representation. The application layer has a type of address called a domain name. **Domain names** are used at the application level because they are much easier for mere mortals to understand and work with than data link or network layer addresses. Thus, DNS has evolved and is in place so that people can understand and more easily recognize the devices in a TCP/IP world.

Simply stated, the DNS matches a Web host's IP address with a more English-like domain name address if that host is going to be accessed by other hosts for such services as Web hosting, FTP, e-mail, and so on. Such a host is usually a server of some type. DNS allows for an IP address to be associated with its domain name address. Like HTTP, FTP, and TCP, DNS is a protocol. To resolve an IP logical address to a DNS address, a sequence of steps is followed. These steps are illustrated in Figure 8.9. (RFCs 882 and 883 describe the DNS implementation. These documents can be found at **www.rfc-editor.org/rfc/rfc882.txt** and **www.rfc-editor.org/rfc/rfc883.txt**.)

DNS is based on a hierarchy of domains. A domain is similar to a directory. Like a directory on a computer's hard drive that can have subdirectories, a domain can have subdomains. This structure of domains with associated subdomains is how the DNS hierarchy is constructed. There are top-level domains and second-level domains. The best known, and original, top-level domains include .com, .edu, .gov, .int, .mil, .net, and .org. ICANN is the Internet organization that controls assignment of top-level domains. ICANN has since considered and accepted other top-level domain names as shown in Figure 8.10, which charts the domain hierarchy. More information on the top-level domain names can be found at **www.icann.org/tlds/**.

DNS servers resolve a domain name, such as **www.woodbury.edu**, to its equivalent IP address. A domain name is resolved when the DNS server matches a client's IP address with a domain name address. In a TCP/IP network, client devices are configured to point to one or more DNS servers. Figure 8.11 shows a Windows 2000 Workstation client-configuration panel.

Figure 8.8

Microsoft Windows–Based DNS Server Being Configured

1. A client browser sends a request to its local primary, DNS server to resolve a domain name address; for example, what is the IP address of **http://www.woodbury.edu?**
2. If the local DNS server does not have this information, the local DNS server sends a request to the root domain server for the required information.
3. The root domain server responds by sending to the local DNS server the IP address of the remote, secondary DNS server responsible for the domain being requested.
4. The local DNS server then contacts the secondary, remote DNS server.
5. The remote DNS server gives to the local DNS server the requested IP address information, for example, 201.14.101.0.
6. The local DNS server then gives this IP address information to its local client.
7. The local client with the required IP address information can now directly request, through its browser, information from the Web server hosting the information for **http://www.woodbury.edu.**
8. The Web server hosting information for **http://www.woodbury.edu** sends to the requesting client browser the requested information.

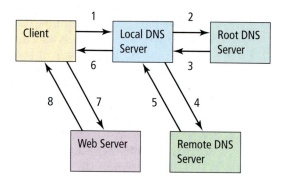

Figure 8.9
Steps in the DNS Resolution Process
Numbers in the graphic represent the sequence of steps followed in order to fulfill a client's request for a Web page.

Note the location where a DNS server can be specified. When a client uses a URL, which is a domain name address, to request a resource, the client must resolve that URL's IP address for the communication to be successful. On the client's side, the component that resolves the address is called the **resolver**.

This process is pretty much invisible to the user. The user enters a URL in a Web browser on the client device. The client device then issues a request to its associated DNS server to resolve, or discover, what IP address is associated with the URL that the user entered. The DNS server may or may not have that information stored in its own local table held in its memory. If the information is available, the DNS server provides the

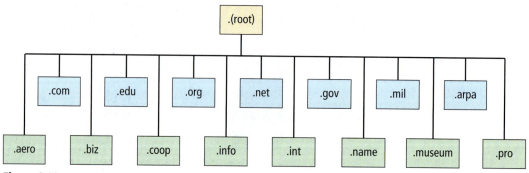

Figure 8.10
The DNS Hierarchy

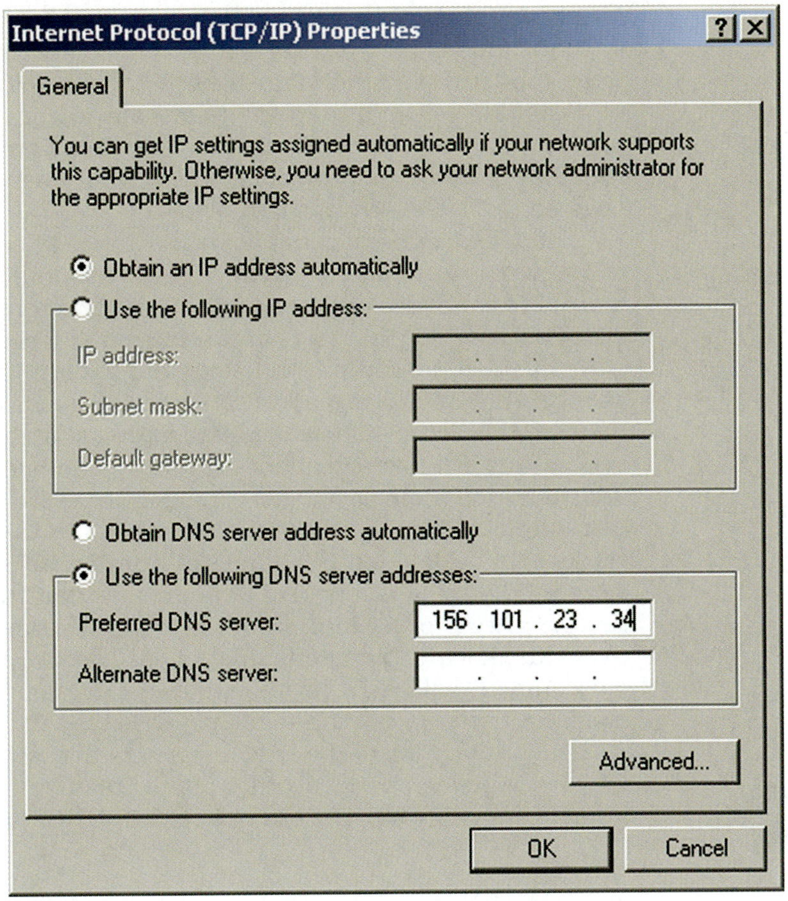

Figure 8.11
Windows 2000 Workstation Client with Its Configured DNS Server

requested information to the client. If it is not available, the DNS server issues its own request to other DNS servers to see if they have the required information. In the event that a bad URL has been entered or if the desired host is not available for some reason, the client is eventually informed of this. If the URL is good and the desired host is available, other protocols, such as HTTP or FTP, take over and deliver the data.

It is not unusual for organizations to have more than one device configured as a DNS server. If an organization has only one DNS server, then clients would not be able to have their URLs resolved if that server were to fail. In simple terms, a failed server would mean no Internet access. Also, in a network with a lot of Web-based requests, having only one DNS server results in bottleneck, because all clients have to go through that single DNS server for address resolution.

Dynamic Host Configuration Protocol Servers

Clients in a TCP/IP network have to be configured so that they can identify their DNS servers. Clients also must have their own IP addresses. Without an IP address, a TCP/IP client cannot function in a TCP/IP network. For very small networks, it is possible for network technicians to manually configure and maintain each client's IP address. In this scenario, the IP addresses are usually fixed, meaning that they can only be changed by a networking technician. This type of unchanging address is called a **static IP address**. However, if the network contains hundreds or thousands of clients, it becomes very complicated and difficult to manually configure and maintain static IP addresses. To address the problem of assigning and maintaining many static client IP addresses, another protocol was developed, **Dynamic Host Configuration Protocol (DHCP)**. As with many other protocols, there is an ongoing Internet work group devoted to DHCP—**www.dhcp.org**.

The term "dynamic" implies than the service is automated. Because the service is automated, it relieves network administrators from having to manually configure and maintain client IP addresses in their enterprise. DHCP is a service that runs on a designated DHCP server. Clients interact with the DHCP server to retrieve and determine their IP addresses. A client configured to use a DHCP server does not have a static IP address. Instead, the client will use dynamic addressing through a DHCP server. To access a DHCP server, clients must be configured with the address or addresses of their DHCP servers. Figure 8.12 shows a Windows 2000 Workstation client that has DHCP enabled. In this example, the client will retrieve its designated IP addresses from an ISP when it connects to that service. The ISP has a pool of IP addresses that the ISP's DHCP server can be configured to allocate. ISPs have specific ranges of IP addresses that they can allocate to customers. A client configured to function in a DHCP environment will, as it boots or powers up, issue a request based on its configuration information to a local DHCP server.

The primary job of the DHCP server is to assign IP addresses, although DHCP servers can perform other related tasks. How a DHCP server assigns an address can vary. For example, some DHCP servers can be configured

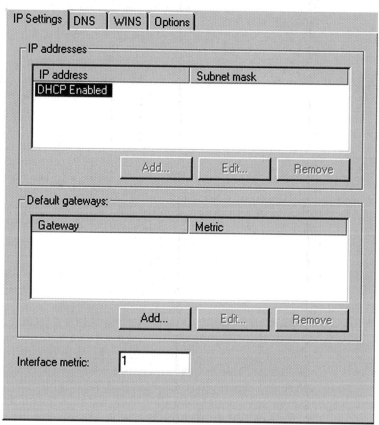

Figure 8.12
Windows 2000 Workstation Client with DHCP Enabled

to assign a specific, fixed IP address to particular clients. This may be useful for host machines that need a stable and unchanging IP address value, for example, routers, Web servers, or FTP servers. In a more typical scenario, a DHCP server is configured to have a pool of IP addresses available to it. This type of DHCP server allocates IP addresses from its pool to client machines as they power up and request addresses. Usually, clients assigned IP addresses in this way are only given a "lease" on the address, meaning at some point the client has to reissue a request to renew its lease on its "temporary" IP address. In such a case, the leased address may or may not be renewed depending on other network variables.

Using port 67 at the server and port 68 at the client, DHCP servers can also be set up to provide information to clients on subnet masking. Most modern desktop operating systems are capable of functioning as a DHCP client. As with Web, e-mail, and FTP servers, open-source code for DHCP is widely available. The most popular implementation, however, is Microsoft's DHCP server. In addition, Novell includes a DHCP server within NetWare, and versions are also available for UNIX and Linux operating systems.

Proxy Servers

Like many of the other types of servers presented thus far, a **proxy server** is a program, or service, that can run on a physical device hosting other types of services or servers. The intent of a proxy server is to provide a measure of security. A proxy server provides security by functioning as an intermediary between a client and a server. This fact should be clearer after the term *proxy* is defined.

Being a proxy literally means having the authority to act for another. Thus, if a person is a proxy, that person has another person's authority to act on his or her behalf. Say that a public figure was concerned for her privacy or safety and did not want to meet with a group of reporters. She might designate a proxy to meet with the reporters. The proxy would then communicate back to the public figure what the reporters wanted her to know. Thus, the proxy acts as a layer between the public figure and the reporters. A proxy server functions in a similar manner.

Proxy servers are commonly used in situations where filtering is desirable. In the case of a network, if a client on the inside of a firewall (a protective program discussed in Chapter 10) wants to communicate with a device outside the firewall, a proxy server could be used. The proxy server takes the client's request from inside the firewall and passes this communication to the device outside the firewall. To the device outside the firewall, the proxy server is the originating communicating device. The original, or true, communicating device is hidden from the receiver. The type of filtering provided by a proxy gives a great deal of assistance to the firewall. In fact, a firewall may have a separate proxy server for each application used by client devices.

Used primarily for Web-based communications, client browsers can be configured to send all of their outgoing requests to a proxy server rather than directly to an Internet server. The proxy server, using its own IP address, not the originating client's address, acts on the client's behalf and passes the client's request to the Internet server. Keep in mind that many clients can go through the proxy. The internal IP addresses of these clients are also hidden. Thus, by using a proxy server's IP address, outsiders are limited in what they can discover about a network's internal architecture. This is a real benefit to security. As with the other server types discussed thus far, both the client and the server must be configured for the proxy service.

Server Clusters

Very small organizations may have only one or two servers, whereas large organizations might have hundreds. One way to take advantage of multiple servers in the enterprise is to connect them together into a group called a **server cluster**. To a client device accessing a server cluster, the servers in the cluster appear to be a single server. A key advantage of having servers participate in a cluster is that the servers in the cluster can share their workload, resulting in the **load balancing** of network traffic. Another advantage of server clusters is that they provide improved fault tolerance. Should one of the servers in the cluster fail, other servers in the cluster can be configured to take over the failing server's responsibilities. This process is referred to as **failover** capability.

Servers participating in a cluster are connected not only physically, but logically as well through their SOS. Depending on the type of SOS, server behavior within the cluster can vary. In a network load-balancing cluster, each server has its own resources (i.e., its own hard drives and applications). Each server in a load-balancing cluster can function as an independent unit, although the servers may share applications and storage. Additionally, servers in the cluster provide each other with updated status information. This means that clustered servers share with each other their current workload demands and other relevant information.

Clients connect to what they see as a single server. Once connected, they can be directed to the server in the cluster that has the smallest workload. In this sense, the clients see a virtual server. A **virtual server** is highly scalable because it is built on a cluster of real servers. The fact that the virtual server is *scalable* means that servers in the cluster can be added or removed as network demands require. The makeup of the virtual server cluster is transparent to the clients using it. Clients see only a single virtual server. Figure 8.13 illustrates the concept of a virtual server in a two-server cluster environment.

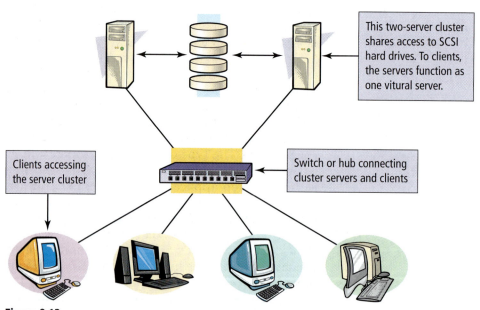

This two-server cluster shares access to SCSI hard drives. To clients, the servers function as one vitural server.

Clients accessing the server cluster

Switch or hub connecting cluster servers and clients

Figure 8.13
To clients, servers in a server cluster appear as one virtual server.

Of course, server clusters can be implemented in a variety of ways. Microsoft includes clustering services in its Windows 2000 Advanced and Datacenter Server products. (You can review the details of Microsoft's server clustering technology at **www.microsoft.com/ntserver/support/faqs/clustering_faq.asp#basics**.) Linux and UNIX versions of clustering also are available. (You can read more about the Linux Virtual Server Project at **www.linuxvirtualserver.org**.) In addition, vendors sometimes team up to develop clustering technologies. A March 10, 2003, article in *Information Week* reports that IBM, Microsoft, and Intel have partnered to produce a server cluster configured to hold more than 100 terabytes of data. The server cluster includes Netfinity servers configured with Intel Pentium III Xeon processors, IBM DB2 Universal Database, and Microsoft Windows 2000 Advanced Server. IBM markets this server cluster as the world's fastest.

System Area Networks

The success of server clusters has prompted the development of a relatively new technology called **system area networks (SANs)**. SANs are so new that standards for the technology are still evolving. A SAN is a local network designed for high-speed interconnection (server to server) in cluster environments using multiprocessing systems and storage area networks. (Storage area networks, also abbreviated as SANs, are discussed in Chapter 9.) SANs almost exclusively use what is called a switched fabric. A switched fabric refers to how ports within a switch are linked so that they can communicate and transfer data. In this instance, a switched fabric refers to the physical ports that enable devices to connect to a switch, not the logical well-known ports that were presented earlier.

An Ethernet switch has physical ports that devices can plug in or connect to. Within the switch, hardware circuitry connects the physical ports. This interconnection creates what vendors call a *switching fabric*. This switching fabric can then provide for high data-transfer rates. **Fibre Channel** is an implementation of a switched fabric that is usually associated with a SAN. A Fibre Channel half-duplex connection can transfer data at 100 Mbps, or 200 Mbps when full-duplex is used. To differentiate Fibre Channel from fiber-optic, note that the spelling of "fibre" is somewhat unusual. Fibre Channel provides a high-speed switched environment in which any device on the network can connect with any other device and then communicate over a dedicated high-speed link. Fibre Channel functions at the physical and data link layers of the OSI and TCP/IP models. Using standard networking hardware elements, Fibre Channel implements much of its functionality in the hardware that it uses rather than programmatically. The Fibre Channel Industry association (**www.fibrechannel.org**) provides links to various products and vendors that support Fibre Channel.

Two organizations particularly involved with SAN technology are Microsoft and a group called Infiniband. Microsoft's Windows 2000 and 2003 Datacenter Server products are SAN compatible. The Infiniband organization is sponsoring a revolutionary approach to SAN architectures. More information on Infiniband can be found at **www.infinibandta.org**. Infiniband proposes a bottom-up network design that provides operating-system-independent communication over a switched network fabric.

Chapter Summary

A server is a device that provides services and resources to other devices called clients. A client is a device that requests services and resources from servers. Virtually all modern desktop operating systems incorporate the ability to run in a peer-to-peer network. In a peer-to-peer network a device can function as a client, a server, or both, depending on how the client is configured. For very small networks this works well; however, for medium- to large-scale networks, the peer-to-peer model is inefficient and difficult to manage.

A server runs a server operating system (SOS) to provide services and resources to clients. Servers are typically physically secured in such a way that only certain authorized personnel can access them. Because of how servers are used, they have specific physical attributes that make them different from clients. These attributes include differences in the physical case, memory, processor, drive interface, and NIC support.

Servers generally have larger and more rugged physical cases than client machines. Because a server has a large physical case, it is easy to upgrade because there is room for expansion bays and slots and more room to work within the case. Servers can support higher RAM capacities than clients, having anywhere from a low end of 128 MB to 4 GB or more. A server's motherboard may have more processor slots than a client motherboard. Whereas a client machine may have only one, or at the most two, CPU slots on its motherboard, a server can have 4, 8, 16, 32, or more CPUs.

Servers typically need to support more drives than a standard desktop machine does. Two common drive interfaces are Integrated Drive Electronics (IDE) and Small Computer System Interface (SCSI). In general, IDE drives are used for user desktop workstations, and SCSI is used for servers or high-performance computers. A SCSI host adapter uses a parallel bus to communicate with the devices attached to it. Each device on the parallel bus has its own unique SCSI identifier number.

The type of NIC card installed on a server can cause or prevent network bottlenecks. If a server has a lot of traffic passing to and through it, it should have a fast, full-duplex NIC. If the NIC card is not adequate for the traffic, bottleneck will result. Network performance can also be improved by having a processor on the NIC. When the NIC has a processor, the NIC puts less work on the server's processor, thereby improving network performance.

If a resource can be networked, a server can probably be configured to manage it. Servers are logical as well as physical. A single device can be configured to run more than one server service. As performance degrades, thought should be given to dividing out server services to separate, physical devices.

File servers control access to file and disk resources. These servers also are usually configured to authenticate users before they can access a resource, thereby providing a level of security. To be effective, a file server must be fast and reliable and have sufficient storage to accommodate user needs. Application servers, which require a front end on the client and a back end on the server, are useful for managing user applications that can be shared across the network. Database servers provide management access control software that makes database records available to users across the network. Database servers can also be configured so that they replicate the database across several locations.

Web servers run software that enables clients to make requests for services from the server. A Web server runs application layer TCP/IP protocols. One such protocol is Hypertext Transfer Protocol (HTTP). Another commonly used protocol is File Transfer Protocol (FTP). Web pages and sites hosted on a Web server are expressed in Hypertext Markup Language (HTML). A Web server is a program. Windows and UNIX-based Web servers are by far the most common servers. For Windows, Microsoft provides Internet Information Server (IIS) for free with its server products. In the UNIX world, the Apache server is quite popular.

Simple Mail Transfer Protocol (SMTP) is an application layer protocol used by TCP/IP. SMTP servers receive outgoing e-mail from clients and transmit it to destination servers. The two most common types of servers used with SMTP are Post Office Protocol Version 3 (POP3) and Internet Message Access Protocol (IMAP). A POP3 server provides basic mailbox services. IMAP is a more sophisticated mailbox service protocol and offers more ways for clients to access and control their e-mail.

Another type of server of particular importance in a TCP/IP environment is a Domain Name System (DNS) server. DNS provides a host's IP address with a more English-like domain name address if that host is going to be accessed by other hosts for such services as Web hosting, FTP, e-mail, and so on. DNS allows for an IP address to be associated with its domain name address. It is not unusual for organizations to have more than one device set up to operate as a DNS server.

Clients in a TCP/IP network have to be configured to identify their DNS servers. These clients also have to be configured with their own IP addresses. Without an IP address, a TCP/IP client cannot function in a TCP/IP network. For large networks, manual configuration of IP addresses is too complicated. Dynamic Host Configuration Protocol (DHCP) solves this problem; the job of the DHCP server is to assign IP addresses.

Proxy servers are used to provide security. A proxy server provides security by functioning as an intermediary between a client and a server. Proxy servers are commonly used in situations where filtering is desirable. With Web-based communications, client browsers are configured to send all of their outgoing requests to a proxy server rather than directly to an Internet server. The proxy server, using its own IP address, not the originating client's address, acts on the client's behalf and passes the client's request to the Internet server.

One way to take advantage of multiple servers in the enterprise is to cluster them into server clusters. To a client device accessing a server cluster, the servers in the cluster appear to be a single server. Servers participating in a cluster are connected not only physically, but also logically through their SOS. When clients connect to what they see as a single server, they can be directed to the server in the cluster with the smallest workload. In this sense, what the clients see is a virtual server. A virtual server is highly scalable because it is built on a cluster of real servers.

The success of server clusters has led to the development of a relatively new technology called system area networks (SANs). SANs standards are still evolving. A SAN is a local network designed for high-speed interconnection in cluster environments (server to server) using multiprocessing systems and storage area networks. Two organizations associated with SAN technology are Microsoft and Infiniband.

8 chapter eight Keywords

Application server **(283)**

Back end **(284)**

Browser **(285)**

Bus **(279)**

Bus mastering **(282)**

Buffers **(282)**

Cache memory **(280)**

Central Processing Unit (CPU) **(279)**

Chassis **(278)**

Client **(275)**

Client/server architecture **(284)**

Database server **(284)**

Dedicated **(276)**

Direct memory access (DMA) **(282)**

Domain name **(289)**

Domain Name System (DNS) server **(289)**

Drive interface **(280)**

Dynamic Host Configuration Protocol (DHCP) **(292)**

E-mail server **(286)**

Failover **(294)**

Fibre Channel **(295)**

File server **(283)**

File Transfer Protocol (FTP) **(285)**

Front end **(284)**

Hypertext Markup Language (HTML) **(285)**

Hypertext Transfer Protocol (HTTP) **(285)**

Integrated Drive Electronics (IDE) **(280)**

Internet Message Access Protocol (IMAP) **(286)**

Load balancing **(294)**

Mailbox **(286)**

Motherboard **(278)**

Network aware **(276)**

Network operating system (NOS) **(276)**

Ports **(285)**

Post Office Protocol Version 3 (POP3) **(286)**

Proxy server **(293)**

Random Access Memory (RAM) **(278)**

Resolver **(290)**

Server **(275)**

Server case **(278)**

Server cluster **(294)**

Server operating system (SOS) **(276)**

Simple Mail Transfer Protocol (SMTP) **(286)**

Small Computer System Interface (SCSI) **(280)**

Static IP address **(292)**

Sticks **(278)**

Symmetric multiprocessing (SMP) **(279)**

System area network (SAN) **(295)**

Uniform Resource Locator (URL) **(285)**

Virtual server **(294)**

Web server **(285)**

Well-known ports **(285)**

Chapter Questions

Short Answer

1. In general, how does a server differ from a client?

2. How might a server's hard drive affect its performance?

3. How does a file server differ from a database server?

4. What is meant by a "virtual server" with regards to server clustering?

Multiple Choice

For each question below select one best answer.

1. In a peer-to-peer network, a device can function as a
   a. client. **b.** server. **c.** a or b **d.** Neither a nor b

2. Peer-to-peer networks are best for networks of what scale?
   a. All networks **b.** Very small networks
   c. Very large networks **d.** None of the above

3. Many modern SOSs only allow servers to function as which of the following?
   a. Servers **b.** Clients **c.** a and b **d.** Neither a nor b

4. As compared with client devices, server cases are usually
   a. smaller. **b.** larger. **c.** about the same. **d.** identical.

5. Which of the following might be in a server's case?
   a. A motherboard with multiple processors
   b. A redundant power supply
   c. An internal surge protector
   d. All the above

6. Which of the following do SMP CPUs share?
   a. A common memory pool **b.** A common I/O bus
   c. Neither a nor b **d.** a and b

7. Compared with RAM, in terms of access cache memory is
   a. slower. **b.** faster. **c.** about the same. **d.** identical.

8. How many devices does IDE support on one interface?
   a. 1 **b.** 2 **c.** 4 **d.** 15

9. How many devices can share an IDE channel?
   a. 1 **b.** 2 **c.** 4 **d.** 15

10. What is the maximum transfer rate of an IDE drive interface?
    a. 100 Mbps **b.** 140 Mbps **c.** 160 Mbps **d.** 260 Mbps

11. What is the maximum transfer rate of a SCSI drive interface?
    a. 100 Mbps **b.** 140 Mbps **c.** 160 Mbps **d.** 260 Mbps

12. How many devices are supported on one SCSI adapter?
    a. 1 **b.** 2 **c.** 4 **d.** 15

13. Which of the following enables a NIC to move data directly from its buffer to system RAM without the direct intervention of the system's main processor?

    a. MAD   **b.** DMA   **c.** ADM   **d.** None of the above

14. Which of the following enables a NIC to temporarily take control of the bus into which it is plugged?

    a. Controlling   **b.** Fetching   **c.** Buffering   **d.** Mastering

15. Which type of server can be used to replicate a database?

    a. File server   **b.** Database server
    c. Application server   **d.** FTP server

16. Servers are

    a. logical.   **b.** physical.   **c.** a and b   **d.** Neither a nor b

17. Which component runs on the client?

    a. The front-end component   **b.** The front-tag component
    c. The back-end component   **d.** The back-tag component

18. Which component runs on the server?

    a. The front end   **b.** The front tag
    c. The back end   **d.** The back tag

19. Which server uses HTTP as its major protocol?

    a. Web server   **b.** E-mail server
    c. Application server   **d.** File server

20. Which server uses SMTP as its major protocol?

    a. Web server   **b.** E-mail server
    c. Application server   **d.** File server

21. Which of the following is used to manage client mailboxes?

    a. POP3   **b.** IMAP   **c.** SMPT   **d.** a and/or b

22. Which of the following primarily is used to transfer files from one device to another?

    a. PTF   **b.** FTP   **c.** HTTP   **d.** HTML

23. Which of the following is the standard port for an HTTP server?

    a. 80   **b.** 25   **c.** 110   **d.** 21

24. Which of the following is the standard port used by an FTP client to create a connection to an FTP server?

    a. 80   **b.** 25   **c.** 110   **d.** 21

25. Which of the following is the standard port used by POP3?

    a. 80   **b.** 25   **c.** 110   **d.** 21

26. Which of the following is the standard port used by SMTP?

    a. 80   **b.** 25   **c.** 110   **d.** 21

27. What layer of the TCP/IP model are domain names associated with?

    a. Network   **b.** Data link   **c.** Transport   **d.** Application

28. What do DNS servers resolve?

    a. Domain names to IP address   **b.** Domain names to MAC addresses
    c. a or b   **d.** Neither a nor b

29. What does URL stand for?

a. Unified Reference Locator **b.** Unified Reformat Locator
c. Uniform Reformat Locator **d.** Uniform Resource Locator

30. Which of the following can be provided by a DHCP server?

a. A subnet mask **b.** An IP address **c.** a or b **d.** Neither a nor b

31. Which port is used by the DHCP server on the server side?

a. 80 **b.** 67 **c.** 68 **d.** 110

32. Which port does the client use in a DHCP communication?

a. 80 **b.** 67 **c.** 68 **d.** 110

33. Where does a proxy server take a client's request?

a. Inside the firewall **b.** Outside the firewall
c. Depends on the client **d.** Depends on the proxy server

34. Which term describes the ability of a server in a cluster to take over a problem server's functions?

a. Failover **b.** Failupon **c.** Overfail **d.** Failsafe

35. When a client accesses a server cluster, how many servers does the client appear to see?

a. 1 **b.** None **c.** It depends on the cluster. **d.** 12

36. Which of the following is a local network designed for high-speed interconnection in server cluster environments?

a. LAN **b.** MAN **c.** SAN **d.** WAN

37. A dedicated server

a. requests resources from a client.
b. provides resources to a client.
c. is often used as a client.
d. cannot be part of a server cluster.

38. In the past, for example, during the late 1980s and early 1990s,

a. servers and clients were very similar.
b. servers were not available.
c. servers and clients were very different.
d. clients were not available.

39. Which of the following is generally true of servers?

a. They are physically secured. **b.** They have rugged cases.
c. They have specialized operating systems. **d.** All the above

40. Which of the following is the most frequently used well-known port?

a. 25 **b.** 21 **c.** 80 **d.** 110

41. Which term is sometimes used to describe RAM modules?

a. Sticks **b.** Cache **c.** ROM **d.** Bus

42. Which of the following can cause a bottleneck at a server?

a. The hard drive **b.** Insufficient RAM
c. The NIC **d.** All the above

43. Which of the following can copy an entire file from the server to the client?

a. Database server **b.** File server
c. Application server **d.** E-mail server

44. Which of the following is used to express, or program, Web pages?

  a. HTTP   **b.** HTML   **c.** FTP   **d.** SMTP

45. Which of the following is true of DHCP servers?

  a. They filter IP addresses.
  b. They dynamically allocate IP addresses.
  c. They filter MAC addresses.
  d. They dynamically allocate MAC addresses.

46. SCSI supports

  a. internal drives only.   **b.** external drives only.
  c. internal and external drives.   **d.** IDE drives.

47. Which of the following is possible for a single physical computer?

  a. It can run only one server service.
  b. It can potentially run multiple server services simultaneously.
  c. It can potentially run multiple server services, but only one at a time.
  d. Servers do not require physical components.

48. Which of the following is true when comparing POP3 and IMAP?

  a. POP3 is more sophisticated.
  b. IMAP requires more resources.
  c. POP3 can permanently maintain a user's e-mail.
  d. IMAP cannot permanently maintain a user's e-mail.

49. Which of the following is true of a proxy server?

  a. It hides a client's IP address.
  b. It reveals a client's IP address.
  c. It uses a client's IP address.
  d. Clients do not interact with proxy servers.

50. What type of address must a client have to access a network TCP/IP Web server?

  a. An IP address only
  b. A DNS address only
  c. An IP or a DNS address, but never both
  d. Both an IP and a DNS address

True or False

For each of the following select either True or False.

1. Many modern desktop operating systems are network aware.

2. Servers are typically physically secured in such a way that casual users cannot access them easily.

3. It is not unusual for important servers to have redundant power supplies.

4. All SOSs are designed to access the same number of CPUs.

5. Cache memory is slower than standard or RAM memory.

6. IDE interfaces can support up to four devices.

7. Devices that share an IDE channel can use the shared channel at the same time.

8. SCSI uses parallel bus capability.

9. All devices on a SCSI interface have the same identifier number.

10. NICs can have their own processors.

11. Synchronization of access should be provided by a file server.

12. Database servers can be configured to replicate a database across a network.

13. When accessing a Web server, the client needs a software component called a browser.

14. Requests come to a Web server over ports.

15. A URL has four potential components.

16. SMTP maintains and manages e-mail mailboxes.

17. An SMTP server cannot run on the same device as a POP3 server.

18. Unlike Web services, e-mail services do not require a client component.

19. SANs were developed prior to server cluster technology.

20. SANs mostly use a switched fabric architecture.

Exercises

Research in Brief

For one or more of the questions below, provide a one- to two-page report based on your findings.

1. This chapter presented the concept of well-known ports in relation to certain TCP/IP functionalities. Research and report back on other types of well-known ports. What are the benefits of using well-known ports? Are there any problems associated with well-known ports? If so, what are they and how can these problems be addressed? In what ways can a network administrator take advantage of well-known ports for supporting network services?

2. SANs are a recent and potentially revolutionary way of connecting devices together in a communications model. Investigate where current research in SAN architecture is going. How can SANs potentially transform data communications? What hurdles must be overcome to implement this technology? What organizations or industries are involved in developing standards for SANs? In your investigation, make sure you do not confuse storage area networks with system area networks; the two are related but different.

3. Many FTP client and server products are available. Select two FTP client and server products. Compare and contrast them. How do they differ? How are they similar? What advantages and disadvantages does each offer? When and where would you recommend one over the other and why?

4. Research server-clustering solutions from such providers as IBM, Compaq, Dell, or other server vendors. How do their solutions differ? In what ways are they the same? What costs are involved for different scales of clusters? Compare and contrast the solutions of at least three different providers.

Sheehan Marketing and Public Relations

President Sheehan has asked you to prepare a report on what would be required for SMPR to host its own Web site and Web server for client and staff access. He wants to know what products are available and which would be best for a business such as SMPR. He also wants to know what hardware and connectivity issues would be involved in hosting a Web site. Should the Web site be hosted in-house or would it be better to use the services of an ISP?

In addition, SMPR needs a more sophisticated e-mail system. You have been asked to evaluate and recommend e-mail server solutions from IBM and Microsoft. You need to evaluate and explain the advantages and disadvantages of their respective products and make a final recommendation. As always, President Sheehan expects to see some type of cost-benefit analysis in your recommendations.

Web References

shopper.zdnet.com

www.crucial.com

www.microsoft.com

www.nwfusion.com/news/tech/2001/1029tech.html

www.intel.com

www.webopedia.com/TERM/B/bus.html

www.scsilibrary.com

httpd.apache.org

www.iana.org/assignments/port-numbers

www.spectorsoft.com

www.elronsoftware.com/pdf/ethicswp.pdf

www.ethix.org

www.rfc-editor.org/rfc/rfc882.txt

www.rfc-editor.org/rfc/rfc883.txt

www.iana.org/domain-names.htm

www.dhcp.org

www.microsoft.com/ntserver/support/faqs/clustering_faq.asp#basics

www.linuxvirtualserver.org

www.fibrechannel.org

www.infinibandta.org

www.sandirect.com/switchsheet.htm

Monitoring Server Performance

Servers are a critical component in today's enterprise systems. Because servers are often used to share and/or distribute resources, they can become a significant bottleneck, negatively affecting enterprise performance, if they are not running properly. Due to their importance, network administrators constantly monitor server performance. Many network monitoring tools are available to network administrators that enable them to monitor server performance.

Reasons for Monitoring a Server

Let's first explore a few reasons why a server needs to be monitored. The following list presents a few of the more important reasons for server monitoring:

- **Hardware failure.** Servers run on computers; computers are machines. Like all machines, computers can suffer from hardware failure. When a server goes down, its resources or the resources that it manages will likely no longer be available. To your user and customer groups, an unavailable server can cause much frustration.

- **Unauthorized access.** Hackers recognize that servers are critical components in the enterprise. Because of their importance, servers are a prime target for hacker intrusion. Network administrators should closely monitor who is accessing server resources.

- **Software failure.** Servers frequently run essential business applications. Should one or more of those applications fail, staff and customers could be negatively affected. When applications are unavailable, the business may be unable to accomplish its work, resulting in financial losses.

- **Other security issues.** Besides unauthorized access, other security issues come into play with server technologies. Servers maintain passwords, contain resources that must be secured, provide directory services, authenticate users, and so on.

- **Port monitoring.** Administrators need to know whether an application or service running on a given IP address and port is running.

- **Content monitoring.** Administrators need to know if content has been altered and if the content delivery mechanism is working properly.

- **Database monitoring.** Administrators need to know if the database server is running and if it is accessible.

As you can see, monitoring server performance is essential. Many tools are available to the network administrator that enable him or her to perform such monitoring.

Network Monitoring Tools

One popular server monitoring tool is the Simple Network Management Protocol, or SNMP. SMNP was presented in Chapter 5. There you learned that devices running SMNP use a file called a MIB (Management Information Base). This MIB can be used to "trap" information, such as a device's functionality and status, unauthorized access attempts, reboots, and other activities that a device might encounter. The information recorded in the MIB can be relayed to a network administrator either through a log file or a paging mechanism. SNMP traps can issue "send" and "get" commands that make this report monitoring possible. Used mostly to monitor hardware, SNMP can also be used to report back on the status of applications.

For SNMP-enabled networks, products are available that enable administrators to monitor traffic flow through network servers. Paessler (**www.paessler.com**) offers a free, though limited, edition of its router graphics software that can report on such things as server CPU utilization and hard drive usage. The PRTG (Paessler Router Traffic Grapher) software is used in Windows environments. For a fee, Paessler offers more sophisticated tracking and monitoring products.

Active Server Monitor (**www.activeservermonitor.com**) is a vendor that can remotely monitor a business's servers. Active Server Monitor, which is available by subscription, can remotely check servers and alert a customer when a failure, whether physical or logical, occurs. Based on the type of service agreement selected, Active Server Monitor might check a server every 1, 5, or 10 minutes, 24 hours a day, 7 days a week.

In an August 25, 2003, article, *InfoWorld* magazine evaluated server-change-detection software from Tripwire. Tripwire (**www.tripwire.com**) is an industry leader in the change-detection software market. Change-detection software enables a network administrator to determine, for example, if employees are installing unauthorized software or are viewing files they should not be accessing, if rogue programs (worms and viruses) have been activated, and other such changes to a system. The Tripwire software is designed to alert network administrators of additions, deletions, and changes to files, applications, and systems. In addition, the software can produce reports of what it is monitoring, and, if properly configured, it can reverse changes that have been detected. At the time of this writing, the Tripwire system costs $595 per server. Tripwire for Servers 4.0 provides coverage for many different platforms, real-time alerts, automatic rollbacks, and Web-based management.

The scale of the enterprise will of course guide the server-monitoring solutions that you pursue. Although free monitoring tools are available, many of the tools are not free. However, before investing money in a product, you should take advantage of the free-trial test periods that many vendors offer for their products. A good site that offers a centralized page of network monitoring tools can be found at **www.slac.stanford.edu/xorg/nmtf/nmtf-tools.html**. This site also offers a link to public domain, open source, monitoring tools. Public domain tools can function very well, although they usually do not come with documentation and/or service support. For example, *sscan* can be used to evaluate hosts to determine if they are vulnerable to exploitation. *JetMon* is used by a server to ping a list of networked devices. Other public domain tools perform similar types of evaluative, troubleshooting, and reporting services.

9 chapternine
Enterprise Solutions

Learning Objectives	After studying this chapter, you should be able to:
	• Know the economic value of data and information.
	• Describe direct attached storage (DAS).
	• Describe storage area networks (SANs).
	• Describe Network-Attached Storage (NAS).
	• Understand virtual private networks (VPNs).
	• Define Voice-over-IP (VoIP).
	• Explain the advantages of Web services.

In Chapter 8, you learned that businesses rely on server technology to meet their networking needs. However, servers and their associated software, hardware, and staffing are not without costs. Ideally, businesses recover these costs from the services and efficiencies that server technologies provide. These services and efficiencies are very often tightly coupled with *enterprise solutions*. Enterprise solutions are designed to allow a business to run its enterprise more efficiently and effectively with regards to cost, service, and security. Chapter 9 explores just a few of these enterprise-level solutions.

The Economic Value of Data and Information

Businesses rely on their data and information resources to provide a vital competitive advantage. Not only must these resources be current and accurate, they must also be readily available to staff and clients. The need to access data and information across the enterprise is transforming how businesses implement storage technologies and how these data and information resources are processed and delivered once they are accessed. Data and information that are freely and easily available to users across the enterprise can give a business a competitive edge, as conceptualized in Figure 9.1.

Figure 9.1
Economics of Data
In a global economy connected through an international infrastructure, an enterprise must be prepared to compete for customers not only from its local industry, but also around the world.

Organizations that are not competitive eventually disappear from the business scene. This chapter examines various enterprise solutions that enable businesses to leverage their data and information resources. Competition among businesses often drives technology in new directions; data communications technology is no exception. Information is a business tool and a competitive weapon. The tremendous growth of data-intensive applications such as e-commerce and Web-based services has driven the development of better enterprise solutions.

Direct Attached Storage

You learned in Chapter 8 that servers are specialized devices that make resources available to clients in the enterprise. One of the main functions of servers is to store data and information. Two evolving storage enterprise solutions reviewed in this chapter are storage area networks (SANs) and Network-Attached Storage (NAS). However, to truly understand the benefits of these two solutions, you need to know about a technology that has been around for several decades—**direct attached storage (DAS)**. DAS is a mature technology that has an important role in today's data communications world. By assessing the shortcomings of DAS as a server tool, you will understand why solutions such as SANs and NAS are being pursued.

DAS is usually associated with magnetic tape, also called "tape," and hard drives. Tape is used extensively by organizations for backing up data and for the off-line storage of data that are not frequently referenced. **Off-line** refers to resources that are not immediately available but that could be made available in a reasonable amount of time (i.e., less than a minute). Tape is the most common DAS technology used to provide off-line service. Data that are immediately available are said to be

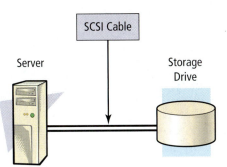

Figure 9.2

Typical DAS Configuration
*In this example, the storage
(hard or tape drive) is directly
attached to the server
computer's processor. I/O
requests access the storage
device directly.*

online. DAS devices, such as a hard drive, are connected by cable to a computer's processor inside a computer's case (see Figure 9.2). This direct connection means that a DAS device is attached to a single computer and, in this discussion, to a single server. As a storage technology, DAS is optimized for single, isolated processors and thereby provides for a lower initial cost.

Regardless of the type of storage device, **input/output (I/O) requests** read and write data from and to the storage device. Storage devices can use a variety of I/O protocols. For a DAS server, the protocol of choice is **Small Computer Systems Interface (SCSI)**. A SCSI command can tell a hard drive to retrieve data from a specific location, or block, on the drive or to mount a specific tape cartridge. SCSI is known as a **block-level I/O protocol** because it specifies block locations on the drives that it accesses. It is possible for SCSI commands to be issued over Ethernet media, Fibre Channel, serial storage architecture (SSA), and standard SCSI parallel cables. Most implementations of DAS devices use standard SCSI cables, such as the one shown in Figure 9.3. A standard SCSI parallel cable should be no longer than 25 meters, which limits how far an external storage

Figure 9.3
*Evolving technologies will likely replace SCSI. Here,
a man shows a standard SCSI cable interface.*

device can be from its direct-connect server. You may recall from Chapter 8 that SCSI supports both internal and external devices.

A DAS server does not permit a second server to directly or simultaneously access its storage drives. This limits a DAS device's ability to perform capacity sharing. With **capacity sharing**, a storage device pools storage space or tape drives with other processors. The ability of a storage technology to pool storage space makes a technology **scalable**, or able to dynamically expand or contract based on network needs. DAS devices do not provide flexible capacity sharing. Additionally, DAS devices do not support data sharing. **Data sharing** is the capability of a storage device to share data and files concurrently with other storage devices. Capacity and data sharing are not the same thing.

Think of capacity sharing as the ability of *multiple* servers to share and pool their multiple storage resources in such a way that a client or user views these resources as a single resource. By appearing as a single resource, capacity sharing in effect creates a **virtualization** of server storage. The term virtualization here means that several physical devices, multiple server hard drives for example, appear as one logical hard drive. In contrast to capacity sharing, think of data sharing as the ability of a *single* server to allow its stored data files and applications to be simultaneously used by other servers. An interesting report related to this topic can be found at **www.clipper.com/research/TCG2003003.pdf**.

Generally, because of its built-in limitations, DAS is best for organizations that have a small number of servers or that have fairly low I/O demands. For a long time, DAS was the only game in town. However, more flexible, though more costly, storage solutions are now available. One such solution is a storage area network.

Storage Area Networks

As its name implies, a **storage area network (SAN)** is itself a network, which is both its advantage and disadvantage. The advantage comes from the efficiencies that a SAN, as a separate network, can bring to storage access and retrieval. The disadvantage comes primarily from the initial cost and complexity of setting up the SAN infrastructure. As with any business solution, the decision of whether to use a SAN will be based on how cost-effective and efficient a SAN would be for the organization.

A SAN is a network of storage devices that other computers, servers, and/or clients can access. This means that enterprise resources such as files, databases, applications, e-mail, or anything else that needs to be stored and retrieved can be removed from the LAN and stored on the SAN. By putting these resources on a SAN, traffic on the LAN is significantly reduced and access to stored data is improved. A LAN in a SAN-configured enterprise has clients and servers as well as an interface, or connection, to the SAN. The connection is typically from the servers to the SAN. Thus, servers are connected to the data network, the LAN, and to the storage network, the SAN. Figure 9.4 illustrates this type of SAN.

SANs are usually implemented with Fibre Channel, although other connecting networking technologies, such as Gigabit Ethernet, are possible. In theory, SANs are independent of the underlying network topology. Recall that a **topology** defines how a network is physically cabled together. Fibre Channel is a high-speed (100 million bytes per second!) switched-fabric technology capable of connecting hundreds or even thousands of devices. (Switched fabric was presented in Chapter 8.) A SAN might be as simple

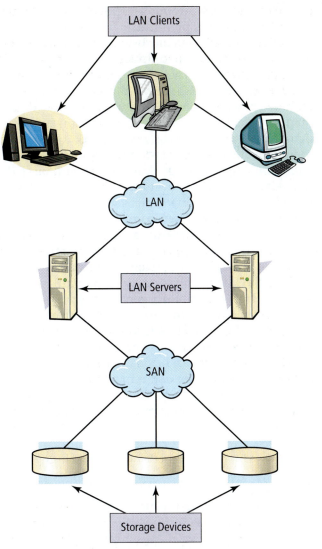

Figure 9.4
Simple SAN Configuration

as a single server connected to a single storage array using Fibre Channel or as complicated as hundreds of servers connected to hundreds of storage arrays. Optimized for storage traffic, SANs manage multiple drives and tape devices as a shared pool, provide a single point of control, and offer specialized backup facilities that reduce server and LAN utilization.

Using technologies such as Fibre Channel, SANs can be far away from the computers or processors that use the stored data. This means that servers do not have to be physically close to the SAN, as they would be with a DAS device in a SCSI setup. Furthermore, because SANs offload I/O traffic from the LAN, higher data availability and improved performance result. As a SAN solution, Fibre Channel is faster than most LAN media, another advantage. Importantly, large numbers of computers, servers, or clients can be connected to the same storage device residing on the SAN, which is not possible in a DAS device configuration.

Note that devices do not have their own separate, physical connection to the SAN. Instead, most devices connect to a server that is connected to the SAN. The result is the virtualization of the SAN to the devices that use it. This means that the devices view the SAN as a single pool of storage resources. Because a SAN appears to be a single pool of storage resources, capacity sharing is possible.

SANs are not just hardware, they also require management software. The SAN management software component must do two things. First, any network topology selected to support the SAN, most probably Fibre Channel, must itself be managed. Managing the topology includes monitoring the storage network, remote maintenance and diagnostics, security management that could involve authentication or encryption, and performance management and fine-tuning. Second, a SAN management component has to provide for management of the stored data itself. Capacity analysis, load balancing, file sharing, data movement, and data backup and restoration are just a few examples of what a SAN software manager must do. Providers of SAN management software include IBM (**www.ibm.com**), Sun Microsystems (**www.sun.com**), Hewlett-Packard (**www.hp.com**), Computer Associates (**www.ca.com**), and Fujistu (**www.fujistu.com**), among others.

SANs may be appropriate in several scenarios. For example, SANs are likely to achieve their best performance in large organizations that have substantial I/O traffic of any type. Organizations that have heavy database activity also are probably good candidates for a SAN. Also, organizations with multiple departments that have cross-dependent data needs may be well suited for a SAN solution. Note that SANs do not have to be implemented corporatewide but can be targeted for specific areas of concern.

Because SANs can be costly to implement and may require significant staff training in their use, organizations usually consider several factors in determining whether a SAN is the right solution for them. An organization may want to consider the following questions before deciding on a SAN solution:

- What applications now in use would justify the implementation of a SAN?

- How is the enterprise currently utilizing its storage and server capacities?

- How many departments and/or locations might be part of or able to take advantage of a SAN?

- If multiple departments and/or locations are expected to participate in the SAN, what are their current storage and connection requirements?

- What business objectives, short-, medium-, or long-term, support the choice of a SAN solution?

- How is the business expected to grow over the short and long term with regards to both the market and geographically?

- What technical staffing resources are available for a SAN implementation, and are other personnel issues involved?

- How have server and storage technologies been budgeted in the past and how will this budget be impacted by a SAN solution?

Network-Attached Storage

Like SANs, **Network-Attached Storage (NAS)** is a recent technology that addresses emerging enterprise storage needs. In some ways, NAS technology is like teaching an old dog to do new tricks—in this case, teaching an old-style file server how to do more, and better, tricks than what file servers of the past were able to perform. NAS can be implemented in conjunction with

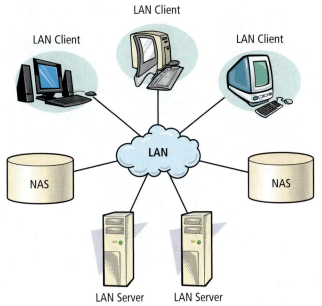

LAN Client

LAN Client

LAN Client

LAN

NAS

NAS

LAN Server

LAN Server

Figure 9.5
Standard NAS Configuration

a SAN, but it can also be a stand-alone solution. Figure 9.5 shows a stand-alone NAS LAN configuration. NAS devices are also referred to as **Network-Attached Storage appliances** (NAS appliances). In general, a NAS appliance is a high-performance storage device that provides shared data and file serving to clients and servers in a LAN. Several factors are driving this push for more, and superior, networked storage solutions.

As mentioned earlier, businesses need to capitalize on their information resources to gain a market advantage over their competitors. A NAS appliance, and a SAN, by providing faster and more reliable access to data and information, allows these resources to be more efficiently utilized. Better and faster storage of data have provided businesses alternative ways to competitively leverage existing data for applications such as data mining, data warehousing, knowledge management, and trend analysis. For such applications, NAS and SANs are very useful. **Data mining** is used to find hidden patterns in data that may be useful for predicting future behavior. Businesses that can predict the future behavior of their market base have a strong competitive edge. For a more detailed look at data mining, be sure to read the "Topic in Focus" at the end of this chapter. **Data warehousing** is a means of viewing a wide variety of data that can offer a comprehensive view of business conditions at a given point in time. **Knowledge management** is a process that businesses follow to generate value from their intellectual property and knowledge-based assets. It involves the creation, dissemination, and utilization of corporate knowledge. **Trend analysis** enables businesses to anticipate where their industry is going. Technologies like the ones identified above, and conceptually illustrated in Figure 9.6, can play a significant role in e-commerce.

These types of applications, however, require data—a lot of it. In order to be fully utilized, the data must not only be stored, but easily accessible as well. Additionally, organizations are pushing to store all data in digital format, including audio, graphics, documents, photography, and video. Finally, as more businesses use the Web for such applications as e-commerce, demand has grown for ways to efficiently and cost-effectively store data and make it easily accessible over the Internet. For many businesses, accessible means, as the saying goes, 24/7.

Figure 9.6

E-commerce

The advent of the WWW has transformed the economics of business, both for the customer and the supplier of a service or product.

NAS appliances have internal, integrated processors that are optimized to manage disk storage. Using either a hub or a switch, a NAS appliance is ordinarily attached to a TCP/IP network, either a LAN or a WAN. However, a NAS appliance must be attached to a network that supports IP-based protocols. Using a stripped-down and proprietary operating system, a NAS appliance's only function is to provide file services to clients or servers. Using specialized file sharing protocols, typically the **Network File System (NFS)** or the **Common Internet File System** (**CIFS**; pronounced "siffs"), networked devices request file services from the NAS appliance. The NAS appliance's internal processor then translates and processes these requests. (The RFC on NFS can be found at **www.faqs.org/rfcs/rfc1094.html**. A brief article on CIFS can be found at **www.microsoft.com/mind/1196/cifs.asp**.)

NFS and CIFS are **file-level I/O protocols**. SCSI, which is also an I/O protocol, is, however, a block-level protocol. NFS and CIFS are both device-independent protocols, meaning that they are not limited to a specific vendor's hardware implementation. NFS's origins are in the UNIX world, whereas CIFS comes from Microsoft's NT operating systems.

NAS appliances can be connected directly to a LAN or WAN or placed on a separate dedicated storage network. The choice depends on how the accessed files are used. For example, if the NAS appliance will house a database or other commonly shared application, it may be preferable to have the appliance on its own network. In that way, servers on the LAN, on behalf of their clients, can interact with the NAS appliance, thereby reducing traffic on the LAN itself. However, if the NAS appliance is used to store individual client files, it may be best to directly connect the NAS appliance to the LAN. Another option is to use a **Network-Attached Storage gateway** (NAS gateway). With a NAS gateway, the NAS appliance has an internal processor but does not have its own integrated storage. Instead, the NAS gateway appliance is connected to, in most cases, a SAN. Figure 9.7 illustrates the NAS gateway concept.

Several benefits of NAS are that it can run on lower-cost Ethernet-based networks, is relatively easy to install, and can automatically assign storage capacity based on user demand. However, NAS only allows resource pooling within the appliance itself. Consequently, there is little, if

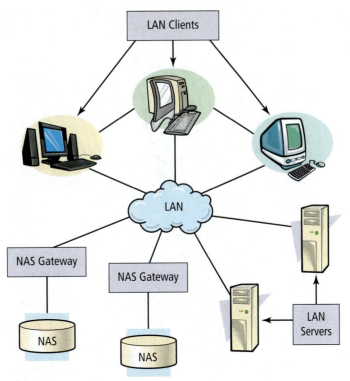

Figure 9.7
NAS Configuration Utilizing a NAS Gateway
*In this configuration, the NAS gateway is a device without
integrated storage. Instead, the NAS gateway connects to
external storage either directly, as in this example, or
through a SAN.*

any, sharing of resources across multiple NAS appliances. An example of
a NAS appliance appropriate for a large enterprise is EMC's Clariion product (**www.emc.com**). For departmental or workgroup solutions,
Quantum (**www.quantum.com**) and Maxtor (**www.maxtor.com**) both
offer a range of products.

Table 9.1 compares the respective characteristics of DAS, SANs,
and NAS.

Table 9.1 Comparison of DAS, SAN, and NAS Technologies

Technology	Separate Network Capable	Most Common Media	I/O Protocol	Supports Capacity Sharing	Supports Data Sharing	Typical Bandwidth
DAS	No	Parallel SCSI	SCSI	Limited	No	40 to 160 Mbps
SAN	Yes	Fibre Channel	SCSI	Yes	With special software	100 to 200 Mbps
NAS	Yes	Ethernet	NFS and CIFS	Yes	Yes	10 Mbps to 1 Gbps
NAS with gateway	Yes	Ethernet	NFS and CIFS	Yes	Yes	10 Mbps to 1Gbps

The Ethical Perspective

Whose Data Is It Anyway?

Businesses have always maintained data on their customers, even if only on paper. With the advent of technologies such as SANs and NAS appliances, businesses are finding that the quantity of data that they can capture, access, and utilize has grown exponentially. This vast quantity of customer data can drive such applications as data mining, data warehousing, knowledge management, and trend analysis. Using database technologies linked by Web services and supported by WAN infrastructures, businesses can access their data from virtually anywhere. In the past, the extent to which businesses collected data on customers was not a controversial issue. Times have changed. Increasingly, customers are becoming concerned, and in some cases alarmed, at the degree of data recording that is taking place.

Much of the data captured by businesses is sensitive and personal in nature: financial, medical, job location and pay, addresses, telephone numbers, driver's license numbers or credit/debit account numbers, and so on. After a business captures such data, is it strictly up to the business as to how those data are used? Can the data, for example, be sold or shared with other businesses? In many cases, at least in the past, the answer has been yes, to the anger and frustration of many consumers. For this reason, consumers have turned to legislative bodies to restrict what businesses may do with the data they capture.

In the United States, the Health Insurance Portability and Accountability Act (HIPPA) of 1996 greatly restricts how, when, where, and to whom a patient's medical history, paper and electronic, can be released. Amazingly, prior to the passage of this act, a patient could have been denied access to his or her own medical records. In July of 2003, the state of California began to enforce a personal privacy act, Senate Bill 1386. This legislation requires a business to inform a customer when his or her name, in conjunction with either a Social Security number, driver's license number, or credit/debit card number, has been accessed by an unauthorized person.

Many businesses believe that legislation of this type puts an unfair economic burden on them. What do you think? Should a business be ethically bound to notify customers if the business shares or sells customer data? Should government bodies regulate such compliance? Should a business be required to give a customer full or limited access to the data that the business stores on that customer?

The content of California's Senate Bill 1386 can be found at **info.sen.ca. gov/pub/01–02/bill/sen/sb_1351-1400/sb_1386_bill_20020926_ chaptered.html**. Details of HIPPA can be found at **www.hhs.gov/ocr/hipaa**. Other states and nations are implementing similar measures.

Virtual Private Networks

In the coming years, storage technologies will play an increasingly critical part in enterprise networking solutions. However, businesses today are looking for ways to leverage existing technologies, such as those provided by the public telecommunications infrastructure. One data communication technology that has proven of great interest to many organizations because of its relatively low cost and ease of implementation is virtual private networking.

A **virtual private network (VPN)** is a private data network that uses a common carrier's public telecommunications infrastructure, at a cost, for private organizational purposes. A VPN can implement privacy through various tunneling and security procedures. **Tunneling** refers to a technique that allows packets from one protocol to be wrapped, or encapsulated, within a second protocol. At the sender's end, the sender's protocol packets are wrapped (encapsulated) in the protocol used by the transmitting infrastructure. The wrapped packets can then be transported over this different packet networking infrastructure. At the receiving end, the packets are unwrapped back into their native, or original, protocol.

Physical private networks are owned, in general, by one organization and used only by that organization. A VPN is very different. Many organizations can concurrently use a common carrier's telecommunications infrastructure for their VPNs. Hundreds, or even thousands, of VPNs, with each VPN completely unaware of the others, can share the carrier's infrastructure. VPNs provide the same capabilities as private leased lines, but at much lower cost. A VPN is in some ways a type of outsourcing. **Outsourcing** refers to one business paying a different business for services rendered. (Many types of services today are outsourced, including manufacturing, call center assistance, payroll services, and even software engineering. For example, Figure 9.8 shows workers processing U.S. health insurance data at an office in Accra, the capital of Ghana.)

Figure 9.8
Outsourcing, especially to foreign countries, has become a controversial and difficult political and social issue.

Businesses that use VPNs have, in effect, outsourced their networking infrastructure. This means that the business paying for the VPN is not responsible for the staffing, management, maintenance, configuration, or security of the VPN's infrastructure. Those issues are left to the common carrier. Of course, that is both an advantage and a disadvantage. For many organizations, having no control over the networking infrastructure can be a problem. A business must carefully weigh the pros and cons of whether to use a VPN.

The popularity of VPNs suggests that for many organizations the advantages outweigh the disadvantages. Selecting a VPN, however, requires some analysis in order to select the most appropriate type of VPN: trusted, secure, or hybrid. Each type of VPN has its own particular characteristics and requirements.

Trusted VPNs

Trusted VPNs preceded secure and hybrid VPNs. Originally, VPNs were circuits that a business leased from a communications carrier. The business had to rely on the carrier's assurances that the carrier's infrastructure was reliable and secure. At first, businesses were slow to adopt VPN. Because few businesses initially utilized VPNs, security was not considered a critical issue. Instead, businesses simply "trusted" the carrier to provide protected and reliable services. This arrangement constituted a "trusted" VPN.

For a trusted VPN, no one other than the carrier can affect the creation or modification of the VPN's path. The path is the series of links between the sender and the receiver that the data traffic flows through. This series of links appears to the business as a cloud (a term you may recall from Chapter 7). With a trusted VPN, many customers can, and are, using the same links within a path. The value of a trusted VPN is that the carrier can be relied on to provide a secure and reliable path. Businesses that use VPN technology should understand that common carriers share each other's infrastructures, therefore a VPN might span the infrastructure of more than one carrier.

Besides having a path, a trusted VPN also carries data. An additional requirement of a trusted VPN is that no one other than the trusted VPN carrier can change, add, or delete data on the trusted VPN. Any change to the data on the path would affect the characteristics of the path itself. Finally, before a trusted VPN path can be established, routing and addressing have to be defined between the sender and the receiver. Figure 9.9 shows a configuration of a possible trusted VPN.

Secure VPNs

Over time, trusted VPNs gained in popularity because they were relatively low in cost and easy to implement. As a result, more businesses began using common carrier infrastructures for transporting more data. Increasingly, businesses using trusted VPNs grew concerned about the security of their data, especially because they had virtually no control over the carrier's infrastructure. To address security concerns, carriers began to incorporate encryption technology into their VPN services.

With such VPN services, the data at the sender's end is encrypted. The encryption can be done by the customer or by the carrier. As the

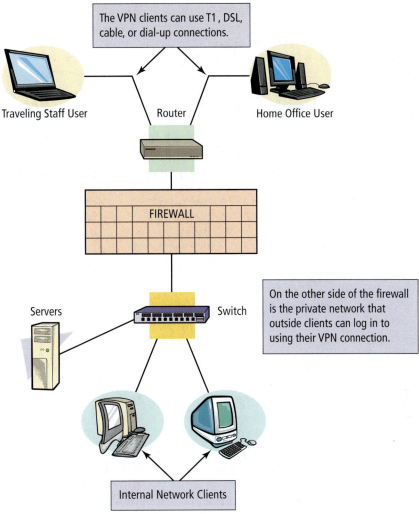

The VPN clients can use T1, DSL, cable, or dial-up connections.

Traveling Staff User

Router

Home Office User

FIREWALL

Servers

Switch

On the other side of the firewall is the private network that outside clients can log in to using their VPN connection.

Internal Network Clients

Figure 9.9
Typical Trusted VPN Configuration

encrypted traffic passes over the VPN, it behaves as though it were in a tunnel that connects the sender and the receiver. If an unauthorized user intercepts the encrypted data, he or she is not able to read it or change it without the receiver being made aware of the intrusion or modification. The receiver, upon receipt of the encrypted data, decrypts it back into its original form. This use of tunneled encryption creates what is called a **secure VPN**. (Chapter 10 examines the topic of encryption in more detail as a means of securing the enterprise.) Figure 9.10 shows the steps in a typical secure VPN transmittal.

By definition, all traffic on a secure VPN must be encrypted and authenticated. Also, all parties must agree on the security characteristics of the VPN. For example, are the security features automated? Are they available 24/7? Are the security features transparent to the user such that the user is not inconvenienced? Will the security features slow network performance? If so, will this slowdown be acceptable to users?

A secure VPN has one or more tunnels. Each tunnel has two end points, one at the sender and the other at the receiver. The administrators of each of the two end points must agree on the characteristics of the tunnel's security properties. Finally, no one outside the VPN should be able to affect the security properties of the VPN.

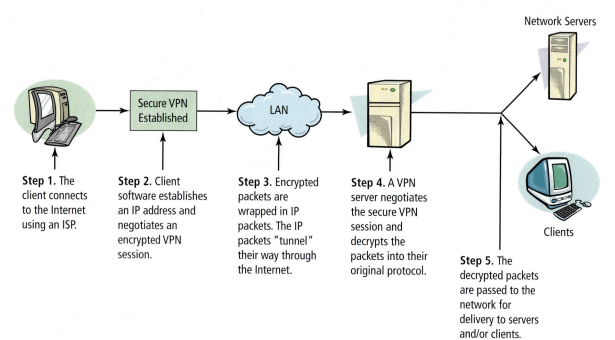

Network Servers

Step 1. The client connects to the Internet using an ISP.

Step 2. Client software establishes an IP address and negotiates an encrypted VPN session.

Step 3. Encrypted packets are wrapped in IP packets. The IP packets "tunnel" their way through the Internet.

Step 4. A VPN server negotiates the secure VPN session and decrypts the packets into their original protocol.

Clients

Step 5. The decrypted packets are passed to the network for delivery to servers and/or clients.

Figure 9.10
Typical Secure VPN Process

Hybrid VPNs

A trusted VPN and a secure VPN are not mutually exclusive. This means that a secure VPN can run as part of a trusted VPN. Between a sender and a receiver, a portion of a communication may be either trusted or secure. Such a pairing creates the third type of VPN technology, the hybrid VPN. The secure part of the **hybrid VPN** can be controlled by the user through secure VPN equipment on site or through the provider of the trusted VPN connection.

Because a hybrid VPN is a combination of trusted and secure VPNs, the boundaries between the two types of VPNs must be well defined. This means that within a hybrid VPN communication, the administrator must be able to determine whether the traffic between a sender and a receiver is part of the secure VPN. The ability to differentiate the traffic is important, because trusted VPN traffic does not use encryption and secure VPN traffic must be encrypted. The type of VPN used will depend on the business, the nature of the data, and the capabilities of the provider.

Using a VPN

This section considers three ways that a VPN might be used. Depending on the enterprise, VPNs can provide secure remote access, intranet access, or extranet access.

Secure remote access is usually offered to staff who are on the road and who need to remotely, but securely, log in to a network and access needed resources such as databases, project management files, and documents. Remote users who use secure remote access usually dial in to the VPN using a standard 56K modem. Today, remote users might also use DSL or cable services to log in.

To access the VPN, the remote user must have a **VPN client** installed on his or her connecting device. The VPN client may perform several functions. A VPN client can negotiate tunnel properties and establish the tunnel. Because the connection is secure, the client authenticates the user and establishes what the user's rights are to the requested resource. The client also establishes security keys for encryption and decryption. Beyond establishing encryption and decryption rules, the data itself must be encrypted and decrypted by the client.

An **intranet**, which is based on the same technology as the Internet, is the internal portion of the enterprise that is primarily for staff access. Intranet access can be useful for connecting remote offices, whether across a city, state, or country. For this type of secure VPN, it is not unusual for intranet access to be filtered first through a firewall or server. The firewall or server can then perform the secure VPN functionalities of tunneling, authentication, and encryption.

An **extranet** is the portion of an enterprise's network that is meant to be shared and accessed by selected customers, suppliers, and/or business partners. This type of VPN access is particularly sensitive because the business is granting access to portions of its network to users who are not formally part of the business. In such a scenario, great care must be taken to ensure that all necessary firewall and security measures are in place. The intent is to precisely limit the resources that are made available through the extranet and to ensure that those using the extranet are in fact authorized to do so.

As you have already read, a VPN requires a tunneling procedure. This tunneling, which is a form of wrapping, or encapsulation, is performed by protocols. The four most common VPN tunneling protocols are Point-to-Point Tunneling Protocol, Layer-2 Tunneling Protocol, Multi-Protocol Label Switching, and Internet Protocol Security. The tunneling protocol used depends on the enterprise's networking protocols; the tunneling protocol must be supported by the networking protocols.

Internet Protocol Security (IPSec), which was standardized by the IETF, is usually associated with secure VPNs. **Point-to-Point Tunneling Protocol (PPTP)** is widely installed because it enables PPP (which you may recall from Chapter 7) to be tunneled through an IP network. PPTP does not change PPP, but is simply a means of carrying PPP communications. Most Windows-based clients automatically support PPTP. **Multi-Protocol Label Switching (MPLS)** is associated with Frame Relay and ATM networks. **Layer-2 Tunneling Protocol (L2TP)** is a Cisco-sponsored protocol that combines the Layer-2 Forwarding Protocol (L2F) with PPTP. L2TP is also an emerging IETF standard. Cisco views L2TP as a key building block for supporting mobile workforce access to VPNs. A detailed discussion of these tunneling protocols is beyond the scope of this text.

Many businesses have found VPNs to be an attractive and effective data communications option. Because of their low cost and benefits, VPNs have found a ready market.

Voice-over-Internet Protocol

Voice-over-Internet Protocol (VoIP) is a technology designed to carry voice communications over digital, packet-switched networks. As an enterprise solution it has received considerable attention over the last few years. VoIP can be combined with VPN for a more complete enterprise solution. Major vendors who provide VoIP solutions include Avaya (**www.avaya.com**), Nortel (**www.nortel.com**), Siemens (**www.siemens.com**), and Cisco (**www.cisco.com**). To some, VoIP offers long-desired benefits. To others, VoIP offers more problems than it resolves. So, is VoIP a blessing or a curse?

VoIP, which is a data service, requires us to remember that voice functionalities must still be supported. These functionalities include supervision, signaling, dialing, voice transmission, call routing, ringing, billing, and administration, among others. Standard voice transmission differs from VoIP in several ways. For example, standard voice is carried as direct current over copper wiring, whereas VoIP sends a bit stream over copper wiring. Standard voice is analog; VoIP is digital. Standard voice transmission is continuous; VoIP uses packets. Figure 9.11 shows an example of Cisco VoIP hardware.

Because voice communication is analog, when you speak and hear a voice communication you hear a smooth flow of sound without the annoyance of dropped sound bites along the way, which can happen when voice is converted into data packets. You may be wondering why anyone would want to convert voice transmission from analog to digital. This transition is being driven by a term you will likely hear much more of in the near future: *convergence*. In this instance, the convergence is between voice and data infrastructures. Chapter 11 looks more closely at convergent technology as a future trend.

Another important factor driving the transition to VoIP is cost. VoIP promises to provide voice-level services at a significant cost savings. The financial advantages of VoIP are alluring and likely to prove irresistible. But how many times have consumers been promised something, particularly involving a technology, that did not live up to its expectations? What is the current status of VoIP?

Figure 9.11
Cisco VoIP Hardware

Traditional analog voice communications use TDM (time-division multiplexing) with Private Branch Exchange hardware. A **Private Branch Exchange (PBX)** functions like a miniature telephone system within the enterprise. The PBX, which is owned by the enterprise, switches calls between enterprise users on lines within the enterprise to a limited number of external phone lines to the common carrier. The common carrier is often a **Public Switched Telephone Network (PSTN)** provider. The PBX connects users to the common carrier's telecommunications infrastructure. The key advantage of a PBX is that it saves the cost of requiring the enterprise to implement individual lines for each user to the telephone company's central office. Also, the PBX gives the organization control and security over its internal voice communications. The PBX sits between the telephone company's technology and the enterprise. In general, layers between the outside world and the enterprise's internal operations provide the organization more control and security over the enterprise.

A PBX functions like a physically isolated network through which all enterprise voice communications must pass. In addition, the PBX box is housed in a specific physical location. This means that call centers that run from a PBX are tied to a specific geographic location. PBX traditionally has been highly proprietary, meaning that an organization has to buy into a specific vendor's PBX implementation, which many view as a disadvantage.

However, another significant benefit of the PBX approach is the high level of security provided. To hack into or secretly record voice conversations carried through a PBX, unauthorized users must have physical access to the PBX box, which is usually physically secured. Or, the unauthorized user must find a way to splice into the phone lines that feed into the PBX.

A disadvantage of the PBX approach is that it requires a separate infrastructure in addition to the one that carries the data of the enterprise. Because voice and data are carried on separate networks, a cost is involved. If voice and data could be transported over a single technology, in this case IP, substantial cost savings can be realized. Recall that IP is a data-based technology. Imagine the following scenario.

Your organization's call center is no longer controlled from a central, physical location. Because IP is used as the voice-delivery mechanism, calls can be managed, accessed, and routed to and from virtually any point that can access the Internet. In addition, because both the voice and data infrastructure are based on IP, a client can seamlessly contact the enterprise using voice, fax, e-mail, chat, or any other Web-based service. This integration of messaging services is called **Unified Messaging (UM).** (UM is examined more closely in Chapter 11.) Because voice and data resources are integrated over the same IP-based network, significant cost advantages are realized. All communications and data pass through the same terminals in the form of integrated voice/data client workstations. In addition, the organization's customer resource management (CRM) software can now use computer-telephone integration technology to link to customer database servers and their applications. This may sound good, but for this scenario to happen several factors must be considered.

First, what is the current network utilization? It is critical for the organization to know current network bandwidth maximums, minimums, and averages, because voice communications can suffer significantly from latency, jitter, and packet loss when carried over an IP infrastructure. Second, network infrastructure elements need to be evaluated to see if they can even be configured to support VoIP. For example, are the Ethernet switches currently in place capable of supporting VoIP traffic?

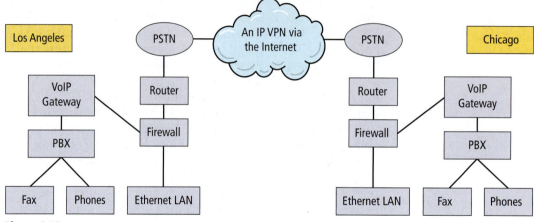

Figure 9.12
Possible VoIP with PBX Configuration

Does the current network support IP-based **Quality of Service (QoS)**? (QoS, as you may recall, enables a network administrator to prioritize packets). In the case of VoIP, it may be necessary to ensure that voice packets have a higher priority than more delay-tolerant traffic. Dropped sound bites are very irritating in a voice conversation!

An organization considering VoIP must know its current and future voice-bandwidth requirements. For example, does the business need to support 100 voice lines or 10,000? Voice traffic, both incoming and outgoing, must be analyzed to determine what level of traffic a VoIP network would have to support. Most PBX-based systems provide statistical information on voice utilization. Traditional PBX voice services that a VoIP solution must provide include call forwarding, call waiting, call return, call hold, call back, call block, and other similar functions.

Security is a particularly sensitive topic with regards to VoIP. PBX-based solutions do not suffer from viruses or denial-of-service attacks, problems associated with IP-based networks running servers. Firewalls, intrusion detection technology, and security practices are critical in protecting the enterprise's voice communications over an IP network. However, VoIP and PBX do not have to be mutually exclusive. In fact, many organizations deploy both. Figure 9.12 illustrates a VoIP network with a PBX configuration.

Vendors of VoIP technology recognize that issues such as security and standardization must be more fully addressed before businesses see VoIP as a total solution. However, the integration and cost savings that VoIP promises will make this a technology that will continue to gain acceptance and implementation.

Web Services

Web services is an umbrella term used to describe technologies that, utilizing the Internet and particularly the WWW, provide access to a host of services for customers, employees, and business partners. Like VPNs and VoIP, Web services are increasingly being viewed as an enterprise technology capable of affecting such areas as business process integration, application integration, and Web-based application development. As an umbrella term, Web services refer to a collection of software components

Figure 9.13
Businesses increasingly view Web services as an additional means of improving the quality of the customer service experience.

designed to dynamically interact with each other using Internet standards. Internet standards are formulated by several organizations. For Web services, three standards organizations in particular must be noted: the **World Wide Web Consortium (W3C)**, the **Organization for the Advancement of Structured Information Standards (OASIS)**, and the **Distributed Management Task Force (DMTF)**. Their respective Web sites are **www.w3.org**, **www.oasis-open.org**, and **www.dmtf.org**.

Web services are enterprise applications that use languages and protocols to enable devices, software, and people to better communicate and collaborate with each other, ultimately to provide better service, conceptualized in Figure 9.13. The trend today is toward a higher integration of data and applications. Integrating data with applications achieves cost efficiencies. Web services can be used to integrate data and applications as well as to access data and applications.

As envisioned by enterprise application technology developers, Web services offer superior access by allowing different interfaces to interact with enterprise resources, particularly data and applications. Web services can be accessed through a client application, such as a browser, or through wireless devices, voice-activated interfaces, Web portals, or other mechanisms. Using Web services, customer database information could be updated through a wireless device, a Web page, or another type of Web service. Also, devices using Web services can communicate with each other, potentially leading to a highly adaptable enterprise infrastructure. Because Web services are based on components, they can be implemented incrementally. Moving to a Web services infrastructure does not have to be an all-or-nothing proposition. But what are Web services based on?

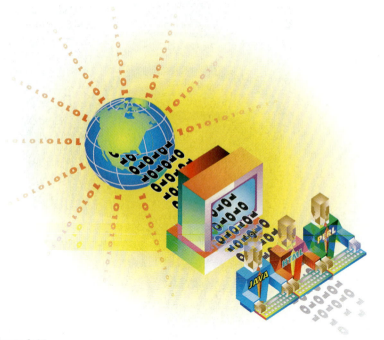

Figure 9.14

Languages such as JAVA, HTML, XML, and PERL are being used to develop Web-based services.

Web service components, like those illustrated in Figure 9.14, are based on protocols and service platforms. The key Web service protocol is **Extensible Markup Language (XML)**. The two key service platforms are Sun Microsystems' **Java 2 Enterprise Edition (J2EE)** and Microsoft's **C#** (pronounced "C sharp"), a programming language within .Net (pronounced "dot net"). .Net is Microsoft's latest application development platform. In addition, Web services are typically tied to a relational database from which data and information are pulled or pushed.

XML is a structured data definition language that was formalized by the W3C for describing Web page content. A number of XML-based languages are used expressly for Web services. Two frequently used XML-based languages are Web Services Description Language and Simple Object Access Protocol. **Web Services Description Language (WSDL)** is used to describe a Web service. **Simple Object Access Protocol (SOAP)** is used to transport data to and from a Web service. Used by programmers to create automated Web-based services, SOAP requests resources from remote software objects using XML over the Internet. SOAP encapsulates its data in an envelope, as shown in Figure 9.15.

Like XML, SOAP is a standard maintained by the W3C (**www.w3.org/TR/SOAP**). A key advantage of SOAP is that it uses two widely implemented protocols, XML and HTTP. Because SOAP automatically supports these two protocols, it enables existing Web-based programs to be more accessible to a greater range of users. It is worth noting that Microsoft's Internet Information Server (IIS) and the open-source Apache Web server, which together direct over half of the world's Internet traffic, are already SOAP enabled.

SOAP is a lightweight protocol that provides for the exchange of structured information in a decentralized, distributed environment. (The term lightweight is used in association with protocols whose functionalities are

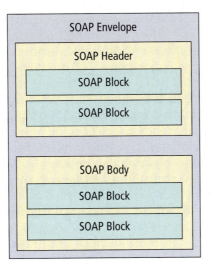

Figure 9.15
The SOAP Envelope
SOAP defines an XML-based structure for transmitting messages. The SOAP envelope structure includes a header with a block and a body with 2 blocks. The SOAP header encapsulates the message and specifies the delivery process. The SOAP body contains the message data, sometimes referred to as the payload.

relatively simple and straightforward.) Web services, by nature, tend to be highly decentralized and distributed. SOAP uses a call/response mechanism, which performs well in a client/server environment. This means that a client application makes a call to a Web server that is somewhere on the Internet. In its call, the client also passes parameters within its request to the Web server. When the Web server receives the client's call, it then provides a response. The request and response are transmitted in the form of XML documents. Figure 9.16 demonstrates this request/response scenario.

Another significant advantage of SOAP is that it allows a device running one kind of operating system to communicate with a device running a different kind of operating system. Because the two devices can be running different operating systems, and yet have a seamless communication, the communication is said to be transparent. This transparent communication can occur because the protocols being used, HTTP and XML, are widely implemented standards used by all major modern operating system platforms. Here we see another example of why standards are so important.

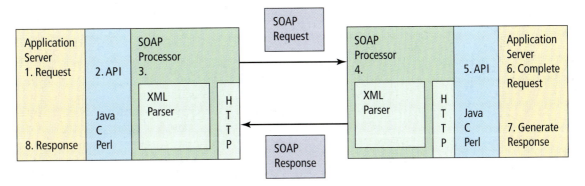

Figure 9.16
Simplified SOAP Request and Response Process
In step 1, a user issues a request to an application server. The request is passed to an Application Programming Interface (API) that uses a programming language such as Java, C, or Perl. Next, the API hands off the request to the SOAP processor, which in turn generates SOAP envelopes. The SOAP envelopes are passed over the Internet using the HTTP protocol. On the receiver's end, a response is generated and ultimately sent back to the requestor, in step 8.

Services such as SOAP enable business-to-business (B2B) partners to electronically share supply information and financial services seamlessly over the Internet. Driving these collaborative partnerships are the cost savings generated by replacing paper-based transactional systems, with their associated time-delay, with virtual systems offering near instantaneous communications. A more detailed discussion on this topic can be found at **msdn.microsoft.com/msdnmag/issues/0300/soap/default.aspx**.

Keep in mind that Web services are not Web applications. Web services are used by Web applications. A **Web application** is typically a browser on a client device, such as a personal computer. A Web service does not, however, have to function through a browser or through a standard desktop computer. For example, a Web service might be a request coming from a cell phone using **Wireless Markup Language (WML)**. WML is an XML-based language used specifically for creating applications capable of running on mobile, handheld devices with small viewing screens. Also, Web services can make requests from other Web services. SOAP makes these service-to-service requests possible. Another important characteristic of a Web service is that the point where a requested transaction begins may not be the point where the interaction ends. This situation is very different from the standard client/server model, where a requested resource is returned to the requesting device.

The intent behind Web services is to bring integration, interoperability, and flexibility to enterprise applications. Vendors are designing tools, devices, and applications with this in mind, in many cases making XML a built-in part of their technology solution. Breaking away from the traditional client/server model in determining how, when, and where, resources can be delivered, Web services represent an evolutionary step in enterprise solution development.

Chapter Summary

Businesses rely on their data and information resources for competitive advantage. Data and information that are not freely and easily available to users across the enterprise can put a business at an economic disadvantage. The tremendous growth of e-commerce and Web-based services has driven the pursuit of better enterprise solutions in data communications.

Direct attached storage (DAS) is a mature technology that has had, and continues to have, an important role in the data communications world. DAS is usually associated with magnetic tape and hard drives. DAS devices, such as a hard drive, are directly connected by cable to a computer's processor inside a computer's case. As a storage technology, DAS is optimized for single, isolated processors, thereby providing for a lower initial cost. However, DAS devices do not support data sharing. Data sharing is the capability of a storage device to share data and files concurrently with other storage devices.

A storage area network (SAN) is a network of storage devices that other computers, servers, and/or clients can access. A LAN in a SAN-configured enterprise will have clients and servers and an interface, or connection, to the SAN. SANs are usually implemented with Fibre Channel, although other networking connection technologies, such as Gigabit Ethernet, are possible. In themselves, SANs are independent of the underlying network topology. Recall that a topology is how a network is cabled together. SANs allow for greater distances between the computers that use the stored data and the data themselves. SANs are not just hardware, they also require a software-based management component. Providers of SAN management software include IBM, Sun Microsystems, Hewlett-Packard, Computer Associates, and Fujistu. SANs are best for large organizations that have substantial I/O traffic of any type.

Network-Attached Storage (NAS) is another recent technology. NAS can be implemented in conjunction with a SAN, but it can also be a stand-alone solution. NAS appliances have an internal, integrated processor optimized to manage disk storage. Using either a hub or a switch, a NAS appliance is ordinarily attached to a TCP/IP network, either a LAN or a WAN. A NAS appliance must be attached to a network that supports IP-based protocols. Network devices use the Network File System (NFS) or the Common Internet File System (CIFS) protocol to make requests from NAS appliances. NAS is a good storage technology for small businesses or for workgroups or departments within a large organization.

A virtual private network (VPN) is a private data network that uses a common carrier's public telecommunications infrastructure. A VPN implements privacy through various tunneling and security procedures. Tunneling is a technique whereby packets from one protocol are wrapped, or encapsulated, within a second protocol. Three types of VPN technologies are trusted VPNs, secure VPNs, and hybrid VPNs. Each type of VPN has its own particular characteristics and requirements.

For a trusted VPN, no one other than the carrier can affect the creation or modification of the VPN's path. No one other than the trusted VPN carrier can change, add, or delete data on the trusted VPN. Before a trusted VPN path can be established, the routing and addressing have to be defined between the sender and the receiver. The use of tunneled encryption creates what is called a *secure* VPN. By definition, all traffic on a secure VPN must be encrypted and authenticated. Also, all parties must agree to the security characteristics of the VPN. A hybrid VPN can be a combination of trusted and secure VPNs. The boundaries between the two VPNs must be well defined. The type of VPN implemented will depend on the business, the nature of the data, and the capabilities of the provider. VPNs can be used to provide secure remote access, intranet access, and extranet access.

Voice-over-Internet Protocol (VoIP) is a data service that is used to carry voice communications. VoIP promises to provide voice-level services at a significant cost savings. Traditional voice communications use time-division multiplexing (TDM) with Private Branch Exchange (PBX) hardware. A PBX functions like a physically isolated network through which all enterprise voice communications pass. PBX offers a high level of security. VoIP allows voice and data to be transported over the same networking infrastructure, which is a strong advantage. An organization considering VoIP needs to know its current, and future, voice bandwidth requirements.

Web services are an enterprise technology that can be used to provide business process integration, application integration, and Web-based application development. As an umbrella term, Web services are software components designed to dynamically interact with each other using Internet standards. Web services integrate data with applications. Because Web services are based on components, they can be implemented incrementally. Web service components are based on protocols and service platforms. The leading Web service protocol is XML (Extensible Markup Language). Two primary web service platforms are Sun Microsystems's J2EE (Java 2 Enterprise Edition) and Microsoft's C#. Web services are typically tied to a relational database. Web services are not Web applications, but they can be used by Web applications. The goal of Web services is to bring integration, interoperability, and flexibility to enterprise applications.

Block-level I/O protocol   **(311)**

Capacity sharing   **(312)**

Common Internet File System (CIFS)   **(316)**

C#   **(328)**

Data mining   **(315)**

Data sharing   **(312)**

Data warehousing   **(315)**

Direct attached storage (DAS)   **(310)**

Distributed Management Task Force (DMTF)   **(327)**

Extensible Markup Language (XML)   **(328)**

Extranet   **(323)**

File-level I/O Protocol   **(316)**

Hybrid VPN   **(322)**

Input/output (I/O) request   **(311)**

Internet Protocol Security (IPSec)   **(323)**

Intranet   **(323)**

Java 2 Enterprise Edition (J2EE)   **(328)**

Knowledge management   **(315)**

Layer-2 Tunneling Protocol (L2TP)   **(323)**

Multi-Protocol Label Switching (MPLS)   **(323)**

Network-Attached Storage (NAS)   **(314)**

Network-Attached Storage (NAS) appliance   **(315)**

Network-Attached Storage (NAS) gateway   **(316)**

Network File System (NFS)   **(316)**

Off-line   **(310)**

Online   **(311)**

Organization for the Advancement of Structured Information Standards (OASIS)   **(327)**

Outsourcing   **(319)**

Point-to-Point Tunneling Protocol (PPTP)   **(323)**

Private Branch Exchange (PBX)   **(325)**

Public Switched Telephone Network (PSTN)   **(325)**

Quality of Service (QoS)   **(325)**

Scalable   **(312)**

Secure remote access   **(322)**

Secure VPN   **(321)**

Simple Object Access Protocol (SOAP)   **(328)**

Small Computer System Interface (SCSI)   **(311)**

Storage area network (SAN)   **(312)**

Topology   **(312)**

Trend analysis   **(315)**

Trusted VPN   **(320)**

Tunneling   **(319)**

Unified Messaging (UM)   **(325)**

Virtualization   **(312)**

Virtual private network (VPN)   **(319)**

Voice-over-Internet Protocol (VoIP)   **(323)**

VPN client   **(323)**

Web application   **(330)**

Web services   **(327)**

Web Services Description Language (WSDL)   **(328)**

Wireless Markup Language (WML)   **(330)**

World Wide Web Consortium (W3C)   **(327)**

Chapter Questions

Short Answer

1. In what ways does a DAS solution differ from a SAN solution?

2. What factors might influence a business to select a SAN solution?

3. How does a standard NAS differ from a NAS with a gateway?

4. What advantages do Web services offer?

5. What factors should a business examine when considering a VoIP solution?

Multiple Choice

For each of the following questions select one best answer.

1. What does DAS stand for?
   a. Direct Area Storage   **b.** Direct Attached Storage
   c. Direct Area Server   **d.** Direct Attached Server

2. Which of the following is DAS usually associated with?
   a. Tape drive   **b.** Hard disk drives
   c. Neither a nor b   **d.** a and/or b

3. Which term refers to data or file resources that are not immediately available?
   a. Online   **b.** Data line   **c.** Off-line   **d.** Inline

4. Which of the following is a DAS server device usually associated with?
   a. SCSI   **b.** IDE   **c.** NFS   **d.** CIFS

5. A SCSI parallel cable should be no longer than
   a. 5 meters.   **b.** 15 meters.   **c.** 25 meters.   **d.** 50 meters.

6. What type of I/O access does SCSI use?
   a. File   **b.** Record   **c.** Byte   **d.** Block

7. Which of the following refers to the ability of a storage device to pool storage space?
   a. Pool sharing   **b.** Capacity sharing
   c. Data sharing   **d.** None of the above

8. What does SAN stand for?
   a. Systematic area network   **b.** Storage area network
   c. Server attached network   **d.** System attached network

9. What network-connecting technology are SANs usually associated with?
   a. Fibre Channel   **b.** Fiber-optic   **c.** SCSI   **d.** Fast Ethernet

10. Which of the following is a major component of SAN management software?
    a. managing the topology
    b. providing wireless access

   c. creating statistical reporting on network traffic

   d. none of the above

11. SANs perform best in

   a. small networks with little I/O traffic.

   b. large networks with little I/O traffic.

   c. large networks with substantial I/O traffic.

   d. a or b

12. What does NAS stand for?

   a. Network-Attached Server **b.** Network-Attached Services

   c. Network-Attached System **d.** Network-Attached Storage

13. What type of processor does NAS use?

   a. External **b.** Internal **c.** Does not use a processor **d.** a or b

14. NFS and CIFS use what type of I/O protocol?

   a. Block **b.** Record **c.** File **d.** Byte

15. Which of the following is true of NFS?

   a. It is relatively easy to install.

   b. It is relatively complex to install.

   c. It can run on low-cost fiber-optic networks.

   d. a or c

16. NAS is

   a. always used with SANs. **b.** never used with SANs.

   c. sometimes used with SANs. **d.** None of the above

17. What does VPN stand for?

   a. Very private network **b.** Virtual public network

   c. Virtual private network **d.** Very public network

18. How many types of VPNs are there?

   a. 1 **b.** 2 **c.** 3 **d.** 7

19. What was the first type of VPN?

   a. Secure **b.** Hybrid **c.** Trusted **d.** Virtual

20. Which type of VPN requires a tunneling protocol?

   a. Secure **b.** Virtual **c.** Trusted **d.** a or b

21. How many end points does a single tunnel have?

   a. 1 **b.** 2 **c.** 4 **d.** None

22. Which tunneling protocol is supported by most Windows-based clients?

   a. PPTP **b.** PPPP **c.** MPLS **d.** IPSec

23. Which tunneling protocol is particularly associated with secure VPNs?

   a. PPTP **b.** PPPP **c.** MPLS **d.** IPSec

24. Which tunneling protocol is associated with Frame Relay and ATM networks?

   a. PPTP **b.** PPPP **c.** MPLS **d.** IPSec

25. VoIP is

   a. analog. **b.** digital. **c.** packetized. **d.** b and c

26. Traditional voice communications are

    a. analog. **b.** digital. **c.** packetized. **d.** b and c

27. VoIP networks can suffer from

    a. virus attacks. **b.** denial of service attacks.
    c. Neither a nor b **d.** Both a and b

28. PBX boxes can suffer from

    a. virus attacks. **b.** denial of service attacks.
    c. Neither a nor b **d.** Both a and b

29. A PBX is usually

    a. owned by the enterprise. **b.** owned by the carrier.
    c. a software tool only.
    d. associated with low-level telephone security.

30. Web services are based on

    a. hardware components. **b.** software components.
    c. Web browsers. **d.** application servers.

31. XML is a(n)

    a. unstructured data definition language.
    b. proprietary data definition language.
    c. closed data definition language.
    d. structured data definition language.

32. Which of the following is true?

    a. XML is based on SOAP. **b.** SOAP is based on XML.
    c. XML and SOAP are not related. **d.** SOAP is based on WML.

33. XML was standardized by

    a. IEFT. **b.** OASIS. **c.** W3C. **d.** None of the above

34. What organization is J2EE associated with?

    a. Microsoft **b.** Sun **c.** IBM **d.** None of the above

35. Web services

    a. are Web applications. **b.** are not Web applications.
    c. can be used by Web applications. **d.** b and c

36. A business's data and information

    a. can be a competitive advantage.
    b. are not a competitive advantage.
    c. are not related to competitive advantage.
    d. are only used for transactional processing.

37. Which of the following is the oldest storage technology?

    a. SAN **b.** DAS **c.** VPN **d.** NAS

38. SCSI is an example of what type of storage technology?

    a. SAN **b.** DAS **c.** VPN **d.** NAS

39. Which term refers to a data file or application that is immediately available?

    a. Online **b.** Data line **c.** Off-line **d.** In-line

40. Which of the following do DAS devices typically support?

    a. Capacity sharing **b.** Data sharing

    c. Resource pooling   **d.** None of the above

41. DAS technology usually connects

    a. one device. **b.** two devices. **c.** four devices. **d.** many devices.

42. A SAN and NAS

    a. are never used in the same network.
    b. are always used in the same network.
    c. may or may not be used in the same network.
    d. are not related in any way.

43. SANs are optimized

    a. for directory services. **b.** for memory access.
    c. for storage traffic. **d.** for protocol conversion.

44. SANs are

    a. hardware. **b.** software. **c.** logical. **d.** a and b

45. A NAS generally

    a. has an open-architecture operating system.
    b. has a proprietary operating system.
    c. does not use an operating system.
    d. has a very complex operating system.

46. From where does NFS originate?

    a. Linux **b.** Microsoft **c.** Unix **d.** Novell

47. From where does CIFS originate?

    a. Linux **b.** Microsoft **c.** Unix **d.** Novell

48. Which of the following is true of VPNs?

    a. They are carried over private telecommunications infrastructures.
    b. They do not use telecommunications infrastructures.
    c. They are carried over public telecommunications infrastructures.
    d. They are carried only with a LAN.

49. Which type of VPN requires encryption?

    a. Trusted **b.** Designated **c.** Public **d.** Secure

50. SOAP makes use of

    a. a response only.
    b. a request only.
    c. a response or a request, but not both within a single communication.
    d. a response and request between a client and server.

True or False

For each of the following select either True or False.

1. Technology is often driven by competition among businesses.

2. Off-line data are inaccessible to users.

3. I/O requests are used to read data but not to write data.

4. SCSI supports both internal and external devices.

5. A SAN is a network.

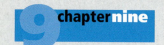

6. Traffic on a LAN is usually increased when SANs are deployed.

7. If implemented, SANs must be implemented corporatewide.

8. NAS is usually associated with a TCP/IP network.

9. A NAS device must be directly connected to a LAN or a WAN.

10. Secure VPNs were introduced prior to trusted VPNs.

11. Trusted VPNs make use of tunneling protocols for security.

12. The different types of VPNs have the same characteristics.

13. Businesses that use VPNs have little control over the infrastructure used to carry the VPNs.

14. No one other than the trusted VPN carrier can change, add, or delete data on the trusted VPN.

15. A trusted and a secure VPN are mutually exclusive.

16. VPNs can be used to supply secure remote access to users.

17. Intranet-access VPNs are commonly configured through a firewall or server.

18. IPSec is an IEEE standard.

19. VoIP is a digital technology.

20. Web services are a collection of software components designed to dynamically interact with each other using Internet standards.

Exercises

Research in Brief

For one or more of the questions below, provide a one- to two-page report based on your findings.

1. Three organizations in particular are associated with Web service protocol standards: the World Wide Web Consortium (W3C, **www.w3c.org**), the Organization for the Advancement of Structured Information Standards (OASIS, **www.oasis-open.org**), and the Distributed Management Task Force (DMTF, **www.dmtf.org**). Investigate one of these organizations. Who makes up the organization's membership? What standards does the organization set? What current projects is the group actively working on? What are the goals and objectives of the organization? Report on your findings.

2. Many organizations use VPNs. When secure VPNs are used, IPSec is the tunneling protocol of choice for encrypting communications. The Virtual Private Network Consortium represents an organization of interested parties who work on and discuss VPNs. Their Web site, **www.vpnc.org**, has much information on IPSec. Visit this organization's Web site and investigate and report on what you discover regarding IPSec. What issues are currently being discussed? Who is participating in the discussion? How is this organization related to standards-setting bodies that affect the Internet and the World Wide Web (WWW)?

3. Many organizations still use DAS devices, particularly small businesses that have data storage needs. Investigate the storage offerings provided by local retail businesses or by online providers and report on the types of SCSI-based DAS solutions for both hard disk drives and magnetic tape. What are the typical costs? What are the installation and configuration issues? What functionalities and capabilities do various DAS devices support? What types of services and warranties do different vendors provide? What types of networks do these devices support?

4. Many believe that XML is the key protocol that future Web services and networking integration will be built upon. As with any other technology, XML has both advantages and disadvantages. Investigate how XML is currently used. In what ways is XML being positioned for future technologies? What are its advantages and disadvantages? How are vendors such as IBM, Microsoft, and Sun, among others, incorporating XML into their technology solutions? Many technologists have expressed concerns about the security of XML as a delivery platform. How are vendors addressing this issue? Based on your research, where and how do you see XML being used 5 years from now?

Case Study

Sheehan Marketing and Public Relations

You have approached SMPR's president with a suggestion that SMPR deploy a SAN at each branch office. Each office uses data, audio, video, and graphic files that are shared by staff at each location. The SAN may incorporate NAS devices, but you have not yet evaluated the solutions provided by various vendors. During your meeting, Mr. Sheehan, the president of SMPR, stated that he agreed with your recommendation. Your next step is to research and provide more detailed specifications on SAN and NAS solutions. What is required to implement a SAN and/or NAS? Which vendor or vendors should be used and why? What are the costs involved? How can SMPR benefit from these technologies?

At each branch location, SMPR has public relations (PR) account executives who increasingly work out of the office. In fact, these PR executives are finding that they often need access to network resources at more than one branch location. You have recommended that PR executives and other remote-access staff be provided with laptops or other mobile technologies that will allow them to use a secure remote access VPN to dial in to SMPR's intranets. President Sheehan has directed you to provide him a report that explains, in simple English, what a secure remote access VPN is. He wants to know how this technology can help agents in the field with their access problems. He is also concerned about the security of client project files and wants to know how you plan to address security.

Web References

www.clipper.com/research/TCG2003003.pdf

www.ibm.com

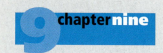

www.sun.com

www.hp.com

www.ca.com

www.fujistu.com

www.faqs.org/rfcs/rfc1094.html

www.microsoft.com/mind/1196/cifs.asp

www.emc.com

www.quantum.com

www.maxtor.com

info.sen.ca.gov/pub/01–02/bill/sen/sb_1351-1400/sb_1386_bill_20020926_chaptered.html

www.hhs.gov/ocr/hipaa

www.avaya.com

www.nortel.com

www.siemens.com

www.cisco.com

www.w3.org

www.oasis-open.org

www.dmtf.org

www.w3.org/TR/SOAP

msdn.microsoft.com/msdnmag/issues/0300/soap/default.aspx

Data Mining

This chapter examined technologies, particularly SANs and NAS, that increasingly enable businesses to store vast quantities of data. Having a mountain of data, however, does not necessarily translate into having useful data. Raw data are not considered information. For data to become information, the data must be transformed. Advances in hardware, software, storage, and database technologies have given businesses a new tool that better allows them to competitively use their mountains of data. This tool is *data mining*.

For many, data mining is a confusing topic. For example, how does data mining differ from such technologies as data warehousing, data marts, and online analytical processing (OLAP)? Data mining complements these other technologies. To better understand data mining, let's first examine these three technologies, beginning with OLAP.

Each of the technologies just mentioned has a particular focus and strength. That is why these technologies complement, and do not replace, each other. OLAP, which is tied to server technologies, focuses on events that have happened in the past. To paraphrase a famous philosopher, only by understanding the past can we prepare for the future. The same holds true for businesses as well. Businesses evaluate and analyze the past behavior of their customers, industry competitors, B2B partners, and staff to make strategic decisions. This is where OLAP comes in. Using software tools, OLAP enables businesses to gain insight about outcomes from data patterns. OLAP tools do not predict behavior, but instead try to *understand* past behavior. By understanding data patterns, businesses can determine how the patterns affect them.

OLAP tools help a business to better understand enterprise data prior to the process of data mining. Whereas OLAP uses data to create a theoretical hypothesis, data mining uses the data to identify patterns that may relate to a potential business problem. Data mining then, helps a business uncover hidden patterns and relationships that can consequently be used to validate a theoretical hypothesis developed by an OLAP tool.

The term *data warehouse* is fairly flexible; depending on whom you ask, you may get a variety of answers as to what one is. Many consider a data warehouse to be a collection of summarized data that has been cleansed, structured, and optimized for access by such technologies as data marts, OLAP, and data mining. To say that data have been "cleansed" means that the data have been checked for missing values, incorrect values, and other syntactical problems. *Syntactics* deals with formal relationships; in this case, the relationship between data fields. Thus, a data warehouse becomes a collection, storage, and staging area for enterprise data. The quantity of warehoused data, however, can be vast. Because data warehouses can be too extensive in the amount of data they offer, data marts have been developed.

A data mart is a segment or category of data that has been extracted from a data warehouse. The data mart groups the data together into a form more specific to, say, a department or workgroup. Departments, using a data mart, can then better customize the data they use. This means that a given department can summarize, sort, select, and structure its data, within its data mart without having to consider data from other departments. In fact, other departments will have their own data marts. Data marts also enable decision support system (DSS) software to reach down to the department level. Significantly, the unit cost of the device that houses the data mart is generally far less than the servers or computers that maintain the potentially huge, centralized data warehouse. A data mart enables a business manager to focus on his or her department when analyzing business problems.

In this discussion, the essential element that differentiates data mining from the other tools mentioned is that data mining looks for hidden patterns in data that might otherwise have gone unnoticed. A variety of data mining models are available. The type of data mining model used depends on the business problem to be resolved. For example, an inferential data mining tool attempts to explain relationships among data, draw inferences from the data, and relate data objects to one other so that a conclusion can be drawn. An associative data mining tool seeks correlations between data attributes. A comparative data mining tool provides comparisons of similarities and differences between data sets. Other models are possible, and different models can be combined to mine the data. The following are just a few of the many vendors that provide data mining solutions:

- IBM Intelligent Miner (**www.ibm.com**)

- Megaputer Intelligence PolyAnalyst (**www.megaputer.com**)

- Oracle 9i Data Mining (**www.oracle.com**)

- SAS Institute Enterprise Miner (**www.sas.com**)

- SPSS Clementine (**www.spss.com**)

Regardless of the data mining tool selected, a business should explore several questions prior to deciding whether data mining is the right solution. For example, is the tool scalable? Is the data mining tool designed for a single or a multiprocessor environment? Are data mining activities restricted by such factors as server hardware memory, processor, and disk storage? These factors will affect scalability. Is the tool being considered compatible with other third-party tools? Very likely, the data mining tool selected will need to work with a business's OLAP, data warehousing, and data mart solutions. Each of these tools may be from a different vendor, hence the importance of compatibility.

Does the business's current infrastructure support the data mining tool being considered? If not, what hardware and software, including licensing, issues need to addressed? What type of budget has been allocated? Is the tool one that is appropriate for the business's particular industry? Also, how will the data mining tool be administered? Are staff trained in the use of the tool? For whom within the organization is the tool intended? Top, middle, or operational managers? Or all three? As you can see, many questions must be asked before a decision can be made.

Securing the Enterprise

Learning Objectives

After studying this chapter, you should be able to:

- Understand the importance of securing the enterprise.
- Identify four components of security.
- Define Redundant Array of Inexpensive Devices (RAID).
- Understand the purpose and use of cryptography.
- Describe asymmetric and symmetric ciphers.
- Explain how firewalls and proxy servers are used in security.
- Know the importance of physical security.
- Explain the benefits of a disaster recovery plan.
- Describe an integrated security system.

Chapter 9 explored a variety of enterprise solutions. Such solutions enable a business to run more effectively and efficiently. However, an enterprise and all of its resources are vulnerable to both internal and external threats. Businesses must take steps to secure their enterprises against attack or disaster. This chapter examines how a business can protect its enterprise against a sometimes menacing world.

The Need for Security

An enterprise is made up of a number of different types of networks of varying size, from LANs to WANs. Once the enterprise is in place, a critical concern becomes how to secure its infrastructure. To many, security

Figure 10.1

*In the event of a natural disaster, such as an earthquake, businesses
must be prepared to recover their data and information technologies.*

is simply preventing unauthorized access to enterprise resources. In practice, however, securing the enterprise means several things. For example, can the enterprise recover in the event of a disaster like the one shown in Figure 10.1? Is the network protected against data tampering? For servers that maintain or provide access to essential data, are recovery plans in place in the event of storage failure? What policies are in place to ensure that enterprise security measures are being followed and adhered to? Are security policies defined? How can customers and staff be confident that data and information concerning them is reliable, accurate, and confidential? Table 10.1 identifies some of the types of security policies that a business should address.

Table 10.1 Types of Security Policies	
Policy	**Description**
Computer use	Appropriate use of organizational computers
Information	Who has access to what information
Backup	Timing and type of backups performed
Staff management	Security policies that restrict employee access to certain resources
Disaster recover	Procedures to follow in the event of a natural or man-made disaster
Incident handling	Steps to follow when unanticipated incidents occur
Account management	Adding, deleting, or modifying systems and users
E-mail	Appropriate use of organizational e-mail systems

Although this chapter addresses a few of the ways an enterprise can implement security, the subject is really a course, and textbook, of its own. To get a sense of the types of vulnerabilities that today's businesses must arm themselves against, visit the SANS (SysAdmin, Audit, Network, Security) Institute Web site (**www.sans.org/top20**). The site offers a changing list of the top 20 vulnerabilities, as identified by the SANS Institute, that organizations must guard against. Another good site that provides computer security recommendations is offered by the National Institute of Standards and Technology (NIST; **www.nist.gov**).

The Components of Security

The questions asked at the beginning of this chapter highlight the types of issues that must be addressed in securing the enterprise. The four key components that define security are confidentiality, access, integrity, and nonrepudiation. These four components are sometimes referred to as the **CAIN principles**.

Confidentiality

Simply stated, **confidentiality** requires that those who should not be able to view a given communication are in fact not able to view it. In a secure enterprise, resources, communications, data, and information are only revealed to those who are authorized to review them. Many users of data communication infrastructures worry that those who should not have access to the infrastructure can view sensitive data.

Confidentiality can be enforced in a number of ways. For example, confidentiality can be enforced through file- and object-level controls. Such controls can be applied, for example, through server operating systems (SOSs) such as Novell's Netware (**www.novell.com**) and Microsoft's Windows 2000/2003 Server products (**www.microsoft.com**). Transmission confidentiality can be implemented through various encryption technologies.

Access

With regard to security, **access** must address two factors. First, access means that information and other enterprise resources are available to authorized users when needed. One way to ensure availability of a resource is to implement **redundancy**. If a resource is duplicated, or redundant, should one duplication fail, the other will still likely be available for access. Of course, redundancy requires additional cost and management. A business will have to analyze which of its resources is best suited for redundancy. Availability, however, is only half of the equation. A second necessary characteristic of access must be that those who do access enterprise resources are authenticated for such access.

Authentication confirms that the user attempting to use a networked resource has the appropriate rights and privileges to that resource. A common means of authentication is the requirement that each user of the enterprise have a user ID and a password, as demonstrated in Figure 10.2. This user ID and password are then directly associated with certain rights, privileges, and restrictions. This type of login requirement is one kind of security policy.

Figure 10.2
A standard network login includes a user ID and password.

Passwords are an important element for validating user access; a network administrator will want to pay close attention to password policies. Ideally, a password should be kept secret, be difficult to guess, and differ from the user ID. A few simple guidelines can help users create passwords that are more difficult for attackers to discover. Although it may be hard to convince users to follow all the suggested rules, combining several of them can make for an effective password policy. Some guidelines for passwords follow:

- Be at least eight characters long

- Be a combination of letters, numbers, and special symbols

- Not be a word found in a dictionary

- Be changed frequently, preferably each month

- Same user should not be able to reuse the password

- Not be the name of a family member, friend, or pet

- Not be a common date such as a birthday, an anniversary, or a holiday

- Be comfortable to type or enter

- Be easy to remember

- Not be written down or kept in a place where others can access it

- Use uppercase and lowercase letters

Additional suggestions compiled by Richard Anderson of Raycosoft for creating good passwords can be found at **www.raycosoft.com/rayco/support/good_password.html**.

SOSs were presented in Chapter 8. One important function of SOSs is user authentication. Part of this authentication often determines, at a fairly fine level, what resources a user will be granted access to. Resources can include data, files, applications, and hardware, such as printers, hard drives, and communication devices. One advantage of server-based authentication is that users can be placed into defined groups. The defined group will have an established security policy. This means that a network administrator does not have to create a separate, unique security policy for each user, but can assign security policy by group identification. Such a scenario is much more efficient.

Furthermore, it is also possible to create *role* security policies. For example, a role security policy can be defined for the position of "Manager of Accounts Payable." Whoever is hired to fill that position can have his or her user ID associated with that **role**. Should that person leave the company, his or her user ID would simply be removed from the "Manager of Accounts Payable" security role policy. In this way, security is defined for the position, or role, not for a specific person, resulting in greater security flexibility.

Integrity

Integrity means that only those who have the right to do so can modify data and information. By applying integrity constraints to data and information, the enterprise attempts to ensure that these resources are not tampered with. Making data available as needed is one thing. The enterprise must also ensure that those who access the data are appropriately limited as to what they can do with the data once they access it. Limiting what can be done to data or an application is the integrity component of security. As an example, you would not expect your bank to allow just anyone to withdraw funds from your checking account. Such an action, the withdrawing of funds from your account without your approval, would lack integrity, besides being very annoying.

Nonrepudiation

Every data communication has a sender and a receiver. In a secure enterprise, users want to be certain that the data and information they receive are in fact from the people who sent it. Additionally, users must be assured that any data or information in transit has not been altered. **Nonrepudiation** means that users know that whoever they are communicating with is indeed who he or she represents himself or herself to be. A customer paying for a commodity over the Internet using a credit card wants to be certain that the vendor is who he or she claims to be and that sensitive financial data are not tampered with in the transaction process.

Nonrepudiation also means that the receipt of a communication can be verified. For example, say that a customer claims that payment was sent for a product using secured technologies, and yet no record of that payment is found. With the proper security technology in place, a business would be able to verify whether the customer's claim is true.

Implementing Security

The four components of enterprise security—confidentiality, access, integrity, and nonrepudiation—can be implemented in various ways. An enterprise that takes its security seriously will make use of several mechanisms and technologies that address one, if not all, of these

Identity Theft and You

Identify theft, depicted in Figure 10.3, occurs when someone obtains key data about another person and then uses that data to impersonate that person. The most common types of data that identity thieves try to obtain are Social Security numbers, driver's license numbers, credit and/or debit card numbers, bank account numbers, and other financial information. Once enough data have been compiled, it is relatively easy for someone you do not know to take over your identity and turn into your evil twin. For many, having one's financial identify stolen is traumatic enough. In some cases, the identify thieves may also commit crimes that then become part of "your" criminal history.

According to a September 2003 report (**www.ftc.gov/os/2003/09/ synovatereport.pdf**) written for the Federal Trade Commission (FTC), 3.23 million consumers, or 1.5 percent of the population, discovered that new accounts had been opened or other frauds, such as renting an apartment or home and obtaining medical care or employment, had been committed using their name. In addition, 6.6 million consumers had their existing accounts compromised by identity theft. On its Web site, the FTC provides useful information on how to guard against identify theft. The Privacy Rights Clearinghouse (**www.privacyrights.org/ index.htm**), a non-profit organization, also provides reports, guidelines, education, and

Figure 10.3
Identify theft results in millions of dollars of cost for businesses and the consumers they serve.

research on securing your personal information. Following are just a few of the security steps recommended by the FTC and the Privacy Rights Clearinghouse:

- Check your credit report at least twice a year.

- Keep your mailbox locked.

- Shred all legal documents and any documents that contain any type of account number that you plan to throw away.

- Place outgoing mail in secure mailboxes.

- Check with your post office if you have not receive mail within four days.

- Destroy preapproved credit card offers and checks and other preapproved documents.

- Avoid using important identification numbers such as a Social Security number whenever possible.

Given the increased risk of identify theft, what measures do you think businesses should follow to protect consumer's identities? In what ways can organizations better secure, inform, and help consumers who have experienced identity theft? What role should the government play?

components. Something to keep in mind, however, is that no technology is perfect. However, when used in combination, multiple security measures can make it much more difficult for an enterprise to be attacked and exposed to security vulnerabilities. This section examines several common security technologies.

Redundant Array of Inexpensive Devices

Especially for medium- to large-scale enterprises, data storage, access, and recoverability are issues of serious concern. Recoverability relates directly to fault tolerance. Something that is **fault tolerant** allows for a degree of fault or failure so that a service or resource remains available in some form or capacity. Redundancy is one way of achieving a degree of fault tolerance. Redundant systems or resources are inherently fault tolerant.

One common storage technology that is used to improve performance, reliability, and recoverability is a **Redundant Array of Inexpensive Devices (RAID)**, like the one shown in Figure 10.4. RAID is also sometimes referred to as a *Redundant Array of Independent Devices* or as a **drive array**. RAID comes in six standardized forms, numbered from 0 to 5. The numbers identify how data are stored and treated. Higher-level numbers do not necessarily imply increased power or speed. The "Topic in Focus" at the end of this chapter provides more detail on this technology solution.

Cryptography

It is important to store data in a manner that makes them easy to access and recover in the event of hardware failure. It is also important to verify that those accessing enterprise data are authorized to do so. Authentication

Figure 10.4
Typical RAID Device for Data Storage

and **digital certificates** are common ways to verify such authorization. In addition, when data are transported across the enterprise, it may be desirable, especially if the data are sensitive, to scramble or jumble the data. In scrambling the data, the intent is to render them useless to anyone who may intercept it. Authentication, certification, and scrambling touch directly on the four components of security previously identified: confidentiality, authentication, integrity, and nonrepudiation.

One technology in particular, cryptography, plays a major role in securing the enterprise. Cryptography is central to many security-based applications. Although cryptographic methods cannot guarantee total security, they are a major component in adequately protecting the enterprise. **Cryptography** is the science of encrypting and decrypting information to ensure that data and information cannot be easily understood or modified by unauthorized individuals. Some of the security functions that cryptographic methods address are authentication, nonrepudiation, privacy, message integrity, and provisions for digital signatures. The following are a few cryptography-related terms:

- **Cryptanalysis**. The process of evaluating cryptographic algorithms to discover their flaws.

- **Cryptanalyst**. A person who uses cryptanalysis to find flaws in cryptographic algorithms.

- **Cryptographer**. A person trained in the science of cryptography.

The field of cryptography is a study unto itself. As a science, it has its own history, methodologies, and, important to our discussion, vocabulary. To understand how a cryptographic method works, a few basic terms must be presented. In addition, the SANS Institute offers a glossary of security terms at its Web site, available at **www.sans.org/ resources/ glossary.php**.

The Vocabulary of Cryptography

A cryptographic method uses an **alphabet**. This alphabet is the set of symbols used in either an input or an output message. The alphabet may be the same for both input and output messages, depending on the cryptographic method. The alphabet can be based on numbers or characters. Using an alphabet, a cryptographic method is applied against data in its raw form. Data in its raw form is referred to as being **plaintext**, or **cleartext**. To transform the data from cleartext to a scrambled or **encrypted** form, a cipher is used. Technically, a **cipher** is a cryptographic encryption algorithm. An algorithm is a mathematical function. Simply stated, a cipher is a mathematical means of transforming data from one form to another. The objective is that if someone should intercept the transformed data, he or she would not be able to use or read it.

Therefore, a cipher is a coding system used to translate cleartext data, based on the cryptographic method's alphabet, into ciphertext. **Ciphertext**, like the example in Figure 10.5, is the encrypted form of the original data. After the cryptographic method is applied, the cleartext message is no longer in its original form. For the cipher's encryption and decryption method to work, however, a key must be defined. The cipher's *key* is used to encode and decode the data. The key is the secret mechanism, or rule, that is used to encrypt or decrypt ciphertext. The key is a secret that is maintained between the sender and receiver of an encrypted message. The sender and receiver of the data must both have access to the key to encode and decode the data. The purpose of this encoding and decoding is to reduce the probability of an attack against the data. An **attack** is the systematic attempt by an unauthorized individual to discover the cleartext form of the data from its encrypted form.

The cipher is the heart of the cryptographic method. A good cipher, or mapping system, should meet two criteria. First, the cipher should make it difficult for an encrypted message to be viewed in its cleartext form without the use of the cryptographic key. As you can imagine, the key must be a controlled secret. Second, the cipher should produce ciphertext that appears to be in a random format to a casual user or to anyone without the key. This means that within the encrypted ciphertext, no ascertainable patterns should be apparent. The alphabetic symbols that appear in the ciphertext should appear with equal frequency. These two criteria, if met, make it very difficult for someone to statistically attack the data to discover the cipher's mapping mechanism. Using a cryptographic method, the sender encrypts and the receiver decrypts. The following list summarizes some important cryptographic terms:

- **Alphabet**. The set of symbols used in either an input or an output message.

- **Asymmetric cipher**. A cryptographic method that uses a key pair: one key to encode data and a second, different key to decode the data.

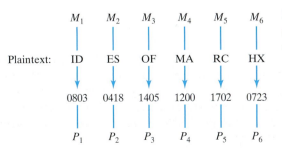

Figure 10.5
Plaintext with its ciphertext equivalent.

- **Certificate Authority**. A trusted third party that manages digital certificates.

- **Cipher**. The mapping scheme used to encode data.

- **Ciphertext**. Encrypted data.

- **Cleartext**. Data and/or information in its raw and unencrypted form.

- **Digital certificate**. A method used to validate a digital signature.

- **Digital signature**. A means of encrypting data, using a specific user's private key.

- **Key**. An algorithm used to encode and decode data.

- **Public Key Infrastructure (PKI)**. A technology that allows for the digital certification of communications.

- **Session key**. A key pair that is changed or renewed periodically.

- **Symmetric cipher**. A cryptographic method that uses the same key to encode and decode data.

One famous cipher is the Caesar cipher, named for Julius Caesar, who used it for encrypting his messages. The **Caesar cipher** used the Latin alphabet. Recall that a cipher works in combination with a key. The key used with the Caesar cipher replaces each letter in a message with the letter that is three positions behind it in the Latin alphabet. Although Julius Caesar used Latin as the cipher, you can easily use his key but use English as the cipher. For example, by using the Caesar key with English as the cipher, the cleartext data "Allen Dooley" encodes to "Doohq Grrohb." Doohq Grrohb is the ciphertext of the cleartext data. In this example, the "A" of Allen is replaced by "D," because "D" is the third letter following the letter "A" in the alphabet. Because you know the key, you can easily convert Doohq Grrohb back to its original cleartext form. What does your name map to using the Caesar key with an English alphabet cipher?

Types of Cryptographic Ciphers

Ciphers fall into one of two major categories: symmetric ciphers and asymmetric ciphers. A sender and a receiver may use one or both forms depending on how enterprise security is configured. With **symmetric ciphers**, the sender and the receiver of a communication must use the same key for encryption and decryption. With **asymmetric ciphers**, the sender and the receiver use different keys for encryption and decryption; however, both parties must agree on the keys that are used. Each category of ciphers has its advantages and disadvantages.

Symmetric Ciphers   Symmetric ciphers require that the sender and the receiver share information on the key used to encode and decode data. The simple act of sharing the key means that symmetric ciphers have a greater security risk than asymmetric ciphers, because multiple parties have access to the key. Also, when the sender and the receiver in a communication are physically distant from each other, a secure exchange of the secret key becomes more difficult. The distance itself is a problem because greater physical distance between the sender and the receiver allows more opportunities for intrusion or attack. Because a symmetric cipher uses a single key, a hacker has a greater probability of discerning the key.

A famous proverb by the Chinese philosopher Sun Tzu holds that if two people share a secret, then it is no longer a secret. With symmetric ciphers, each party using the cipher must share and maintain the secrecy of the key. The advantage of symmetric ciphers is that they are normally faster to compute than asymmetric ciphers. When speed is critical, as with real-time applications, symmetric ciphers provide an edge.

Asymmetric Ciphers With asymmetric ciphers, two separate keys are used, a public key and a private key. Together, they are known as a **key pair**. One of the keys is used for encryption, the other for decryption. The **public key**, as its name implies, is made public for anyone to use. The **private key** is known only to its owner, and it can be managed locally by its owner. Both the sender and the receiver have public keys and private keys. Figure 10.6 describes a communication between Jack and Jill using asymmetric encryption.

In Figure 10.6, when the sender, Jack, wants to send a message to Jill, Jack encrypts his message using Jill's public key. Jill's public key is available, or published, for anyone to use. Jack sends his encrypted message to Jill. When Jill receives the message, she uses her private key to decrypt the message. Only Jill has her private key, so only she can decrypt the message. The situation is reversed when Jill sends a message to Jack.

Jack and Jill can both change, and republish, their public keys for anyone to use whenever they want. Jack and Jill can also change their own private keys whenever they want. Changing private keys frequently is one way to improve security, because the private key becomes a moving target, making it difficult for someone to discover. Public keys can be freely distributed without compromising security. Secure communication with multiple parties only requires the exchange of public keys. However, one concern with regards to asymmetric ciphers is authenticating the user of a public key. Is that user who he or she claims to be? Also, asymmetric ciphers take longer to process, and therefore may not be suitable for time-sensitive applications.

Session Keys One way to combine the benefits of both symmetric and asymmetric ciphers is to create a session key. A **session key** uses a key pair that is renewed, or changed, periodically. When a sender and a receiver establish a connection for communication, a **session** is established. With

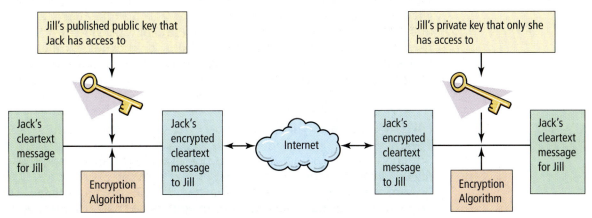

Figure 10.6
Jack and Jill Using Public and Private Key Encryption
Using Jill's published public key with his encryption algorithm, Jack encrypts his message to Jill and sends it over the Internet. On her end, Jill uses her private key to decrypt the message that Jack has sent her.

a session key approach, the message, which is the largest part of the communication, is carried using a symmetric cipher, which makes for faster processing. To maintain security, an asymmetric cipher is used to pass and/or update the shared keys for the symmetric process. During the communication, data are encrypted and decrypted using this one-time session key pair. When the communication terminates, the session key pair is also terminated. The session key is so named because it is created and used during a communication session between a sender and receiver.

Public Key Infrastructure

This discussion of cryptography has been important because it is the basis of a technology that is used to authenticate and enable the digital certification of communications. This technology is **Public Key Infrastructure (PKI)**. PKI creates key pairs that establish confidential communications. In doing so, PKI uses digital certificates to enforce two criteria. First, only the owner of a digital certificate may possess the private key that corresponds to a certified public key. Second, an unauthorized user who intercepts the digital certificate cannot use it to discover the private key. PKI is based on asymmetric ciphers using public and private keys. SOSs such as Windows 2000/2003 incorporate PKI as part of their functionality.

A **digital signature** is not an electronic form of a handwritten signature. Rather, a digital signature is a means of encrypting data using a specific user's private key. This digital signature is used to determine if the sender of a message is in fact who he or she says he or she is. The receiver of a message with a digital signature can validate that message using the sender's public key. If the data in the message have been changed in any way, the digital signature will fail, and the receiver will know that the message is not valid. A third party called a **Certificate Authority (CA)** usually manages digital certificates and the ability to use them. The Certificate Authority binds private keys to public keys and guarantees that the digital signature used in a secure communication is valid. VeriSign (**www.VeriSign.com**) is one of the best-known Certificate Authorities. VeriSign offers a tutorial on PKI at **verisign.netscape.com/security/pki/understanding.html**.

Technologies such as PKI support not only confidentiality and authentication, but nonrepudiation as well. A highly secure, cryptographic PKI process can verify whether an event has occurred. In a maximum cryptographic scenario, it is possible to determine, based on digital signatures, whether an event indeed took place, and if it did take place, at what date and time and by what device. Such technology provides evidence that a user of the enterprise infrastructure did, or did not, explicitly request a specific action. Especially for financial applications, such electronic evidence is necessary.

Putting It All Together

Although the preceding discussion has described public and private keys, digital signatures, digital certificates, and Certificate Authorities, it can still be hard to clearly see how all of these technologies are interrelated. This section seeks to put these technologies in context so that you may more clearly understand how they support each other. Keep in mind that all of the keys, signatures, and certificates that have been discussed are created through security encryption software that both the sender and the receiver are using.

If a user wants to send a message over the Internet and be assured of a secured communication, the user will likely use some type of encryption technology. That encryption technology may use a single private key. If a single private key is used, that one key will be used to both encrypt and decrypt the data. An advantage of using only one key is that the encryption/decryption process will be faster. The disadvantage is that using only one key makes the communication more vulnerable to attack.

If the sending user instead uses a private key and a public key (a key pair), one key will be used to encrypt the data and the other key to decrypt it. In this case, the sending user is the creator and owner of the key pair. The private key is a secret and known only to the sending user. The sending user shares the public key with anyone who wants to communicate with the sending user. The public and private keys have two different values. Although the public key is public, someone accessing the sending user's public key cannot use that public key to discover the sending user's private key. When the sending user sends a message that has been encrypted with the private key, the receiver can decrypt the message with the sender's public key. In turn, the recipient can use the sender's public key to encrypt a message that will be sent back to the original sending user. Once the message is sent back to the original user, he or she uses the private key to decrypt the message. A security system using private and public key pairs is complicated, but the added complexity also makes the system more difficult to attack.

So how do digital signatures relate to private keys and public keys? If a person distributes his or her public key information over the Internet, how can you be certain that he or she is in fact the owner and creator of that public key? Or, after you have received a message from that person, how can you be certain that the message has not been tampered with before you have received and reviewed it? This is where the digital signature comes in. The sender uses a software-driven mathematical formula called a hashing algorithm to process the message. A result is derived. The sender attaches this result to the message and sends the hashed message to you over the Internet. Each message sent by that sender will have its own unique digital signature generated based on the sender's hashing formula. Each digital signature is unique. Ideally, no two messages going through a hashing formula will produce the same hashing result.

At your end, you receive the sender's message. Using the public key that the sender made available to you, software on your end runs the received message through the same hashing formula used by the sender. The result derived by your software is compared with the result derived by the sender's software. Recall that the sender sent you a hashed result as well as the message. If your derived hashed result is equal to the sender's derived hashed result, you know that the message you received has not been tampered with. This comparison of the hashed result is the digital signature.

Given how digital signatures work, where then does the Certificate Authority come in? Simply stated, a Certificate Authority is a trusted third party that validates electronic messages. The job of the Certificate Authority is to verify to you, the receiver, that the public key sent by the sender is in fact from the sender. Certificate Authorities are an essential part of the PKI. A number of Certificate Authorities are listed at **www.pki-page.org**. Figure 10.7 shows where a Certificate Authority would be positioned in a secure communication.

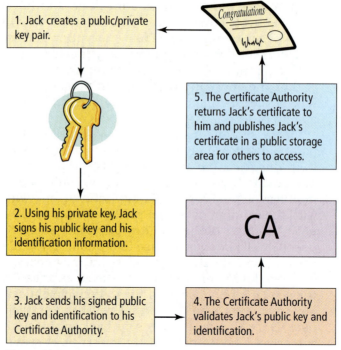

Figure 10.7
The Certificate Authority Process

Other Forms of Encryption

This chapter has looked at forms of encryption that enable the exchange of secure communications. Other forms of encryption for other purposes are also possible. A popular application-level authentication service is provided by Kerberos, an encryption technology developed by the Massachusetts Institute of Technology (MIT). The purpose of Kerberos is to provide a centralized authentication service, usually server based, that authenticates users to servers and servers to users. Such authentication is very useful in a distributed environment where a user may need to gain access to the network from various workstations. Using a service such as Kerberos, a user can log in to the network from multiple locations and still be authenticated to use network services.

Another widely used tool used in e-mail applications is Pretty Good Privacy, or PGP as it is more commonly known. Paul Zimmerman developed PGP and made its source code and documentation freely available over the Internet. Hugely successful, PGP offers businesses a standardized approach for e-mail encryption. An additional factor in PGP's success is that it supports many operating system platforms, including DOS, Windows, Unix, and Macintosh. A white paper on cryptography, the second chapter of which was written by Paul Zimmerman, is available at **www.pgp.com/products/whitepapers/index.html#cryptography**.

Firewalls and Proxy Servers

With the use of RAID, essential data can be better protected. Using cryptographic methods such as PKI, confidentiality and authentication can be improved. Additional technologies used to secure the enterprise against attack or intrusion are **firewalls** and **proxy servers**. Sometimes firewalls and proxy servers are implemented in combination with one another. Keep in mind that no intrusion security technology is perfect. Even so,

Figure 10.8
This graphic conceptually illustrates the purpose of a firewall.

firewalls and proxy servers are an important security component used by many organizations.

Firewalls primarily serve as a barrier, as depicted in Figure 10.8. A firewall can be a barrier between the outside world and the enterprise or between networks within the enterprise. When configured as a barrier between the outside world and the enterprise, a firewall keeps out unauthorized individuals who are attempting to attack or penetrate the enterprise.

A firewall placed between networks within the enterprise helps to isolate sensitive or critical data and applications from unauthorized staff. For example, an organization may have its financial services, such as payroll and/or accounts receivable, on a separate network. A firewall can be placed between the financial network and other networks of the enterprise to protect the financial network's resources from unauthorized internal access. Figure 10.9 demonstrates how a firewall might be positioned.

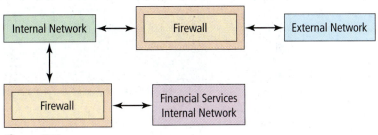

Figure 10.9
Standard Firewall

Where does the term *firewall* come from? In building construction, it is not unusual to erect an interior or exterior wall of fire-resistant materials. This fire-resistant wall becomes a firewall, or a barrier. A firewall is installed to prevent a fire from spreading to other areas of a building. Network firewalls perform a similar service, but in this instance the fire being controlled is unauthorized access to networked resources. The **trusted network** is inside the firewall. The **untrusted network** is outside the firewall. Portions of the untrusted network are also sometimes referred to as the **demilitarized zone (DMZ)**.

For a firewall to be effective, it must meet three requirements. First, all traffic that passes between the trusted and untrusted networks must pass through a firewall. Second, the firewall must be configured so that only authorized traffic can pass through it. By passing all traffic through the firewall, both trusted and untrusted traffic is filtered. A successful firewall prevents unauthorized traffic from reaching the trusted network. Third, a firewall must be able to protect itself from attack and penetration. Those trying to break into a network know that firewalls are in place to protect that network. Because firewalls are a first line of defense, they themselves are targets of attack. If the firewall is successfully attacked, network resources will be vulnerable.

Firewalls may be hardware, software, or more commonly, a combination of the two, like the Cisco firewall shown in Figure 10.10. Two broad approaches can be followed in determining how firewalls should be configured. The stricter, and more secure, approach is that any traffic not specifically permitted is denied. The second, and more open, approach is that any traffic not specifically denied should be permitted. In a large enterprise, a combination of the two approaches can be implemented. Something that must be pointed out, however, is the role of the user in establishing these policies.

It is not unusual for users to think that access should not be restricted. From a security manager's perspective though, access should be highly restricted. This difference of opinion between users and the security manager can cause conflict. It is essential that any security measures implemented be clearly communicated to the affected user groups in language that is user-friendly and nondemeaning. Remember, your users are not security specialists. Essential to the communication should be an explanation of why enforced security measures are needed. Users can also be brought into the discussion as to how security measures might be improved and if procedures or policies can be developed that might allow for more flexibility.

Figure 10.10
A Cisco series PIX Firewall 525.

With the first, more restrictive traffic-screening approach, an enterprise starts from a totally secure environment and gradually opens access as access needs are discovered. This approach can take time to fully implement and will likely frustrate users of the enterprise who do not get immediate access to the resources they need until the firewall has been properly configured. Such an approach emphasizes security over access. With the second, more open traffic-screening approach, the enterprise's firewalls are configured to prevent certain types of traffic as intrusions or attacks are encountered, not before. This technique is more of a wait-and-see approach and elevates ease of access over security. For portions of the enterprise that are critical or particularly sensitive, starting from an open access model and gradually restricting access is probably not a good idea.

You know that firewalls filter traffic, but how? A firewall can be configured to filter traffic in four general ways. These four methods are not mutually exclusive; a particular firewall may incorporate more than one filtering methodology. The four types of filtering a firewall might perform are packet, application, circuit-level, and stateful packet inspection. The following discussion briefly examines each of these filtering methods.

Packet-Filtering Firewalls

Packet-filtering firewalls provide basic, low-level filtering. This type of firewall drops or passes packets based on their destination and source addresses or ports. Routers can provide this type of packet filtering. A packet-filtering firewall inspects the header of each packet that passes through it. Based on the packet's header information, the packet is either passed to its next hop along its network path or it is rejected and dropped. Generally, this type of firewall is relatively easy and inexpensive to set up, but is limited in its filtering capabilities. Figure 10.11 illustrates the concept of a packet-filtering firewall.

With a packet-filtering firewall, one port of the firewall accepts outside traffic. Another port passes accepted packets to their next destination. Before a packet is allowed to traverse the accepting and passing ports, a set of packet-filtering policy rules is applied to that packet. Packet-filtering policy rules can be based on a range of source or destination addresses, types of network protocols (e.g., TCP, UDP, or ICMP), or port numbers being used in the communication. In Chapter 8, you learned that in a TCP/IP network logical ports are associated with various types of network requests.

Packet-filtering firewalls are usually able to handle large amounts of network traffic because they have little overhead. They have less overhead because, unlike other firewalls, packet-filtering firewalls do not rely on proxies or require complicated hardware or software configuration setups. However, a packet-filtering firewall will fail if its internal table of valid and invalid ports and/or addresses is incorrect. Also, packet-filtering firewalls are susceptible to an attack called **address spoofing**. Address spoofing

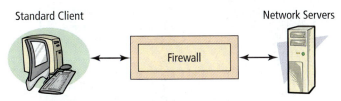

Standard Client   Network Servers

Firewall

Figure 10.11
Packet-Filtering Firewall
A packet-filtering firewall evaluates packets that filter through it and based on packet-filtering rules denies or allows access.

occurs when a filter is tricked into believing a packet is coming from a device with one address when in fact it is coming from a different address. In such a scenario, the originator's true address has been forged or "spoofed." Because proxies are not used, traffic from a client is sent directly to a server if the client's traffic passes the firewall. This direct communication between a client and server leaves the server exposed and vulnerable to attack.

Application-Filtering Firewalls

Application-filtering firewalls are also called proxy firewalls or application-layer gateways. This type of firewall provides for higher-level screening of traffic from specific applications, such as FTP and e-mail. An application-filtering firewall can perform more sophisticated evaluation and authentication of the packets that it filters. As with a packet-filtering firewall, policy rules must be configured that tell the application firewall how to perform. Policy rules are implemented by proxies. (Recall the discussion of proxy servers in Chapter 8.) Each protocol filtered by an application-filtering firewall must have its own proxy. If using an application-filtering firewall, proxies for the following protocols are required: FTP, HTTP, SMTP, and Telnet. Figure 10.12 illustrates the concept of an application-filtering firewall.

The necessity for proxies makes application-filtering firewalls more complex to set up and manage. Application-filtering firewalls are also susceptible to SYN and ping packet flooding. SYN stands for "synchronized" and is a type of packet used by a requesting device to establish a session with a receiving device. SYN packets initiate a TCP connection. The receiver of such a packet is supposed to respond with a SYN ACK (acknowledgment) using the source address contained in the originating SYN request packet. However, in a **Synchronized (SYN) attack**, the SYN source address is forged with, in most cases, a non-existent or fake address. Typically, the attacker floods the receiving device, often a server, with a continuous stream of forged SYN requests. The targeted device, flooded with unanswerable packets, is no longer capable of fulfilling requests from legitimate users.

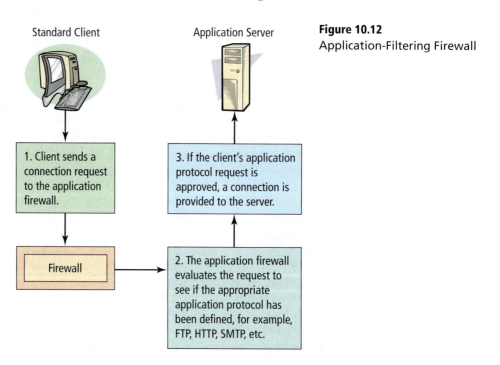

Figure 10.12
Application-Filtering Firewall

Standard Client

Application Server

1. Client sends a connection request to the application firewall.

3. If the client's application protocol request is approved, a connection is provided to the server.

Firewall

2. The application firewall evaluates the request to see if the appropriate application protocol has been defined, for example, FTP, HTTP, SMTP, etc.

Ping attacks are similar to SYN attacks in that the attacker is attempting to flood the network with bogus communication traffic. In Chapter 6, you learned how ping can be used as a diagnostic tool. When one device pings another, the receiving device, if available, responds back. In a ping flood attack, thousands, even millions, of ping packets using a forged source address overwhelm a receiving device, often a server of some type. Network bandwidth can potentially be entirely consumed by attack traffic as the attacker and the targeted device exchange responses to millions of bogus packets.

The general term that defines the types of attacks just described is **denial-of-service (DoS) attack**. The goal of a denial-of-service attack is to make network resources unavailable to legitimate users. Common types of services targeted by denial-of-service attackers include access to information, applications, systems, and communications. When an enterprise's infrastructure is overwhelmed with an attacker's packet flooding, a denial-of-service to the legitimate users often results.

Circuit-Filtering Firewalls

A **circuit-filtering firewall**, also called a circuit-level gateway, evaluates not only a packet's source and destination addresses, but also the circuits that have been established for the packet's communication. This type of firewall is useful for connection-oriented TCP communications, but not connectionless UDP communications. A proxy server is a common example of a circuit-filtering firewall. For example, a circuit-filtering firewall relays TCP connection information from a trusted network device to an untrusted network device. To the untrusted device, the source address at the other end of the connection is the circuit-filtering firewall, not the true communicating, trusted device.

In this way, by supplying its own address, the circuit-filtering firewall functions as a proxy for the trusted communicating device on the inside of the firewall. Once connections are established, the circuit-filtering firewall typically passes TCP packets from one connected device to the other without examining the contents of the packets. The security is in allowing the connection to be established in the first place. Also, when circuit-filtering firewalls are used, communications are outbound, from a trusted internal device to an outside untrusted device. Because communications are not inbound, resulting in less flexible communication, this limitation can be a disadvantage.

Stateful Packet Inspection

Stateful packet inspection combines the advantages of packet filtering with the advantages of application filtering, resulting in compromise between the two. Stateful packet-inspection firewalls are not as fast as packet-filtering firewalls or as secure as application-filtering firewalls, but provide some of the benefits of both.

A standard packet-inspection firewall examines each packet in a communication stream, evaluates that packet's header information, but not its content, and either passes or drops the packet based on filtering rules. Stateful packet-inspection firewalls, on the other hand, can examine packet contents. Also, stateful packet-inspection firewalls continuously evaluate packets to determine if a valid connection has been opened for them from inside of the network. If there is a valid connection for the packet or packet stream, the stateful-packet inspection firewall lets the packet through, otherwise the packet is dropped.

In effect, the stateful packet-inspection firewall evaluates source and destination IP addresses, source and destination ports, and packet sequence numbers to determine if the packet belongs to a currently opened connection. The stateful packet-inspection firewall also compiles information about a communication in a packet-state table. For added security, a stateful packet-inspection firewall can close off ports used in a communication until connection to the specific port is requested. This is important because many attacks come through open, logical, and usually well-known ports through a process called *port scanning.*

A **port scanning** application searches for Internet-connected devices and looks for access to open, logical port services. Recall from Chapter 8 that with TCP/IP, thousands of logical ports are used for particular types of services. A malicious program can hide its intent by making a request through an innocent port service identifier. Although software-driven port scanning is not illegal, this technique is often used by attackers searching for an open or weak part of a network's infrastructure. Closing ports when they are not in use can significantly improve a networked organization's internal security.

NetworkWorld (**www.nwfusion.com**) in its August 25, 2003, edition reported on a survey conducted by the magazine on port attacks over a 2-week period. Over the 2-week period, attacks were generated from 99 countries, with the highest number of attacks, in order, coming from China, the United States, South Korea, Brazil, and Germany. Of the 180,000 port attacks detected, 78 percent were targeted at port 80, which is used by most Web page transfers. Other popular ports targeted for attack were ports 139, 445, and 135. The article also reported that 45 to 55 percent of suspicious activity encountered was from hackers scanning for open targets. Hackers specifically searched for weak networks where they could find computers that they could hijack to relay spam, store illicit files, or take over as launching points for future attacks. A free port scanning utility that you can use to detect if your ports are being scanned is available from **www.ntutility.com/freeware.html**. An easy-to-navigate site with reviews and information on firewalls in general can be found at **www.firewallguide.com/software.htm**. Finally, for the home or small business user, Zone Alarm (**www.zonealarm.com**) offers a free version of its popular firewall product.

Physical Security

A network is not only logically vulnerable, but physically at risk as well. Although tools such as cryptography and firewalls are useful in securing the enterprise, physical security is also important. With **physical security**, physical access to sensitive network components is limited, such as the servers shown in Figure 10.13. For example, it is ill advised to place a critical server in an open area where it could easily be accessed, damaged, or stolen. Additionally, damage or theft may not come from someone outside the organization, but from within.

A few common-sense guidelines can go a long way towards providing adequate physical security. Specialized devices such as servers, routers, and switches should be housed in wiring closets. These closets should be secured by locks or other physically restricting mechanisms and only accessible to technicians and staff whose job functions require such access. A policy should be in place to identify who has access, by what means, when, and for what purpose. When physical keys or badges are issued to permit entry to secured rooms, this information must be accurately documented and maintained. Intruder detection systems that work by alarm or other means of notification can also be installed.

Figure 10.13
Secured Server Farm
This server farm uses a locked chain link fence as one means of physical security.

If possible, expensive equipment should be physically secured so that it cannot be easily moved. Any media that might possibly contain sensitive data must be closely monitored and should be wiped clean of all data before being openly released. When storage media used by the enterprise are either sold or donated, such media should have all their contents physically erased and tested for deletion prior to being released. Similar deletion or cleaning of content should occur with user workstations that are moved or assigned from one user to another or when a user leaves the organization. Once again, these actions must be documented.

A set of network security policies and procedures that explicitly define guidelines for protecting network resources and that address organizational vulnerabilities is essential. Part of the network security policy should clearly specify job responsibilities, by title and function, for all areas of enterprise security. Such a document should describe how access is given, to whom, under whose authority, and under what conditions. It should also be specified how access is either denied or taken away. Security should be determined by such factors as who you are, what you do, what resources you require, and why.

Physically securing the enterprise is an obvious task, yet it is often overlooked. Clear and thoroughly defined security policies and procedures with well-maintained documentation are an invaluable asset to a network administrator.

Disaster Recovery Planning

Physical security is important to the day-to-day operations of the enterprise. When designing physical security implementations, the enterprise can exercise a degree of control over such factors as unauthorized access or damage and theft of network resources. What cannot be controlled, though, are disasters—power blackouts, fires, floods, earthquakes, tornados, or some other catastrophe, natural or man-made. However, it is possible to prepare the enterprise to withstand, or at least survive, a disaster. A **disaster recovery plan (DRP)** must be an integral part of enterprise network planning. Having a disaster recovery plan in place is only half the solution. You must also be confidant that the plan works. Businesses should periodically put their disaster recovery plan into action by performing the procedures defined in the plan to determine whether they will work. Finding a flaw in the disaster recovery plan after a disaster has occurred is too late.

A first step in creating a disaster recovery plan is determining the degree of recovery essential for the business to continue as a functioning entity. For some enterprises, full-scale redundancy may be needed, although such a scenario is relatively rare. It is more likely that only select business-critical data, applications, and services will need to be functioning within hours, if not sooner, after a disaster occurs.

Many organizations make use of facilities called hot spots. A **hot spot** is an alternative facility where an organization can restore all or a portion of its business-critical systems within a short amount of time. The hot spot could be a branch office or a separate organization that has entered into a disaster recovery plan agreement with the organization. For example, two organizations in the same industry, say, auto parts manufacturing, in different cities may have an agreement to be a hot spot for each other in the event of a natural disaster. The advantage of partnering with an enterprise in the same industry is that each is likely to have a similar data communications infrastructure. Table 10.2 summarizes the steps in implementing a disaster recovery plan.

For a disaster recovery plan to work, some degree of redundancy is required. Critical data, information, and applications must be backed up and shipped to secure locations, usually off-site. (A good Web site for comparing vendor backup solutions can be found at **www.storage forum.be/market.html**.) Backups are best shipped off-site, preferably to a different city, so that they may be available for recovery at another

Table 10.2	The Disaster Recovery Plan (DRP) Development Process	
Step	**Description**
1. Define planning groups	Planning groups must include key users from each business unit or operational area.
2. Establish priorities	The DRP must address essential business processes, technology, networks, systems, and services. It must identify functions that are mission critical, important, or minor.
3. Develop a recovery strategy	The recovery strategy should cover the facts of surviving a disaster. The DRP should identify the people, facilities, network services, communication equipment, applications, clients and servers, support, and maintenance contracts that are required for the business to survive.
4. Develop verification measures and procedures	Does the DRP work? Measures should be identified and carried out that prove the disaster recover strategy meets its goals and objectives.
5. Implement the plan	The DRP should be documented and communicated to all who are essential to its success. The DRP should periodically be tested to determine that it works.

location. Keeping backups at the same facility where a disaster may occur is self-defeating. If the facility is destroyed, very likely any backups it contained will also be destroyed or unavailable. Two types of backup are incremental and full. **Incremental backups** only back up files or data that have changed since the last backup was made. With a **full backup**, all files and data are backed up completely and fully regardless of whether the files or data have been modified. Incremental backups take less time to create, but more time to restore. Full backups take more time to create, but less time to restore. Consider the following scenario.

On Monday morning at 6:00 A.M., the customer database is given a full backup. This means that all data on the customer database are saved and stored. The backup in this case is a full copy of the original customer database at that point in time. Beginning at 8:00 A.M., transactions begin to be applied to the original customer database: customers are added or deleted or existing data are modified, such as customer phone numbers, addresses, or balance changes. Assume that 1,000 such transactions take place each day of the week. By the following Monday, 7,000 changes have been made to the original customer database. If another full backup is made, those changes are then captured and stored on this latest copy of the customer database.

In this scenario, if a problem occurred in the middle of the week—for example, Wednesday—and the customer database had to be restored from the previous Monday's backup, potentially 3,000 transactions would be lost because the backup was not current. The business could, to address this problem, make a full backup of the customer database at the end of each day. In this way, all transactions could be fully recovered. However, making a full backup takes time.

If a business used an incremental backup approach, the scenario would be different. Again, assume a full backup is made at 6:00 A.M. on Monday. At the end of Monday's business processing day, an incremental backup is performed. This incremental backup would only back up data on those customers who had changes applied against their accounts for that Monday. On Tuesday, another incremental backup is made, and again, only changes made on that Tuesday are captured and stored. On Wednesday, a third incremental backup is made. Then, say a disaster strikes and the database has to be recovered and restored. The business would first restore the full backup from Monday and then the incremental backups from Monday, Tuesday, and Wednesday, in that order. The transactions for those days would be recovered. The ability to recover transactions is critical to a business. Figure 10.14 illustrates the full-backup scenario and Figure 10.15 illustrates an incremental backup.

The timing of the backups also has to be considered. Two different sets of data may require two different backup-timing cycles. Depending on the resource and how it is used, backup may occur on a daily, weekly, monthly, or other time-framed basis. Knowing how your organization uses its data and applications is essential for planning the timing of backup cycles.

With more redundancy, greater expense is usually involved. But, with greater redundancy, the potential for fuller recovery is also improved. Balancing expense with recovery is why thorough analysis is needed to determine what functionalities truly are essential for the business to survive.

This text has repeatedly emphasized the need for, and usefulness of, good documentation. In the event of a disaster, good documentation can mean the survival or death of a business. In the disaster recovery plan, instructions must outline who does what, where, when, and how in the event of a disaster. A disaster is not a time for guesswork or for determining how and where essential organizational functions and staff are to

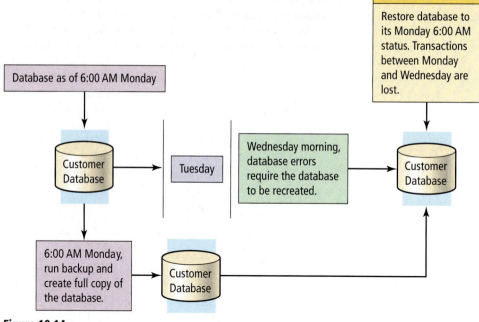

Figure 10.14

Full Backup Recovery

In this scenario, unless a full backup is made each day, all transactions that took place between Monday 6:00 AM and the time of Wednesday's database recovery are lost. Full backups are longer to create, but shorter to recover if done frequently. In this particular example, two days of missing data are probably not tolerable.

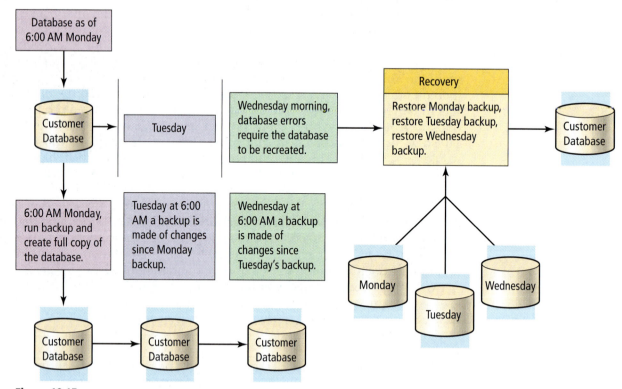

Figure 10.15

Incremental Backup Recovery

In this scenario, all transactions between Monday and Wednesday's last incremental backup are recovered. Some transactions may still have been lost, but far fewer than in our full backup example. Incremental backups are faster to create, but longer to recover.

respond. Some organizations contract out the design of their disaster recovery plan to vendors who specialize in this field. DRP vendors perform risk analysis and auditing of enterprise functionalities to determine what functions and data are essential to enterprise survival. An easy to read disaster recovery guide can be found at **www.disaster-recovery-guide.com**.

Integrated Security Systems

Securing the enterprise depends on a combination of technologies, tools, and planning. These components must work together in an integrated manner to be effective. The larger and more complex the organization, the likelier that the organization will have a staff of experts whose job is to design, implement, and maintain an integrated security system. An **integrated security system** should incorporate preventive, detective, and reactive measures that are internal and external to the enterprise. Such a system is not a disaster recovery plan, but the disaster recovery plan is included within it.

Successful integrated security systems are adaptive, meaning that the organization must continually educate itself on changing security threats. Integrated security systems can include such elements as logical perimeter security gates using firewalls and proxies, surveillance systems to control access, fire and intrusion detection, and other systems, such as the face scanning technology shown in Figure 10.16. As with a disaster recovery plan, vendors are available to design and implement integrated security systems. An example of such a vendor is Integrated Security Systems (**www.disaster-recovery-guide.com**).

Figure 10.16
Face Scanning
An integrated security system might utilize such recently introduced technologies as face scanning systems.

Creating a security plan is a balancing act: Too much security gets in the way of doing business, yet too little leaves the enterprise vulnerable to attack. The goals of an integrated security system should be directly linked to the goals of the organization. Such a system must identify and prioritize critical enterprise assets and the level of protection these assets require. Integrated security systems need to allow for detection and response to threats, and yet be flexible enough for users of enterprise resources to function. Although perfect security is not possible, and probably not practical, good security is a must.

The four critical components of security are confidentiality, access, integrity, and nonrepudiation. These four components are sometimes referred to as the CAIN principles. Technologies that address the CAIN principles make it more difficult for an enterprise to be attacked and exposed to security vulnerabilities.

A common storage technology used to provide improved performance, reliability, and recoverability is Redundant Array of Inexpensive Devices, or RAID. RAID is also referred to as a Redundant Array of Independent Devices or a drive array. RAID comes in six standardized forms, numbered from 0 to 5. RAID numbers identify how each RAID solution stores and treats data. Higher RAID numbers do not necessarily imply increased power or speed. As a storage security solution, RAID can be implemented as hardware, software, or a combination of the two.

Cryptography plays a major role in securing the enterprise and is central to many security-based applications. Cryptography is the science of using encryption and decryption to ensure that data and information cannot be easily understood or modified by unauthorized individuals. Cryptographic methods address several security features: authentication, nonrepudiation, privacy, message integrity, and digital signatures.

At the heart of the cryptographic method is the cipher. A successful cipher makes it difficult for an encrypted message to be viewed in its cleartext form without the use of the cryptographic key. Also, a cipher must produce ciphertext that appears random in format to a casual user or to anyone without the key. Two major branches of cryptography are symmetric and asymmetric cryptography. One way to combine the benefits of both symmetric and asymmetric ciphers is to create a session key, which is a key pair that is renewed or changed periodically.

Firewalls primarily serve as a barrier. A firewall can be a barrier between the outside world and the enterprise or between networks within the enterprise. When configured as a barrier between the outside world and the enterprise, a firewall prevents unauthorized individuals from successfully attacking or penetrating the enterprise. A firewall placed between networks within the enterprise isolates sensitive or critical data and applications from internal staff access. Firewalls may be hardware, software, or a combination of the two. Firewalls can be configured to provide four types of filtering: packet, application, circuit-level, and stateful packet inspection.

A network is not only logically vulnerable, but physically at risk as well. Physical security addresses the day-to-day physical security of the enterprise. A set of network security policies and procedures needs to be defined that explicitly detail guidelines for protecting network resources and addresses organizational vulnerabilities. Security access should be determined by such factors as who you are, what you do, what resources you require, and why.

A disaster recovery plan (DRP) must be an integral part of enterprise network planning. Businesses should periodically put their DRPs into action

by performing the procedures defined in the plan to determine whether they work. A first step in creating a DRP is determining the degree of recovery essential for the business to continue as a functioning entity. For a DRP to work, some degree of redundancy is required. The DRP plan should provide instructions that outline who does what, where, when, and how in the event of a disaster.

An integrated security system should incorporate preventive, detective, and reactive measures that are internal and external to the enterprise. Successful security systems are also adaptive. The goals of an integrated security system should be directly linked to the goals of the organization.

Access **(345)**

Address spoofing **(359)**

Alphabet **(351)**

Application-filtering firewall **(360)**

Asymmetric cipher **(352)**

Attack **(351)**

Authentication **(345)**

Caesar cipher **(352)**

CAIN principles **(345)**

Certificate Authority **(354)**

Cipher **(351)**

Ciphertext **(351)**

Circuit-filtering firewall **(361)**

Cleartext **(351)**

Confidentiality **(345)**

Cryptography **(350)**

Demilitarized zone (DMZ) **(358)**

Denial-of-service (DoS) attack **(361)**

Digital certificate **(350)**

Digital signature **(354)**

Disaster recovery plan (DRP) **(364)**

Drive array **(349)**

Encrypted **(351)**

Fault tolerant **(349)**

Firewall **(356)**

Full backup **(365)**

Hot spot **(364)**

Incremental backup **(365)**

Integrated security system **(367)**

Integrity **(347)**

Key pair **(353)**

Nonrepudiation **(347)**

Packet-filtering firewall **(359)**

Physical security **(362)**

Ping attack **(361)**

Plaintext **(351)**

Port scanning **(362)**

Private key **(353)**

Proxy server **(356)**

Public key **(353)**

Public Key Infrastructure (PKI) **(354)**

Redundancy **(345)**

Redundant Array of Inexpensive Devices (RAID) **(349)**

Role **(347)**

Session **(353)**

Session key **(353)**

Stateful packet inspection **(361)**

Symmetric cipher **(352)**

Synchronized (SYN) attack **(360)**

Trusted network **(358)**

Untrusted network **(358)**

Chapter Questions

Short Answer

1. What guidelines should be followed in establishing a password policy?

2. Briefly describe the key differences between symmetric and asymmetric cryptography.

3. What elements make for a good disaster recovery plan?

4. In general, what purpose does a firewall serve?

Multiple Choice

For each of the following questions select one best answer.

1. How many components make up the CAIN principles?
   a. 2   **b.** 4   **c.** 6   **d.** 8

2. Which of the following requires that communications not be observed by unauthorized individuals?
   a. Confidentiality   **b.** Integrity   **c.** Access   **d.** Nonrepudiation

3. As a security component, has how many factors should access address?
   a. 1   **b.** 2   **c.** 3   **d.** 4

4. Which of the following is a common means of authentication?
   a. User ID   **b.** Password   **c.** a and/or b   **d.** Neither a nor b

5. Which security component refers to only those with the proper authority being able to modify data?
   a. Confidentiality   **b.** Integrity   **c.** Access   **d.** Nonrepudiation

6. Which of the following ensures that you can verify that a person has received a communication that you have sent?
   a. Confidentiality   **b.** Integrity   **c.** Access   **d.** Nonrepudiation

7. What is another term for a RAID?
   a. Disk rack   **b.** Disk adapter   **c.** Drive rack   **d.** Drive array

8. Which of the following is fault tolerance often associated with?
   a. Nonredundancy   **b.** Redundancy   **c.** Low cost   **d.** Vulnerability

9. What type of security policy is associated with the appropriate use of an organization's computers?
   a. Information   **b.** Computer use   **c.** Backup   **d.** Incident handling

10. What type of security policy is associated with who has access to what information?
    a. Information   **b.** Computer use   **c.** Backup   **d.** Incident handling

11. DRPs prepare for what type of disaster?
    a. Natural   **b.** Man-made   **c.** a and/or b   **d.** Logical

12. File- and object-level controls can provide

    a. confidentiality **b.** access **c.** integrity **d.** nonrepudiation

13. Which of the following can be provided through redundancy?

    a. Confidentiality **b.** Access **c.** Integrity **d.** Nonrepudiation

14. Which of the following confirms that a user has a right to a resource?

    a. Confidentiality **b.** Redundancy **c.** Authentication **d.** Integrity

15. Which of the following is a characteristic of a good password?

    a. It is at least eight characters long. **b.** It is easy to remember.
    c. It can be written down for later use. **d.** a and b

16. What type of security policy might be defined for a "Manager of Payroll"?

    a. Title **b.** Description **c.** Role **d.** Group

17. Which security component ensures that only those who have the right to do so can view data?

    a. Confidentiality **b.** Integrity **c.** Access **d.** Nonrepudiation

18. Which of the following ensures that a communication is from the person who claims to have sent it?

    a. Confidentiality **b.** Integrity **c.** Access **d.** Nonrepudiation

19. A tight security policy might include how many of the CAIN principles?

    a. 2 **b.** 3 **c.** 4 **d.** 6

20. What term describes when someone uses another person's personal data with criminal intent?

    a. Data theft **b.** Information theft
    c. Responsibility theft **d.** Identify theft

21. Which of the following is true of redundant systems?

    a. They are inherently faulty.
    b. They are inherently fault tolerant.
    c. They are risk faulty.
    d. They are subjectively fault tolerant.

22. What is the science of encrypting and decrypting data and information called?

    a. Cryptodynamics **b.** Cyrptomechanics
    c. Cryptography **d.** Cryptics

23. Which of the following is a set of symbols used in cryptography in an input or output message?

    a. Ciphertext **b.** Cleartext **c.** Alphabet **d.** Cipher

24. Which of the following is the encrypted form of the original data?

    a. Ciphertext **b.** Cleartext **c.** Alphabet **d.** Cipher

25. Which of the following is the raw, or decrypted, form of the original data?

    a. Ciphertext **b.** Cleartext **c.** Alphabet **d.** Cipher

26. What is the coding system used to translate an encrypted message?

    a. Ciphertext **b.** Cleartext **c.** Alphabet **d.** Cipher

27. Which of the following must be used in conjunction with a cipher?

   a. Numbers   **b.** Characters   **c.** Keys   **d.** None of the above

28. Which of the following is a set of symbols that a cryptographic system may be based on?

   a. Numbers   **b.** Characters   **c.** Neither a nor b   **d.** a or b

29. When using cryptography, the sender of the message

   a. encrypts the message.   **b.** decrypts the message.
   c. formats the message.   **d.** None of the above

30. Ciphers fall into how many main categories?

   a. 1   **b.** 2   **c.** 3   **d.** 4

31. What type of cipher requires the sender and receiver to use the same set of keys?

   a. Bimetric   **b.** Symmetric   **c.** Asymmetric   **d.** Remetric

32. What type of cipher is used when the sender and receiver share a public but not a private key?

   a. Bimetric   **b.** Symmetric   **c.** Asymmetric   **d.** Remetric

33. Which type of cipher is computed more quickly?

   a. Bimetric   **b.** Symmetric   **c.** Asymmetric   **d.** Remetric

34. What does PKI stand for?

   a. Private Key Issue   **b.** Public Key Issue
   c. Private Key Infrastructure   **d.** Public Key Infrastructure

35. PKI can be used to create a digital

   a. station.   **b.** value.   **c.** signature.   **d.** None of the above

36. Which of the following is a third party that manages digital certificates?

   a. Verifying Authority   **b.** Certificate Authority
   c. Password Authority   **d.** The Certifier

37. Which of the following is the least sophisticated type of firewall?

   a. Packet filtering   **b.** Application filtering
   c. Circuit filtering   **d.** Stateful packet inspection

38. Which type of firewall is associated with proxy servers?

   a. Application filtering   **b.** Circuit filtering
   c. a or b   **d.** Neither a nor b

39. Which of the following refers to the network inside a firewall?

   a. Trusted   **b.** Untrusted   **c.** Secured   **d.** Unsecured

40. Firewalls may be based on

   a. hardware.   **b.** software.   **c.** a and/or b   **d.** Neither a nor b

41. What type of security is implemented by placing a server within a secured wiring closet?

   a. Logical security   **b.** Disaster recovery plan
   c. Physical security   **d.** None of the above

42. Which of the following is a plan that you must create but hope never to use?

   a. Allocation recovery plan   **b.** Assistance recovery plan
   c. Disaster resource plan   **d.** Disaster recovery plan

43. Which of the following is an alternative facility where an organization can restore and run some of its business-critical applications in the event of a disaster?

   a. Cold spot   **b.** Hot spot   **c.** Secure spot   **d.** Recovery spot

44. Which type of security system incorporates all elements of enterprise security?

   a. Integrated security system   **b.** Failsafe security system
   c. Integrated application security   **d.** Security integrated application

45. Technically, a cipher is

   a. a cryptographic plaintext encryption.
   b. a cryptographic encryption algorithm.
   c. a hardware element.
   d. associated with application-filtering firewalls.

46. What is a private and public key combination referred to as?

   a. Key duet   **b.** Key algorithm   **c.** Key set   **d.** Key pair

47. What is PKI based on?

   a. Symmetric ciphers   **b.** Asymmetric ciphers
   c. Only private keys   **d.** Only public keys

48. Which of the following is used to validate a digital signature?

   a. Authority   **b.** Digital Authority
   c. Security Authority   **d.** Certificate Authority

49. Which of the following is supported by PKI?

   a. Confidentiality   **b.** Authentication
   c. Nonrepudiation   **d.** All the above

50. Which of the following is PGP most often associated with?

   a. HTTP   **b.** FTP   **c.** E-mail   **d.** Telnet

True or False

For each of the following select either True or False.

   1. User IDs and passwords are often used for user authentication.

   2. In terms of security, confidentially and access are the same.

   3. When something is fault tolerant, it is more likely to fail.

   4. Nonrepudiation implies that someone who has received a communication cannot be verified as having received it.

   5. RAID stands for Reduced Array of Inexpensive Devices.

   6. The components of security must all be applied in equal measure.

   7. Cryptography is central to many security-based applications.

   8. A cryptographic alphabet is always based on letters or characters.

   9. Cleartext and plaintext are synonyms.

   10. Ciphertext is the encrypted form of the original data.

   11. A cipher should produce ciphertext that appears in a nonrandom format.

12. Symmetric ciphers are faster than asymmetric ciphers.

13. Firewalls primarily serve as barriers.

14. Application-filtering firewalls often make use of proxies.

15. Firewalls cannot be attacked.

16. Address spoofing is an attack based on a packet's destination address.

17. Good physical security does not require documentation.

18. Disaster recovery plans commonly use forms of redundancy.

19. Incremental backups are slower to create but faster to restore.

20. An integrated security system is essentially a disaster recovery plan.

Exercises

Research in Brief

For one or more of the questions below, provide a one- to two-page report based on your findings.

1. RAID is an important storage-recovery technology. Many vendors supply RAID-based solutions. Choose one of the standardized RAID levels and research two vendors who provide solutions for that RAID level. What are the advantages and disadvantages of the solution? What costs are involved? What technology is used? What types of questions should a business ask of itself when selecting a RAID solution?

2. Cryptography is an essential tool in e-commerce applications because of its importance in implementing financial security. In the United States, controversy exists over whether U.S.-based cryptography technologies should be sold outside of the country. For a long time, U.S. vendors of sensitive cryptographic technologies were unable to sell them outside the country. Investigate and report on arguments for and against the for-profit sale of U.S.-based cryptographic methods to the world at large. Based on your findings, what would you recommend and why?

3. Research and select at least two cryptographic applications that could be useful for the small business user. Compare and contrast the functionalities, costs, benefits, and/or disadvantages of the two products. Which of the two products would you recommend and why?

4. More and more home users are using "always on" connections to the Internet. These types of connections leave the user vulnerable to external attack. Investigate and compare at least two firewall products targeted at the home user. Report on their functionalities, costs, benefits, and any disadvantages. Which of the two products would you recommend and why?

376   **Part 4** | Integrating the Enterprise

Case Study

Sheehan Marketing and Public Relations

You are not surprised to learn that SMPR has no disaster recovery plan in place for any of its offices. You realize that this lack of disaster planning is a critical issue that must be addressed as soon as possible. Although you have not addressed this topic specifically with the company president, you believe the time is now right to present this problem to Mr. Sheehan.

To fully inform Mr. Sheehan about SMPR's disaster recovery options, you have decided to prepare a detailed report on disaster recovery planning "best practices." This report will require you to seek out and investigate what disaster recovery experts recommend be included in a disaster recovery plan. Besides this general report that details what must be included in a disaster recovery plan and why, you want to include a brief section that highlights two potential vendor-based solutions. In addition to the written report, you have also decided to make an oral presentation with simple visual elements to SMPR management on your findings.

Finally, Mr. Sheehan has also asked that you provide him a brief memo that explains what a firewall is and whether such a technology would be a good idea for SMPR.

Web References

www.sans.org/top20

www.nist.gov

www.novell.com

www.microsoft.com

www.raycosoft.com/rayco/support/good_password.html

www.ftc.gov/os/2003/09/synovatereport.pdf

www.privacyrights.org/index.htm

www.sans.org/resources/glossary.php

www.VeriSign.com

verisign.netscape.com/security/pki/understanding.html

www.pki-page.org

www.pgp.com/products/whitepapers/index.html#cryptography

www.nwfusion.com

www.ntutility.com/freeware.html

www.firewallguide.com/software.htm

www.zonealarm.com

www.storageforum.be/market.html

www.disaster-recovery-guide.com

Redundant Array of Inexpensive Devices

RAID's (Redundant Array of Inexpensive Devices) key purpose is to provide redundancy of stored data. By providing data redundancy, RAID increases the probability that an organization will be able to recover lost or damaged data. Being able to recover lost or damaged data may determine whether a business survives or fails. In some cases, for example financial institutions such as banks, a business can be held legally liable if it is unable to recover lost or damaged customer data. The degree of recovery possible depends on the form of RAID implemented, which in turn will likely be selected on how critical full data recovery is. As with most technology solutions, there is no one answer for all business scenarios.

As a storage security solution, RAID (Redundant Array of Inexpensive Devices) can be implemented as hardware, software, or a combination of the two. In general, hardware RAID solutions are faster but more expensive, whereas software solutions are cheaper but slower. Frequently, RAID levels 3 and higher are implemented using hardware due to performance requirements. If hardware based, a RAID controller card is used or an independent RAID drive array is implemented. If a controller card is used, the card, which is connected by cable to the RAID hard drives, is plugged into an available server's expansion slot. The advantage of a separate RAID controller card is that the card has its own processor and memory. Because the RAID card has its own resources, it does not have to use the server's processor or memory to perform its functions, improving overall server performance.

If instead an independent RAID drive array is used, it will also have its own processor and memory. In addition, the drive array unit will contain bays into which the RAID hard drives can be placed. Usually, an independent RAID drive array allows for easier expandability and greater storage capacity due to the number of drives the array can potentially hold. The drive array unit is then connected to a server. RAID drive arrays are often based on SCSI technology. More expensive RAID drive arrays have a backplane.

The backplane provides power to the hard drives and also connects the drives directly to the unit's SCSI bus, such that separate cables are not required. At an added expense, RAID drive arrays can also support *hot swappable drives*. Hot swappable drives, however, need to be of the same type and configuration. The advantage of a hot swappable drive is that it can be removed or inserted without powering down the RAID unit. This means that if one of the hard drives in the array fails, the failing drive can be replaced without taking down the entire array. The type of RAID level implemented determines whether such hot swappable drives can be used. The following discussion briefly outlines the six standardized RAID levels, 0 through 5.

RAID Level 0

RAID Level 0, also referred to as simple diskstriping, usually uses block-level striping but can also be configured for byte-level striping. The term striping refers to spreading out blocks of each file across multiple disks. A block is generally composed of 512 bytes. A byte is composed of eight bits. Block-level striping is preferred with data files containing small data records. Small data records will likely fit within one block. Therefore when a block is retrieved, it would probably contain the entire record. Because the entire record has been accessed, no additional data retrieval or storage operations will be required. The fewer data retrieval and storage operations performed, the more efficient the process.

Byte-level striping is preferred for large data records, because multiple drives can be read in parallel if a large record spans more than one drive. Assuming a three-drive RAID 0 array, block A is written to the first drive, block B to the second, and block C to the third. Block D then writes again to the first drive, block E to the second drive, and so on. In this example the file is "striped" across three drives.

The interesting thing about RAID 0 is that, in reality, it provides no redundancy, and therefore no fault tolerance, making it a potentially dangerous RAID choice. The advantage of RAID 0 is that it offers the best performance in terms of data access, because no overhead is involved for data recovery. Overhead is not involved because error checking is not performed. Also, drives can be accessed in parallel for read and write operations. However, for the multiple drives in a RAID 0 array, should one drive fail, the entire array fails. This means that data on all of the drives of the array become unavailable should one drive fail. The result of this type of failure is a lack of fault tolerance. Because there is no fault tolerance, when implementing RAID 0 an enterprise must make sure that regular backups are performed so that data can be recovered if the array fails.

RAID Level 1

RAID 1 can be implemented with disk mirroring or disk duplexing. Both provide a level of fault tolerance, with disk duplexing being superior. With a mirrored RAID 1, a single hard drive controller manages two hard drives. As data are written to one drive, the data are copied, or mirrored, to the second drive as well. Should one drive fail, the second drive is available for data recovery. However, should the hard drive controller fail, then both drives in the array become unavailable.

Although two drives are used in the array, the enterprise does not get double the performance or double the storage. Two 20-GB drives that are mirrored or duplexed store the same set of 20 GB data, thus disk utilization is very inefficient. Furthermore, when a write operation is performed, both drives are written to simultaneously, resulting in single drive speed performance. On the other hand, when a read operation is performed, the array can alternate between the two drives, improving read access performance.

Unlike a mirrored RAID 1, a duplexed RAID 1 has separate hard drive controllers for each hard drive. Should one drive fail, the second drive is still available. In addition, should one of the hard drive controllers fail, the second hard drive controller remains available, so a single hard drive controller failure does not bring the array down. Disk duplexing provides better fault tolerance because both a hard disk drive and a hard disk drive controller can fail yet data can still be accessed on the array. Of course, should both drives or both controllers fail, then the array fails, but such duplicated failure is less likely to occur in a duplexed RAID 1.

RAID Level 2

RAID level 2 uses some of its arrayed drives only for data and some only for error-correcting codes (ECCs). ECCs allow data to be reconstructed in the event of a data drive failure. But, multiple ECC drives also puts the array at greater risk, because if one ECC drive fails, all of them fail. Such a scenario is not secure. In practice, RAID 2 is rarely implemented because it is slow, disk intensive, and unreliable in the manner in which the ECC disks are configured.

RAID Level 3

RAID 3 uses data striping at the byte level, but with the addition of parity checking. Unlike RAID 1, which has no automated error-correcting mechanism, RAID 3 uses parity for data recovery. And, unlike RAID 2, RAID 3 uses only one of the drives in its array for parity checking, not several. At a minimum, RAID 3 requires three drives, two for data and one for parity. More than two data drives can be supported. Should a data drive in the array fail, the parity drive can be used to rebuild that failed drive's data. However, the single parity drive is itself a weakness. Should the single parity drive fail, data drives cannot be reconstructed.

RAID Level 4

RAID 4 closely resembles RAID 3, except that RAID 4 uses block-level data striping instead of byte-level data striping. As with RAID 3, one drive is used for parity, and two or more drives are used for data. Like RAID 2, RAID 4 is not often implemented because RAID 5 is faster and more reliable. Physically RAID 4 is similar to RAID 3, except that the parity drive is block rather than byte based.

RAID Level 5

RAID 5 also uses data striping at the block level, but unlike RAID 3 or 4, parity or ECC information is distributed among the disks that make up the array. Because RAID 3 and 4 use a single parity drive, that drive becomes a bottleneck in terms of access performance, meaning that each write operation has to wait its turn for its parity data to be written to the parity drive. With RAID 5, distributed parity writing removes the single parity drive bottleneck, resulting in improved write performance. RAID 5's distributed parity also results in better rebuild of lost or damaged data, when required. Read performance, however, in a RAID 5 array can suffer because drives in a RAID 5 array contain both data and parity information. When the array is accessed for a read operation, drive heads have to bypass, or jump over, parity information maintained on the drive. Bypassing the parity information takes time, and, as the saying goes, time is money.

Of the various forms of standardized RAIDs just considered, RAIDs 1 and 5 are the most commonly implemented. RAID 1 serves well for smaller organizations. RAID 5 is better suited for medium- to large-scale enterprises. Other nonstandardized and proprietary forms of RAID also exist.

chapter eleven

Trends in Business Data Communications

Learning Objectives

After studying this chapter, you should be able to:

- Identify the elements of convergence in data communications.
- Understand how convergence affects security, privacy, and ethics.
- Define unified messaging (UM).
- Describe three leading wireless implementations.
- Explain three ways in which IPv6 differs from IPv4.
- Name four emerging career areas related to data communications.

It is essential for businesses to secure their data communications infrastructures. Businesses not only depend on their data communications resources for their own purposes, but customers, vendors, and business partners depend on these resources as well. Businesses also need to keep abreast of where new technologies are leading so that they do not lose their competitive advantage. Although many businesses do not want to run their operations on the leading of edge of technology, and for good reason, it is important for a business to know what tools its competition could be planning to use. This chapter explores some of these leading-edge technologies.

The Convergence of Pervasive Networking

Do you know where your SPOT is? SPOT stands for **Small Personal Object Technology**. If you do not currently have a SPOT, you will probably have one in the near future. A SPOT does not require a spray can of cleanser, but instead uses bytes of digital data to retrieve news articles, the latest stock quotes, customer contact data, recent movie reviews, and other information. This text began with the idea that in the future instant communications, regardless of a person's location, will be available at the push of a button—perhaps the button of a jacket, wallet, purse, or key chain.

When networking technologists discuss **convergence**, they are talking about the integration of data, voice, and video, all carried seamlessly over one infrastructure. And more to the point, all of these elements will be accessible from many types of devices, not just from a desktop or laptop computer. SPOT is intended to build networking intelligence into any device, small or large, inexpensive or expensive, high or low power.

The issue of power is critical to the development of SPOT devices. Many users of laptop computers or other battery-operated mobile devices appreciate these devices' portability, but fault them for their inability to power themselves for long periods of time. To succeed, SPOT devices must be smart in how they consume power and extend it. In a very real sense, the goal of always being "plugged in" means not having to plug a communications device into a power supply every few hours or even every few days. With the ideal SPOT device, users will not have to think about the availability of the device, wondering how many minutes of usage are left. Convenience will be a major characteristic of such devices. To see how SPOT technology may be incorporated into a watch, visit **www.microsoft.com/resources/spot/product.mspx**. Of course, such devices are not yet available, but this chapter concerns the future—where technology is heading, not necessarily where it is now.

Communication technology is on the road to invisible mobility, offering devices that are always there but never seen. Users will carry communication technologies with them in unobtrusive places, such as a bracelet on their wrist. Of course, such pervasive technologies will raise new social and work-related issues. Many already believe that the blurring between home and office has gone too far.

Many employees are already available to or in contact with the corporate office by mobile phone, fax, electronic pager, and e-mail. This type of connectivity will only increase in the near future. Mobile technologies are not only transforming how business is done, but also how employees work, causing them to take more work into their homes and private spaces. Some think that this may be too much of a good thing. If employees can be contacted anywhere, what will prevent the office from contacting its employees from literally anywhere at any time, even when they are on vacation?

Mobile technologies are creating what is often considered pervasive, and some say invasive, computing. **Pervasive computing** refers to technology so prevalent, and easy to use, that the technology becomes a second thought, or nearly invisible to the user. Three issues of particular concern involving pervasive computing are security, privacy, and ethics. Consider security. The more available the enterprise's information infrastructures, the more open they are to attack. For customers and employees who need to access the enterprise from any location, a major challenge then becomes how to adequately authenticate and validate these users. Undoubtedly, more types of personalized identification information will be required from users, along with new ways of validating this information.

Requiring users to provide more information that may be easily accessible from an open access-from-anywhere network raises questions of privacy. Identify theft is already a major issue today. Will users of a data communications infrastructure that is accessible from anywhere be willing to provide sensitive data about themselves, such as passwords, account numbers, financial data, addresses, or other privileged information, in order to verify who they are to the network? The distinction between personal privacy and the communication infrastructure's need to verify users will require a difficult and controversial balancing act. This discussion of privacy, and how it can be used or abused, ties directly to ethics.

The Ethical Perspective

A Chip for Every Body?

An organization in Florida, Applied Digital Solutions (**www.adsx.com**), offers a technology called the **VeriChip**. This intelligent chip is about the size of a grain of rice, similar to the one depicted in Figure 11.1. The intent is for the VeriChip to be implanted directly into a body, perhaps a pet's, a child's, or maybe even your own. The VeriChip can be used to store security, health, financial, or other types of information about the host into which it is implanted. It can also be used for tracking. However, is it possible for this chip and the information it contains to be used for purposes other than for which it was intended? The potential problem with such technologies that allow you to be tracked and identified wherever you are, is the very fact that these technologies can track and identify you wherever you are.

This is something of a paradox, and to many a frightening future. Users of these technologies that are now on our doorstep will want assurances that these technologies will not, or cannot, be used in a manner for which they were not intended. The problem with technology, however, is that once it is unleashed it can sometimes be difficult to control. And can any technology truly be guaranteed against abuse? Probably not.

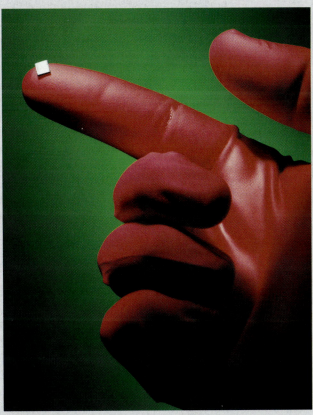

Figure 11.1
Body Microchip
Could there be a microbody chip in your future?

What do you think about technologies such as those offered by Applied Digital Solutions? Could such embedded body chips be used unethically? Should those who are incarcerated for serious crimes have a chip implanted? Would such implantation be a violation of basic human rights?

The convergence of voice, video, and data into a seamless infrastructure will require technologies that can support such convergence. Users will require persistent connections to high-speed wired and wireless networks; therefore, better and highly reliable delivery technologies will be needed. These delivery technologies will have to be invisible and reliable, as reliable as hearing a dial tone on a telephone. Also, protocols that can support these different types of applications must be created.

Session Initiation Protocol

One protocol getting a lot of notice in the convergence industry is **Session Initiation Protocol (SIP)**. The IETF has a workgroup devoted to SIP (**www.ietf.org/html.charters/sip-charter.html**). In addition, such heavyweight players as Microsoft, IBM, Siemens, and Cisco Systems view SIP as the protocol that will deliver real-time communications for IP-based voice, video, data, and instant messaging. The role of **instant messaging (IM)** as a communications tool has become a major consideration. According to the Yankee Group (**www.yankeegroup.com**), a communications and networking research and consulting firm, by 2005 there will be 80 million IM users in the United States alone. IM has become a major contender in the enterprise-application realm. Three protocols are evolving for the corporate use of IM: SIP, **Security Assertion Markup Language (SAML)**, and **Extensible Messaging and Presence Protocol (XMPP)**.

SIP will be used for establishing, modifying, and terminating IM communications on an IP-based network. SAML will be used to enable the exchange of security credentials between communications. SAML comes from XML, which you may recall from Chapter 9. XMPP will allow for interoperability between enterprises. Like SAML, XMPP is also an XML-based specification. OASIS offers links to recent articles and research related to XML on its Web site (**xml.coverpages.org**).

Unified Messaging

Besides IM, another application that has caught the corporate world's attention is unified messaging. **Unified messaging (UM)** is an umbrella term used to describe systems that offer access to e-mail, voice, and fax messages through a unified application. Such a system is designed to work through a single common interface, most likely through an existing e-mail client application. Some consider UM to be one of the next "killer applications" that will gain wide acceptance in the corporate infrastructure. The term **killer application** is used to describe a service, program, or application that will have mass appeal. By having mass appeal, vendors of killer applications expect to achieve substantial economic profit by selling them to consumers.

Being able to receive a message as a voice mail, a fax, or an e-mail sounds like a fairly simple request. But for many users, multiple messaging systems are likely involved. One voice-mail system is used for a desk or land phone. A second voice-mail system is needed for a cell or mobile phone. A third system is needed to receive faxes. And yet a fourth system is required for e-mail. Then, of course, consider that a single user might have multiple land phones, mobile phones, faxes, and e-mail accounts. As you can see, getting a message to a user can be more complicated than it initially appears. With UM, all of the various messaging systems are rolled into one system, with one access point—the user's e-mail inbox. Of course, although one access point may provide user convenience, it might also provide hacker convenience as well. With UM, the topics presented in Chapter 10—digital signatures, digital certificates, and security in general—become even more important.

So how does UM actually work? First, a message sent to the user, whether fax, voice, or e-mail, is placed in the appropriate e-mail server's message space. For organizations using traditional PBX voice systems, voice messages from the PBX are copied to a UM storage location. Finally, all messages are ultimately routed to the user's e-mail inbox. UM vendors currently include Avaya Inc., Nortel Networks, and Cisco Systems, among others. (Their Web sites are, respectively, **www.avaya.com**, **www.nortel.com**, and **www.cisco.com**.) The products supplied by these vendors are designed to route messages to a user's e-mail server, perhaps a Lotus Notes, Figure 11.2, or Microsoft Exchange server. From the server, messages can then be routed to the user's e-mail client application, such as Microsoft Outlook or Yahoo.

In this scenario, all messages, regardless of their source, are ultimately digitized. Users can listen to voice messages, print faxes, or simply view text messages through their e-mail client; the messages are simply e-mail attachments. Web-based e-mail clients enable users to access their messages from virtually anywhere in the world where a Web connection can be made. The goal of UM is to integrate all of the different communication technologies so that they work as an integrated whole.

As an example, IBM plans to tie its Lotus Software Dominos platform to its WebSphere application server and its DB2 database to create an integrated application, database, and messaging environment. Microsoft

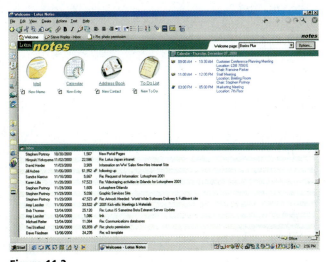

Figure 11.2
Lotus Notes is an example of an application that might utilize unified messaging.

has plans for closely coupling its Exchange Server product to its .Net Web services platform. Novell plans to integrate its GroupWise software to collaborate with its application Web services. Many vendors are aggressively seeking ways to marry relational database technologies to UM applications. Database technologies permit a more generalized format for message storage and allow for more powerful querying, reporting, and data mining. Relational databases are already used extensively by most organizations, another advantage. Database languages, especially SQL, are being modified to work closely with such protocols as SOAP and J2EE, two protocols presented in Chapter 9. Figure 11.3 gives a high-level concept of UM.

The promise of UM is that users of communication technologies using different media and different devices will be able to communicate with anyone, anywhere, at any time. This works both ways, of course, because the user will both send and receive messages. UM reduces the number of places users must check for all their messages—fax, voice, or e-mail—to one portal. And, with UM, users can send and receive messages from a single interface.

In practice, a UM application allows a telephone call to switch from voice to data mode while the connection is in progress. In such a scenario, tying a UM technology to a database can be a real payoff. As a client calls in, the UM application, through its database connection, identifies the client by his or her telephone number. If the customer is using a display

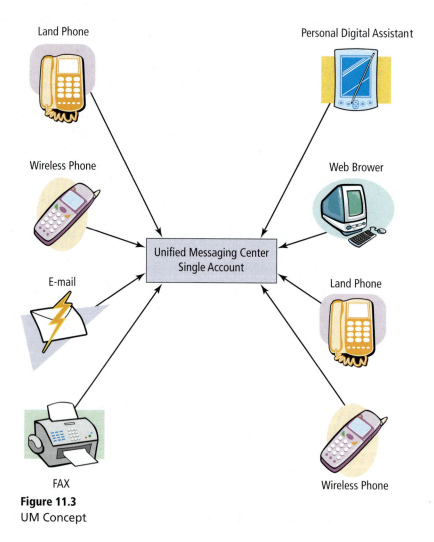

Figure 11.3
UM Concept

device of some type to place a call, the UM application can automatically respond with appropriate information based on the client's previous communications with the business. Information can be tracked and stored for improved marketing response to client needs.

UM will utilize text-to-speech capabilities so that messages can be read back to the user, or the reverse, verbal messages translated into their text equivalents. A user may want a printed copy of a voice message, so a speech-to-text capability might be convenient. This technique of translating from one form to another can be used, for example, for converting text to fax or speech to fax. Flexibility of message manipulation is the end result.

UM providers will have to create solutions that are also flexible enough to accommodate traditional services, such as PBX, until they are replaced by completely digital solutions. Because such services will be digital, scaling the services to expand or contract becomes much simpler. Very likely, as with many technologies today, vendors of UM tools will rely on open-architecture models and protocols. So whether you are a corporate employee, a home-based worker, or a student, UM services are likely to be in your near future.

Wireless Implementations

Applications such as IM and UM are increasingly expected to be accessible from anywhere. Being able to access such communications from anywhere frees users from wire-based connections. Wireless communications by way of satellite and terrestrial microwave have been available for decades. What has changed is the pervasive use of wireless technologies by the average person. Wireless-access technologies are no longer just for the big guys. However, vendors of wireless implementations have had trouble convincing the mass market that their products are practical. Critical concerns about early wireless solutions were their limited bandwidth capacity, narrow geographic scope, lack of security, and, importantly, lack of reliable standards. Each of these areas now has been addressed, with varying degrees of success.

As with UM, wireless communication is being positioned as one of the next major killer applications, provided the technology can be implemented to support it. Many think the time for wireless has finally arrived. Three emerging wireless-based technologies have sparked wide interest: 3G, 802.11, and Bluetooth. In scope, these three technologies scale from the worldwide to the personal. Let's start by looking at 3G, a wide-area technology, and end with Bluetooth, whose focus is more personal.

Third-Generation Wireless

3G stands for "third generation." The name implies that there has been a first and a second generation, which is in fact true. Like 3G, 1G and 2G were designed for wide-area mobile communications and relied on cellular technologies. However, 1G and 2G were designed for voice-based analog communications. First introduced in Norway in 1981, 1G, or first-generation, systems used analog modulation and only provided voice transmission. Using frequencies around 900 MHz, 1G systems eventually made their way to the United States and other parts of

Europe. 2G, or second-generation, systems were introduced in the early 1990s. They rely on a frequency band of 900 to 1800 MHz. 2G systems provided voice and limited data services and used digital modulation for improved audio quality. A bridge between 2G and 3G, 2.5G, improved on data-carrying capacity by better utilizing the Global System for Mobile Communications (GSM).

Today's customers of mobile appliances, including cell phones, want these devices to support more than just a simple voice conversation. Users seek a mobile appliance, like the one shown in Figure 11.4, that gives them a richer multimedia experience. Users want mobile communications devices that support sound, graphics, video, text, and photography, all in real time. 1G and 2G cellular networks were never intended for these types of communications. Although 2G and 2.5G networks are still very common, 3G networks promise to deliver on multimedia capabilities. To support multimedia data, though, greater bandwidth must be provided. This is why 3G is significant. A 4G solution is currently under development. Table 11.1 summarizes 1G through 4G systems.

Legacy 1G and 2G networks use equipment that typically runs at a bandwidth of 19.2 Kbps, which is perfectly adequate for simple voice communications. In contrast, 3G systems have a minimum speed of 144 Kbps and a maximum speed of 2 Mbps. These speeds support many types of data

Figure 11.4
This wireless HandSpring PDA is an example of a device that can utilize 3G technology.

Table 11.1 Summary of 1G to 4G Systems

Generation	Characteristics
1G	• First analog cellular systems
	• Initiated in the early 1980s
	• Uses Advanced Mobile Phone System (AMPS), Nordic Mobile Telephone (NMT), and Total Access Communication System (TACS)
	• Delivers only voice information
	• Conflicting world standards
2G	• First digital cellular systems
	• Initiated in the early 1990s
	• Uses GSM, CDMA, Digital AMPS (DAMPS), and Personal Digital Communication (PDC)
	• Delivers mostly voice, limited data delivery
	• Conflicting world standards
2.5G	• Enhanced version of 2G
	• Capable of greater data delivery capacity
3G	• Current worldwide standard
	• Uses Universal Mobile Telecommunications System (UMTS)
	• Supports packet- and circuit-switching networks
4G	• Next-stage generation, still in research phase

beyond voice and offer a dramatic improvement in bandwidth capacity over legacy 1G and 2G networks. What is slowing the rapid move to a totally 3G-based world? Two critical factors are preventing the widespread use of 3G technologies.

First, businesses have already invested billions of dollars on 2G and 2.5G technologies. A business will not abandon a heavily invested technology without good reason. For many businesses, the level of service provided by 2G and 2.5G communication infrastructures may not be perfect, but it is adequate for immediate needs. Spending tens of thousands, even millions, of dollars to upgrade to the latest, greatest technology simply to have it does not make financial sense. Not every business needs or desires to give its employees the capability of zapping a live video feed from their work cubicle, or wherever they may be, to a colleague halfway around the world or to Mom in Iowa.

Second, 3G is a still-emerging technology. For many network administrators, the term *emerging technology* translates into "do not go there." Emerging technologies can provide real and immediate benefits, but they can also result in disaster. In addition, the cost of adopting an emerging technology may mean little or no technical support from vendors. Then there is the problem of finding qualified staff, and those who are qualified are likely to be very expensive. Finally, buying into a technology that ends up not being the worldwide standard can be very costly, as well as embarrassing. Investing in an emerging technology is something of a gamble.

Keep in mind that 3G standards are still being defined, appliances are still being created and refined, full-featured services that can utilize 3G are not yet entirely in place, and potential customers are not yet fully informed. As you have read, being at the cutting edge of technology can be perilous for a business: either the business will move ahead of its competition with the advanced performance of the newest technology or the unproven technology will fail and competitors will overtake the business. In the case of 3G, though, all trends point to implementation and acceptance, especially once standards are finalized. For example, an April 7, 2003, front-page article in *InfoWorld* calls out a significant fact regarding CDPD (cellular digital packet data) networks. Of the last two major providers of CDPD services—AT&T and Verizon—AT&T plans to discontinue service of CDPD in June of 2004. CDPD is a 2G technology. As the saying goes, the writing is on the wall, or in the case of 3G, in the air.

Based on UMTS (Universal Mobile Telecommunications System) technology, 3G is geared to provide broadband, packet-based transmission of digitized voice, video, and text at speeds that offer a consistent set of services to mobile users wherever they are in the world. That's the big picture. UMTS, which is itself based on GSM (Global System for Mobile Communications), is endorsed by major standards-setting bodies and manufacturers around the world. Once UMTS is completely implemented, mobile devices can be constantly connected to the Internet, wherever they may be. A combination of terrestrial wireless and satellite transmission will make this connectivity possible. You can find out much more about 3G and UMTS at **www.umtsworld.com**.

Three data rates have been proposed for the various types of 3G-based application traffic: 144 Kbps for automotive, 384 Kbps for pedestrian, and 2 Mbps for interior, meaning within a building. 3G also supports several characteristics required for multimedia communications, most notably the following:

- Fixed- and variable-rate bit traffic

- Bandwidth on demand

- Asymmetric data rates in forward and reverse links

- Multimedia mail storage and forwarding

- Broadband access of up to 2 Mbps

Using 3G services, businesses can take advantage of such alternative billing methods as pay per bit, fixed flat rate, and symmetric or asymmetric bandwidths, among other possibilities. Such alternatives enable 3G providers to offer more than a one-size-fits-all solution, resulting in a wider market base. Because 3G's UMTS foundation offers higher bandwidth capacities than traditional 1G and 2G networks, new services, such as on-demand video conferencing, will be more practical and cost-effective. In a 3G world, a user can expect to experience the same level of bandwidth and connectivity as he or she would find at the office, but have the convenience of working from home. Finally, perhaps the most important characteristic of 3G technologies is that they are a single family of worldwide wireless and mobile standards. Figure 11.5 illustrates how a 3G scenario might work.

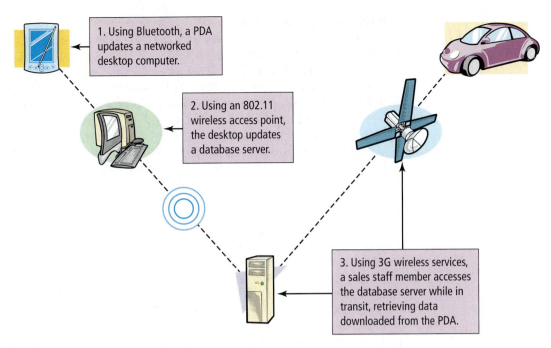

Figure 11.5
3G, 802.11, and Bluetooth

The Wireless Local Area Network

As you have learned, 3G is a big-picture technology that offers users world-wide mobility. In contrast, **wireless local area networks (WLANs)** have a geographic scope closer to traditional LAN territory: a room, a building, or a campus. Today, WLAN implementations are being driven by the 802.11 family of protocols. You may recall that the IEEE is the standards-setting body that formulates LAN protocols under the 802 heading. By now you are also familiar with two 802-based LAN technologies: Ethernet (802.3) and token ring (802.5). WLANs use three 802-based protocols. They are, from oldest to newest, 802.11b, 802.11a, and 802.11g. As a group, 802.11 WLANs are often referred to as **Wi-Fi (wireless fidelity)** solutions. Figure 11.6 shows a wireless PC card that might enable a user to connect to a wireless LAN. Let's look at some of the characteristics of each of these WLAN protocols.

Figure 11.6
Wireless PC cards allow users the mobility of roaming with their equipment.

802.11b

The **802.11b** WLAN operates at 2.4 GHz, and although it has a "b" designation, it is in fact older than 802.11a. The 802.11b protocol supports a maximum throughput of 11 Mbps per channel, and up to three nonoverlapping channels are possible. The range of an 802.11b WLAN is 328 feet, which is significantly roomier than an 802.11a implementation. However, compared with an 802.11a WLAN, 802.11b is relatively slow. The 802.11b solution offers two main advantages: equipment is generally inexpensive and it is compatible with proposed 802.11g technologies. For businesses that cannot wait for an 802.11g WLAN, 802.11b may be the preferred solution because it provides an easier future upgrade path to 802.11g.

802.11a

The **802.11a** protocol, operating at around 5 GHz, is newer than 802.11b. It offers a maximum throughput per channel of 54 Mbps. An 802.11a WLAN can support up to 12 separate nonoverlapping channels within a range of 80 feet. In a small area, 802.11a provides for relatively high performance. For larger spaces, 802.11a is not a practical solution. Additionally, 802.11a is not compatible with older 802.11b equipment or with equipment being developed for 802.11g. Organizations that do not currently have a WLAN but that want one might prefer to wait for 802.11g's stabilization rather than buy into a protocol that is already obsolete.

802.11g

Like 802.11b, the **802.11g** protocol operates at around 2.4 GHz. Also, like 802.11b, 802.11g supports three nonoverlapping channels, but the channels have a maximum throughput of 54 Mbps, significantly better than 802.11b's 11 Mbps. In addition, an 802.11g WLAN can span 328 feet. This makes the 802.11g solution faster than 802.11b and capable of covering more floor space than 802.11a. Also, because 802.11b equipment can interoperate with 802.11g equipment, prior 802.11b equipment investments are not a total loss. A major hurdle for 802.11g had been its lack of formal ratification by the IEEE. Many businesses do not want to buy into a nonformalized standard, fearing they would end up with equipment and solution investments that are not based on the final standard.

WAP and WEP

Two protocols associated with WLANs and wireless devices are **Wireless Application Protocol (WAP)** and **Wired Equivalent Privacy (WEP)**. WAP is transforming how wireless mobile devices communicate and has proven very successful. WEP, however, has shown through its widely reported and demonstrated weaknesses that securing the WLAN is more challenging than it had first appeared.

WAP, rather than being a single protocol, is more like an application environment that uses a set of communication protocols to create applications that run on mobile devices, such as cell phones and PDAs (Personal Digital Assistants). As a wireless technology, WAP offers several benefits. First, it is an open standard and is network-platform independent. This platform independence allows many vendors of varying technologies to develop tools that can run on a variety of devices and software. To create a WAP application, Wireless Markup Language (WML) is used. WML is based on XML, which was introduced in Chapter 9. You may have noticed that XML and its associated offspring seem to be popping up in every corner of the data communications world.

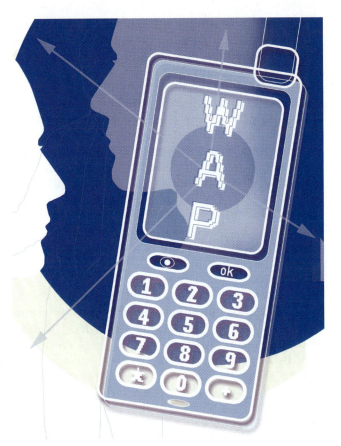

Figure 11.7
WAP is used particularly for small display interfaces, such as those found on handheld devices.

Using WML, WAP applications make efficient use of small-screen displays, like that depicted in Figure 11.7, which are common on mobile devices, and they enable micro-browser-based navigation with one hand. WAP is flexible enough to accommodate a basic two-line text message on a simple screen or a fully featured graphics display. Besides WML, WAP applications also use standards-based protocols such as UDP and IP. UDP and IP, in terms of delivery and bandwidth requirements, are much more efficient than TCP with its connection-oriented characteristics.

Although WAP has proven itself to be a successful wireless solution, WEP has not. The intent behind WEP was good; it sought to provide a measure of security for wireless communications. Unfortunately, WEP has proven to be a bad implementation of good idea. WEP is an encryption standard that is bundled with Wi-Fi protocols. Although WEP encryption is based on the same Secure Socket Layer (SSL) security used by Web browsers, in practice, WEP is easily broken or hacked into. This means that WEP security is in fact not secure. Because of this, businesses that use WLANs should not base secure communications on the embedded WEP protocol.

A major concern of most organizations that decide to pursue a wireless solution is how secure their enterprise data and information will be. Keep in mind that wireless communications are "in the air." Anyone with the proper equipment can intercept a wireless communication. You read in Chapter 10 that cryptographic technologies are used extensively to secure the enterprise. In a wireless world, cryptographic measures are crucial. The threat to a WLAN is not only that communications can be intercepted, but also that the network and its resources may be at risk. In a wireless world, organizations that take their security seriously will implement layers of security so that if one approach or avenue is breached, another wall is in place to prevent unauthorized access.

In response to wireless security concerns, the IEEE is currently working on **802.11i**, a new security protocol that addresses the problems of WEP. Using Temporal Key Integrity Protocol (TKIP), 802.11i ensures that a TKIP key varies for each packet in a communication through key mixing. Furthermore, the Wi-Fi Alliance (**www.wi-fi.org**), which includes such members as Microsoft, Intel, Cisco, and Apple, has proposed a standard of its own called Wi-Fi Protected Access (WPA). WPA works by frequently refreshing the master key in a secure communication, reducing the chance that intercepted packets by unauthorized users can be decoded. Security in a WLAN also will likely need to include such technologies as VPNs and tunneling.

Bluetooth

Whereas 3G is global and 802.11 is local, the focus of **Bluetooth** is personal. Bluetooth (**www.bluetooth.com**) is a wireless implementation that creates a Personal Area Network (PAN). Using low-power radio transmissions, various networked devices (e.g., cameras, printers, scanners, keyboards, or other near-area devices, such as the wireless mouse shown in Figure 11.8) can be connected without cables and maintain a network connection even as the networked device is being moved locally, say as a user crosses the room to look out a window. The intent of Bluetooth is not to enable users to wander 10,000 feet away from their networks with their Bluetooth devices, but rather no more than 1 to 1,000 feet, although a 4,000 foot radius is in the works.

Because Bluetooth is based on radio transmission, it does not suffer from the line-of-sight limitations of infrared-based wireless implementations. However, radio transmissions are susceptible to interference and security breaches. Any radio receiver tuned in to a Bluetooth device's frequency can pick up the communication being carried. To compensate for potential interference and interception, Bluetooth does two things. First, short data packets are used. Shorter data packets result in less potential interference from outside sources, because less can go wrong within the

Figure 11.8
Wireless Bluetooth Enabled Mouse

packet. Also, if the packet has to be retransmitted, because it is short, retransmission is less of a problem. Bluetooth transmits at 1 Mbps. Security is provided by Bluetooth's use of **frequency hopping** at approximately 1,600 hops per second. This frequency of hops in a transmission goes a long way toward ensuring that signals will not be intercepted. In addition, besides frequency hopping, Bluetooth can use encryption technologies as well as an authentication mechanism. For the business, the home user, or the road warrior, Bluetooth enables mobility by doing away with cables and wires that would otherwise have to be carted around. Supporting both data and voice, Bluetooth bridges telephone and mobile computing devices.

Hot Spots

In Chapter 10, the term *hot spot* was used to describe an alternative facility that a business could use to restore and run critical data, applications, and communications. In the wireless world, a **hot spot** is something else entirely. To a wireless user, a hot spot is a location remote from the office or home where the user can access the Internet. Hot spots are increasingly showing up in airports, hotels, bookstores, and, very famously, in coffee shops such as Starbucks. As the wireless revolution continues, users of the technology will demand and expect to have inexpensive and easy access to high-speed Internet connections from wherever they are. Hot spots are used for this purpose. Users connecting to a Wi-Fi hot spot usually pay a fee for the service provided.

Recognizing that they could make a profit by offering Wi-Fi access to roaming users, many businesses, large and small, are hopping onto the hot spot bandwagon. Hot spot providers require relatively simple software, hardware, and something like a DSL connection, and, voilá, they are in business. Users of the hot spot need the necessary client software, and of course a wireless device, to connect to the WLAN. Once connected, a user could, for example, initiate a VPN connection to his or her corporate office and have a secure communication. A popular vendor of hot spot software for both users and providers is Boingo. On their Web site (**www.boingo.com**), one can find a link that lists hot spot locations throughout the United States. Boingo also offers client software that allows the wireless user to "sniff out," or find, Wi-Fi networks.

Of course, not all those attempting to tap into, or sniff out, a WLAN are doing so as authorized users. Individuals who want to locate WLANs in order to penetrate the network also use **sniffing** software. These individuals may simply be on a fishing expedition, intending no direct harm, but they may also be attempting to steal or damage network resources such as data, information, and applications. The process of seeking out WLANs, usually in a car or truck, for purposes of unauthorized penetration is called **war driving**. *PCWorld* reported in a September 2002 article on a massive war drive at **www.pcworld.com/news/article/0,aid,104802,00.asp**. Informed WLAN administrators are well aware of this practice, however, and place layers of security between their WLAN resources and the outside world.

IPv6 and the New Internet

Technologies such as 3G, 802.11, and Bluetooth derive much of their appeal by providing all-time access to the network of all networks—the Internet. As connectivity technologies have evolved, it should be no surprise to discover that the Internet also has evolved. The Internet we know and love, IPv4, has been around, at least in a very basic form, since the late 1960s. For a computer-based technology, this is truly ancient. But, the long life that IPv4 has enjoyed says a great deal about how well designed it was and how reliable and flexible a technology it is. But, as you probably know, all good things must come to an end. To many, the end of the road for IPv4 is close at hand. Gradually replacing IPv4 is the new and improved Internet, IPv6 (Internetworking Protocol version 6), also known as **IPng (Internetworking Protocol, next generation)**. Why is IPv4 being retired? How does IPv6 differ from IPv4? The following text explores these very questions.

IPv4 Limitations

The Internet was initially designed primarily as a tool for researchers, scientists, and engineers to more easily exchange data and information with each other. Who could have foreseen that their creation, **IPv4**, would turn into one of the most wildly popular communication technologies the world has ever seen? Also, at that time the types of data that IPv4 was created to carry were fairly simple: text and numbers. Today, the IPv4 infrastructure transmits much more complex types of data, including video, audio, graphics, and voice. IPv4 can do this, but not as efficiently as desired or required in today's world of instant mass communications. The very popularity of IPv4 has also resulted in the rapid depletion of an essential element needed by any entity that wants an Internet presence, namely an IP address.

IPv4 uses a two-level, hierarchical addressing scheme. Part of an IPv4's address is used to identify the specific host or client device on a network, and part as the identifier for the network itself, as you read in Chapter 5. As you may recall, IPv4 address classes are A, B, C, D, and E. This type of addressing scheme is not able to meet the needs of the numbers and types of networks now in place. As an example of this inefficiency, you know that a Class A IP address has one network identifier but up to 16 million host addresses. A Class C IP address has only 254 usable host addresses. The first class offers far too many host addresses, and the second class, for most organizations, offers far too few. Keep in mind, though, that what IPv4 was designed for and how it ended up being used are two very different things.

IPv4 can carry transmit multimedia data, but not very well. Multimedia data were never provided for in the IPv4 architecture because at that time such data did not exist. Also, and very importantly, IPv4 does not inherently provide for encryption and authentication, two technologies critical to securing the enterprise. Instead, encryption and authentication technologies had to be designed around the limitations of IPv4. Of course, it would have been more efficient for such capabilities to have been designed into the architecture, but that would have required a fortune teller.

The wireless revolution is well on its way to being a resounding success. What will likely stop this multi-billion-dollar revolution in its tracks, however, is the lack of IP addressing. Wireless devices and the WLANs they run on must have IP addresses to fulfill their promise. Without an IP address, there is no connectivity. Workarounds using techniques such as subnetting and supernetting have helped extend IP addresses, but such techniques can only take IPv4 so far. Many believe this limit has been reached. And finally, many countries outside of the United States and Europe were not part of the initial IP address giveaway. For these countries, the lack of IP addresses means literally having no Internet presence.

Fortunately, all of these problems have been apparent for some time. In response, the Internet engineering community began in the early 1990s to develop a solution. That solution, now ready for gradual implementation, is IPv6. IPv6 has been designed to take into careful consideration all of the present limitations of IPv4. A forum has been created for IPv6. You can visit this forum at **www.ipv6forum.com**.

IPv6 Address Notation

A notable feature of an IPv4 address is that it is limited to a 32-bit, or 4-byte, value. The binary equivalent of an IPv4 address is often expressed in a dotted-decimal format, for example, 192.37.113.12. **IPv6** uses 128 bits, or 16 bytes. Because of the length of the IPv6 address, the dotted-decimal format has been dropped. Instead, IPv6 addresses are expressed in what is called a hexadecimal-colon notation. **Hexadecimal** is the Base-16 numbering system and is more efficient for expressing large numbers.

You may recall from Chapter 5 that a decimal 15 is expressed as F in hexadecimal, using one character instead of two, making hexadecimal more efficient. Thirty-two hexadecimal digits can represent the 128 binary bits of a 16-byte IPv6 address. Going from 128 to 32 is pretty efficient, don't you think? The rule is that four binary bytes require two hexadecimal digits to be expressed. Therefore, 16 binary bytes can be expressed in 8 groups of 4 hexadecimal digits. A colon is used to separate each set of four hexadecimal digits from each other. Here is an example of a possible IPv6 address:

DA3F:38C7:1934:EC8B:5671:0000:A690:21FD

In the IPv6 addressing scheme, each 128-bit address string uniquely identifies one single networked device on the worldwide Internet. As in IPv4, there is a network and host portion embedded within the 128-bit address. But, unlike IPv4, with IPv6 there is much greater flexibility in assigning network and host portions within the 128-bit string. Another difference that IPv6 makes in its addressing scheme is that only three address types are allowed: unicast, multicast, and anycast. Within these three address types, an additional characteristic called the address *type prefix* is used. The type prefix specifies the purpose of the address.

IPv6 Addressing Types

A **unicast address** defines one specific networked or host device. No two devices can use the same unicast address, with two exceptions: the unspecified unicast address and the loopback unicast address. The **unspecified address**, represented by two colon characters (::), is used by a device when it powers up if it does not know its own IP address. The unspecified unicast address is used by that device to send a message to available routers on the local link that asks for addressing information. In this way, a device that does not know its address can learn what its address is. The unspecified address is composed entirely of zeros.

The **loopback address** is composed entirely of zeros, except for the very last bit, which is set to one. The loopback unicast address is represented as two colons followed by a one (::1). A device uses the loopback unicast address to test itself to determine whether it has been properly configured for communication without having to go out to the network. In effect, the device uses the loopback address to make sure that its software layers have been correctly set up to allow for communications.

A **multicast address** is used when a message needs to be sent to a group of devices that may or may not be on the same *type prefix*. The use of the multicast and anycast addresses in IPv6 eliminates the need for broadcast packets. This is an advantage, because broadcast packets, which go to all devices on a network, consume a lot of bandwidth, and are therefore inefficient. In a multicast IPv6 world, devices have to **subscribe** to, or sign up with, a multicast group to receive the multicast transmission. For devices not on the same physical network that participate in a multicast group, routers must be configured as subscribers so that they can pass the multicast traffic on to its intended destination.

Unlike a multicast address, the **anycast address** is for a group of devices that are of the same type prefix. The anycast address is new to IPv6. A packet addressed to an anycast address is delivered to the closest device with that address's anycast type prefix.

IPv6 Packet Format

IPv6 packets can have three components: a required header, an optional extension header, and the message, or **payload**. The required header is fixed at 40 bytes. With IPv6, the header has been redesigned to make processing time faster for intermediate routers and the ultimate destination devices. Six fields from the old IPv4 header have been eliminated, three fields have been updated, and two fields have been added. Of the two added fields, the class field supports packet prioritization, and the flow field has been left open for future interpretation. All packets are encapsulated at the data link layer.

The required base header includes the IP version number and source and destination addresses, as well as such important values as class value and payload length. The class value, as mentioned earlier, allows for prioritization. Prioritization values are especially important because they allow IPv6 to provide Quality of Service (QoS). A QoS component can be critical when a network is congested and higher-priority data must be transmitted before lower-priority data. With IPv6, congestion-controlled and non-congestion-controlled traffic can be identified. IPv4 does not have this built-in capability.

With congestion-controlled traffic, packets may be delayed, lost, or received out of sequence. This type of traffic is assigned a priority from 0 to 7, with 7 being the highest. For non-congestion-controlled traffic, which is important for applications such as real-time audio or video, priority numbers from 8 to 15 are assigned. Generally, data that can experience more packet loss, because it contains more redundancy, might be assigned a lower priority value, for example, 8, whereas less redundant data is given a higher number, perhaps 12. The idea here is that IPv6 allows the network administrator to fine-tune the delivery of data packets so that what is most important gets through first.

From IPv4 to IPv6

The transition from IPv4 to IPv6 will not happen over a year or two, more likely it will take at least a decade. Considering the huge implementation base of the current IPv4 infrastructure, moving seamlessly into the newly designed IPv6 architecture will be a challenge. With this in mind, the IPv6 design team has put together a set of guidelines to assist in the transition to the new Internet. Their recommendations take three approaches: dual stack, tunneling, and header translation.

The **dual-stack approach** has IP devices running both IP stacks, meaning both IPv4 and IPv6. Running dual stacks is seen as a transitional phase to gradually move from one platform to the other. Running dual stacks requires more processing overhead, but it also allows IPv4 devices to communicate through and with IPv6 devices. More than likely, the most important devices in the dual-stack approach will be network routers. Dual-stack routers will probably be a common means of translating between the old and new Internet architectures. Essential to the dual-stack approach is the DNS. When a device sends or receives a packet, the DNS should be able to determine whether an IPv4 or an IPv6 packet is being processed.

Tunneling is recommended when two IPv6 devices want to communicate but must pass through an IPv4 network. In such a scenario, the IPv6 packets are encapsulated into an IPv4 format, traverse the IPv4 infrastructure, and then are ultimately translated back into their original IPv6 form. Two types of tunneling could be implemented: automatic and configured. With automatic tunneling, if the receiving device already uses a compatible IPv6 address, no reconfiguration is required. If the receiving device does not support IPv6, then configured tunneling is required. In this scenario, routers translate between IPv6 and IPv4. In this way, the receiving device ultimately receives the packet in the format that it understands.

Finally, with **header translation**, the assumption is that the sender needs to send an IPv6 packet through an IPv6 infrastructure, but that the receiver is still on IPv4. This scenario assumes that most of the Internet has transitioned to IPv6. In this example, the header format is changed through header translation from IPv6 into an IPv4 header. In such a case, the IPv6 mapped address is changed to an IPv4 address by evaluating the right-most 32 bits from the originating IPv6 address. Recall that an IPv4 address is 32 bits in length. The receiving IPv4 device can then process the communication.

In this discussion of addressing, it must be pointed out that the IETF has defined two types of IPv6 addressing techniques that can embed IPv4 addresses: compatible and mapped. An IPv6 compatible address has its first 96 bits set to zero, followed by a 32-bit IPv4 address. A compatible address is used when an IPv6 device wants to communicate with another IPv6 device over an IPv4 region. An IPv6 mapped address sets its first 80 bits to zero and the next 16 bits to one; the final 32-bits contain the embedded IPv4 address. A mapped address travels through IPv6 networks to the ultimate IPv4 device. Compatible and mapped addresses travel through networks of the opposing sorts. Both will be required in the transition from IPv4 to IPv6.

Careers in Data Communications

This text has discussed the many technologies that make up the data communications infrastructure. Within the field of data communications, which is itself a subfield of telecommunications, many career paths can be followed. As with other professional areas, people generally follow a series of job steps in pursuing a data communications career.

Entry-level staff might begin by working a help desk, responding to customer or staff questions, and arranging for technical help to be sent out. From the help desk, the next step would be network technician. Network technicians, like the one shown in Figure 11.9, go out in the field

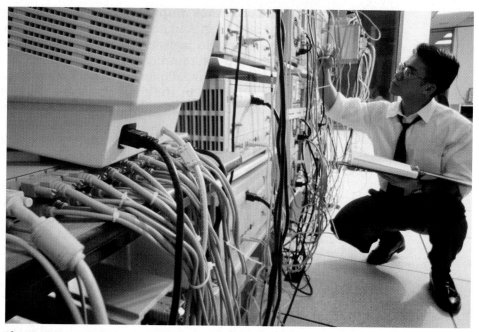

Figure 11.9

Entry-level data communication positions often require networking technicians to go out in the field to configure and maintain elements of the infrastructure.

and configure, maintain, and troubleshoot problems encountered by customers or staff. From network technician, it is possible to move into the area of network architect or designer. Network architects work on creating and overseeing the data communications infrastructure that supports the enterprise. Depending on the person's interest, a network architect might pursue entry into LAN or WAN management, supervising a staff. From there, the next step would be into senior management, overseeing multiple functional areas.

In 2002, *Network World*, a leading communications technology magazine, surveyed more than 1,600 organizations for average annual salaries by general job title. The salaries listed are from that survey and reflect salaries for those with several years experience:

- Help Desk Operator—$49,700
- Network Technician—$56,340
- Network Architect—$69,910
- LAN/WAN Manager—$65,180
- Senior Management—$108,820

The survey also reported a direct relationship between educational level and potential earned income. Following are average base salaries for data communications professionals according to their educational level:

- High school diploma—$61,680
- Associate's degree—$63,800
- Bachelor's degree—$70,830
- Graduate degree—$82,080

From the data, it appears that education pays for itself in the long run, so those long hours of study that you have been investing in this and other courses will have a reward. According to survey respondents, formal education was more important, and earned a higher pay rate, than professional certifications. Professional certifications were viewed more as "icing on the cake" rather than as essential requirements. Table 11.2 provides a list of popular data-communications-oriented certifications. At the end of this chapter, the "Topic in Focus" provides more detail on the various certifications available to networking technologists. Uniformly, survey respondents also rated oral and written communication skills as a necessity.

Although there is no crystal ball that can tell you what areas in data communications will have the greatest demand for staff over the next 5 years, some pretty good predictions can be made. The following four career areas involving data communications will have a greater demand for qualified staff than the available supply. Specialists in these areas will likely be at the top of everybody's list of "must have" technologists.

First, XML experts are going to be hugely popular. XML, or one of its derivatives, is driving much of the future technology underlying operating systems, development platforms, applications, and protocols. Second, wireless implementations are still in their infancy. Professionals who know how to configure, maintain, and develop wireless solutions will find themselves welcome at many, many places. The wireless revolution will also require more professionals in security. Therefore, third, security specialists will be courted and pursued by many organizations. Fourth and finally, IPv6 is on its way, and few are proficient in configuring IPv6 networks. Those who can work in both IPv4 and IPv6 will find that they are a rare group who will be much in demand as the transition from the old Internet to the new Internet takes place.

Table 11.2   Popular Networking Certifications

Vendor	Certification	Number of Exams
CompTIA	A +	2
CompTIA	Network +	1
Cisco	Cisco Certified Network Associate (CCNA)	1
Cisco	Cisco Certified Network Professional (CCNP)	1
Cisco	Cisco Certified Internetwork Expert (CCIE)	2
Microsoft	Microsoft Certified Professional (MCP)	1
Microsoft	Microsoft Certified Systems Engineer (MCSE)	7
Novell	Certified NetWare Administrator	1
Novell	Certified NetWare Engineer	6

When networking technologists discuss convergence and pervasive computing, they are most likely discussing the integration of data, voice, and video all carried seamlessly over one infrastructure. Communication technology is also on the road to invisible mobility. Three issues of particular concern involving pervasive computing are security, privacy, and ethics. The convergence of voice, video, and data into a seamless infrastructure will require protocols and technologies that can support such a convergence. One protocol in particular that is getting a lot of notice in the convergence industry is SIP, or Session Initiation Protocol.

With unified messaging (UM) all of the various messaging systems used by an enterprise are rolled into one system with one access point—the user's e-mail inbox. All messages, regardless of their source, will ultimately be digitized. The promise of UM is that it will allow users of different communication technologies who are operating different media and different devices to communicate with anyone, anywhere, at any time.

Wireless implementations by way of satellite and terrestrial microwave have been available for decades. Three emerging wireless-based technologies include 3G, 802.11, and Bluetooth. 3G stands for "third generation," and 3G standards are still being defined. Three types of data rates have been proposed for 3G-based application traffic: 144 Kbps for automotive, 384 Kbps for pedestrian, and 2 Mbps for indoor traffic.

Three important wireless local area network (WLAN) protocols are, from oldest to newest, 802.11b, 802.11a, and 802.11g. 802.11g was officially formalized in June of 2003. As a group, these types of WLAN protocols are also referred to as Wi-Fi (wireless fidelity) solutions. Two protocols associated with WLANs and wireless devices are WAP (Wireless Application Protocol) and WEP (Wired Equivalent Privacy). Bluetooth is a wireless implementation that creates a Personal Area Network (PAN) using low-power radio transmissions. To a wireless user, a hot spot is a location remote from the office or home where a user can access the Internet. Hot spots are increasingly popping up in airports, hotels, bookstores, and, very famously, in coffee shops such as Starbucks.

The current version of the Internet is known as IPv4. The Internet was initially designed primarily as a tool for researchers, scientists, and engineers to more easily exchange data and information with each other. IPv4 uses a two-level, hierarchical addressing scheme. IPv4 can be used to carry multimedia data, but not very well. To address the limitations of IPv4, IPv6 has been designed from the ground up. IPv6 uses 128 bits, or 16 bytes, in its addresses. IPv6 addresses are expressed in what is called a hexadecimal-colon notation. IPv6 uses three types of addresses: unicast, multicast, and anycast. IPv6 packets may have three components: a required header, an optional extension header, and the message, or payload.

Careers in data communications range from help desk to senior management. A recent *Network World* survey of more than 1,600 organizations revealed that formal education was considered highly important, as were communication skills.

3G **(387)**

802.11a **(392)**

802.11b **(392)**

802.11g **(392)**

802.11i **(394)**

Anycast address **(398)**

Bluetooth **(394)**

Convergence **(382)**

Dual-stack approach **(399)**

Extensible Messaging and Presence
Protocol (XMPP) **(384)**

Frequency hopping **(395)**

Header translation **(399)**

Hexadecimal **(397)**

Hot spot **(395)**

Instant messaging (IM) **(384)**

Internetworking Protocol Next Generation
(IPng) **(396)**

IPv4 **(396)**

IPv6 **(397)**

Killer application **(384)**

Loopback address **(397)**

Multicast address **(398)**

Payload **(398)**

Pervasive computing **(382)**

Session Initiation Protocol (SIP) **(384)**

Security Assertion Markup Language
(SAMP) **(384)**

Small Personal Object Technology
(SPOT) **(381)**

Sniffing **(395)**

Subscribe **(398)**

Tunneling **(399)**

Unicast address **(397)**

Unified messaging (UM) **(384)**

Unspecified address **(397)**

VeriChip **(383)**

War driving **(395)**

Wi-Fi (wireless fidelity) **(391)**

Wired Equivalent Privacy (WEP) **(392)**

Wireless Application Protocol (WAP) **(392)**

Wireless local area networks (WLANs) **(391)**

Short Answer

1. How does WAP differ from WEP?

2. What components might be present in a UM solution?

3. How does Bluetooth differ from 3G?

4. Describe at least one characteristic that differentiates IPv6 from IPv4.

Multiple Choice

For each of the following questions select one best answer.

1. Which of the following is convergence associated with?
   a. Data **b.** Voice **c.** Video **d.** All the above

2. What does SIP stand for?
   a. Serial Initiation Protocol
   b. Session Initiation Protocol
   c. Serial Implementation Protocol
   d. Session Implementation Protocol

3. What does UM stand for?
   a. Ultimate messaging **b.** Undefined messaging
   c. Unified messaging **d.** Unified media

4. Which of the following can be part of a UM system?
   a. Voice **b.** Fax **c.** E-mail **d.** All the above

5. What technology is 3G based on?
   a. UMTS **b.** SMTU **c.** MTUS **d.** TMUS

6. Which 3G data rate is targeted at automotive use?
   a. 100 Kbps **b.** 144 Kbps **c.** 384 Kbps **d.** 2 Mbps

7. Which 3G data rate is targeted at pedestrian use?
   a. 100 Kbps **b.** 144 Kbps **c.** 384 Kbps **d.** 2 Mbps

8. Which 3G data rate is targeted at indoor traffic?
   a. 100 Kbps **b.** 144 Kbps **c.** 384 Kbps **d.** 2 Mbps

9. How many nonoverlapping channels does 802.11a support?
   a. 2 **b.** 3 **c.** 10 **d.** 12

10. What radio-band range does 802.11a operate in?
    a. 2 GHz **b.** 2.4 GHz **c.** 5 GHz **d.** 8Ghz

11. How many nonoverlapping channels does 802.11b support?
    a. 2 **b.** 3 **c.** 10 **d.** 12

12. What radio-band range does 802.11b operate in?
    a. 2 GHz **b.** 2.4 GHz **c.** 5 GHz **d.** 8Ghz

13. How many nonoverlapping channels does 802.11g support?
    a. 2 **b.** 3 **c.** 10 **d.** 12

14. What radio band range does 802.11g operate in?

  a. 2 GHz **b.** 2.4 GHz **c.** 5 GHz **d.** 8Ghz

15. Which of the following is the security protocol currently being worked on by the IEEE for 802.11 networks?

  a. 802.11i **b.** 802.11s **c.** 802.11x **d.** 802.11z

16. What language is a WAP application written in?

  a. MWL **b.** WML **c.** ABL **d.** SOAP

17. What rate do Bluetooth devices transmit at?

  a. 1 Kbps **b.** 1 Mbps **c.** 2 Mbps **d.** 10 Mbps

18. How many bits make up an IPv6 address?

  a. 100 **b.** 120 **c.** 128 **d.** 264

19. How many bytes make up an IPv6 address?

  a. 8 **b.** 12 **c.** 15 **d.** 16

20. How many hexadecimal digits can be expressed in a two-byte hexa-decimal notation?

  a. 2 **b.** 4 **c.** 6 **d.** 8

21. Which character is used in IPv6 address notation?

  a. * **b.** : **c.** ! **d.** .

22. How many address types does IPv6 support?

  a. 1 **b.** 2 **c.** 3 **d.** 24

23. Which type of IPv6 address is used when a message needs to be sent to a group of devices that may or may not have the same type prefix?

  a. Fixedcast **b.** Anycast **c.** Unicast **d.** Multicast

24. Which type of IPv6 address is used when a message needs to be sent to a group of devices that have the same type prefix?

  a. Fixedcast **b.** Anycast **c.** Unicast **d.** Multicast

25. Which term describes a device running both IPv4 and IPv6?

  a. Multistack **b.** Dual stack **c.** Duo stack **d.** Variable stack

True or False

For each of the following select either True or False.

  1. Convergence involves data, voice, and video.

  2. Security is not an issue with pervasive computing.

  3. SIP can be used to establish and terminate an IM session.

  4. UM provides for the integration of multiple message systems.

  5. UM can be used for voice but not for fax messaging.

  6. 3G is capable of supporting various types of multimedia data.

  7. 3G provides one data rate for all forms of communication.

  8. 802.11 is a standard formalized by the IEEE.

  9. 802.11a and 802.11b are compatible protocols.

10. 802.11a offers a throughput of 54 Mbps per channel.

11. 802.11b provides for three nonoverlapping channels.

12. 802.11b is compatible with 802.11g.

13. 802.11g supports a throughput of 54 Mbps.

14. 802.11g provides for 12 nonoverlapping channels.

15. WAP is network-platform dependent.

16. WML is based on SOAP.

17. WEP is recognized as being very secure.

18. IPv6 address notation uses a colon.

19. IPv6 packets have a fixed header component.

20. One way to move from IPv4 to IPv6 is through a technique called dual stacks.

Exercises

Research in Brief

For one or more of the questions below, provide a one- to two-page report based on your findings.

1. SPOT is a new concept for mobile devices. Microsoft in particular is involved in establishing SPOT as a common technology platform. Investigate how and where Microsoft plans to utilize this technology. What other organizations are involved in SPOT?

2. The IEEE is working on the 802.11i security protocol for wireless networks. Research what the 802.11i protocol will do. How close to ratification is the standard? What types of security is 802.11i positioned to address?

3. Many vendors offer UM solutions. Evaluate UM solutions from two vendors. Compare and contrast them with regards to cost, functionality, and their advantages and disadvantages. Of the two, which would you recommend and why?

4. IPv6 will change how we use the Internet. Research how organizations are planning to transition form IPv4 to IPv6. What problems are predicted, if any? What issues have to be addressed for the transition? How is IPv6 being viewed in terms of the capabilities it will offer?

Case Study

Sheehan Marketing and Public Relations

Your time with SMPR has proven to be a valuable learning experience, but now you feel you need more of a challenge. You have decided to look into changing jobs. Prepare a resume that details what you have

accomplished at SMPR. Identify the ways that you will pursue your job search. For the geographic area that you are interested in working, identify what job opportunities are available. You may want to visit the *Network World* Web site, using DocFinder identification number 1425, to find salary information (**www.nwfusion.com**).

Web References

www.microsoft.com/resources/spot/product.mspx

www.adsx.com

www.ietf.org/html.charters/sip-charter.html

www.yankeegroup.com

www.avaya.com

www.nortel.com

www.cisco.com

www.umtsworld.com

www.wi-fi.org

www.bluetooth.com

www.boingo.com

www.pcworld.com/news/article/0,aid,104802,00.asp

www.ipv6forum.com

www.nwfusion.com

Career Certifications

Research shows that having a formal degree, whether an Associate's degree from a community college, a bachelor's degree from a university, or a graduate-level Master's degree, can significantly increase your future earning power. These formal degrees pay for themselves in the long run. However, for many in the technical fields, including programming, database and applications development, and especially data communications, career certifications may also play a factor in one's potential career advancement. Career certifications may affect base salaries, bonuses, promotions, or other job-related areas. Certifications require that an individual take and pass one or more technical examinations, depending on the certification being sought.

In general, each exam costs approximately $100, and you are charged each time you retake an exam. However, if your college or university has an academic partnership with a vendor that offers a certification, such as Cisco, Microsoft, or Novell, it may be possible to get a student discount. To register and sit for an exam, you must go to a recognized testing center, such as Prometric (**www.prometric.com**). Prometric has testing centers nationwide. Although you can locate an exam site and register for an exam online, you must go to the testing center, with appropriate identification, to take an exam. The following career certifications are appropriate for those in the data communications field. Keep in mind, however, that certifications have to be kept up-to-date. Very likely, you will probably have to retake an upgrade certification exam to maintain your credentials about every two years.

CompTIA's A + Certification

Some consider CompTIA's A + (pronounced "A Plus") certification to be the first level of certification for a computer technologist. The certification is meant to be vendor neutral and concentrates on two technical areas: (1) the hardware that make up a standard desktop computer and (2) the software (operating system and drivers) that a standard desktop computer would use. The term *standard desktop computer* refers to a PC computer, not a Macintosh. To become A + certified, one must pass two exams, one covering each technical area. The exams can be taken on the same day or on different days. The exams are updated periodically, and you have until the next update to take the second exam. Visit CompTIA's Web site (**www.comptia.com**) for the latest update on their exams.

The Core Hardware exam tests that an examinee has the basic knowledge to install, configure, upgrade, troubleshoot, and repair a standard desktop computer. This exam will typically have between 20 to 30 questions that must be completed in 30 minutes. Basic hardware networking is also tested in this exam. The Operating System (OS) exam requires the examinee to demonstrate basic proficiency with a command line prompt and with installing, configuring, upgrading, troubleshooting, and repairing a Windows 9x, Windows 2000, and Windows XP computer. This exam also has 20 to 30 questions that must be answered in a 30-minute timeframe. Each exam costs approximately $100, and if you need to retake an exam, you must pay for each sitting.

CompTIA's Network + Certification

CompTIA also offers a foundation certification in basic networking called Network + (again, pronounced "Network Plus"). This certification is for technology professionals with at least 9 months of experience in network support or administration. The intent of the certification is to demonstrate technical abilities in networking administration and support and knowledge of media, topologies, protocols and standards, network implementations, and network support. This certification is also meant to be vendor neutral. Network + is a single exam, again costing approximately $100 per attempt.

Cisco Certifications

Cisco (**www.cisco.com**) is a major provider of technologies that power the Internet and networking infrastructures. Cisco offers several stages of certification. First-level Cisco certification is for the Cisco Certified Network Associate, or CCNA. For this certification, students usually take a series of four classes that prepare them for the CCNA exam. The CCNA exam requires students to demonstrate first-level knowledge of Cisco routers and switches and their installation and configuration. Second-level Cisco certification is referred to as Cisco Certified Network Professional, or CCNP. Prior to taking the CCNP exam, one must already be a CCNA. CCNP certification indicates advanced knowledge of Cisco-based networks. The CCNP demonstrates that a network professional can install, configure, and troubleshoot LANs and WANs for enterprise organizations with networks having 100 to more than 500 devices. The exam focuses on topics related to security, converged networks, QoS, VPNs, and broadband technologies. To prepare for CCNP certification, four classes are usually required. The third level of Cisco certification is for the Cisco Certified Internetwork Expert, or CCIE. To sit for this exam, you must already be a CCNP. Also, the CCIE has a required hands-on lab component where the test taker must, at a Cisco facility, manually configure and troubleshoot Cisco equipment.

Microsoft Certifications

Microsoft also offers varying levels of certification. First-level certification leads to Microsoft Certified Professional, or MCP, certification. The most likely beginning MCP certification for a networking technologist is certification in Microsoft's Workstation or Server operating systems. An MCP certification can be applied toward Microsoft's next higher networking-oriented certification, the Microsoft Certified Systems Engineer, or MCSE. To become an MCSE, an MCP must pass an additional six to seven exams. With each exam successfully passed, the candidate becomes an MCP in that exam area. After all exams are passed, the candidate becomes an MCSE. As with other vendor certifications, Microsoft's certification requirements change over time. It would be best to visit Microsoft's Web site (**www.microsoft.com**) to find out the most current requirements for MCP and MCSE certification. As with other types of certification, there is a fee for each exam taken.

Novell Certifications

Like Cisco and Microsoft, Novell (**www.novell.com**) offers several levels of certification. First-level certification is to become a Certified NetWare Administrator, or CNA. A CNA is certified to provide support in Novell's NetWare Server Operating System for users in various work environments, including professional offices and small businesses, work groups or departments, and corporate information services. The next level of Novell certification leads to the Certified NetWare Engineer, or CNE. For CNE certification, a candidate will have to pass an additional five exams. Check Novell's Web site for the latest certification testing requirements.

Index

Slave, 280
Sliding windows buffer, 97, 124–127
Sliding windows flow control, 94, 96–97, 124–127
SLIP (Serial Line Internet Protocol), 253–254
Small Computer System Interface (SCSI), 280–281,
    282, 311–312
Small Personal Object Technology (SPOT), 381–382
SMDS (Switched Multimegabit Data Services), 228
SMDS Interface Protocol (SMDSIP), 228
SMP (symmetric multiprocessing), 167
SMTP (Simple Mail Transfer Protocol), 183, 286
Sniffing, 395
SNMP (Simple Network Management Protocol),
    307–308
  defined, 183
  standards-setting body for, 16
SOAP (Simple Object Access Protocol), 328–330
Software. *See also* Network/server operating systems
  defined, 131
  piracy, 155
Software keys, 65
SOS. *See* Server operating system (SOS)
Source service access point (SSAP), 94
Spectrum, 87–88
Splitter, 260
SPOT (Small Personal Object Technology), 381–382
Sputnik, 7
SSAP (source service access point), 94
Standard ASCII, 54
Standard DB-25 connector pins, 44, 45
Standard Ethernet, 146–148
Standards. *See also* 802 entries
  de facto, 15
  defined, 15–16
  ISO 2110, 44, 45
  RS232, 71
Standards-setting bodies, 11, 13, 15–16
Star topology, 132–133
Stateful packet inspection, 361–362
Static IP address, 261–262, 292
Statistical time-division multiplexing (STDM), 74–75
Sticks, 278
Stop-and-wait acknowledgment repeat request, 102
Stop-and-wait flow control, 94, 95–96
Storage
  direct attached, 310–312, 317
  Network-Attached, 314–317
Storage area networks (SANs), 312–314, 317
Store-and-forward switch, 113
STP (shielded twisted pair), 61
Striping, 378–380
Subnet, 186
Subnet addressing, 194–196
Subnet mask
  default, 193, 194
  defined, 187
  defining, 192–197
Subnetting, 187
Subnetwork architecture, 187–188
Subscribe, 398
Subscriber, 250

Supernet mask, 197
Supernetting, 196–197
SVC (switched virtual circuit), 247
Switched Ethernet, 148–151
Switched Multimegabit Data Services (SMDS), 228
Switched network, 242
Switched virtual circuit (SVC), 247
Switches
  backbone network, 211–218
  Cisco layer 3 8500 series, 145
  cross-point, 114
  cut-through, 114
  data link layer, 113–114
  defined, 113
  edge, 243
  Ethernet, 148–151
  local area network, 144–145
  multilayer, 145
  store-and-forward, 113
  wide area network, 242–243
Switching, 242–243
Switching fabric, 295
Switching services
  Asynchronous Transfer Mode, 213, 252–253
  circuit, 243–244
  datagram packet, 246–247
  Digital Subscriber Line, 258–262
  Frame Relay, 213, 250–252
  ISDN, 258, 272–273
  overview, 242–243
  packet, 244–246
  Point-to-Point Protocol, 253–256
  Switched Multimegabit Data Services, 228
  trunk carrier services, 256–258
  virtual-circuit packet, 247
  X.25, 247–249
Symbol rate, 50
Symmetric cipher, 352–353
Symmetric Digital Subscriber Line (SDSL), 258–262
Symmetric multiprocessing (SMP), 167
SYN attack, 360
Synchronous protocols, 104–105
Syntactics, 341
System area networks (SANs), 295

T

TA (terminal adapter), 272
Tape, 310
TCP. *See* Transmission Control Protocol/Internet
    Protocol (TCP/IP)
TCP/IP. *See* Transmission Control Protocol/Internet
    Protocol (TCP/IP)
TDM (time-division multiplexing), 73–74, 325
TE-1 (Terminal Equipment-1), 272–273
TE-2 (Terminal Equipment-2), 272–273
Telecommunications, 11
Telecommunications Competition and Deregulation
    Act, 7
Telemetry, 9–11
Telepole, 220–221

Credits

Chapter 1 Page 3: Figure 1.2; from Myrleen Ferguson Cate/PhotoEdit. Page 4: Figure 1.4; from Stephen Simpson/Getty Images, Inc.–Taxi. Page 5: Figure 1.5; from Sebastian Quigley/Dorling Kindersley Media Library. Page 7: Figure 1.7; from Getty Images, Inc.–Hulton Archive Photos. Page 8: Figure 1.8; from Cybergeography.org. Page 9: Figure 1.9; from Donald E. Carroll/Getty Images, Inc.–Image Bank. Page 10: Figure 1.10; from Intermec Technologies Corporation. Page 13: Figure 1.12; from EyeWire Collection/Getty Images, Inc.–Photodisc.

Chapter 2 Page 61: Figure 2.14; from Belkin Components/Belkin Corporation. Courtesy of the Belkin Corporation. Page 64: Figure 2.16; from CMCD/Getty Images, Inc.–Photodisc.

Chapter 3 Page 111: Figure 3.12; from 3Com Corporation. Reproduced with permission of 3Com Corporation. Page 112: Figure 3.13; from Proxim, Inc. Page 114: Figure 3.15; from Cisco Systems. The materials have been reproduced by PERC with permission of Cisco Systems, Inc. COPYRIGHT ©2004 CISCO SYSTEMS, INC. ALL RIGHTS RESERVED.

Chapter 4 Page 130: Figure 4.1; from Edward Rozzo/Corbis RF. Page 131: Figure 4.2; from AP/Wide World Photos. Page 135: Figure 4.6; from 3Com Corporation. © 3 Com Corporation. Page 136: Figure 4.7; from Intel Corporation Museum Archives & Collection. Photo courtesy of Intel Corporation. Page 138: Figure 4.8; from Tony Freeman/Corbis/Stock Market. Page 139: Figure 4.9; IBM Corporation. Courtesy of International Business Machines Corporation. Unauthorized use not permitted. Page 142: Figure 4.11; from Phil Banko/Corbis/Stock Market. Page 143: Figure 4.12; Dell, Inc. © 2004 Dell Inc. All Rights Reserved. Page 145: Figure 4.13; Cisco Systems. The materials have been reproduced by PERC with permission of Cisco Systems, Inc. COPYRIGHT ©2004 CISCO SYSTEMS, INC. ALL RIGHTS RESERVED. Page 146: Figure 4.14; Cisco Systems. The materials have been reproduced by PERC with permission of Cisco Systems, Inc. COPYRIGHT ©2004 CISCO SYSTEMS, INC. ALL RIGHTS RESERVED. Page 153: Figure 4.19; from Red Hat, Inc. Page 156: Figure 4.20; from August Stein/Getty Images, Inc–Artville LLC.

Chapter 5 Page 172: Figure 5.1; from NCSA Media Technology Resources. NCSA Media Technology Resources, University of Illinois at Urbana-Champaign. Page 176: Figure 5.5; from Tom Wagner; Corbis/SABA Press Photos, Inc. Page 184: Figure 5.13; from Charles Schwab & Company, Inc.

Chapter 6 Page 219: Figure 6.7; Black Box Corporation. Page 220: Figure 6.8; from RON CHAPPLE; Getty Images Inc.–Taxi. Page 222: Figure 6.9; from CMCD/Getty Images, Inc.–Photodisc. Page 224: Figure 6.11; from Mark Richards/PhotoEdit. Page 227: Figure 6.12; from Bonnie Kamin/PhotoEdit.

Chapter 7 Page 251: Figure 7.6; from Spots on the Spot. Page 254: Figure 7.9; from Unidentified/Dorling Kindersley Media Library. Page 254: Figure 7.10; from ZOOM Telephonics, Inc. Courtesy of Zoom Telephonics Inc. Page 261: Figure 7.13; from D–Link Systems, Inc. Page 272: Figure 7.14; from 3Com Corporation. ©3Com Corporation.

Chapter 8 Page 276: Figure 8.1; from The Small System Journal. Page 277: Figure 8.2; from Microsoft Corporation. Screen shot reprinted by permission from Microsoft Corporation. Page 277: Figure 8.3; from AP/Wide World Photos. Page 279: Figure 8.4; from Nick Rowe/Getty Images, Inc.–Photodisc. Page 281: Figure 8.5; from CMCD/Getty Images, Inc.–Photodisc. Page 289: Figure 8.8; from Microsoft Corporation.

Chapter 9 Page 310: Figure 9.1; from Spots on the Spot. Page 311: Figure 9.3; from Erik Dreyer/Getty Images Inc.–Stone Allstock. Page 316: Figure 9.6; from Robin Jareaux/Getty Images, Inc.–Artville LLC. Page 319: Figure 9.8; from REUTERS/Kwaku Sakyi–Addo/ Corbis/ Bettmann. © Reuters NewMedia Inc./CORBIS. Page 324: Figure 9.11; from Cisco Systems. The materials have been reproduced by PERC with permission of Cisco Systems, Inc. COPYRIGHT ©2004 CISCO SYSTEMS, INC. ALL RIGHTS RESERVED. Page 327: Figure 9.13; from Spots on the Spot. Page 328: Figure 9.14; from August Stein/Getty Images, Inc–Artville LLC.

Chapter 10 Page 344: Figure 10.1; from Robert F. Bukaty/AP/Wide World Photos. Page 346: Figure 10.2; from Daisuke Morita/Getty Images, Inc.–Photodisc. Page 348: Figure 10.3; from AP/Wide World Photos. Page 350: Figure 10.4; from Advanced Computer & Network Corporation. Page 351: Figure 10.5; from PH ESM. 1999 Prentice Hall. Page 357: Figure 10.8; from Spots on the Spot. Page 358: Figure 10.10; from Cisco Systems. The materials have been reproduced by PERC with permission of Cisco Systems, Inc. COPY-RIGHT ©2004 CISCO SYSTEMS, INC. ALL RIGHTS RESERVED. Page 363: Figure 10.13; from Raimund Koch. © Raimund Koch. Page 367: Figure 10.16; from Jockel Finck/AP/Wide World Photos.

Chapter 11 Page 383: Figure 11.1; from JAMES PORTO/Getty Images, Inc.–Taxi. Page 385: Figure 11.2; from Lotus Development Corp. Courtesy Lotus Development Corporation. Page 388: Figure 11.4; from palmOne, Inc. palmOne, Zire, Tungsten, Treo, logos, stylizations, and design marks associated with all the preceding and trade dress associated with palmOne, Inc. ™ products, are among the trademarks or registered trademarks owned by or exclusively licensed to palmOne, Inc. Page 391: Figure 11.6; from Farallon Communications, Inc. Page 393: Figure 11.7; from Jacey Debut Art/Digital Vision Ltd. Page 394: Figure 11.8; from Microsoft Corporation. Reprinted with permission from Microsoft Corporation. Most current version of this product located on the Microsoft web site at http://www.microsoft.com/presspass/images/gallery. Page 400: Figure 11.9; from Keith Brofsky/Getty Images, Inc.–Photodisc.